P9-DMW-608

Essential System Administration

Essential System Administration

Æleen Frisch

O'Reilly & Associates, Inc.
103 Morris Street, Suite A
Sebastopol, CA 95472

Essential System Administration
by Æleen Frisch

Copyright © 1991 O'Reilly & Associates, Inc. All rights reserved.
Printed in the United States of America.

Editor: Mike Loukides

Printing History:

October 1991:	First Edition.
January 1992:	Minor corrections.
August 1992:	Minor corrections.
January 1993:	Minor corrections.

Nutshell Handbook and the Nutshell Handbook logo are registered trademarks of O'Reilly & Associates, Inc.

Many of the designations used by manufacturers and sellers to distinguish their products are claimed as trademarks. Where those designations appear in this book, and O'Reilly and Associates, Inc. was aware of a trademark claim, the designations have been printed in caps or initial caps.

While every precaution has been taken in the preparation of this book, the publisher assumes no responsibility for errors or omissions, or for damages resulting from the use of the information contained herein.

This book is printed on acid-free paper with 50% recycled content, 10-15% post-consumer waste. O'Reilly & Associates is committed to using paper with the highest recycled content available consistent with high quality.

ISBN: 0-937175-80-3   [11/94]

Table of Contents

Figures

Tables

Preface

UNIX Versions Discussed
Audience
Organization
Conventions Used in this Handbook
Acknowledgments
We'd Like to Hear From You

This book covers basic UNIX system administration. "Basic" refers to the funda-mental and essential tasks a system manager performs, not necessarily merely beginning or simple ones. The goal in this book is to make administering UNIX systems straightforward by providing you with exactly the information you need—not just an overview that gets you started but leaves you hanging when the first complication arrives and not a lot of extraneous information to wade through in order to find what you actually need. More than just command syntax is con-sidered, of course; this book will also cover the UNIX structure and the guiding assumptions which will enable you to place these commands in context.

This book will also offer some advice on system administration strategies and procedures; I won't be shy about letting you know what my opinion is. But really I'm much more interested in giving you the information you need to make informed decisions for your own situation than in providing a single, univocal view of the "right way" to administer a UNIX system. It's much more important that you know what the issues are concerning, say, system backups, than that you adopt anyone's specific philosophy or scheme. When you know the issues, you'll be in a position to decide what's right for you and your system.

More and more, UNIX system administration means taking care of multiple computers, often from more than one manufacturer. While UNIX is widely lauded in marketing brochures as the "standard" operating system "from microcomputers to supercomputers"—and I must confess to having written a few of those brochures myself—this is not at all the same as there being a "standard" UNIX. At this point, UNIX is hopelessly plural, and nowhere is this plurality more evident than in system administration. Before going on to discuss how this book addresses that fact, let's take a brief look at the UNIX universe.

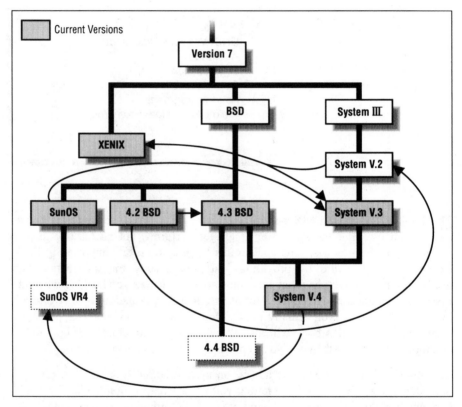

A UNIX Genealogy (Simplified)

The preceding figure attempts to capture the current state of things. It illustrates a simplified UNIX genealogy, with an emphasis on influences and family relationships (albeit Faulknerian ones) rather than on strict chronology and historical accuracy. It begins at an arbitrary point in time, with UNIX Version 7, and traces the major lines of descent from that point. The SunOS, Stardent UNIX, and Interactive UNIX, three main versions of UNIX are described in the following list:

• XENIX: The first microcomputer UNIX version, and still in widespread use, (XENIX was derived from Version 7 and converted to System V Release 2 gradually over time. XENIX then in turn influenced System V Release 3 when many of its capabilities were merged into V.3.2.

• BSD: The Berkeley Standard Distribution was the first UNIX version to support virtual memory. Many BSD-based UNIX operating systems are in current use; some are derived from the most recent release, 4.3 BSD, and some from the previous version. Thus, although 4.2 BSD is technically an ancestor of 4.3 BSD, it lives on (thrives!) in many commercial implementations and so has equal status in the chart.

The best known BSD-based operating system is of course SunOS (Release 4.1 and earlier), which also introduced many new capabilities to the UNIX world, most notably the Network File System (NFS). SunOS will be used as an example for BSD behavior at various points in this book. Differences between SunOS and standard BSD will also be pointed out when appropriate. Otherwise, all discussion of BSD can be assumed to apply to SunOS.

• System V: Derived from System III,* and now including a few features introduced by BSD (e.g, virtual memory support, the C shell), there are a multitude of extant versions of System V. The two major variations which we will consider are System V Release 3 (V3) and System V Release 4 (V.4). V.3 itself exists in several sub-versions, and commercial implementations derived from earlier versions lack features found in V.3.2. To further complicate the picture, many vendors freely intermix BSD features with standard System V.

System V Release 4 is often described as a merger of the System V and BSD lines, but this is not quite accurate. V.4 incorporates the most important features of BSD and SunOS into System V. The union is a marriage and not a merger, however, with some but not all characteristics from each parent dominant in the offspring (as well as a few whose origins no one is quite sure of).

Even as V.4 promises to bring some uniformity and standardization to this myriad of UNIX flavors—many vendors have promised V.4 support in their next release—great diversity will inevitably remain for several reasons. First, the changeover to V.4 is proceeding slowly and will continue to be very gradual. Older versions will remain around for quite a while. Secondly, since even V.4

---

*The movement from Version 7 to System III is a simplification of strict chronology and descent. System III was derived from an intermediate release between Version 6 and Version 7, and not every Version 7 feature appears in System III.

doesn't standardize all potential features of a modern production operating system (e.g., a batch system, asynchronous I/O), vendors will continue to develop their own versions of them. Finally, some of the alternate UNIX threads will continue to develop despite the existence of V.4; OSF/1 and 4.4 BSD are two well-known alternatives.

UNIX Versions Discussed

What should be clear from the preceding discussion is that all these standard UNIX versions are abstractions that exhibit significant variations by the time they are implemented on real systems. Even when you know what standard version your computer's operating system is derived from, there is no guarantee that it is either completely standard or completely missing features from the other standard versions. We've tried to be very careful in this book to cover not only the differences between the major UNIX versions, but also to mention variations in actual implementations whenever relevant.

We'll be concentrating on the shaded versions in the chart: namely, those versions of UNIX still in wide use in current operating system releases.* We will use these implementations as models in this book:

- *For System V*: Interactive UNIX System V.3.2/386, running on a 80386-based microcomputer system, is our model V.3 system. We'll refer to it simply as "V.3" most of the time, when its features truly are generic; we'll denote it as "Interactive UNIX" when an Interactive-specific feature is discussed.

  From time to time, we'll also look at Stardent UNIX Release 3.01 Revision A, running on a Titan 3020 ("P3"). Stardent UNIX is based on an earlier version of V.3 than Interactive UNIX, and represents a minimal implementation of the System V Release 3 "standard." It also includes many BSD and proprietary features; we'll mention a couple of the latter at appropriate points.

  The designation "V.4" will refer to the 3B2 AT&T version of System V Release 4 (although almost none of the discussion here is specific to the 3B2).

- *For BSD*: The generic 4.3 BSD examples come from Multiflow Computer's TRACE/UNIX Version 4.1 (on a TRACE 14/300). Although Multiflow is no longer in business, their 4.3 BSD port was almost completely standard. Naturally, no Multiflow-specific features are discussed. Generic 4.3 BSD will be

---

*This is not to say that there aren't still many computers running older versions, but their owners probably have system administration for them figured out by now.

designated as "BSD." From time to time, we'll discuss differences between 4.3 BSD and 4.2 BSD, but not all such differences are noted.

We'll also discuss SunOS Release 4.1 on a Sun 4 (denoted as "SunOS"), both as a BSD example and in order to point out some of its own unique extensions. When I use the designation BSD, you can assume that the discussion applies to SunOS as well unless it's specifically stated otherwise.

- *For XENIX*: We'll use SCO's XENIX System V for the 80386, Release 2.3.3 (running on a 386), designated as "XENIX." As its full name emphasizes, XENIX is essentially a System V-based version of NIX at this point, so much of the discussion of vanilla System V applies to XENIX as well.

- *For AIX*: Finally, we'll also consider a new UNIX version that's especially important in the workstation market: IBM's AIX Release 3.1 Revision 03.01.0005.0012 (commonly referred to as 3005), running on an RS/6000 540, which we'll refer to as "AIX 3.1." AIX 3.1 is a System V-based operating system, but supports very large numbers of features from V.4 and BSD, in addition to many unique features. Note that earlier versions of AIX are quite different from Release 3.1, and our discussion will not apply to them.

Now that may seem like a lot of systems to consider, but juggling several UNIX versions isn't really that difficult. A lot of people do it every day, in fact, and this book is designed to reflect that reality. Indeed, it is quite common for sites to have at least one system in each UNIX flavor.

When there are significant differences between the versions, I've made extensive use of headers and other devices to indicate which version is being considered. You'll find it easy to keep track of where we are at any given point and even easier to find out the specific information you need for your version. In addition, the book will continue to be useful to you when you get your next, different UNIX system—and sooner or later you will . . .

Audience

This book will be of interest to:

- Administrators of UNIX computer systems. The book does not assume previous system administration experience.

- Workstation and microcomputer users. For small, stand-alone systems, there is often no distinction between the user and the system administrator. And even if your workstation is part of a larger network with its designated administrator, in practice many system management tasks for your workstation will be left to you.

- Users of UNIX systems who are not full-time system managers but who perform administrative tasks periodically.

This book assumes that you are familiar with UNIX user commands: that you know how to change the current directory, get directory listings, search files for strings, edit files, use I/O redirection and pipes, and so on. If you need help at this level, consult the Nutshell Handbooks *Learning the UNIX Operating System* (O'Reilly & Associates, 1989) and *UNIX in a Nutshell* (O'Reilly & Associates, 1990).

If you have previous UNIX experience but no administrative experience, several sections in Chapter 1, *Introduction to System Administration*, will show you how to make the transition from user to system manager. If you some have system administration experience but are new to UNIX, Chapter 2, *The UNIX Way*, will explain the UNIX approach to major system management tasks. Chapter 2 will also be helpful to current UNIX users who are unfamiliar with UNIX file, process, or device concepts.

This book is not designed for UNIX wizards. Accordingly, it stays away from topics like writing device drivers and customizing the UNIX kernel.

Organization

As noted previously, the first two chapters of the book provide some essential background material required by different types of readers. The next several chapters discuss various aspects of everyday system operation, while later chapters focus on major UNIX subsystems and configuration issues.

Chapter 1,   *Introduction to System Administration*, describes some general principles of system administration and then discusses the administrative uses of several common UNIX commands. By the end of this chapter, you'll be thinking like a system administrator.

Chapter 2,   *The UNIX Way*, considers the ways that UNIX structure and philosophy affect system administration. It discusses how UNIX handles various operating system functions, including file privilege and protection, process creation and control, and device handling. This chapter closes with an overview of the UNIX system directory structure and important configuration files.

Chapter 3,   *Startup and Shutdown*, describes how to boot up and shut down UNIX systems. It also considers UNIX boot scripts in detail, including how to modify them for the needs of your system.

Chapter 4,   *User Accounts*, details how to add new users to a UNIX system. It also discusses UNIX login initialization files and groups.

Chapter 5,   *Security*, provides an overview of UNIX security issues and solutions to common problems, including how to use UNIX groups to allow users to share files and other system resources while maintaining a secure environment. It also discusses optional security-related facilities like dialup passwords.

Chapter 6,   *Automating Routine Tasks*, discusses how UNIX shell scripts and the *cron* system may be used to automate many routine operations. Monitoring and managing disk usage is used as an extended example.

Chapter 7,   *Managing System Resources*, discusses tools designed to monitor CPU usage and control process execution. It then discusses memory performance and managing system paging space and concludes with a look at the disk quota system available in some UNIX implementations.

Chapter 8,   *Filesystems and Disks*, discusses how discrete disk partitions become part of the UNIX filesystem. It begins by describing the disk mounting commands, filesystem configuration files, and the *fsck* utility, which is used to check filesystem integrity. It also considers UNIX disk partitioning schemes and describes how to add a new disk to a UNIX system.

Chapter 9,   *Backups and Restore*, begins by considering several possible backup strategies before going on to discuss the various backup and restore services that UNIX provides.

Chapter 10,   *Terminals and Modems*, discusses UNIX handling of serial lines, including how to add and configure new serial devices.

Chapter 11,   *Printers and the Spooling Subsystem*, discusses printing on UNIX systems, including day-to-day operation and configuration issues.

Chapter 12,   *TCP/IP Network Management*, provides an overview of UNIX networking capabilities. While not an exhaustive discussion of TCP/IP or NFS by any means, this chapter will enable you to add new hosts to an existing network and to mount disks remotely via NFS.

Chapter 13,   *Accounting*, describes the UNIX accounting services.

The appendix, *Bourne Shell Programming Overview*, is designed for readers unfamiliar with Bourne shell (*/bin/sh*) programming. Virtually all UNIX system scripts are written for the Bourne shell. This appendix reviews major Bourne shell programming structures, taking examples from actual UNIX system scripts.

The *Bibliography*,

lists specialized works that may be of interest to some readers.

Conventions Used in this Handbook

The following typographic conventions are used in this book:

Italic
: is used for UNIX pathnames, filenames, program names, command names, options, and parameters, usernames, groupnames, attributes, and keywords in normal text. It is also used to emphasize new terms and concepts when they are introduced. Finally, italic is used to highlight comments in command examples.

`Constant Width`
: is used in examples to show the contents of files or the output from commands.

`Constant Bold`
: is used in examples to show commands or other text that would be typed literally by the user. For example, **rm foo** means to type "rm foo" exactly as it appears in the text or example.

`Constant Italic`
: is used in examples to show variables for which a context-specific substitution should be made. The variable *`filename`*, for example, would be replaced by some actual filename.

$
: is the prompt for the Bourne and Korn shells. It is used in generic UNIX and System V-specific examples.

%
: is the C shell prompt and is used in examples designed to illustrate (Bx-specific behavior.

#
: is the prompt for the *root* user (also called the superuser). It is used in examples for commands which must be executed as the superuser.

. . .   stands for text (usually computer output) that has been omitted for clarity or to save space.

The notation CTRL-X and ^X indicate the use of *control* characters. CTRL-X means to hold down the CONTROL key while hitting the "x" key.

Acknowledgments

Many people have helped this book at various points in its successive incarnations. It began life as a system administration manual written by O'Reilly and Associates (and specifically Tim O'Reilly) for the Massachusetts Computer Corporation (MASSCOMP) in the early 1980s. This version served as the starting point for Multiflow Computer's *Guide to TRACE/UNIX System Administration*. Mike Loukides (now of ORA) wrote the manual's first version, and I took over the work when I joined Multiflow in 1987. At Multiflow, Mike Loukides, Chris Dodd (Intel), Doug Gilmore (Silicon Graphics), Ben Cutler (Equator Technologies), Bob Colwell (Intel), and Chris Ryland (Em Software) were especially helpful to me (although but a few traces remain of that work).

Jim Binkley (EASE Inc.), Tan Bronson (Microvation Consultants), Clem Cole (Cole Computer Consulting), Dick Dunn (eklektix), Laura Hook (United Technologies), Mike Loukides, and Tim O'Reilly read the finished manuscript of the present work and provided perceptive and helpful suggestions; this book has profited greatly from their comments. I owe a special debt to Mike Loukides and Tim O'Reilly for their patient guidance through this work's progressive evolution.

The section entitled "Making the Physical Connection," in Chapter 10, *Terminals and Modems*, is reprinted with minor changes from the Nutshell Handbook *Managing uucp and Usenet*.

Mike Frisch (Lorentzian, Inc.) and Tan Bronson gave me access to various UNIX systems, enabling me to experience many of the variations and intricacies of the UNIX universe.

Finally, my thanks also go to Kismet McDonough for copyediting the manuscript, Ellie Cutler for writing the index, Chris Reilly for designing the illustrations, and the rest of the excellent production group at O'Reilly and Associates for putting the finishing touches on this book.

We'd Like to Hear From You

We have tested and verified all of the information in this book to the best of our ability, but you may find that features have changed (or even that we have made mistakes!). Please let us know about any errors you find, as well as your suggestions for future editions, by writing:

```
O'Reilly & Associates, Inc.
103 Morris Street, Suite A
Sebastopol, CA 95472
1-800-998-9938 (in the US or Canada)
1-707-829-0515 (international/local)
1-707-829-0104 (FAX)
```

You can also send us messages electronically. To be put on the mailing list or request a catalog, send email to:

info@ora.com   (via the Internet)
uunet!ora!info   (via UUCP)

To ask technical questions or comment on the book, send email to:

bookquestions@ora.com   (via the Internet)

1

Introduction to System Administration

The System Administrator's Job
Becoming Superuser
Communicating with Users
Essential Administrative Tools
Menu Interfaces for System
Administration

The System Administrator's Job

A plausible, even traditional, way to begin a book like this is to provide a list of system management tasks. I'm not sure such lists are really worth much, although I will provide one in a moment. I think they leave out too many intangibles, the sort of things that take up a lot of time or energy, but never make it into job descriptions. Lists also tend to suggest that system management has some sort of coherence across the vastly different environments where people find themselves responsible for or taking care of computers. There are similarities, of course, but what is important on one system won't necessarily be on another at another site, or on the same system at a different time. And systems that are very different may have similar system management needs, while nearly identical systems in different environments might have very different ones.

But now to the list. In lieu of an idealized list, I offer the following unordered recitation of the things I spent the most time doing in my previous full-time system administration position, managing several superminicomputers:

- Adding new users.

- Adding toner to electrostatic plotters.

- Doing backups.

- Restoring files from backups that users had accidentally deleted or trashed.

- Answering user questions ("How do I send mail?"), usually not for the first or last time.

- Monitoring system activity and trying to tune system parameters to make overloaded systems have the response time of an idle system.

- Moving jobs up in the print queue, after more or less user whining, pleading or begging, contrary to stated policy (about moving jobs, not about whining).

- Worrying about system security and plugging the most noxious security holes I had inherited.

- Installing programs and operating system updates.

- Trying to free up disk space (and especially contiguous disk space).

- Rebooting the system after a crash (always at late and inconvenient times).

- Figuring out network glitches ("Why isn't *hamlet* talking to *ophelia*?"). Occasionally, this involved physically tracing the Ethernet cable around the building, checking it at each node.

- Rearranging furniture to accommodate new equipment. Installing said equipment.

- Figuring out why a program/command/account suddenly and mysteriously stopped working since yesterday, even though the user changed nothing.

- Fixing—or rather, trying to fix—corrupted CAD/CAM data files.

- Going to meetings.

- Adding new systems to the network.

- Writing scripts to automate as many of the above activities as possible.

As this list indicates, formal system management is truly a hodgepodge of activities, and involves at least as many people skills as computer skills. While I'll offer some advice along these lines in a moment, interacting with people is best learned by watching others, emulating their successes, and avoiding their mistakes.

Currently, I set up and look after much smaller systems—workstations and microcomputers—but it's surprising how many of these same activities I still have to do. Adding toner may now mean changing a toner cartridge in a laser printer, backups now go to floppy disk and cartridge tape rather than 9-track tape, and user problems and questions are in different areas but are still very much on the list. And while there are (thankfully) no meetings, there's probably even more furniture moving.

Some of these topics—moving furniture and going to/avoiding meetings, most obviously—are beyond the scope of this book. Other topics, like system tuning, are touched on only briefly; in these cases, it's because the topic is huge, and I'll usually point you in the direction of another book. This book will cover most of the ordinary tasks that fall under the category of "system administration." The discussion will be relevant to you whether you've got a single 386 machine, a room full of mainframes, or a building full of networked workstations. Not all topics will apply to everyone, but I've learned not to rule out any of them *a priori* for a given class of user. For example, it's often thought that only big systems need accounting, and this is usually true, but every so often I run across a microcomputer system that needs to be able to bill its several customers individually. The moral is: take what you need and leave the rest; you're the best judge of what's relevant and what isn't.

I've touched briefly on some of the nontechnical aspects of system administration. These dynamics will probably not be an issue if it really is just you and your 386 (or you and your Cray, for that matter), but if you interact with other people at all, they will come up. It's a cliché that system administration is a thankless job—one widely-reprinted cartoon has a user saying "I'd thank you but system administration is a thankless job"—but things are actually more complicated than that. As another cliché puts it, system administration is like keeping the trains on time; no one notices except when they're late.

System management seems often to involve a tension between authority and responsibility on the one hand and service and cooperation on the other. The extremes seem easier to maintain than any middle ground; fascistic dictators who rule "their system" with an iron hand, unhindered by the needs of users, find their opposite in the harried system managers who jump from one user request to the next, in continual interrupt mode. The trick is to find a balance between being accessible to users and their needs, and sometimes even their mere wants, while still maintaining your authority and sticking to the policies you've put in place for the overall system welfare. The goal is to provide an environment where users can get what they need to do done, in as easy and efficient a manner as possible, given the constraints of security, other users' needs, the inherent capabilities of the system, and the realities and constraints of the human community in which it is located.

The key to successful, productive system administration is knowing when to solve a CPU-overuse problem with a command like:

```
# ps -ef | awk '$1==chavez {print $2}' | xargs kill -9      (System V)
# kill -9 `ps aux | awk '$1==chavez {print $2}'`            (BSD)
```

(which blows away all of user *chavez*'s processes) and when to use:

```
$ write chavez
You've got a lot of identical processes going.
Any problem I can help with?
^D
```

and when to walk over to her desk and talk with her face-to-face. The first approach displays UNIX finesse as well as administrative brute force, and both are certainly appropriate—even vital—at times. At other times, a simpler, less aggressive approach will work better to resolve your system's performance problems as well as the user's confusion. It's also important to remember that there are some problems no UNIX command can address.

To a great extent, successful system administration is a combination of careful planning and habit, however much it may seem like crisis intervention at times. The key to really handling a crisis well is having had the foresight and taken the time to anticipate and plan for exactly the emergency that has just come up (or at least some approximation of it). And many crises can be prevented altogether by a determined devotion to carrying out all the careful procedures you've designed: changing the root password regularly, faithfully making backups (no matter how tedious), logging out and clearing the terminal screen as a ritual, testing every change several times before letting it loose, sticking to policies you've set for users' benefit—whatever you need to do for your system. (On the other hand, I try always to remember, as Emerson said, that "a foolish consistency is the hobgoblin of little minds.")

As far as making changes to the system goes, I've adopted an attitude I heard from a friend who worked in a museum putting together ancient pottery fragments: always make it reversible. The museum did this so that if better reconstructive techniques were developed decades from now, they could undo the current work and use the better method. As far as possible, I've tried to do the same with computers, adding changes gradually and preserving a path by which to back out of them.

A simple example of this sort of attitude in action concerns editing system configuration files. UNIX systems rely on many configuration files, and every major subsystem has its own files (all of which we'll get to in their own time). Many of these will need to be modified from time to time. I impose the following rules on myself whenever I change a configurations file (well, almost every time anyway):

- Never modify the original copy of the configuration file, either as delivered with the system or as you found it when you took over the system. I always copy these files right away, appending the suffix *.dist* to the filename; for example:

```
# cd /etc
# cp rc rc.dist
# chmod a-w rc.dist
```

  I write-protect the *.dist* file so I'll always have it to refer to.

- Never modify the current configuration file without copying it first (so undesirable changes can be undone). I add a suffix like *.old* or *.sav* to the filename for these copies.

- *Always* test the changes.

Of course, testing won't always find every bug or prevent every problem, but it will eliminate the most obvious ones.

The remaining sections of this chapter discuss some important administrative tools. The first describes how to become the superuser (the UNIX privileged account). The next two discuss using familiar commands for system administrative purposes. Since I believe a good system manager needs to have both technical expertise and an awareness of and sensitivity to the user community (of which he's a part), both UNIX communication commands and administrative uses for common commands like *find* and *grep* are covered, in separate sections. The goal of these discussions—as well as of this chapter as a whole—is to highlight how a system manager thinks about system tasks and problems, rather than to provide literal, cookbook solutions for common scenarios.

Becoming Superuser

On a UNIX system, the *superuser* is a privileged account with unrestricted access to all files and commands. The username of this account is *root*. Many administrative tasks require superuser status.

There are two ways to become the superuser. The first is to log in as *root* directly. The second way is to execute the command *su* while logged in under another username. After entering the *su* command, the system will prompt you for the root password. If you type the password correctly, the system will display a pound sign (#), indicating that you have successfully become superuser, and that the rules normally restricting file access and command execution do not apply. For example:

```
$ su
Password:                          ...Not echoed...
#
```

If you typed the password incorrectly, the operating system will print the word "Sorry" and return the normal prompt. You may exit from the superuser account with a CTRL-D. On systems/shells with job control, you may stop the shell and place it in the background with the *suspend* command, and restart it later using *fg*.

On most UNIX systems, any user who knows the root password may become superuser at any time by using *su*. However, on BSD systems, only users who are members of group 0 (the *wheel* group) may use *su* to become the superuser. Under SunOS, if the *wheel* group has a null user list in the group file (*/etc/group*), then any user may *su* to root; otherwise, normal BSD rules apply.

Unlike some other operating systems, the UNIX superuser has all privileges all the time: access to all files, commands, etc. Therefore, it is all too easy for a superuser to crash the system, destroy important files, and create havoc inadvertently. For this reason, those who know the superuser password (including the system administrator) should *not* do their routine work as superuser. *Only use superuser status when it is needed.*

I try to avoid logging in directly as *root*. Instead, I *su* to *root* only as necessary, exiting from or suspending the superuser shell when possible. Alternatively, in a windowing environment, you can create a separate window in which you *su* to *root*, again executing commands there only as necessary. The *root* account should *always* have a password; this password should be changed periodically. Only experienced UNIX users with special requirements should know the superuser password. To set or change the superuser password, become superuser and execute the following command:

```
# passwd
```

The system will then ask you to type the old superuser password, and then ask you to type the new password twice. The root password should also be changed whenever someone who knows it stops using the system for any reason (e.g., transfer, new job, etc.), or if there is any suspicion that an unauthorized user has learned it.

Communicating with Users

The commands discussed in this section are simple and familiar to most UNIX users. For this reason, they're often overlooked in system administration discussions. However, I believe you'll find them to be an indispensable part of your repertoire.

Interactive Communication with Users

A system administrator frequently needs to send a terminal screen message to a user. *write* is one way to do so:

```
$ write username [tty]
```

where *username* indicates the user to whom you wish to send the message. If you want to *write* to a user who is logged in more than once, the *tty* argument may be used to select the appropriate terminal or window. You can find out where a user is logged in using the *who* command (and also the *finger* command under BSD). Once the *write* command is executed, communication is established between your terminal and the user's terminal: lines that you type on your terminal will be transmitted to him. End your message with a CTRL-D. Thus, to send a message to user *martin* for which no reply is needed, execute a command like this:

```
$ write martin
...One or more lines of message text...
^D
```

The user at the other terminal may establish two-way communication with you by issuing his own *write* command. Communication may be broken by either party with a CTRL-D. At that point, *write* sends "EOT" (end of transmission) to the other terminal and exits.

write may also be used over a network by appending a hostname to the username. For example, the command below initiates a message to user *chavez* on the host named *hamlet*:

```
$ write chavez@hamlet
```

The *rwho* command may be used to list all users on the local network.

The *talk* command is a more sophisticated version of *write* which is available under BSD, V.4, and AIX 3.1. It formats the messages between two users in two separate windows on the terminal screen. The recipient is notified that someone is calling her, and she must issue her own *talk* command to begin communication. Figure 1-1 illustrates the use of *talk*.

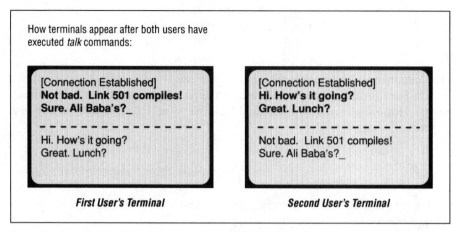

Figure 1-1. Two-way Communication with talk

Users may disable messages from both *write* and *talk* by using the command *mesg n* (they can include it in their *.login* or *.profile* initialization file). Sending messages as the superuser will override this command. Be aware, however, that sometimes users have good reasons for temporarily turning off messages. For example, a user might execute *mesg n* before generating a report on a printing terminal. If such situations are common on your system, you'll want to limit messages sent as superuser to those of a truly urgent nature. In general, the effectiveness of terminal messages is inversely proportional to their frequency.

Sending a Message to All Users

If you need to send a message to every user on the system, you can use the *wall* command. *wall* stands for "write all" and allows the administrator to send a message to all users simultaneously.

To send a message to all users, execute the command:

```
$ wall
...Followed by the message you want to send, terminated with CTRL-D on a separate line...
^D
```

UNIX will then display a phrase like:

```
Broadcast Message from root on console ...
```

on every terminal in use, followed by the text of your message. Similarly, the *rwall* command sends a message to every user on the local network.

Anyone can use this facility; it does not require superuser status. As with *write* and *talk* above, you will need to send the message as the superuser to override any users' *mesg n* commands. A good example of such a message would be to give advance warning of an imminent but unscheduled system shutdown.

The Message of the Day

Login time is a good time to communicate certain types of information to users. It's one of the few times that you can be reasonably sure of having a user's attention (sending a message to the terminal screen won't do much good if the user isn't at the terminal). The file */etc/motd* is the system's message of the day. Whenever anyone logs in, the system will print the contents of this file on the terminal. You can use it to display system-wide information such as maintenance schedules, news about new software, an announcement about someone's birthday, or anything else considered important and appropriate on your system. This file should be short enough so that it will fit entirely on a typical terminal screen. If it isn't, users won't be able to read the entire message as they log in.

On BSD systems, users can disable the message of the day by creating a file named *.hushlogin* in their home directories.

System V Local System News

For less timely or less critical information, the directory */usr/news* (*/var/news* under V.4) may be used as a system news repository. Any user with write access to the directory may place a file there. The *news* command is used to read news placed there. The creation time of the file *$HOME/.news_time* is used by *news* to determine the items to display; all files created after it will be displayed.

The *news* command concatenates all the relevant news files together, preceding each file by a header line displaying the filename and user ID of the user who created it:

```
Ping_Pong_Tourney (chavez) Fri Feb 15 12:19:38 1991

A new ping-pong tournament is organizing. Send me mail if
you want to be in it.
```

```
GrpMtg_Reschedule (williams) Fri Feb 15 14:09:21 1991

The compiler group meetings for the next three weeks will
be held at 10:15, instead of 10, in conference room C.
```

If filenames are carefully chosen, they can serve as quasi-subject lines for the news items.

Users must run the *news* command to see the news messages. Hence, if your system decides to use news as a serious information exchange method, it is a good idea to put a *news* command in users' initialization files when creating new accounts. Since news items are not limited in length, *news* ought to be piped to *more*:

```
$ news | more
```

If you don't want the news facility on your system, remove write access from the news directory. (If you delete the directory entirely, the *news* command will fail with an ugly error message.)

NOTE

The news facility described above has no connection to the Usenet network news system.

Sending Mail to a Group of Users

For non-urgent or lengthy messages, the mail system is the easiest way to communicate with users. It is also the most convenient way of sending a message to an arbitrary group of users all at once. It is preferable to the message of the day facility when the information you need to send is too lengthy for one terminal screen or when users will want to be able to refer to it at a later date.

To send mail to a group of users, you must first create a distribution list containing the usernames of the members of the group. (Note that "group" is used here merely to refer to a collection of users. It need not—and generally won't—correspond to a UNIX group.) System distribution lists are stored in ASCII form in the file */usr/lib/aliases* (sometimes stored in */etc* or as */usr/lib/mail.aliases*). New lists may be created by editing this file.

Distribution lists are specified in the file in the following format:

   aliasname: *username1, username2, username3,* ...

where *aliasname* is the name by which you will refer to the distribution list. The alias name is followed by a colon and the list of users to include in that distribution list, separated by commas. Any line beginning with white space is interpreted as a continuation line, so the username list may continue across several lines. Another popular format is to place each username on a separate line for ease of reading. The following example shows a simple */usr/lib/aliases* file, showing various possible formats:

```
chemists: priestley, dalton, davy, lavoisier, faraday

physicists:
  faraday,
  planck,
  einstein,
  curie

everybody: chemists, physicists, lamarck, root
```

Note that users may be placed in more than one list: *faraday* belongs to both chemists and physicists, for example. It is also legal for an alias to be a member of another distribution group; for example, *everybody* includes *physicists* and *chemists* among its user list.

A hostname may be appended to the username to specify mail on a given system:

```
curie:
  \curie@radium
```

The initial backslash inhibits any further aliasing of the name (to prevent mail bouncing back and forth among hosts forever).

The UNIX mail facility does not access the */usr/lib/aliases* file directly. Instead, it uses the binary files */usr/lib/aliases.dir* and */usr/lib/aliases*. These random access databases speed up the alias expansion process. Once you have edited the */usr/lib/aliases* file, you must update the binary files by using the *newaliases* command:

```
# newaliases
```

Any changes you make to the */usr/lib/aliases* file will not take effect until this command is executed. You may want to run *newaliases* in the background because it can take a while to complete.

Once your distribution lists are set up and installed, they may be used like any other username in mail commands by any user on the system. For example, to send a mail message to every user in the *chemists* list above, you could use the following command:

```
% mail chemists
. . . Text of message, ending as usual with a CTRL-D . . .
```

When the message is processed, the alias *chemists* will be expanded to the list of users in the */usr/lib/aliases* file. Duplicates are removed automatically.

You may want change the alias for *postmaster* in the */usr/lib/aliases* file; by default, it is set to *root*. If you do not use the *root* account as your primary account, it may be more convenient for it to be set to the username you do use.

Essential Administrative Tools

This section will consider ways that some common user commands can be used as tools to obtain information relevant to system administration and to perform basic administrative tasks. We'll use *grep* and *find* as examples.

The *grep* command searches its input for lines containing a given pattern. Users commonly use *grep* to search files. That is undoubtedly familiar to you already. What might be new is some of the ways *grep* is useful in pipes with many administrative commands. For example, if you want to find out about all of a certain user's current processes, pipe the output of the *ps* command to *grep* and search for her username:

```
% ps -aux | grep chavez
chavez    8684 89.5  9.627680 5280 ?  R N  85:26 /u/j90/1988
root     10008 10.0  0.8 1408  352 p2 S      0:00 grep chavez
chavez    8679  0.0  1.4 2048  704 ?  I N    0:00 -csh (csh)
chavez    8681  0.0  1.3 2016  672 ?  I N    0:00 /usr/nqs/scl
chavez    8683  0.0  1.3 2016  672 ?  I N    0:00 csh -cb rj90
chavez    8682  0.0  2.6 1984 1376 ?  I N    0:00 j90
```

This example uses the BSD version of *ps*, using the options which list every single process on the system,* and then uses *grep* to pick out the ones belonging to user *chavez*. If you'd like the header line from *ps* included as well, use a command like:

```
% ps -aux | egrep 'chavez|PID'
```

---

*Under System V, the corresponding command is *ps -ef*.

Now that's a lot to type every time, but you could define an alias if you use the C shell:

```
% alias pu "ps -aux | egrep '\!:1|PID'"
% pu chavez
USER     PID %CPU %MEM   SZ RSS TT STAT  TIME COMMAND
chavez  8684 89.5  9.627680 5280 ?  R N  85:26 /u/j90/1988
. . .
```

Another useful place for *grep* is with the *man -k* command, used to list manual pages concerning a given topic (not available under XENIX and most V.3 versions). I recently was trying to figure out where the error log file was on a new system—the machine kept displaying annoying messages from the error log indicating that disk 3 had had a hardware failure. Now I knew that, and it was even already fixed. I tried *man -k error*: 64 matches; *man -k log* was even worse: 122 manual pages. But *man -k log | grep error* produced only 9 matches, including a nifty command to blast error log entries older than a given number of days.*

Another common command of great use to a system administrator is *find*. *find* is one of those commands that you wonder how you ever lived without—once you learn it. It has one of the most obscure manual pages in the UNIX canon, so I'll spend a bit of time explaining its syntax (skip ahead if it's already familiar).

find locates files having certain common characteristics, which you specify, anywhere on the system that you tell it to look. *find* has the following syntax:

```
# find  starting-dir(s)  matching-criteria-and-actions
```

Starting-dir(s) is the set of directories where *find* should start looking for files. *find* searches all directories underneath the listed directories. Thus, specifying / as the starting directory would search the entire filesystem.

The *matching-criteria* tell *find* what sorts of files you want to look for. Some of the most useful are shown in Table 1-1.

---

*It's probably worth mentioning how to get *man -k* working if your system says it supports it, but nothing comes back when you use it. This command (and its alias *apropos*) uses a data file */usr/man/whatis*, which usually has to be created by the system administrator (and also needs to be updated from time to time). The command to do so is:

```
# catman -w &
```

It takes quite a while, so you'll probably want to run it in the background.

Table 1-1. find Matching Criteria

Option	Meaning
-atime n	File was last accessed exactly *n* days ago.
-mtime n	File was last modified exactly *n* days ago.
-size n	File is exactly *n* 512-byte blocks long.
-type c	Specifies the file type: *f*=plain file, *d*=directory, etc.
-fstype typ	Specifies filesystem type: *4.2* or *nfs* (BSD/V.4 with NFS only).
-name nam	The filename is *nam*.
-user usr	The file's owner is *usr*.
-group grp	The file's group owner is *grp*.
-perm p	The file's access mode if *p*.

Now these may not seem all that useful—why would you want a file accessed exactly three days ago, for instance? However, you may precede all time periods and sizes with a plus sign (meaning "more than") or a minus sign (meaning "less than") to get more useful criteria. Here are some examples:

```
-mtime +7      ...Last modified more than 7 days ago...
-atime -2      ...Last accessed less than 2 days ago...
-size +100     ...Larger than 50K...
```

You can also include wildcards with the *-name* option, provided that you quote them. For example, the criteria *-name '*.dat'* specifies all filenames ending in *.dat*.

Multiple conditions are joined with AND by default. Thus, to look for files last accessed more than two months ago and last modified more than four months ago, you would use these options:

```
-atime +60 -mtime +120
```

Options may also be joined with *-o* for OR combination, and grouping is allowed using escaped parentheses. For example, the matching criteria below specifies files last modified more than seven days ago or last accessed more than 30 days ago:

```
\( -mtime +7 -o -atime +30 \)
```

An exclamation point may be used for NOT (be sure to quote it if you're using the C shell). For example, the matching criteria below specify all *.dat* files except *gold.dat*:

```
\! -name gold.dat -name \*.dat
```

The *actions* options tell *find* what to do with each file that it finds that matches all the specified criteria. Some available actions are shown in Table 1-2.

Table 1-2. find Actions

Option	Meaning
-print	Display pathname of matching file.
-exec cmd	Execute command on file.
-ok cmd	Prompt before executing command on file.
-mount (System V)	Restrict the search to the filesystem of the starting directory.
-xdev (BSD)	Restrict the search to the filesystem of the starting directory.
-prune (BSD)	Don't descend into directories encountered.

Commands must end with an escaped semicolon (\;). The form "{}" may be used in commands as a placeholder for the pathname of each found file. For example, to delete each matching file as it is found, specify the following option:

```
-exec rm {} \;
```

There are no spaces between the opening and closing braces.

Now let's put the parts together. The command below lists the pathname of all C source files under the current directory:

```
$ find . -name \*.c -print
```

The starting directory is "." (the current directory), the matching criteria specify filenames ending in *.c*, and the action to be performed is to display the pathname of each matching file. This is a typical user use for *find*. Other common uses include searching for misplaced files and feeding file lists to *cpio*.

find has many administrative uses, including:

• Monitoring disk use.

• Locating files that pose potential security problems.

• Performing recursive operations (especially useful under System V).

For example, *find* may be used to locate large disk files. The command below displays a long directory listing for all files under */chem* larger than 1000 blocks (approx. 500K) that haven't been modified in a month:

```
$ find /chem -size +1000 -mtime +30 -exec ls -l {} \;
```

To search for files not modified in a month or not accessed in three months, use this command:

```
$ find /chem -size +1000 \( -mtime +30 -o -atime +120 \) \
   -exec ls -l {} \;
```

Such old, large files might be candidates for tape backup and deletion if disk space is short.

If desired, *find* can delete files automatically as it finds them. The following is a typical administrative use of *find*: to automatically delete old junk files on the system:

```
# find / \( -name a.out -o -name core -o -name '.CKP.*' \
   -o -name '.BAK.*' -o -name '#*#' \) -type f -atime +14 \
   -exec rm -f {} \; -o -fstype nfs -prune
```

This command searches the entire filesystem and removes various editor backup files, core dump files, and random executables (*a.out*) that haven't been accessed in two weeks and that don't reside on a remotely mounted filesystem. The logic is messy: the final *-o* option OR's all the options that preceded it with those that followed it, each of which is computed separately. Thus, the final operation finds files that match either of two criteria: the filename matches, it's a plain file, and it wasn't accessed for 5 days; or the filesystem type is NFS (meaning a remote disk). If the first criteria set is true, the file gets removed; if the second set is true, a "prune" action takes place, which says "don't descend any lower into the directory tree." Thus, every time *find* comes across an NFS-mounted filesystem, it will move on, rather than searching its entire contents as well.

Matching criteria and actions may be placed in any order, and are evaluated from left to right. For example, the following *find* command lists all regular files under the directories */u* and */u1* which are larger than 500K and were last accessed over 30 days ago (done by the options through *-print*); additionally, it removes those named "core":

```
# find /u /u1 -type f -atime +30 -size +1000 -print \
   -name core -exec rm {} \;
```

find also has security uses. For example, the following *find* command lists all files that have SUID or SGID access set (see the section, "The SUID and SGID Access Modes," in Chapter 5, *Security*:

```
# find / -type f \( -perm -2000 -o -perm -4000 \) -print
```

The output from this command could be compared to a saved list of SUID and SGID files, in order to locate any newly-created ones requiring investigation:

```
# find / \( -perm -2000 -o -perm -4000 \) -print | \
  diff - files.secure
```

find may also be used to perform the same operation on a selected group of files. For example, the command below changes the ownership of all the files under user *chavez*'s home directory to user *chavez* and group *physics*:

```
# find /u/chavez -exec chown chavez {} \; \
  -exec chgrp physics {} \;
```

As a final example of the creative use of ordinary commands, consider the following dilemma. A user tells you his workstation won't reboot. He tells you he was changing his system's boot script but may have deleted some files in */etc* accidentally. You go over to it, type *ls* and get a message about some missing shared libraries. How do you poke around and find out what files are there?

The answer is to use the simplest UNIX command there is, *echo* (which is simple enough not to need shared libraries), along with the wildcard mechanism built into every shell. To see all the files in the current directory, just type:

```
$ echo *
```

which tells the shell to display the value of "*", which of course expands to all files not beginning with a period in the current directory.

By using *echo* together with *cd* (also a built-in shell command), I was able to get a pretty good idea of what had happened. I'll tell you the rest of this story in Chapter 3, *Startup and Shutdown*.

Menu Interfaces for System Administration

I'd like to conclude this introductory chapter with a brief look at the growing trend toward menu-driven system administration interfaces on UNIX systems.

There have been many efforts in recent years to standardize and simplify UNIX system administration. The growing popularity of workstations, which to some extent make every user an administrator, has fueled these efforts. Many UNIX versions now provide menu interfaces for system administration, designed to allow even relative novices to perform routine administrative tasks.

Unfortunately, there is as yet no standard way of setting up or invoking such menu systems. Currently, XENIX calls its command *sysadmsh*, under System V it is *sysadm,* and AIX 3.1 provides SMIT (System Management Interface Tool), invoked with the *smit* command.

Menus can sometimes be quite useful. You don't need to worry about getting tricky command syntax just right because the program does it for you. But if you know the command you want to run, it's usually faster just to enter it yourself.

Most menu interfaces provide some sort of shortcut startup command to get you to the exact screen you want to work with. For example, to go directly to the interface to the *mkfs* command, you could use one of these startup commands:

```
# sysadm make      V.4 uses task keywords to specify menus.
# smit mkfs         AIX 3.1 uses command names.
```

AIX 3.1 in particular has adopted a consistent naming convention across a wide range of administrative commands. These commands use the prefixes *mk* (make), *ch* (change), *ls* (list), and *rm* (remove) and append the object to be acted on to complete the command name: *mkuser, chuser, lsuser, rmuser* for working with user accounts; *mkfs, chfs, lsfs, rmfs* for working with filesystems, and so on. Thus, it's often possible to guess the name of the command you want and, using SMIT's quick startup mode, get right to the command screen you need.*

```
Current fast path:
  "mkdev"
```

If the screen doesn't have a fast path, the second line will be blank. Press Cancel (ESCAPE 3) to return to the menu.

Most of the menu interfaces are basically shells that construct and run the same commands that you would enter at the command line. There is a misconception, especially with AIX 3.1's SMIT, that somehow these programs are doing additional things that the raw commands alone won't do. That isn't true for any of the specific UNIX versions we're considering, although some menu choices may execute more than one command. Some of the confusion in AIX 3.1 comes from the fact that a few commands do more than they do in other UNIX versions. More specifically, some AIX 3.1 commands update both the traditional UNIX ASCII configuration files and the device information database maintained by AIX 3.1's Object Data Manager (ODM). It isn't SMIT that is doing things differently, it's the seemingly-familiar command that is, whether entered by you or by SMIT.

AIX 3.1 and V.4 configuration files present another dilemma for the administrator, especially those who have experience managing other UNIX systems. Current documentation for both of these versions generally discourages the practice of editing these files directly. Rather, they suggest using the command interfaces

---

*When you're at a SMIT screen, you can display the argument you need to start up SMIT at that screen by pressing F8 (or ESCAPE 8):

that they provide. In real life, it's often much faster to just edit the files directly, and in many cases this will work fine. However, in some cases, all of the data is not stored in the configuration file any more. For example, shadow password files hold actual user passwords. In other cases, the command interfaces perform other actions in addition to modifying the configuration file (such as also updating the device database maintained by the Object Data Manager under AIX 3.1). Check the relevant manual pages carefully before assuming that you can simply change a configuration file under V.4 or AIX 3.1 the way you can under BSD or V.3.

One disadvantage of menu interfaces is that all command functionality is not available through the menu system. Often only the most frequently-used commands and/or options are. You'll still need to execute some versions of commands by hand.

However, the best argument against menu interfaces is that using them slows down the process of learning the underlying commands that they call. This may not be important if your administrative duties really are limited to keeping just your own workstation running. However, if you have any responsibility for other systems—or to other users—then it's vital that you know how the administrative commands work. One way to make the transition from menus to commands (or to menus plus commands) is to use the built-in equivalent command display feature available in some menu systems. For example, under AIX 3.1's SMIT, pressing F6 (or ESCAPE 6) will display the command it will execute; this feature allows you to look at the command being generated by the menu system before it is run. In this way, you can learn the associated UNIX commands or, if you are already have some experience with UNIX administrative commands, you can use it to check up on the menu system to make sure that it is really using the option combination you want to use. Unfortunately, the V.4 menu system has no comparable facility.

All in all, menu interfaces are great when they save you time and effort, but relying on them to lead you through every situation will inevitably lead to frustration and disappointment.

2

The UNIX Way

Files
Processes
Devices
The UNIX Filesystem Layout

While I've avoided presenting you with a list of standard system management tasks, it is fairly easy to list the most important issues and concerns system managers face, regardless of the type of system they have. Almost every system manager has to deal with users' accounts, system startup and shutdown, peripheral devices, system performance, security—the list could go on and on. While the commands and procedures you'd use in each of these areas vary widely with different computer systems, their general approaches to such issues can at times be remarkably similar. For example, the process of adding users to a system has the same basic shape everywhere: add the user to the system databases, allocate some disk space for him, assign a password to the account, and so on. Naturally, the commands to perform these tasks are different for different systems.

In other cases, however, even the *approach* to an administrative task or issue will change from one computer system to the next. For example, "mounting disks" doesn't mean the same thing on a UNIX system that it does on, say, a VMS system or on an MVS system (where they're not always even called disks). No matter what operating system you're using—UNIX, VMS, MVS, DOS—you need to know something about what's happening inside, at least more than an ordinary user does. Like it or not, a sytem administrator is generally called on to be the resident guru. If you're responsible for a multi-user system, you'll need to be able to answer questions, come up with solutions that are more than just band-aids, and so on. Even if you're only responsible for your own workstation, you'll find yourself dealing with aspects of the computer's operation that most ordinary users can simply ignore. In either case, you need to know a fair amount about how UNIX really works, both to manage your system and to navigate the eccentric and sometimes confusing byways of the often jargon-ridden technical documentation.

This chapter will explore the UNIX approach to some basic computer entities: files, processes, and devices. In each case, it will discuss how the UNIX approach affects system administration procedures and objectives. The chapter concludes with an overview of the standard UNIX directory structure. If you have managed non-UNIX computer systems, this chapter will serve as a bridge between the administrative concepts you know and the specifics of UNIX. If you have some familiarity with user-level UNIX commands, this chapter will show you their place in the underlying operating system structure, enabling you to place them in an administrative context. If you're already familiar with things like file modes, inodes, special files, and fork-and-exec, you can probably skip this chapter.

Files

Files are central to UNIX in ways that are not true for other operating systems. Commands are executable files, usually stored in predictable locations in the directory tree. System privileges and permissions are controlled almost exclusively via access to files. Device I/O and file I/O are not distinguished at the highest levels. Even most interprocess communication occurs via file-like entities. Accordingly, the UNIX view of files and its standard directory structure are among the first things a new administrator needs to know about.

Like all modern operating systems, UNIX has a hierarchical (tree-structured) directory organization, known collectively as the *filesystem*.* The base of this tree is a directory called the *root directory*. The root directory has the special name / (the slash character). On UNIX systems, all user-available disk space is combined into a single directory tree under /, and the physical disk a file resides on is not part of a UNIX file specification. We'll discuss this topic more in the section entitled "Devices," later in this chapter.

---

*Or *file system*—the two forms refer to the same thing.

Access to files is organized around file ownership and protection. Security on a UNIX system depends to a large extent on the interplay between the ownership and protection settings on its files and its user account and group* structure (as well as factors like physical access to the machine). The following sections discuss the basic principles of UNIX file ownership and protection.

File Ownership

UNIX file ownership is a bit more complex than it is under some other operating systems. Files have both a user owner and a group owner. However, the UNIX scheme is different than just allowing you to specify file access for members of your own group separately from the access applying to the rest of the world. What is unusual about UNIX file ownership is that these two owners are decoupled. A file's group ownership is independent of the user who owns it. Although a file's group owner is often, perhaps even usually, the same as the primary group of its user owner (except on BSD systems, as we'll see), in principle the user owner of a file need not even be a member of the group that owns it. There is no necessary connection between them at all. In such a case, when file access is specified for a file's group owner, it applies to members of that group and not to other members of its user owner's primary group; they are treated simply as part of the "world."

The motivation behind this group ownership of files is to allow file protections and permissions to be organized according to local needs. The key point here is flexibility. Since UNIX lets users be in more than one group, you are free to design groups as you need them. Files can be made accessible to completely arbitrary collections of the system's users. Group file ownership means that giving someone access to a entire set of files and commands is as simple as adding her to the group that owns them; similarly, taking access away from someone else involves removing him from the relevant group.

To consider a more concrete example for a moment, suppose user *chavez*, who is in the *chem* group, needs access to some files usually used by the *physics* group.

---

*On UNIX systems, individual user accounts are organized into *groups*. Groups are simply collections of users and are defined in the configuration files */etc/passwd* and */etc/group*. The mechanics of defining groups and designating users as members of them are described in Chapter 4, *User Accounts*. Using groups effectively to enhance system security is discussed in Chapter 5, *Security*.

UNIX allows users to be members of more than one group. If this is the case, then the group to which a user's account was assigned when created (in the file */etc/passwd*) is known as the user's *primary group*. Other groups are *secondary groups*.

There are several ways you can give her access:

- Make copies of the files for her. If they change, however, her copies will need to be updated. And if she needs to make changes too, there will end up being two versions.

- Make the files world-readable. Unfortunately, this opens up the possibility that someone you don't want to look at the files will see them.

- Make *chavez* a member of the *physics* group. This is the best alternative and also the simplest. It involves changing only the group configuration file. The file permissions don't need to be modified at all, since they already allow access for *physics* group members.

Displaying File Ownership

To display a file's user and group ownership, use the long form of the *ls* command, selected with *–l* (V.4) or *–lg* (BSD):[*]

```
$ ls -l
-rw-------  1 root     system      120 Mar 12 16:10 gold
-rw-------  1 chavez   chem         84 Feb 28 16:10 silver
-rw-------  1 chavez   physics     512 Jan  2 16:10 bronze
```

Columns three and four display the user and group owners for the listed files. For example, we can see that the file *gold* is owned by user *root* and group *system*. The other two files are both owned by user *chavez,* but they have different group owners; *silver* is owned by group *chem* while *bronze* is owned by group *physics*.

Who Owns New Files?

When a new file is created, its user owner is the user who creates it. Its group ownership is more complicated and varies on different UNIX systems:

- Under System V, the group owner is the current group of the user who creates the file.

- On BSD-based systems, the group owner is the same as the group owner of the directory in which the file is created.

---

[*]The *–g* option (used in conjunction with *–l*) is quite different between System V and BSD. Under BSD, *–g* says to include the group owner along with the user owner. Under System V, it says to display *only* the group owner.

Both SunOS and AIX 3.1 use the System V group ownership rules by default, but allow BSD-style group inheritance from the directory by setting the SGID attribute on the directory. See the section entitled "SGID Access on Directories (AIX 3.1 and SunOS)," later in this chapter for information on setting this attribute.

Changing File Ownership

If you need to change the ownership for a file, use the *chown* and *chgrp* commands. The *chown* command changes the user owner of a file or group of files:

```
# chown new-owner file(s)
```

where *new-owner* is the username (or user ID) of the new owner for the specified files. For example, to change the owner of the file *brass* to user *martin*, execute this *chown* command:

```
# chown martin brass
```

If you need to change the ownership of an entire directory subtree, under BSD and V.4 you can use the *-R* option (for *recursive*). Otherwise, use *find*. For example, the following commands change the user owner to *martin* for the directory */home/iago/new/mhg* and all files contained underneath it:

```
# chown -R martin /home/iago/new/mhg     or
# find /home/iago/new/mhg -print | xargs chown martin
```

Under System V, either the file's owner or the superuser may change file ownership; on BSD systems, only the superuser may change file ownership. AIX 3.1 follows the BSD practice, and XENIX follows the System V practice.*

The *chgrp* command may be similarly used to change a file's group ownership:

```
$ chgrp new-group file(s)
```

where *new-group* is the group name (or GID) of the desired group owner for the specified files. *chgrp* also supports the *-R* option under BSD and V.4. Non-*root* users must be both the owner of the file and a member of the new group to change a file's group ownership under BSD and its derivatives.

The BSD *chown* command lets you change both the user and group owner in a single operation, using this format:

```
# chown new-owner.new-group file(s)
```

---

*Under V.4, the system administrator may specify whether non-*root* users are allowed to change file ownership by setting the value of the kernel parameter *RSTCHOWN* and building a new kernel.

For example, to change the user owner to *chavez* and the group owner to *chem* for *chavez*'s home directory and all the files underneath it, use this command:

```
# chown -R chavez.chem /u/chavez
```

The AIX 3.1 version of *chown* also works this way. V.4 offers this version of the command as part of its BSD compatibility. See the section entitled "Processes," later in this chapter on how to make the BSD version the default *chown* command under V.4.

File Protection

Once ownership is set up properly, the next natural issue to consider is how to protect files from unwanted access (or the reverse: how to allow access to those people who need it). The protection on a file is referred to as its *file mode* on UNIX systems. File modes are set with the *chmod* command; we'll look at *chmod* after discussing the file protection concepts it relies on.

Types of File and Directory Access

UNIX supports three types of file access: read, write, and execute, designated by the letters *r*, *w*, and *x* respectively. Table 2-1 shows the meanings of those access types.

Table 2-1. File Access Types

Access	Meaning on File	Meaning on Directory
r	View file contents.	Search directory contents (e.g., to use *ls*).
w	Alter file contents.	Alter directory contents = delete files in it.
x	Run executable file.	Make it your current directory (*cd* to it).

The file access types are fairly straightforward. If you have read access to a file, you can see what's in it. If you have write access, you can change what's in it. If you have execute access and the file is an executable program, you can run it. To run a script, you need both read and execute access, since the shell has to read the commands to interpret them. Running a compiled program means loading it into memory and beginning execution, so you don't need read access.

The corresponding meanings for directories may seem strange at first, but they do make sense. If you have execute access to a directory, then you can *cd* to it (or include it in a path that you want to *cd* to). You can also access files in it by name. To use the *ls* command without any arguments, however, you also need read access to the directory. This is consistent since a directory is just a file whose contents are the names of the files it contains, along with information pointing to their disk locations. To access a directory location, you don't necessarily need to know what's in it, but to list its contents, you do. Thus, to *cd* to a directory, you need only execute access, but to run any command that operates on any of the directory's files without explicitly listing their pathnames, you need read access as well (e.g., *ls* without arguments or any command with wildcards).

Table 2-2 illustrates the workings of these various access types by listing some sample commands and the minimum access you would need to successfully execute them.

Table 2-2. File Protection Examples

Command	Minimum Access Needed	
	(on file itself)	(on directory file is in)
cd /u/chavez	N/A	x
ls /u/chavez/.c*	none	r
ls −s /u/chavez/.c*	none	rx
cat runme	r	x
cat >>runme	w	x
runme	x (if binary)	x
runme	rx (if script)	x
rm runme	none	xw

Some items in this list are worth a second look. For example, you need only read access to do a simple *ls,* but if you include the -s option (which lists file sizes), then you need execute access as well. This is because the file sizes must be determined from the disk information, which requires logically moving to the directory. Any operation that involves more than simply reading the list of filenames from the directory file is going to require execute access.

Note especially that write access on a file *is not required* to delete it; write access to the directory where the file resides is sufficient (although in this case you'll be asked whether to override the protection on the file):

```
$ rm copper
rm: override protection 440 for copper? y
```

If you answer *yes,* the file will be deleted (the default response is *no*). What is happening here is that deleting a file actually means removing its entry from the directory file (among other things), which is a form of altering the directory file. The moral is that write access to directories is very powerful, and should be granted with care.

Given these considerations, we can summarize the different options for protecting directories as shown in Table 2-3.

Table 2-3. Directory Protection

Type of Access	Result
No access	Does not allow any activity of any sort within the directory or any of its subdirectories under any conditions.
Execute access only	Lets users work with programs in the directory that they already know about, but hides all others.
Execute and read access	Lets a user work with programs in the directory and list the contents of the directory, but does not let the user create or delete files in the directory.
Execute, read, and write access	Lets a user work with programs in the directory, look at the contents of the directory, and create or delete files in the directory.

Access Classes

UNIX defines three basic classes of access to files for which protection may be specified separately:

User access (*u*)   Access granted to the owner of the file.

Group access (*g*)   Access granted to members of the same group as the group owner of the file.

Other access (*o*)   Access granted to everyone else (except *root*).

UNIX file protection specifies what access types are available to members of each of the three access classes for the file or directory.

The long version of the *ls* command also displays file permissions in addition to user and group ownership:

```
$ ls -l
-rwxr-xr-x  1 root    system     120 Mar 12 16:10 gold
-r--r--r--  1 chavez  chem        84 Feb 28 16:10 silver
-rw-rw-r--  1 chavez  physics    512 Jan  2 16:10 bronze
```

The set of letters and hyphens at the left end of each line represents the file's mode. The ten characters are interpreted as indicated in Figure 2-1.

	File Type	User Access			Group Access			Other Access		
	−	r	w	x	r	−	x	r	−	x
Position	1	2	3	4	5	6	7	8	9	10
Read Access		●			●			●		
Write Access			●			●			●	
Execute Access				●			●			●

Figure 2-1. Interpreting File Modes

The first character indicates the file type; it is a hyphen for plain files and a *d* for directories (see the section entitled "File Types," later in this chapter for a discussion of the other possibilities). The remaining nine characters are arranged in three groups of three. Moving from left to right, the groups represent user, group, and other access. Within each group, the first character denotes read access, the second character write access, and the third character execute access. If a certain type of access is allowed, then its code letter will appear in the proper position within the triad; if it is not granted, a hyphen will replace it.

For example, in the previous listing, read access and no other is granted for all users on the file *silver*. On the file *gold,* the owner—in this case, *root*—is allowed read, write, and execute access while all other users are allowed only read and write access. Finally, for the file *bronze,* the owner (*chavez*) and all members of the group *physics* are allowed read and write access while everyone else is granted only read access.

Setting File Protection

The *chmod* command is used to specify the protection mode for files:

```
$ chmod access-string(s) file(s)
```

chmod's second argument is an *access-string* which states what permissions you want to set (or remove) for the listed files. An access-string has three parts: the code for one or more access classes, the operator, and the code for one or more access types.

Figure 2-2 illustrates the structure of an *access-string*. To create an access-string, you choose one or more codes from the access class column, one operator from the middle column, and one or more access types from the third column. Then you concatenate them together into a single string (no spaces). For example, the access string "u+w" says to add write access for the user owner of the file. Thus, to add write access for yourself for a file you own (*lead,* say), use the command:

```
$ chmod u+w lead
```

To add write access for everybody, use the *all* access class:

```
$ chmod a+w lead
```

To remove write access, use a minus sign instead of a plus sign:

```
$ chmod a-w lead
```

You can specify more than one access type and more than one access class. For example, the access string "g-rw" says to remove read and write access from the group access. The access string "go=r" says to set the group and other access to read-only (no execute access, no write access), changing the current setting as needed. And the access string "go+rx" says to add both read and execute access for both group and other users.

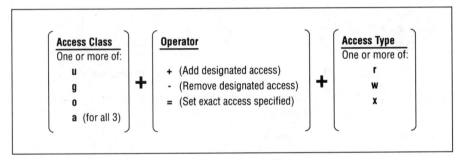

Figure 2-2. Constructing an Access String for chmod

It's also legal to have more than one set of operation-access type pairs for any given access class specification. For example, the access string "u+x-w" adds execute access and removes write access for the user owner. You can combine multiple access strings by separating them with commas (no spaces between them). Thus, the following command adds write access for the file owner, and removes write access and adds execute access for the *group* and *other* classes for the files *bronze* and *brass*:

```
$ chmod u+w,og+r-w bronze brass
```

Under BSD and V.4, the *chmod* command also supports a *recursive* option (*-R*), to change the mode of a directory and all files under it. For example, if user *chavez* wanted to protect all the files under her home directory from everyone else, she could use the command:

```
$ chmod -R go-rwx /u/chavez
```

Specifying Numeric File Modes

The method for specifying file modes just described uses *symbolic* modes, since key letters are used to refer to each access class and type. The mode may also be set as an *absolute* mode by converting the symbolic representation used by *ls* to a numeric form. Each access triad (for a different user class) is converted to a single digit by setting each individual character in the triad to 1 or 0, depending on whether that type of access is permitted or not, and then taking the resulting three-digit binary number and converting it to a decimal number (which will be between 0 and 7). Here is a sample conversion:

user			group			other			
r	w	x	r	-	x	r	-	-	*...Access Class...*
									...Mode...
1	1	1	1	0	1	1	0	0	*...Convert to binary...*
	7			5			4		*...Convert to digit...*
				754					*...Corresponding absolute mode...*

To set the protection on a file to match those above, you specify the 754 numeric file mode to *chmod* as the access string:

```
$ chmod 754 pewter
```

Specifying the Default File Mode

You can use the *umask* command to specify the default mode for newly created files. Its argument is a three digit numeric mode that represents the access to be *inhibited*—masked out—when a file is created. Thus, the value it wants is the octal complement of the desired numeric file mode. To determine this, you simply figure out the numeric equivalent for the file mode you want to get and then subtract it from 777. For example, to obtain the mode 751 by default, compute 777 - 751 = 026; this is the value you give to *umask*:

```
$ umask 026
```

Once this command is executed, all future files created will be given this protection automatically. You usually put a *umask* command in the system initialization file and in the individual initialization files you give to users when you create their accounts (see the section entitled "Initialization Files," in Chapter 4, *User Accounts*).

Additional Access Modes

The simple file protection modes described previously do not exhaust the UNIX possibilities. Table 2-4 lists the other defined file modes.

Table 2-4. Additional File Access Modes

Code	Name	Meaning
t	Sticky bit	Keep executable in memory after exit.
s	Set UID	Set process user ID on execution.
s	Set GID	Set process group ID on execution.
l	File locking	Set mandatory file locking on reads/writes to this file (System V only).*

The *t* access type turns on the *sticky bit* (the formal name is *save text mode,* which is where the *t* comes from), which tells the UNIX operating system to keep an executable image in memory even after the process that was using it has exited. This feature is used infrequently in current UNIX implementations. It was designed to minimize startup overhead for frequently-used programs like *vi*, and is still used on a few systems.

When the set user ID (SUID) or set group ID (SGID) access mode is set on an executable file, processes which run it are granted access to system resources based upon the file's user or group owner, rather than based on the user who created the process. We'll consider these access modes in detail in the section entitled "Processes," later in this chapter.

---

*Under SunOS, turning on SGID access on a file and turning off execute access results in mandatory file locking on that file (instead of the default advisory locks).

Save Text Access on Directories (AIX 3.1 and SunOS)

The sticky bit has been given a new meaning when it is set on directories in some UNIX implementations, including SunOS and AIX 3.1. In these implementations, if the sticky bit is set on a directory, then a user may only delete files which she owns or for which she has explicit write permission granted, even when she has write access to the directory (thus overriding the default UNIX behavior). This feature is designed for use with directories like */tmp,* which are world-writable, but where it may not be desirable to allow any user to delete files at will.

The sticky bit is set using the user access class. For example, to turn on the sticky bit on */tmp,* use this command:

```
# chmod u+t /tmp
```

Oddly, UNIX displays the sticky bit in the other execute access slot in long directory listings:

```
$ ls -ld /tmp
drwxrwxrwt   2 root        8704  Mar 21 00:37  /tmp
```

SGID Access on Directories (AIX 3.1 and SunOS)

SGID access on a directory has a special meaning under SunOS and AIX 3.1. When this mode is set, it means that files created in that directory will have the same group ownership as the directory itself (rather than the user owner's primary group), emulating the default behavior on BSD systems. This is useful when you have groups of users who need to share a lot of files. Having them work in the same directory, which has the SGID attribute, means that correct group ownership will be automatically set for new files, even if the people in the group don't share the same primary group.

To place SGID access on a directory, use a command like:

```
# chmod g+s /pub/chem2
```

How to Recognize a File Access Problem

The first rule of thumb about any user problem that comes up is: it's usually a file ownership or protection problem. Seriously, though, most problems users encounter that aren't the result of hardware problems are file access problems. The classic tip-off for a file protection problem is something that worked yesterday, or last week, or even last year, but doesn't today. In order to work properly, programs and commands must have access to the input and output files they use, any scratch areas they access, and any permanent files they rely on, including the special files in */dev* (which act as device interfaces).

When a problem arises, it can come from either the file permissions being wrong, or the protection being correct but the ownership (user and/or group) being wrong.

The trickiest problem of this sort I've ever seen was at a customer site where I was conducting a user training course. Suddenly, the main text editor stopped working. It would seem to start up fine, and then bomb out when it got to its initialization file. But it worked fine for *root*. The system administrator admitted to "changing a few things" the previous weekend, but didn't remember exactly what. I checked the protections on everything I could think of, but found nothing. I even checked the special files (used for lowest level disk access) in */dev*. My company ultimately had to send out a debugging version of the editor, and the culprit turned out to be */dev/null*! There were at least three morals to this story:

- For the local administrator: always test every change before going on to the next one—multiple, random changes almost always wreak havoc.

- For me: if you *know* it's a protection problem, check the permissions on *everything*.

- For the person who wrote the editor: *always* check the return value of system calls (but that's another book).

If you suspect a file protection problem, try running the command or program as *root*. If it works fine, it's *definitely* a protection problem.

A common, inadvertent way of creating file ownership problems is by accidentally editing files as *root*. When you save the file, the file's owner is changed by some editors. The most obscure variation on this effect that I've heard of is this: someone was editing a file as *root* using an editor that automatically creates backup files whenever the edited file is saved. Creating a backup file meant writing to the directory where the file being edited resides in order to add another entry. This caused the ownership on the *directory* to be set to *root*. Since this happened in the directory used by *uucp* (the UNIX-to-UNIX copy facility), and correct file and directory ownership are crucial for *uucp* to function, what at first seemed to be an innocuous change to an inconsequential file broke an entire UNIX subsystem. *chown uucp* on the directory fixed everything again.*

---

*Clearly, the system itself was somewhat "broken" as well, since adding a file to a directory should never change the directory's ownership.

Mapping Files to Disks

This section will change our focus from files as conceptual entities to files as collections of data on disk. Users need not be aware of the actual disk locations of files they access, but administrators need to have at least a basic conception of how UNIX maps files to disk blocks in order to understand the different file types and the purpose and functioning of the various filesystem commands.

An *inode* (pronounced "eye-node") is the data structure on disk that describes and stores a file's attributes, including its location. When a disk partition is initially prepared to accept files, a specific number of inodes are created. This becomes the maximum number of files of all types, including directories, special files, and links (discussed later) that can exist there, typically, one inode for every 2 to 8 KBytes of actual file storage. This is more than sufficient in most situations.[*] Inodes are given unique numbers, and every distinct file has its own inode. When a new file is created, an unused inode is assigned to it.

Information stored in inodes includes the following:

* User owner and group owner ID's.

* File type (regular, directory, etc., or 0 if unused).

* Access modes (permissions).

* File creation, access, and modification times.

* Inode modification time.

* Number of links to the file (see the section entitled "Links," later in this chapter).

* Size of the file.

* Disk addresses where the file's contents are actually stored.

For very large files, some of the disk addresses in the inode point to *indirect blocks*, which hold addresses of data blocks, rather than actual data. In BSD filesystems, some of the addresses in the inode can point to *double indirect blocks*: blocks holding the addresses of indirect blocks, still two steps away from

---

[*]There are a couple of circumstances where this may not hold. One is the disk partition containing the directory */usr/spool/news*. News files are typically both very small and inordinately numerous, and their numbers have been known to exceed normal inode limits. A second potential problem situation occurs with facilities that make extensive use of symbolic links for functions such as source code control, again characterized by many, many tiny files. In such cases, you can run out of inodes long before disk capacity is exhausted. You will want to take these factors into account when preparing the disk; see the section entitled "Making a New Filesystem," in Chapter 8, *Filesystems and Disks*.

the actual file contents. Addresses in System V inodes can point to triple indirect blocks.

Thus, inodes store all available information about the file *except* its name and directory location. Additional information is stored in inodes in some UNIX implementations. For example, AIX 3.1 includes access control list information in the inode.

File Types

Under UNIX, everything is a file: the operating system even represents I/O devices as files. Therefore, there are several different kinds of files, each with a different function.

Plain Files

Plain files are files containing data, normally called simply "files." These may be ASCII text files, binary data files, executable program binaries, program input or output, and so on.

Directories

A *directory* is a binary file containing a list of the other files it contains (possibly including other directories). Directory entries are filename-inode pairs. This is the mechanism by which inodes and directory locations are associated; the data on disk has no knowledge of its location within its filesystem.

Special Files

Special files are the mechanism used for device I/O under UNIX. They reside in the directory */dev* (and its subdirectories under System V).

There are two types of special files: *character special files*, corresponding to character or raw device access, and *block special files*, corresponding to block I/O device access. Character special files are used for unbuffered data transfers to and from a device; in contrast, block special files are used when data is transferred in fixed-size chunks known as *blocks*. Both kinds of special files exist for some devices (including disks). Character special files generally have names beginning with "r" (for "raw")—*/dev/rdisk0a*, for example—or reside in sub-directories of */dev* whose names begin with "r"—*/dev/rdsk/c1d1s5*, for example. The corresponding block special files have the same name minus the "r": */dev/disk0a*, */dev/dsk/c1d1s5*. Special files are discussed in more detail in the section entitled "Devices," later in this chapter.

Links

A *link* is a mechanism that allows several filenames to refer to a single file on disk. There are two kinds of links: hard links and symbolic (soft) links. A hard link associates two (or more) filenames with an inode. Hard links all share the same disk data blocks while functioning as independent directory entries. For example, the command:

```
$ ln index hlink
```

will create an entry in the current directory named *hlink* with the same inode number as *index*. Hard links may not span disk partitions, since inode numbers are only unique within a given device.

Symbolic links, on the other hand, are pointer files that name another file elsewhere in the filesystem. A symbolic link is a file which points to another pathname in the filesystem. Symbolic links may span physical devices, since they point to a UNIX pathname, not to an actual disk location.

Symbolic links are available in BSD-based versions of UNIX, in AIX 3.1, and in V.4. A few versions of V.3 also implement this feature. They are created with the *-s* option to *ln*.

The two types of links behave similarly, but are not identical. As an example, consider a file *index* to which there is a hard link *hlink* and a symbolic link *slink*. Listing the contents of any of them with a command like *cat* will result in the same output. For both *index* and *hlink*, the disk contents pointed to by the addresses in their common inode will be accessed and displayed. For *slink*, the disk contents referenced by the address in its inode will point to *index*, *index*'s inode will be accessed next, and finally its data blocks will be displayed.

In directory listings, *hlink* will be indistinguishable from *index*. Changes made to either file will affect both of them, since they share the same disk blocks. However, moving either file with the *mv* command will not affect the other one, since moving a file only involves altering a directory entry (remember that pathnames are not stored in the inode). Similarly, deleting *index* will not affect *hlink*, which will still point to the same inode. If a new file in the current directory named *index* is subsequently created, there will be no connection between it and *hlink* since when the new file is created, it will be assigned a free inode. Although they are initially created via an existing file, hard links are "linked" only to an inode, not to the other file. In fact, all regular files are technically hard links.

By contrast, a symbolic link *slink* to *index* will behave differently. The symbolic link will still appear in directory listings, but will be very small (*hlink* is naturally the same length as *index*), and it will be marked as a link with an "l" as the first character in the mode string:

```
% ls -l
-rw------- 1 chavez  5228 Mar 12 11:36 index
-rw------- 1 chavez  5228 Mar 12 11:36 hlink
lrwxrwxrwx 1 chavez     5 Mar 12 11:37 slink -> index
```

Changes made under either name will affect the contents of *index*. Deleting *index* will also break access via the symbolic link; *slink* will point nowhere. But if another file *index* is subsequently recreated, *slink* will once again be linked to it.* Figure 2-3 illustrates the differences between hard and symbolic links.

In the first picture, *index* and *hlink* share the inode N1 and its associated data blocks. The symbolic link *slink* has a different inode, N2, and therefore different data blocks. The contents of inode N2's data blocks refer to the pathname to *index*. Accessing *slink* thus eventually reaches the data blocks for inode N1.

When *index* is deleted (in the second picture), *hlink* is associated with inode N1 by its own directory entry. Accessing *slink* will generate an error, however, since the pathname it references does not exist. When a new *index* is created (in the third picture), its gets a new inode, N3. This new file clearly has no relationship to *hlink*, but does act as the target for *slink*.

For more information, see the *ln* manual page, and experiment with creating and modifying linked files.

Sockets (BSD and V.4)

A socket is a special type of file used for communications between processes. It may be thought of as a communications end point, tied to a particular system port, to which processes may attach. For example, the socket */dev/printer* is used by processes to send messages to the program *lpd* (the line-printer spooling daemon), informing it that it has work to do. Sockets are a BSD feature that has been included in V.4.

Named Pipes (System V, SunOS)

Named pipes are pipes opened by name by applications. They are a System V feature (also supported by SunOS), and they often reside in the */dev* directory. Named pipes are another mechanism to facilitate interprocess communication.

---

*Symbolic links are actually interpreted only when accessed, so they can't really be said to point anywhere at other times. But conceptually, this is what they do.

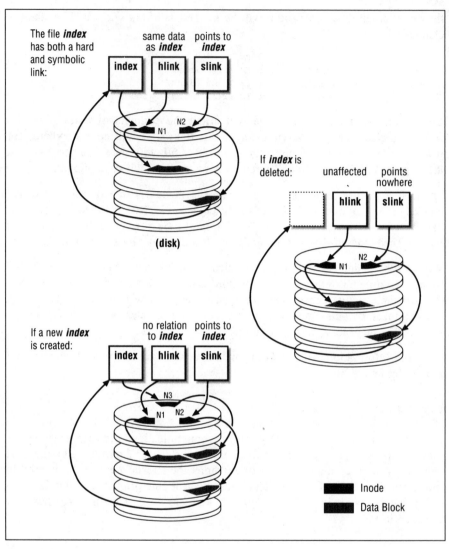

Figure 2-3. Hard Versus Symbolic Links

Using ls to Identify File Types

The long directory listing (produced by the *ls -l* command) identifies the type for each file it lists via the initial character of the permissions string:

-     Plain file (hard link).

d   Directory.

l   Symbolic link.

b   Block special file.

c   Character special file.

s   Socket.

p   Named pipe.

For example, the following *ls* output includes each of the file types discussed above, in the same order:

```
-rw-------- 1 chavez  28 Mar 12 11:36 au.dat
-rw-------- 1 chavez  28 Mar 12 11:36 hlink.dat
drwx------ 2 chavez 512 Mar 12 11:36 bad_data
lrwxrwxrwx 1 chavez   8 Mar 12 11:37 zn.dat -> gold.dat
brw-r----- 1 root     0 Mar  2 15:02 /dev/disk0a
crw-r----- 1 root     0 Jun 12  1989 /dev/rdisk0a
srw-rw-rw- 1 root     0 Mar 11 08:19 /dev/log
prw-------- 1 root     0 Mar 11 08:32 /usr/lib/cron/FIFO
```

Note that the *-l* option also displays the target file for symbolic links.

In some circumstances, you can use the *-i* option to *ls* to determine the equivalent file in the case of hard links. Using *-i* tells *ls* to display its inode number along with each filename. Here is an example:

```
$ ls -i /dev/mt0 /dev/mt/*
  290 /dev/mt0          293 /dev/mt/c0d6ln
  292 /dev/mt/c0d6h     291 /dev/mt/c0d6m
  295 /dev/mt/c0d6hn    294 /dev/mt/c0d6mn
  290 /dev/mt/c0d6l
```

From this display, we can determine that the special files */dev/mt0* (the default tape drive for many commands including *tar*) and */dev/mt/c0d6l* are equivalent, since they both reference inode number 290.

ls can't distinguish between text and binary files (both are "regular" files). You can use the *file* command to do so. Here is an example (the output is taken from a Stardent UNIX system):

```
# file *
appoint:      Stardent 500/3000 series demand paged not stripped
bin:          directory
clean:        symbolic link to bin/clean
fort.1:       empty
gold.dat:     ascii text
intro.ms:     [nt]roff, tbl, or eqn input text
run_me:       commands text
xray.c:       ascii text
```

The file *appoint* is an executable image; the additional information provided for such files differs from system to system. Note that *file* tries to figure out what the contents of ACSII files are, with varying success. If you're running V.3, V.4, or SunOs, you can customize the *file* command to recognize other file types by editing the file */etc/magic*.

Processes

A *process* is a single program that is running in its own virtual address space. It is distinct from a job or a command, which, on UNIX systems, may be composed of many processes working together to perform a specific task. Simple commands like *ls* are executed as a single process. A complex command containing pipes will execute one process per pipe segment. For UNIX systems, managing CPU resources must be done in large part by controlling processes, since the resource allocation and batch execution facilities of other operating systems are underdeveloped or missing.

Process Types

UNIX processes may be of several types:

Interactive processes

> Processes initiated from and controlled by a terminal session. Interactive processes may run either in the *foreground* or the *background*. Foreground processes remain attached to the terminal; the foreground process is the one with which the terminal communicates directly. For example, typing in a UNIX command and waiting for its output means running a foreground process. While a foreground process is running, it alone can receive direct input from the terminal.

For example, if you run, say, the *diff* command on two quite large files, you will be unable to run another command until it finishes (or you kill it with CTRL-C).

BSD popularized *job control* within the UNIX world, implemented in its C shell. The Korn shell also supports job control. V.4 makes C shell-style job control available in all three shells, via the *jsh* version of the Bourne shell. Job control allows a foreground process to be sent to the background. When this happens, the process is temporarily stopped, and terminal control returns to its parent process (usually a shell). The background job may be restarted and continue executing unattached to the terminal session that launched it. Or it may be eventually brought to the foreground, and become once again the terminal's current process. Processes may also be initially started as background processes.

The following inset reviews the methods for controlling foreground and background processes.

Batch processes

Processes which are not associated with a terminal. Rather, they are submitted to a queue, from which jobs are executed sequentially. SunOS and System V have a very primitive *batch* command, but vendors whose customers require queueing have generally implemented something more substantial. Some of the best known are the Network Queueing System (NQS), developed by NASA and used on some high performance computers including Crays, and Hewlett-Packard's TaskBroker, a network-based process scheduling system which attempts to distribute the aggregate CPU load to unused workstations in the network.

Daemons* Server processes, usually initiated at boot time, that wait in the background until some process requires their service. For example, network daemons are idle until some process requests network access.

---

*Daemon is an old word, dating back to ancient Greece. More recently, the poet Yeats wrote at length about daemons, defining them as that which we continually struggle against yet paradoxically need in order to survive, simultaneously the source of our pain and of our strength, even in some sense, the very essence of our being. For Yeats, the daemon is "of all things not impossible the most difficult."

UNIX Job Control

Command	Meaning	Example
&	Run command in background.	`% long_cmd &`
^Z	Stop foreground process.	`%^Z` `Stopped`

jobs	List background processes.	`% jobs`
		`[1] - Stopped  vi`
		`[2] - big_job &`
		`[3] + Stopped long_cmd`

%n	Refers to background job number n.	`% fg %1`
%?str	Refers to the background job command containing str.	`% fg % ?ls`
bg	Restart stopped background process.	`% bg` `[3] long_cmd &`
fg	Bring background process to foreground.	`% fg %1`
kill	Shell version of UNIX command.	`% kill %2`

~^Z	Suspend *rlogin* session.	`hamlet>> ~^z`
		`Stopped`
		`duncan>>`

~~^Z	Suspend second level *rlogin* session.*	

*Useful for nested *rlogin*'s; each additional tilde says to pop back to the next highest level of *rlogin*. Thus one tilde pops all the way back to the lowest level job (the local job), two tildes pops back to the first *rlogin* session, and so on.

Process Attributes

UNIX processes have many associated attributes. Some of the most important are:

Process ID (PID) A unique identifying number used to refer to the process.

Parent Process ID (PPID)
        The PID of the process's parent process.

Nice Number   A number indicating the process's priority relative to other processes. This needs to be distinguished from its actual execution priority, which is dynamically changed according to its nice number and recent resource usage. See the section entitled "Controlling Execution Priorities," in Chapter 7, *Managing System Resources,* for a detailed discussion of nice numbers and their effect on execution priority.

TTY   Terminal (or pseudo-terminal) device associated with the process.

Real and Effective User ID (RUID, EUID)

A process's real UID is the UID of the user who started it. Its effective UID is the UID which is used to determine the process' access to system resources (such as files and devices). Usually the real and effective UID's are the same, and the process accordingly has the same access rights as the user who launched it. However, when the SUID access mode is set on an executable image, then the EUID's of processes executing it are set to the UID of the file's user owner, and they are accorded corresponding access rights.

Real and Effective Group ID (RGID, EGID)

A process's real GID is the user's primary or current group. Its effective GID, used to determine the process' access rights, is the same as the real GID except when the SGID access mode is set on an executable image. The EGID's of processes executing such files are set to the GID of the file's group owner, and they are given corresponding access to system resources.

The Life Cycle of a Process

A new process is created in the following manner. An existing process makes an exact copy of itself, a procedure known as *forking*. The new process, called the *child process*, has the same environment as its *parent process*, although it is assigned a different process ID. Then, the image in the child process' address space is overwritten by the one it will run; this is done via the *exec* system call. (Hence, the often-used phrase *fork-and-exec*.) The new program (or command) completely replaces the one inherited from the parent. However, the environment of the parent still remains, including the values of environment variables, the assignments of standard input, standard output, and standard error, and its execution priority.

Let's make this picture a bit more concrete. What happens when a user runs a command like *grep*? First, the user's login process (assuming he's not running any subshell) forks, creating a new process to run the command. Normal shell initialization takes place; thus, if the user is running the C shell, or the Korn shell with the environment variable ENV defined, then the appropriate initialization file is executed (see the section entitled "Initialization Files," in Chapter 4, *User Accounts*). Then, the new process exec's *grep*, overlaying the shell's image with *grep*'s, which starts to execute. When the *grep* command finishes, the process will die.

This is the way that all UNIX processes are created. The ultimate ancestor for every process on a UNIX system is the process with PID 1, *init*, created during the boot process (described in the section entitled "The UNIX Boot Process," in Chapter 3, *Startup and Shutdown*). *init* creates many other processes (all by fork-and-exec). Among them are one or more executing the *getty* program. The *getty*s are each assigned to a different terminal; they display the login prompt and wait for someone to respond to it. When someone does, the *getty* process exec's the *login* program, which validates user logins among other activities. Once the username and password are verified,[*] *login* exec's the user's shell. Note that the user's final login shell is the same process as the *getty* that was watching the unused terminal; the process has changed identity twice by exec'ing a new program (without forking). This same process will create new processes to execute commands the user types. Figure 2-4 illustrates UNIX process creation.

When any process exits, it sends a signal to its parent process telling it so. So, when a user logs out, her login shell sends a signal to its parent *init* as it dies. This will let *init* know that it's time to create a new *getty* process for the terminal. *init* will fork again and start the *getty*, and the whole cycle will repeat itself again and again as different users use that terminal.

SUID and SGID File Access and Process Execution

The purpose of the SUID and SGID access modes is to allow ordinary users to perform a wider range of functions with fewer access privileges. For example, on many systems the *df* command is owned by the same group as owns the disk special files in */dev*. *df* has SGID access, allowing any user to retrieve and display the current status of the system's filesystems. When users execute the *df* command, their effective GID is set to that of the group owner of *df* (on BSD systems, it is often group *operator*). At all other times, they won't have access to the disk special files.

---

[*]If the login attempt fails, then *login* exits, sending a signal to its parent process, *init*, indicating it should create a new *getty* process for the terminal.

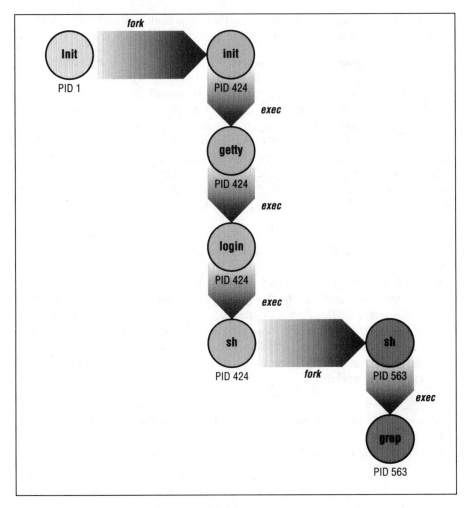

Figure 2-4. UNIX Process Creation: fork and exec

Another example of SUID and SGID access is the *uucp* facility, which allows users to copy files between loosely interconnected UNIX systems, and is often used to transfer files between completely unrelated sites. To prevent *uucp* from being a security risk, the *uucp* programs belong to the special user *uucp* and the special group *daemon* (or group *uucp* on some systems). Whenever users execute one of these programs, they temporarily give up their own user ID and group, and become the *uucp* user and a member of the *daemon* group. If UNIX is installed and configured correctly, the *uucp* user has sharply limited privileges—*uucp* can only execute a few commands and access a single directory. Furthermore, other users on the system have limited access to the *uucp* directories and therefore cannot manipulate *uucp*'s files without using *uucp* itself. Thus, anyone who uses *uucp* is limited to what *uucp* is allowed to do.

SUID and SGID access are also used by the spooling system, by programs like mailers, and by programs like *write* that send messages directly to other users' terminals. However, SUID programs are also notorious security risks. SUID usually means SUID to *root,* and the danger is that somehow, through program stupidity or their own cleverness or both, users will figure out a way to retain their inherited *root* status after the SUID program ends. In general, SUID access should be avoided since it involves greater security risks than SGID and almost any function can be performed by using the latter in conjunction with carefully designed groups. See Chapter 5, *Security*, for a more detailed discussion of the security issues involved with SUID and SGID programs.

The Relationship Between Commands and Files

The UNIX operating system does not distinguish between commands and files in the ways that some systems do. Aside from a few commands which are built into each UNIX shell, UNIX commands are executable files stored in one of several predictable locations. Access to commands is exactly equivalent to access to these files. There is no other privilege mechanism. Even I/O is handled via *special files*, stored in the directory */dev*, which function as interfaces to the device drivers. All I/O operations look just like ordinary file operations from the user's point of view.

UNIX uses *search paths* to locate the executable's images for commands that users enter. A search path is simply an ordered list of directories to look in for commands. A faulty search path is the most common cause for "Command not found" error messages.

Search paths are stored in the PATH environment variable. Here is a typical PATH:

```
$ echo $PATH
/usr/bin:/usr/ucb:/bin:/usr/local/bin:.:$HOME/bin
```

The various directories in the PATH are separated by colons. The search path is used whenever a command name is entered without an explicit directory location. As an example, consider the command below:

```
$ od data.raw
```

The *od* command is used to display a raw dump of a file. To locate this command, the operating system will first look for a file named *od* in the directory */usr/bin*. If such a file exists, it will be executed. If there is no *od* file in */usr/bin*, then */usr/ucb* will be checked next, followed by */bin* (where *od* is in fact located). If it were necessary, the search would continue in */usr/local/bin*, the current directory, and finally the *bin* subdirectory of the user's home directory.

The order of the directories in the search path is important when more than one version of a command exists. Such effects come into play most frequently when both the BSD and the System V versions of commands are available on a system. In this case, you should put the directory holding the versions you want to use first in your search path. For example, if you want to use the BSD versions of commands like *ls* and *ln* on a V.4 system, then put */usr/ucb* ahead of */usr/bin* in your search path. Similarly, if you want to use the System V-compatible commands available under SunOS, put */usr/5bin* ahead of */usr/bin* and */usr/ucb* in your search path. These same considerations will obviously apply to users' search paths that you define for them in their initialization files (see the section entitled "Initialization Files," in Chapter 4, *User Accounts*).

Most of the UNIX administrative utilities are located in the directories */etc* and */usr/etc* (*/sbin* and */usr/sbin* with V.4). These directories typically aren't in the search path unless you put them there explicitly. When executing administrative commands, you can either add these directories to your search path or provide the full pathname for the command, as in the example below:

```
# /etc/chown chavez /u/chavez
```

I'm going to assume in my examples that the administrative directories have been added to the search path. Thus, I won't be including the full pathname for any of the commands I'll be discussing.

Devices

One of the strengths of UNIX is that users don't need to worry about the specifics of devices very often. They don't need to know, for example, what disk drive a file they want to access physically sits on. And the UNIX special file mechanism allows many device I/O operations to look just like file I/O. As we've noted, the administrator doesn't have these same luxuries, at least not all of the time. This section discusses UNIX device handling and then surveys the special files used to access them. We'll use disk drives as an example in our discussion of devices under UNIX.

As we've noted before, UNIX merges all user accessible files into a single hierarchical directory structure. The files contained in it may be spread across several different disk drives.

On most UNIX systems, disks are divided into one or more fixed-size *partitions*: physical subsets of the disk drive which are separately accessed by the operating system. There may be several partitions or just one on each physical disk. The disk partition containing the root directory is called the *root disk* (although it needn't comprise an entire disk drive). The root disk is the first one *mounted*, early in the UNIX boot process, and the remaining disk partitions are mounted afterwards.

On many operating systems, mounting a disk refers to the process of bringing the device online, making its contents available. For UNIX, it means something more. Like the overall UNIX filesystem, the files and directories physically located on each disk partition are themselves arranged in a tree structure.* An integral part of the process of mounting a disk partition involves merging its local directory structure into the total UNIX directory hierarchy. Once this is done, the files physically residing on that device may be accessed via the usual UNIX slash-separated pathname syntax; UNIX takes care of mapping pathnames to the correct physical device and data blocks.

For administrators, however, there are a few times when the disk partition must be accessed directly. The actual *mount* operation is the most common of them. On UNIX systems, all physical devices are accessed via *special files*, located in */dev*. A special file associates a location, type, and access mode with a specific device. As such, it functions as a pointer to a device driver. Thus, for a given device, there may be more than one special file, corresponding to different modes of accessing the device. For example, disk partitions may be accessed in two modes: block mode and raw (or character) mode. Character access mode does unbuffered I/O, generally making a data transfer to or from the device with every *read* or *write* system call. Block devices do buffered I/O on a block basis, collecting data in a buffer until it can transfer an entire block of data at one time.

For devices which support multiple access modes, there will be a special file corresponding to each one. For example, the disk partition containing the root filesystem under BSD typically corresponds to the special files */dev/disk0a* and */dev/rdisk0a*, specifying the first partition on the first disk (disk 0, partition a), accessed in block and raw mode respectively.†

---

*For this reason, each separate disk partition may also be called a *filesystem*. This "filesystem" is used to refer to both the overall system directory tree (as in "*the* UNIX filesystem"), comprised of every user-accessible disk partition on the system, and to the files and directories on individual disk partitions (as in "build *a* filesystem on the disk partition" or "mounting the non-root filesystem*s*"). Whether the overall UNIX directory tree or an individual disk partition is meant will be clear from the context.

†The names given to the two types of special files are overdetermined. For example, the special file */dev/disk0a* is referred to as a *block special file*, and */dev/rdisk0a* is called a *character special file*. However, block special files are also sometimes called *block devices*, and character special files may be referred to as *character devices* or *raw devices*.

CAUTION

Most commands require one or the other type of special file.

As an example of the use of special files to access disk partitions, consider the *mount* commands below:

```
# mount /dev/disk0a /
# mount /dev/disk1e /home
```

Naturally, a command to mount a disk partition will need to specify the physical disk partition to be mounted—*mount*'s first argument—and the location to place it in the filesystem—the second argument.* The first command makes the files in the first partition on drive 0 available, placing them at the root of the UNIX filesystem. The second command accesses a partition from drive 1, placing it at */home* in the overall directory tree. Thus, files in the top-level directory on this second disk partition will appear in */home*. Top-level directories on the disk partition become subdirectories of */home*, and so on. The *mount* command is discussed in greater detail in the section entitled "Mounting and Dismounting Filesystems," in Chapter 8, *Filesystems and Disks*.

Fixed Disk Special Files

Special file names are highly implementation-dependent. Under BSD, special files to access disk partitions have the following form:

/dev/disknx	*Block device.*
/dev/rdisknx	*Character (raw) device.*

where *n* is the disk number (beginning at 0) and *x* is a letter from *a* to *h* designating the partition on the physical disk. The partitions have conventional uses, and not all partitions are used on every disk (see the section entitled "Disk Partitions," in Chapter 8, *Filesystems and Disks*, for more details). The *a* partition on the root disk contains the root filesystem; this is usually the only disk that will have an *a* partition. *b* partitions are conventionally used as swap partitions. On the root disk, other partitions might be used for various system directories: for example, *e* for */tmp*, *g* for */usr*, *h* for */home*, and so on.

---

*In fact, on most UNIX systems, mount is smarter than this. If you give it a single argument—either the physical disk partition or a directory within the UNIX filesystem—it will look up the the other argument in a table. But you can always supply both arguments, which means that you can rearrange your filesystem at will. (Why you would want to do so is another question.)

The *c* partition often refers to the entire disk as a whole, including areas that should be accessed only by the kernel (such as the partition information at the beginning of the drive). Thus, on most BSD-based systems, the *c* partition is never used in commands.

Sometimes, the "disk" portion of the special file names will vary. For example, under SunOS, the block special files for hard disks connected via the SCSI interface are */dev/sdna*, */dev/sdnb*, and so on, where *n* is the drive number.

System V employs a similar naming philosophy, although the actual names differ. Special filenames for disk partitions are of the form:

```
ckdmsn
```

where *k* is the controller number, *m* is the drive number on that controller, and *n* is the partition number on that drive (all numbers start at 0).* Character and block special files have the same names, but are stored in two different subdirectories of */dev*: */dev/dsk* and */dev/rdsk* respectively. Thus, the special file */dev/dsk/c1d0s2* is the block special file for the third partition on the first disk on controller 1. The corresponding character device is */dev/rdsk/c1d0s2*. System V partition numbers also have conventional uses: 0 refers to a root partition, 1 is a swap partition, 2 is used for user filesystems, 3 is used for the */stand* filesystem on the boot device (the mount point for the kernel filesystem), 6 refers to the entire disk, 7 is the boot partition (which stores the programs used to read in and start the kernel), 8 is used for */var*, and 9 for */home*. As with the BSD partitions, not every partition is used for every disk.

The first three characters of the special file name are omitted for controller 0: */dev/dsk/0s1*, for example.

Both XENIX and AIX 3.1 allow the system administrator to specify names for the special files for filesystems when they are created (although in completely different ways). Special files have names of the form:

```
/dev/name
/dev/rname       ...XENIX only...
```

where **name** is chosen when the filesystem is created. Under XENIX, the special files */dev/root* and */dev/rroot* are used to access the root filesystem.

---

*Names in this format, known as *controller-drive-section identifiers*, are used for all disk and tape devices under V.4, although sometimes there are links to more mnemonically-named special files.

Figure 2-5 illustrates the similarities among disk special file names.

	BSD	System V.4	SunOS	Interactive UNIX
File Name	/dev/rdisk0d	/dev/rdsk/c1d0s2	/dev/rsd0d	/dev/rdsk/0s2
Raw Access Mode	/dev/**r**disk0d	/dev/**r**dsk/c1d0s2	/dev/**r**sd0d	/dev/**r**dsk/0s2
Device Type	/dev/r**disk**0d	/dev/r**dsk**/c1d0s2	/dev/r**sd**0d	/dev/r**dsk**/0s2
Drive #	/dev/rdisk**0**d	/dev/rdsk/c1d**0**s2	/dev/rsd**0**d	/dev/rdsk/**0**s2
Disk Partition	/dev/rdisk0**d**	/dev/rdsk/c1d0**s2**	/dev/rsd0**d**	/dev/rdsk/0**s2**
Controller Number		/dev/rdsk/**c1**d0s2		

Figure 2-5. Disk Special File Names

Other disk special files may be present in */dev*. For example, Stardent UNIX allows several disks to be combined into a single logical disk, which it calls a *disk farm*, accessed via special files of the form */dev/farm/farm* n.

Special Files for Other Devices

Other device types have special files named differently, but according to these same basic conventions. Some of the most common are summarized in Table 2-5 (they will be discussed in more detail as appropriate in later chapters). Note that in general the block special files are listed; there will, of course, be character special files for many of them as well.

Table 2-5. Common UNIX Special File Names

Special File Form	Example	Device/Use
*/dev/fd**	*/dev/fd0*	Floppy disk.
/dev/mtn	*/dev/mt2*	Generic tape device.
*/dev/*stn*	*/dev/nst0*	SunOS SCSI tape drive.

Table 2-5. Common UNIX Special File Names (continued)

Special File Form	Example	Device/Use
/dev/ttyn /dev/term/n	/dev/tty01 /dev/term/01	Serial line (hardwired terminal). V.4 terminal (sometimes linked to /dev/ttyn).
/dev/tty[p-s]n	/dev/ttyp1	Virtual terminal (used for network sessions, windows, etc.)
/dev/pts/n	/dev/pts/12	V.4 virtual terminal (sometimes linked to /dev/tty[p-s]n).
/dev/console /dev/hft /dev/ega /dev/vga		Console terminal. AIX 3.1 graphics terminal. XENIX video terminal interfaces.
/dev/tty		Synonym for each process' controlling TTY. Can be used to ensure output goes to the terminal, regardless of any I/O redirection.
/dev/mem /dev/kmem		Map of physical memory. Map of kernel virtual memory.
/dev/winn /dev/mouse	/dev/win00	SunOS window device. Mouse interface.
/dev/ramn /dev/swap	/dev/ram00	RAM disk. Swap device.
/dev/null		Null device: output written to it is discarded; reads from it always return nothing (0 characters, 0 bytes, etc.)

The UNIX Filesystem Layout

Now that we've considered the UNIX approach to major system components, it's time to acquaint you with the structure of the UNIX filesystem. Here, then, is a brief tour. We will begin with the root directory and its most important subdirectories.

The basic layout of traditional UNIX filesystems is illustrated in Figure 2-6, which shows an idealized BSD directory structure.

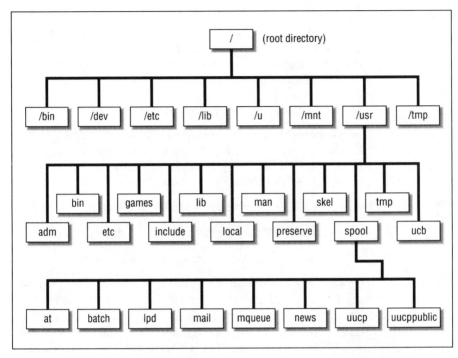

Figure 2-6. BSD Directory Structure

The layouts under V.3, XENIX, and AIX 3.1 are quite similar. We will point out differences as we proceed:

/   The root directory. This is the base of the filesystem's tree structure; all other files and directories, regardless of their physical disk locations, are logically contained within the root directory. This process is described in detail in the section, "Mounting and Dismounting Filesystems," in Chapter 8, *Filesystems and Disks*.

/bin   Command binaries directory. This directory includes executable public programs that are part of the UNIX operating system and its utilities. Other directories which hold UNIX commands are */usr/bin* and (in many UNIX versions) */usr/ucb*.

/dev   Device directory, containing special files as described previously. The */dev* directory is divided into subdirectories in some V.3 implementations and in standard V.4. Each subdirectory holds special files of a given type and is named for the type of devices it contains: *dsk* and *rdsk* for disks accessed in block and raw mode, *mt* and *rmt* for tape drives, *term* for terminals, *pts* and *ptc* for pseudo-terminals (the latter three under V.4 only), and so on.

/etc   System configuration files and executables. This directory contains many administrative files and configuration files. It also contains the executable binaries for most administrative commands. A few additional commands are stored in */usr/etc*. Among the most important files in */etc* are the system boot scripts. Under SunOS, most administrative commands are in */usr/etc*.

Under System V, */etc* also contains a subdirectory *default* which holds files containing default parameter values for various commands (such as the */etc/default/su* file discussed in Chapter 1, *Introduction to System Administration*).

Under AIX 3.1, */etc* contains two additional directories of note:

/etc/objrepos   Stores the device configuration databases.

/etc/security   Stores most user account databases.

/lib   This directory contains library files for the C and other programming languages. Standard runtime library files have names of the form *lib*x*.a*, where *x* is one ore more characters related to the library's contents: *libc.a* = C language library, *libX11.a* = X Windows library, and so on. Some library files are also stored in */usr/lib*.

/lost+found   Lost files directory. Disk errors or incorrect system shutdown may cause files to become *lost*: lost files refer to disk locations that are marked as in use in the data structures on the disk, but that are not listed in any directory (e.g., a non-empty inode that isn't listed in any directory). When the system is booting, it runs a program called *fsck* that, among other things, finds these files. There is a *lost+found* directory on every disk partition; */lost+found* is the one on the root disk.

/mnt   Mount directory. An empty directory conventionally designed for temporarily mounting disk partitions.

/u   This directory is a conventional location for users' home directories. For example, user *chavez*'s home directory would often be */u/chavez*. The name is completely arbitrary, however, and is often changed by the local site. Another common name for this direc-

tory is */home*, which is the name defined under V.4. On older systems, user home directories were placed under */usr*.

/usr   This directory contains subdirectories for spooling, mail, locally generated programs, executables for user commands, and other parts of the UNIX system. The subdirectories of */usr* are discussed in more detail in the next section.

/tmp   Temporary directory, available to all users as a scratch directory. The system administrator should see that all the files in this directory are deleted occasionally. Normally, one of the UNIX startup scripts will clear */tmp*.

The /usr Directory

The directory */usr* contains a number of important subdirectories:

/usr/adm   Administrative directory (home directory of the special *adm* user). This directory contains the UNIX accounting files and various system logging files.

/usr/bin   Command binary files and shell scripts. This directory contains public executable programs that are part of the UNIX system, similar to */bin*. On many systems, executables for layered products are also sometimes stored in */usr/bin* (or subdirectories under it).

/usr/etc   On most systems, a few additional administrative commands are stored here. Under SunOS, the administrative commands usually found in */etc* are stored here.

/usr/games   This directory contains the standard UNIX games collection. Some sites choose to remove this directory.

/usr/include   Include files. This directory contains C-language header files which define the C programmer's interface to standard system features and program libraries. For example, it contains the file *stdio.h*, which defines the user's interface to the C standard I/O library. The directory */usr/include/sys* contains operating system include files.

/usr/lib   Library directory, for public library files. Among other things, this directory contains the standard C libraries for mathematics and I/O. This directory may also contain certain configuration files for UNIX services such as mail. Finally, subdirectories of */usr/lib* contain command and configuration files for various standard UNIX facilities like *uucp* and *lex* and optional software products.

/usr/local Local files. By convention, the directory /usr/local/bin is reserved for any public executable programs developed on your system.

/usr/man Manual pages directory. This directory contains the online version of the UNIX reference manuals. It is divided into subdirectories for each section of the manual. Under BSD and some System V implementations, /usr/man contains several mann subdirectories holding the raw source for the manual pages in that section and the catn subdirectories storing the processed versions. The latter can be cleared to save space; they will be filled only as manual pages are actually accessed. If present, the file /usr/man/whatis contains a database used by the whatis and apropos (man -k) commands.

The significance of the sections is described in the following table. Programs developed at your installation can be documented according to the UNIX manual page format and included in the online manual.

Contents	BSD Section	System V Section
User commands.	1	1
System calls.	2	2
C and other library routines.	3	3
Special files, device drivers, hardware.	4	7
Configuration files.	5	4
Games.	6	6 or 1 or N/A
Miscellaneous commands.	7	5
Administration commands.	8	1M
Maintenance commands.	8	8

An older organizational scheme is used by many System V systems. It adds another layer of structure to the BSD plan. The directories /usr/man and /usr/catman both have several subdirectories of the form x_man, where x is a code letter indicating the directory's contents: a for administrative, p for programming, u for user commands (other codes are present on some systems). Under each of these directories there are several subdirectories named mann or catn, holding the actual manual pages.

/usr/spool   Spooling directory. This directory contains subdirectories for UNIX subsystems that provide different kinds of spooling services. Some of the tools using */usr/spool* are *uucp*, the print spooling system, and the *cron* facility.

/usr/ucb   A directory that contains standard UNIX command originally developed at the University of California, Berkeley. This directory sometimes includes subdirectories for separate file types (*bin* for binaries, *lib* for libraries, and so on).

/usr/5bin   Under SunOS, executables for System V-compatibility commands are stored here.

/usr/lpp   Under AIX 3.1, "licensed program products" (optional products) are stored in subdirectories of */usr/lpp*. Another important subdirectory is */usr/lpp/bos* (for "base operating system"), which holds information about the current operating system release.

System V.4 Filesystem Organization

System V.4 reorganizes the UNIX directory structure in several ways. Besides adding new subdirectories to */dev* for terminal devices (discussed previously), the following major changes occur:

- Executable files are moved out of */etc* into a new directory named */sbin* or to */usr/sbin* (which was formerly named */usr/etc*). However, many systems set up links to the old locations, so the commands may seem to be in both places.

- Virtually all system configuration files are placed in */etc*. Some new subdirectories are created there to organize files by facility.

- Certain types of static data files (such as the online manual pages, font directories, the files for *spell*, and the like) are stored in subdirectories under */usr/share*. The name "share" reflects the idea that such files could be shared among a group of networked systems, eliminating the need for separate copies on every system.

- A new top-level directory, */var*, holds the volatile spooling directories formerly placed under */usr/spool*. If *var* is placed on a separate disk partition (or even a separate disk) from the root disk partition, then the latter can remain relatively static after initial system setup. This is an important step toward full support for readonly system disks. SunOS also uses a */var* directory.

- The contents of */bin* and */lib* are moved to */usr/bin* and */usr/lib* respectively.

The basic layout of the V.4 filesystem is illustrated in Figure 2-7.

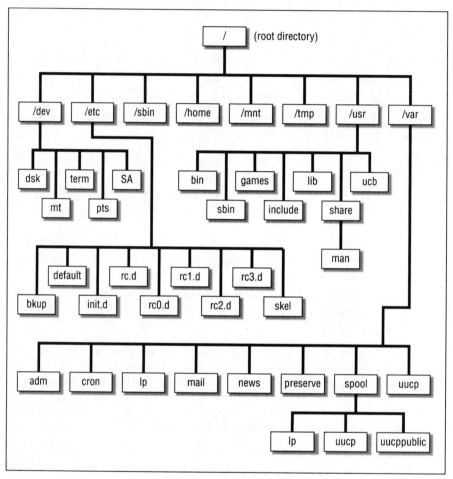

Figure 2-7. Typical V.4 Directory Structure

3

Startup and Shutdown

The UNIX Boot Process
Starting a Boot
UNIX Initialization Scripts
Shutting Down a UNIX System
When the System Crashes
When the System Won't Boot

Keeping the system running is the most visible aspect of system administration. You're the one they call when the system crashes. This chapter will discuss the normal UNIX booting and shutdown processes. Shutting down and bringing up a UNIX system are actually very simple. What will require more careful consideration is the myriad of system configuration files which perform and control these processes.

NOTE

Even if your system is a single-user microcomputer system, normal UNIX startup and shutdown will still be important to you. *All* UNIX systems need to use the built-in shutdown procedures; you can't just turn them off like you can, say, a 386-based system running DOS. And every system administrator needs to have at least a conceptual understanding of the startup process to be able to recognize, at a minimum, when something goes awry.

The UNIX Boot Process

Bootstrapping is the full name for the process of bringing a computer system fully to life and ready for use. The name comes from the fact that a computer needs its operating system in order to be able to do anything, but must also somehow get the operating system started all on its own, without having the operating system to do it. Hence, it must "pull itself up by its own bootstraps." *Booting* is short for bootstrapping, and is the term I'll use.*

The basic boot process is very similar for all UNIX systems, although the mechanisms used to accomplish it varies quite a bit between System V and BSD. The process begins when some instructions stored in ROM (permanent, non-volatile memory) are executed. This can be initiated automatically when power is applied. On many systems, if the front panel key is in a certain position, often labeled "Normal" or "On," then the system will begin booting automatically when it is powered on (this is called *autobooting*).

These ROM instructions may also begin executing in response to a command entered on the system console (see the section entitled, "Starting a Boot," later in this chapter). These instructions are used to start up the system's *boot program*: a program stored in a predictable location on disk (often block 0 of the root disk) or from a file server via the network (in the case of diskless workstations). The boot program is responsible for loading the UNIX *kernel*—that part of the UNIX operating system that remains running at all times when the system is up—into memory. The kernel image itself, usually named *unix* (System V) or *vmunix* (BSD), is almost always stored in the root directory.†

The ROM program is basically just smart enough to figure out if the hardware devices it needs are accessible—can it find the system disk, or the network, for example—and to load and initiate the boot program before handing off control to it. The boot program often performs additional hardware checking, including for the presence of expected system memory and major peripheral devices.

---

*IBM has traditionally referred to the bootstrapping process as IPL (initial program load). This term occasionally shows up in AIX 3.1 documentation.

†System V.4 complicates this basic picture a bit. Under V.4, there are two boot programs, *mboot* and *boot*, and booting is in three stages: *mboot* executes first, started by the firmware (ROM) booting instructions. *mboot* starts *boot*, which loads and starts *unix*. The boot programs are stored in partition 7 of the root disk, and the kernel *unix* and the system configuration file *system* are stored in partition 3. The presence of these two partitions, and the files within in them, is what defines a bootable disk under V.4. See the section entitled "Disk Partitions" in Chapter 8, *Filesystems and Disks*, for a further discussion of V.4 disk layouts and disk partitions.

Once control passes to the kernel, it prepares itself to run the system by initializing its internal tables. The kernel will also complete the hardware diagnostics that are part of the boot process. Minimally, this includes testing the memory system to be sure all expected memory is present and accessible. Some systems do much more elaborate hardware checks, verifying the status of virtually every device and detecting new ones added since the last boot and automatically creating their associated special files.

When all is ready, the kernel verifies the integrity of the root filesystem and then mounts it. It then starts the *init* program as the process with PID 1 (process 0, which forks to create process 1, is really part of the kernel itself). As we've seen, *init* is the ancestor of all subsequent UNIX processes and the direct parent of user login shells (see the section entitled "The Life Cycle of a Process," in Chapter 2, *The UNIX Way*.

init does the rest of the work needed to prepare the system for users. This includes mounting the remaining local disk partitions, performing some filesystem cleanup operations, turning on the major UNIX subsystems such as accounting and the print service, starting the network (including mounting remote file-systems), and enabling user logins. These activities are specified and carried out by means of the system *initialization scripts*, Bourne shell programs stored in */etc* or its subdirectories and executed by *init* at boot time. These files are organized very differently under System V and BSD, but they accomplish the same purposes, including the following tasks:

- Checking the integrity of the filesystems, using the *fsck* utility.

- Mounting local disks.

- Designating paging areas.

- Performing filesystem cleanup activities: checking disk quotas, preserving editor recovery files, deleting temporary files in */tmp* and elsewhere.*

- Starting system server processes (*daemons*) for subsystems like printing, mail, accounting, error logging, and *cron*.

- Starting networking daemons and mounting remote disks (if applicable).

- Enabling user logins by starting *getty* processes and, under BSD, removing the file */etc/nologin* if present.

---

*Unlike most UNIX versions, AIX 3.1 does not clear */tmp* at boottime. AIX 3.1 takes care of clearing */tmp* via the *skulker* script run nightly by *cron* (although it is not initially enabled). See "The AIX 3.1 skulker Script," in Chapter 8, *Filesystems and Disks*.

The initialization files are described in detail in the section entitled "UNIX Initialization Scripts," later in this chapter.

Once these activities are complete, users may log in to the system. At this point, the boot process is complete, and the system is said to be in *multi-user mode.*

Single-user Mode

Once *init* takes control of the booting process, it can place the system in *single-user mode* instead of completing the initialization tasks required for multi-user mode.

Single-user mode is a system state designed for administrative and maintenance activities which require complete and unshared control of the system. To initiate single-user mode, *init* forks to create a new process, which then executes the Bourne shell (*/bin/sh*), executing as user *root.* The prompt in single-user mode is the number sign (#), the same as for the superuser account, reflecting the *root* privileges inherent in it. Single-user mode is sometimes called *maintenance mode*, especially on microcomputers.

Another situation when the system might enter single-user mode occurs if there are any problems in the boot process that the system cannot handle on its own. Examples of such circumstances include filesystem problems that *fsck* cannot fix in its default mode and errors in one of the system initialization files. The system administrator must then take whatever steps are necessary to resolve the problem. Once this is done, booting may continue to multi-user mode by entering a CTRL-D, terminating the single-user mode shell:

```
# ^D                          Continue boot process to multi-user mode.
Tue Jul 14 14:47:14 EDT 1987  Boot messages from the initialization files.
. . .
```

Alternatively, rather than picking up the boot process where it left off, the system may be rebooted from the beginning. This procedure is described in the section, "Rebooting UNIX," later in this chapter.

Single-user mode represents a minimal system startup. Although you will have root access to the system, many of the normal system services are not available at all or are not set up. On a mundane level, the search path and terminal type are often not set correctly. Less trivially, no daemons are running, so many UNIX facilities are shut down (e.g., printing). Finally, only the root filesystem is mounted. Therefore, only commands that physically reside on the root filesystem will be available initially. This limitation is especially noticeable if */usr* has been set up as a separate disk partition from the root filesystem (as is the trend on many newer systems). Sometimes if the */usr* filesystem is not mounted, even commands stored in the root filesystem (in */bin*, for example) won't work because they use shared libraries under */usr*.

Of course, under normal circumstances, you can just mount the other filesystems by hand; we'll discuss this in the section entitled "Mounting and Dismounting Filesystems," in Chapter 8, *Filesystems and Disks*. If there is some problem with the */usr* filesystem, however, you will have to make do with the tools that are available. For example, for such situations, however rare and unlikely, you should know how to use the *ed* editor in case *vi* is not available.

On older UNIX systems, where no password is required to gain access, single-user mode can be a significant security problem. If someone gained physical access to the system, he could crash it (by hitting the reset button, for example), and then boot to single-user mode via the console and be automatically logged in as *root* without having to know the root password. On more modern systems, various safeguards are provided. For example, many systems now require that the root password be entered before granting system access in single-user mode; if it is not entered, then booting continues to multi-user mode (where passwords are always required). On other systems, a front panel key position—often labeled "Secure" (versus "Normal") or "Standard" (versus "Maintenance" or "Service")—will disable booting to single-user mode. Such security features are often described on the *init* or *boot* manual pages.

System V Run-levels

At any given time, a BSD system can be in one of three conditions: off (not running, whether or not there is power), single-user mode, and multi-user mode (normal operating conditions). These three conditions may be thought of as three implicitly-defined system states.

Although conceptually System V systems work and feel similarly, things are actually more complicated there. System V explicitly defines a series of system states, called *run-levels*, designated by a one-character name (usually a number). At any given time, the system will be at one of these states, and can be sent to another one using various administrative commands. The defined run-levels are listed in Table 3-1.

Table 3-1. System V Run-levels

Run-level	Name and Uses
0	Powerdown state: conditions where it is safe to turn off the power.
1	Administrative state.
s or S	Single-user mode.
2	Multi-user mode: the normal operating state for isolated, non-networked systems.
3	Remote File Sharing (RFS) state: defined as the normal operating state for systems on networks, possibly sharing disks with other systems. Run-level 3 is thus the networked state, irrespective of whether networking/file sharing occurs via RFS, TCP/IP and NFS, or some other protocol.
4	User-definable system state: a currently unused run-level, which can be set up and defined locally.
5	Firmware state: used for some types of maintenance activities and for running diagnostics, and for booting from an alternate disk (i.e., not the root disk). The V.4 firmware state has its own password, distinct from the root password. On 3B2 systems, it may also be accessed via a *floppy key*, a special floppy disk containing system-identification information, used if the firmware password is forgotten or unavailable. Obviously, the floppy key needs to be stored in a secure location.
6	Shutdown and reboot state: used to reboot the system from some running state (s, 2, 3, or 4). Moving to this state causes the system to be taken down (to run-level 0) and then immediately rebooted back to its normal operating state.

In many implementations, states 1 and s are not distinguishable in practice, and not all states are predefined by all System V implementations. State 3 is the defined normal operating mode for networked systems. Note, however, that many System V systems collapse run-levels 2 and 3, supporting all networking functions at run-level 2 and ignoring run-level 3. We will use both run-levels in our examples.

The command *who -r* may be used to display the current run-level and the time it was initiated:

```
$ who -r
.     run-level 3  Mar 14 11:14   3   0   S          Previous run-level
```

This system was taken to run-level 3 from run-level S on March 14th.

Now for some concrete examples. Let's assume a system whose normal, every-day system state is state 3 (networked multi-user mode). When you boot this system after the power has been off, it moves from state 0 to state 3. If you shut the system down to single-user mode, it moves from state 3 through state 0 to state s. When you reboot a system, it moves from state 3 through state 6 and state 0, through state 2 and back to state 3.

Moving between run-levels is handled by *init*. Each run-level is controlled by its own set of initialization files. We'll look at them in detail in the section entitled "System V Initialization Files," later in this chapter.

Starting a Boot

Many systems can be configured to boot automatically when power comes on or after a crash. When autobooting is not enabled, booting is initiated by entering a simple command in response to a prompt: sometimes just a carriage return, sometime a *b*, sometimes the word *boot*. When a command is required, you often can tell the system to boot to single-user mode by adding a *-s* option to the boot command, for example:

```
> b -s
```

On some systems, booting manually is a two-stage process. In the first phase, you give a command to the hardware monitor program to load a boot program which is, in effect, a mini-operating system, often called a *stand-alone shell*. You then enter a second command to the stand-alone shell to load UNIX:

```
>  b                                Boot to stand-alone shell.
$$ unix                             Boot UNIX.
```

A generic startup sequence is shown in the following example; it is a composite of several systems, although it is labeled as for a mythical computer named the Urizen, a mid-1990's system running a BSD-style operating system. While it does not correspond exactly to any existing system, it does illustrate the usual elements of booting on UNIX systems, under both System V and BSD. (Comments are in italics.)

```
> b                                 Initiate boot process (to multi-user).

Urizen Ur-UNIX boot in progress...  This is a Urizen computer running Ur-UNIX.
testing memory                      Check the hardware.
checking device
loading vmunix                      Read in the kernel executable.

Urizen Ur-UNIX* Version 9.1.3: Fri Jul 15 19:05:46 EDT 1995
      *UNIX is a trademark of AT&T Technologies
```

```
Copyright (c) 1995 Blakewill Computer, Ltd.
All rights reserved                      UNIX kernel is running now.

real mem = 2147483648                    Total physical memory.
avail mem = 2018634629                   Total memory available for use.
using 512 buffers containing 4194304 bytes of memory
Ethernet address = 8:0:20:7:58:jz        Ethernet address of system.
Multiuser reboot in progress...          Means "Be patient."
Tue Jul 15 14:45:28 EDT 1997
checking filesystems                     Verify filesystem integrity with fsck.
/dev/disk0a: 7956 files, 195173 used, 35898 free
/dev/disk0a: (2226 frags, 4209 blocks, 1.0% fragmentation)
/dev/rdisk2d: 1764 files, 290620 used, 110315 free
/dev/rdisk2d: (555 frags, 13720 blocks, 0.1% fragmentation)
/dev/rdisk1g: 2012 files, 193518 used, 37553 free
/dev/rdisk1g: (185 frags, 4671 blocks, 0.1% fragmentation)
Root on /dev/disk0a fstype 4.2           Indicates disk partitions used as /,
Adding /dev/disk1b as swap device        for paging and for crash dumps.
Adding /dev/disk2b as swap device
Using /dev/disk1b as dump device
checking quotas: done.                   Messages produced by startup scripts.
preserving editor files                  Many start server processes.
starting local daemons: routed sendmail.
enabling logins                          Remove the /etc/nologin file.
clearing /tmp
standard daemons: update cron accounting.
starting network daemons: rwhod inetd printer.
Tue Jul 15 14:47:45 EDT 1997             Display the date, again.

Urizen Ur-UNIX 9.1 on hamlet            The hostname is hamlet.
login:                                   UNIX is running in multi-user mode.
```

Filesystem Checking

Filesystem checking is one of the most important boottime activities. It is performed by the *fsck** utility. In most cases, *fsck* does its work automatically, repairing any minor inconsistencies it finds. Occasionally, however, fsck finds more serious problems, requiring administrator intervention. This section introduces *fsck* and its role in the boot process.

System V and BSD have very different philosophies of filesystem verification. Under BSD, the normal practice is to check all filesystems on every boot. In contrast, under System V filesystems are not checked if they were unmounted normally when the system last went down (although the boot script may ask whether to check them anyway). System V uses the *fsstat* command to determine whether

---

*Variously pronounced as "fisk" (like the baseball player Carlton), "ef-es-see-kay," "ef-es-check," and in less genteel ways.

a filesystem was unmounted cleanly or not. If not—as would be the case after a crash—*fsck* will be run on that filesystem.

The BSD approach is the more conservative, taking into account that filesystem inconsistencies can very occasionally crop up at times other than system crashes. On the other hand, the System V approach results in much faster boots.

If the system is rebooting after a crash, it is quite normal to see many messages indicating minor filesystem discrepancies that have been repaired. By default, *fsck* will only fix problems if the repair cannot possibly result in data loss. If *fsck* discovers a more serious problem with the filesystem, it will print a message describing the problem and leave the system in single-user mode; you must then run *fsck* manually to repair the damaged filesystem. For example (from a BSD system):

```
/dev/disk2e: UNEXPECTED INCONSISTENCY;            Message from fsck.
    RUN fsck MANUALLY
Automatic reboot failed . . . help!              Message from /etc/rc init. file.
#                                                Single-user mode.
# /etc/fsck -p /dev/disk2e

                                                 Many messages from fsck . . .
BAD/DUP FILE=2216 OWNER=190 M=120777             Mode shows the file is a symbolic link,
    S=16 MTIME=Apr 16 14:27 1991                 so deleting it will cause no data loss.
CLEAR? y

*** FILE SYSTEM WAS MODIFIED ***
# ^D                                             Resume booting.
Root on /dev/disk0a  fstype 4.2
```

In this example, *fsck* found a file whose inode address list contained duplicates or addresses of known bad spots on the disk. From the owner UID (190) and inode number, you can find out which file it is. In this case, the troublesome file was a symbolic link, so it may be safely removed (although the user who owned it will need to be informed). This example is intended merely to introduce you to *fsck*; the mechanics of running *fsck* are described in detail in the section entitled "Checking a Filesystem with fsck," in Chapter 8, *Filesystems and Disks*.

UNIX Initialization Scripts

This section discusses the UNIX initialization files: command scripts that perform most of the work associated with taking the system to multi-user mode. Although similar activities take place under System V and BSD, the mechanisms by which they are initiated are quite different.

Understanding the initialization scripts in place on your system is a vital part of system administration. You should have a pretty good sense of where they are located and what they do. That way, you'll be able to recognize any problems at boottime right away, and know what corrective action to take. Also, from time to time you'll probably need to modify them to add new services (or to disable ones you've decided you don't need).

NOTE

For security reasons, the system initialization scripts (and any old or saved copies of them) should be owned by *root* and not be writable by anyone but the owner.

BSD Initialization Files

System initialization under BSD-based operating systems is controlled by the files */etc/rc* and */etc/rc.local*. During a boot to multi-user mode, *init* executes the *rc* script which, in turn, executes *rc.local*. If the system is booted to single-user mode, *rc* executes when the single-user shell is exited. (By default, XENIX systems use only *rc*.)

Your system is shipped with standard versions of *rc* and *rc.local*. At some point, you may want to modify either file. As a precaution, *before modifying them in any way*, copy these files to the files */etc/rc.dist* and */etc/rc.local.dist*, and write-protect these copies:

```
# cp /etc/rc /etc/rc.dist
# cp /etc/rc.local /etc/rc.local.dist
# chmod a-w /etc/rc*.dist
```

Both *rc* and *rc.local* are Bourne shell (*/bin/sh*) scripts. Programming for the Bourne shell is similar to programming for the C shell (*/bin/csh*), but there are some significant differences. If you're used to the C shell, some Bourne shell constructs will be somewhat opaque at first. As a convenience, Bourne shell programming features are summarized in the Appendix.

Although the contents of these initialization files vary from system to system, there is substantial commonality among them. The discussion that follows describes generic initialization files, but much of it will apply to most systems. Check the initialization files on your own system to learn about its setup and eccentricities.

Filename Variations Under SunOS and AIX 3.1

Some BSD-based operating systems use additional initialization files. SunOS, for example, uses the additional files */etc/rc.boot* and */etc/rc.single*. *init* runs *rc.boot* first, which takes care of setting the hostname and checking the filesystems. *rc.boot* runs *rc.single*, which finishes mounting the non-root filesystems. If the system is booting to single-user mode, control passes to the single-user shell from *rc.single*. *rc* runs next when booting to multi-user, or when the single-user shell is exited, and it runs *rc.local*. *rc.single* is run by one of the other two scripts to finish mounting the filesystems. Some of the commands discussed in this section appear in these additional files under SunOS.

Technically, AIX 3.1 is a System V-based operating system, but it has designed its initialization files so that they can be organized and administered in the BSD manner. AIX 3.1 breaks *rc.local* into a sequence of initialization files, each devoted to a single subsystem (all stored in */etc*): *rc.net* (general network configuration); *rc.tcpip* (starts TCP/IP and local daemons); *rc.nfs* (starts NFS); *rc.ncs* (starts the Network Computing Service); *rc.pci* (DOS interface). Note that some AIX 3.1 initialization files are Korn shell scripts (*/bin/ksh*). ▪

Local Initialization: /etc/rc

rc often begins by defining HOME and PATH shell variables to be used by the rest of the shell script:

```
HOME=/; export HOME
PATH=/bin:/usr/bin:/usr/ucb:/etc:/usr/etc
```

It then executes the command *fsck -p* to check the filesystem's consistency. The *-p* option stands for "preen" and says to make any needed repairs that will cause no loss of data; virtually all repairs are of this type. Here is a typical invocation of *fsck*:

```
if [ -r /fastboot ]; then          Does this file exist?
    rm -f /fastboot
    echo Fast boot ... skipping disk checks >/dev/console
elif [ $1x = autobootx ];          Was rc passed the parameter "autoboot"?
then    init invokes rc with this option.
    echo Automatic reboot in progress... >/dev/console
    fsck -p >/dev/console
    case $? in                     Check fsck exit code.
    0)                             Normal exit.
        date >/dev/console
        ;;
    2)                             fsck failed on root disk.
        exit 1
        ;;
    4)                             fsck fixed problems on root disk.
        /etc/reboot -n
```

```
        ;;
    8)                                      fsck failed on non-root disk.
        echo "Automatic reboot failed... help!" >/dev/console
        exit 1
        ;;
   12)                                      Someone typed CTRL-C.
        echo "Reboot interrupted" >/dev/console
        exit 1
        ;;
    *)
        echo "Unknown error in reboot" > /dev/console
        exit 1
        ;;
    esac
else                                     If the parameter to rc wasn't "autoboot."
    date >/dev/console
fi
```

First, *rc* checks to see whether the file */fastboot* exists. This file is created when
the *-f* option is specified to the *shutdown* command, requesting a "fast reboot"
(see the section entitled "BSD Shutdown and Fast Reboot," later in this chapter).
rc does not run *fsck* if the file */fastboot* exists; in this case, the system will be rein-
itialized without checking the disks because it knows the system was shut down
cleanly.

CAUTION

Don't try to create */fastboot* yourself. This could lead to serious filesystem errors if a crash or a power failure occurred before the next normal
startup. Although it is time-consuming, *fsck* must run after *any* abnormal
shutdown (including an incorrectly executed operator shutdown). If it
does not, the contents of your filesystem may be compromised.

Next, if the first parameter passed to *rc* by *init* was "autoboot," which says that
this is a boot to multi-user mode, *fsck* runs (with the *-p* option). The case statement checks the status value returned by *fsck* (denoted by "$?"), and performs the
appropriate action for each potential return value as shown in Table 3-2.

Table 3-2. fsck Return Values

Return Value	Meaning	Action
0	Success.	Display the date.
2	Failure on root disk.	Exit to single-user mode.
4	Errors corrected on root disk.	Reboot the system.
8	Failure on non-root disk.	Exit to single-user mode.
12	*fsck* interrupted.	Exit to single-user mode.

If *fsck* cannot fix a disk on its own, you will need to run it manually when it dumps you into single-user mode. Fortunately, this is rare. That's not just talk, either. I've had to run *fsck* manually only a handful of times over the many hundreds of times I've rebooted UNIX systems, and those times occurred almost exclusively after crashes due to electrical storms.

If *rc* was passed some parameter other than "autoboot" or no value at all, then *fsck* won't run.

If all goes well during the file system check, *rc* checks the existence and size of the password lock file, */etc/ptmp*. This file is created by the *vipw* command, which is used to edit the system password file, */etc/passwd*, where user accounts are defined. This section of *rc* is designed to recover the password file in the event that someone was editing it when the system went down.

```
if [ -s /etc/ptmp ]; then          Someone was editing the password file.
    if [ -s /etc/passwd ]; then        If passwd is non-empty, keep it.
        ls -l /etc/passwd /etc/ptmp >/dev/console
        rm -f /etc/ptmp
    else                           Otherwise rename the lock file.
                                   Just delete an empty lock file.
        (echo 'passwd file recovered from ptmp') >/dev/console
        mv /etc/ptmp /etc/passwd
    fi
elif [ -r /etc/ptmp ]; then
    (echo 'removing passwd lock file') >/dev/console
    rm -f /etc/ptmp
fi
```

If the password lock file exists and is not empty (*-s* checks for a file of greater than zero length), then someone was editing */etc/passwd* when the system crashed or was shut down. If */etc/passwd* exists and is not empty, *rc* assumes that it hasn't been damaged, prints a long directory listing of both files on the system console, and removes the password lock file. If */etc/passwd* is empty or does not exist, then *rc* restores */etc/ptmp* as a backup version of */etc/passwd* and prints the message "passwd file recovered from /etc/ptmp" on the console.

If */etc/ptmp* exists but is empty, *rc* deletes the lock file, since its presence would otherwise prevent you from using *vipw*, and prints the message "removing passwd lock file" on the console.

Next come a variety of activities preparing the system for users:

```
mount -at 4.2                          >/dev/console 2>&1
        (echo -n 'checking quotas: ')  >/dev/console
quotacheck -a -p                       >/dev/console 2>&1
        (echo 'done.')                 >/dev/console
quotaon -a

/bin/ps -U                             >/dev/console 2>&1
```

```
rm -f /etc/nologin
if [ -f /dev/ttyp0 ]; then
    chown root /dev/tty[pqrs]*
    chmod 666 /dev/tty[pqrs]*
fi
```

The *mount* command mounts all local filesystems. The options to *mount* say to mount all known filesystems that are type "4.2" (named at the 4.2 BSD release). Next, disk quotas are checked and enabled, using the *quotacheck* and *quotaon* commands respectively. If disk quotas are not in use, then these lines will be commented out (have a "#" as their initial character). Disk quotas are discussed in Chapter 7, *Managing System Resources*.

The script then updates a database used by the *ps* command, and removes the */etc/nologin* file, which disables user logins. */etc/nologin* is created automatically when the system is shut down normally. It may also be created as needed by the system administrator. If this file is not empty, its contents will be displayed to users when they attempt to log in.

rc next resets the ownership and protection of all virtual terminal special files. When a user initiates a login session using one of these devices, the ownership is changed to her username and to group *tty*; ownership changes back to the default (*root* and group 0 usually) when the session ends normally. When the system needs a virtual terminal device, it uses the first one available with default ownership and protection. The commands in *rc* take care of the case where a session didn't end normally and ownership and protection weren't reset properly, suggesting that the device is still in use, even though it can't be because the system is just coming up.

At about this point, *rc.local* runs (discussed in the next section); when it returns, *rc* performs a few more housekeeping functions, including:

*   Preserving editor files from *vi*, *ed*, and other *ex*-based editors, which enable users to recover some unsaved edits in the event of a crash. These editors place checkpoint files in */tmp* during editing sessions; the preserve utility saves its work in the directory */usr/preserve*.

*   Clearing the */tmp* directory. This can be simple:

    ```
    (cd /tmp; rm -f ./*)
    ```

or complex:

```
(cd /tmp; find . ! -name . ! -name lost+found ! \
   -name quotas -exec rm -r {} \;)
```

The second form might be used when */tmp* is located on a separate disk partition from the root filesystem to avoid removing important files and subdirectories.

* Removing *uucp* lock files. Here is a simple command:

```
rm -f /usr/spool/uucp/LCK.*
```

rc may also include other *uucp*-related commands.

* Enabling swap partitions and/or paging files, via the *swapon -a* command.

* Starting local server processes. These usually include:

— *update*: a process which periodically updates the superblocks of all filesystems by running the *sync* command, ensuring that they are fairly up-to-date should the system crash (see the section entitled "Guaranteeing Disk Accuracy," later in this chapter). Don't disable the *update* daemon or you will seriously compromise filesystem integrity.

— *cron*: a facility to execute commands according to a pre-set schedule (see Chapter 7, *Managing System Resources*).

— accounting: via the *accton* command. If accounting is not enabled, the relevant commands will be commented out.

At the beginning of this process, *rc* writes a message like *standard daemons:* to the console. As each server is started, its name is written to the system console, on the same line as the header message. After all daemons have been started, a period is displayed. The final line looks like this:

```
standard daemons: update cron accounting.
```

During a boot, a partial version of this line will indicate what daemons have been started so far.

* Starting some network server processes. Commands to do this are usually of the form:

```
if [ -f server pathname ]; then
   server-start-cmd; (echo -n ' server-name') >/dev/console
fi
```

There may also be additional commands before the server is started. For example, here is a typical way to start *lpd*, the line printer spooling daemon:

```
if [ -f /usr/lib/lpd ]; then
        rm -f /dev/printer /usr/spool/lpd.lock
        /usr/lib/lpd; (echo -n ' printer') >/dev/console
fi
```

The *if* command checks whether the daemon program is present in the filesystem. If it is, the printer lock file is removed (if present) and then the daemon is started. Lastly, a message indicating this is sent to the system console. Like those for the local daemons, the messages for the network daemons are also displayed on a single line on the console, labeled with the heading:

```
network daemons:
```

At this point, the boot process is complete and the system will enter multiuser mode and allow users to log in.

Network Initialization: /etc/rc.local

Somewhere in the middle of its execution, *rc* runs the script */etc/rc.local*, which performs many network initialization tasks.

After setting its own PATH variable, *rc.local* begins by setting the system's network name and address, enabling it to communicate with other hosts on the local network, other UNIX systems connected to it via *uucp*, and other external networks like the Internet. The crucial part of *rc.local* for these purposes looks something like the following:

```
HOSTNAME=hamlet
hostname $HOSTNAME
ifconfig lo0 localhost
ifconfig en0 $HOSTNAME -trailers arp up
ifconfig en0 broadcast brcast
hostid $HOSTNAME
```

The first line sets the variable HOSTNAME to the name of the local system, in this case *hamlet*. The *ifconfig* commands initialize the network interface parameters; the first parameter to *ifconfig* will vary, depending on your system's exact networking and hardware configuration. Those listed above (*en0* and *lo0*) are common names for Ethernet connections; others include *ie0* and *le0* (SunOS) and *et0* (some System V). Networking is described in more detail in Chapter 12, *TCP/IP Network Management*. The *hostname* and *hostid* commands set the system's alphabetic and numeric network identifiers respectively. Both are commonly set to the local system name.

The vast majority of *rc.local* consists of initializing various network services and starting their associated daemons. These may include the following programs shown in Table 3-3.

Table 3-3. Network Daemons Started by /etc/rc.local

Daemon(s)	Purpose
named *routed*	The name server and route daemons, which provide dynamic remote hostname and routing data for TCP/IP.
timed	Manages synchronization between different system clocks on a local network. If invoked with the *-M* flag, this system can act as a *timed* master, assumed to have the correct time to which all other time daemons will synchronize themselves. At least one system on the network must have the *-M* flag; otherwise, *timed* will be ineffective.
sendmail	The mail daemon, responsible for routing mail locally and via the network.
nfsd *biod*	NFS daemons, which service file access requests from remote systems. Both take an integer parameter indicating how many copies of the daemon are created. *rc.local* also typically executes the *exportfs -a* command, which makes local filesystems available to remote systems via NFS.
ypbind *ypserv*	NIS daemons, which implement the NIS-distributed database service, allowing networked systems to share a common set of configuration files.

A typical command from this portion of *rc.local* looks like:

```
if [ -f /etc/routed ]; then
    /etc/routed;  echo -n ' routed' >/dev/console
fi
```

In this example, *rc.local* starts the route daemon *routed* only if its executable file exists.

Networking is described in more detail in Chapter 13, *Accounting*. If you aren't planning to use some of these services, you should disable the appropriate part of *rc.local* by placing a comment character (#) in front of the appropriate lines. For example, to disable the route daemon, *routed*, edit the lines we looked at previously to look like this:

```
#if [ -f /etc/routed ]; then
#    /etc/routed;          echo -n ' routed'    >/dev/console
#fi
```

On the other hand, if you need to start any local software during initialization, you should add the commands necessary to do this at this point.

System V Initialization Files

System V organizes the initialization process in a much more complex way, using what amounts to three levels of initialization files. On a boot, when *init* takes control from the kernel, it scans its configuration file, */etc/inittab*, to determine what to do next. This file defines *init*'s actions whenever the system enters a new run-level; it contains instructions to carry out when the system goes down (run-level 0), when it boots to single-user mode (run-level s), when booting to multi-user mode (run-level 2 or 3), when rebooting (run-level 6), and so on.

Typically, the commands to execute at each run-level are stored in an initialization file named *rcn*, where *n* is the run-level number. The files are located in the directory */etc* under V.3 and */sbin* under V.4. The various *rcn* scripts in turn execute additional files in subdirectories of */etc* named *rcn.d*. For example, when the system is booted to run-level 2, *init* reads the */etc/inittab* file, which tells it to execute *rc2*. *rc2* will then execute the scripts stored in the directory */etc/rc2.d*. Similarly, when a system is rebooted, it moves first from run-level 2 to run-level 0 and executes *rc0* and the scripts in */etc/rc0.d*, and then it moves to run-level 2, again executing *rc2* and the files in */etc/rc2.d*.

A simple version of the System V rebooting process is illustrated in Figure 3-1 (assuming run-level 2 as the normal operating state).

The init Configuration File

As we've seen, top-level control of changing system states is handled by the file */etc/inittab*, read by *init*. This file contains entries which tell the system what to do when it enters the various defined system states. Entries are of the form:

> *cc:states:action:process*

where *cc* is a unique, two-character label identifying each entry (although some newer implementations raise this limit to 14 characters); *cc* is case-sensitive. *States* is a list of run-levels to which the entry applies; if *states* is blank, the entry applies to all of them. *Process* is the command to execute, and *action* indicates how *init* is to treat the process started by the entry. When the system enters a new state, *init* processes all entries specified for that run-level in the *inittab* file, in the order they are listed in the file.

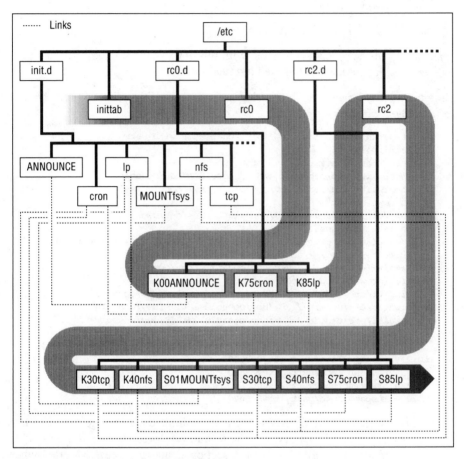

Figure 3-1. Rebooting Under System V

The possible *action* keywords are:

wait   Start the process and wait for it to finish before going on to the next entry for this run state.

respawn   Start the process and automatically restart it when it dies (used for *getty* terminal line server processes).

once   Start the process if it's not already running. Don't wait for it.

boot   Only execute entry at boottime; start the process but don't wait for it.

bootwait   Only execute entry at boottime and wait for it to finish.

initdefault   Specify the default run-level (the one to reboot to). Usually set to 2 or 3.

sysinit   Used to initialize the console.

off   If the process associated with this entry is running, kill it. Also used to comment out unused terminal lines.

Comments may be included by placing a number sign in the first column. Here is a sample *inittab* file:

```
# set default init level -- multi-user mode with networking
is:3:initdefault:
# check root filesystem on boots
fs::bootwait:/etc/bcheckrc </dev/console >/dev/console 2>&1
br::bootwait:/etc/brc </dev/console >/dev/console 2>&1
# shutdown script
r0:056:wait:/etc/rc0 >/dev/console 2>&1 </dev/console
# run-level changes
r1:1:wait:/etc/shutdown -y -iS -g0 >/dev/console 2>&1 </dev/console
r2:23:wait:/etc/rc2 >/dev/console 2>&1 </dev/console
r3:3:wait:/etc/rc3 >/dev/console 2>&1 </dev/console
# off, firmware and reboot states
of:0:wait:/etc/uadmin 2 0 >/dev/console 2>&1 </dev/console
fw:5:wait:/etc/uadmin 2 2 >/dev/console 2>&1 </dev/console
rb:6:wait:/etc/uadmin 2 1 >/dev/console 2>&1 </dev/console
# terminal initiation
co:12345:respawn:/etc/getty console console
t0:234:respawn:/etc/getty tty0 9600
t1:234:respawn:/etc/getty tty1 9600
t2:234:off:/etc/getty tty2 9600
t3:234:respawn:/etc/getty tty3 9600
```

This file is organized in six major sections (delimited by comments). The first one, consisting of a single entry, sets the default run-level, in this case, networked multi-user mode (state 3). The second section contains processes started when the system is booted. In the sample file, this consists of running the scripts */etc/bcheckrc*, whose main function is to run *fsck* on the root filesystem, and */etc/brc*, which performs additional initialization activities at boottime (not all System V systems use */etc/brc*). Each script is allowed to complete before *init* goes on to the next *inittab* entry.

The third section specifies the commands to run whenever the system goes down, either during a system shutdown and halt (to run-level 0), a shutdown to the firmware state (run-level 5) or during a reboot (run-level 6). In all cases, the script */etc/rc0* is executed, and *init* waits for it to finish before proceeding.

The fourth section, headed "run-level changes," specifies the commands to run when system states 1, 2, and 3 begin. For state 1, the *shutdown* command listed in the sample file takes the system to single-user mode (see the section entitled "The System V shutdown Command," later in this chapter for details). For state 2, *init* executes the initialization script */etc/rc2*; for state 3, *init* executes */etc/rc2* followed by */etc/rc3*. In all three states, each process is allowed to finish before *init* goes on to the next entry.

Some (especially older) System V systems execute the initialization file */etc/rc1*, when the system enters state 1 instead of a *shutdown* command like the one above. Others use an additional initialization directory, */etc/rc.d*, when entering a multi-user state.

The fifth section specifies the commands to run when the system enters states 0, 5, and 6. In all three cases, *init* runs the *uadmin* command, which initiates system shutdowns. The arguments to *uadmin* specify how the shutdown is to be handled. The meaning of argument sets used in the sample *inittab* file are shown in Table 3-4.

Table 3-4. Arguments to the uadmin Command

Arguments	Final State	Meaning
2 0	Off	Halt the processor.
2 1	Firmware	Manual reboot.
2 2	Reboot	Automatic reboot.

The final section initializes the system's terminal lines. It is discussed in Chapter 10, *Terminals and Modems*.

System V Initialization Scripts

As we've seen, *init* typically executes a script named *rcn* when entering run-level *n* (*rc2* for state 2, for example). Although the boot (or shutdown) process to each system state is controlled by the associated *rcn* script, the actual commands to be executed are stored in a series of files in the directory */etc/rcn.d*. Thus, when the system enters state 0, *init* runs *rc0* (as directed in the *inittab* file), which in turn runs the scripts in *rc0.d*.

The contents of a typical */etc/rc2.d* directory (on a system that doesn't use a separate run-level 3) are listed below:

```
$ ls -C /etc/rc2.d
K30tcp          S15preserve     S30tcp      S50RMTMPFILES     S85lp
K40nfs          S20sysetup      S35bsd      S70uucp
S01MOUNTFSYS    S21perf         S40nfs      S75cron
```

All filenames begin with one of two initial filename characters (S and K), followed by a two-digit number, and end with a descriptive name. The *rc* scripts execute the K-files (as I'll call them) in their associated directory in alphabetical order, followed by the S-files, also in alphabetical order. In this directory, files would be executed in the order *K30tcp, K40nfs, S01MOUNTFSYS, S15preserve*, and so on, ending with *S75cron* and *S85lp*. K-files are used to kill processes (and perform related functions) when a system state starts up; S-files are used to start processes and perform other initialization functions.

The files in the *rc*.d* directories are usually links to files in the directory */etc/init.d*, where the real files live. For example, the file *S30tcp* from the *rc2.d* directory listed previously is actually a link to */etc/init.d/tcp*. You see how the naming conventions work: the final portion of the name in the *rc*.d* directory is the same as the filename in the */etc/init.d* directory.

The file *K30tcp* is also a link to */etc/init.d/tcp*. The same file in */etc/init.d* is used for both the kill and start scripts for each subsystem. The K and S links can be in the same *rc* subdirectory, as is the case for the TCP/IP initialization file, or in different subdirectories. For example, in the case of the print spooling subsystem, the S-file might be in *rc2.d* while the K-file is in *rc0.d*.

The same file in */etc/init.d* can be put to both uses because it is passed a parameter indicating whether it was run as a K-file or an S-file. Here is an example invocation, from an *rc2* script:

```
# If the directory /etc/rc2.d exists, run the K-files in it ...
if [ -d /etc/rc2.d ]; then
    for f in /etc/rc2.d/K*
    {
        if [ -s ${f} ]; then
# pass the parameter "stop" to the file
            /bin/sh $f stop
        fi
    }
# and then the S-files:
    for f in /etc/rc2.d/S*
    {
        if [ -s ${f} ]; then
```

```
# pass the parameter "start" to the file
        /bin/sh ${f} start
    fi
  }
fi
```

Notice that when a K-file is executed, it is passed the parameter "stop"; when an S-file is executed, it is passed "start." The script file will use this parameter to figure out whether it is being run as a K-file or an S-file.

Here is a sample lowest-level script file, */etc/init.d/cron*, which controls the *cron* facility. It doesn't matter whether you know what *cron* is or not; you'll still be able to see the basic structure of a System V initialization file:

```
#!/bin/sh
case $1 in
# commands to execute if run as "Snncron"
'start')
# remove lock file from previous cron
rm -f /usr/lib/cron/FIFO
# start cron if executable exists
if [ -x /etc/cron ]; then
    /etc/cron
    echo "starting cron."
fi
;;
# commands to execute if run as "Knncron"
'stop')
pid=`/bin/ps -e | grep ' cron$' | sed -e 's/^  *//' -e 's/ .*//'`
if [ "${pid}" != "" ]; then
    /bin/kill ${pid}
fi
;;
esac
```

The first section in the case statement is executed when the script is passed "start" as its first argument (when it's an S-file); the second section is used when it is passed "stop," as a K-file. The startup commands remove an old lock file and then start the *cron* daemon if its executable is present on the system. The shutdown commands figure out the process-ID of the *cron* process and kill it if it's running.

The file */etc/init.d/cron* might be linked both to */etc/rc2.d/S75cron* and */etc/rc0/K75cron*. The *cron* facility will then be started by *rc2* during multi-user boots and stopped by *rc0* during system shutdowns and reboots.

Sometimes scripts are even more general, explicitly testing for the conditions under which they were invoked:

```
. . .
set `who -r`
if [ $8 != "0" ]              The return code of the previous state change.
then
    exit
fi
case $arg1 in
'start')
    if [ $9 = "2" -o $9 = "3" ]    The previous run-level.
    then
        exit
    fi
    echo "Starting process accounting"
    /usr/lib/acct/startup
    ;;
. . .
```

This file uses various parts of the output from *who -r*. It tests to see if the current system state was entered without errors, exiting if it wasn't, and what the immediately previous system state was, again exiting if it was a multi-user state. These tests ensure that accounting will be started only during a successful boot, and not when single-user mode has been entered due to boot errors or when moving from on multi-user state to another.

Non-root filesystems are typically mounted by */etc/rc2.d/S01MOUNTFSYS*. Here is a simple example of this script:

```
cd /
/etc/mountall /etc/fstab
```

mountall is another shell script which calls *fsck* and *mount*. Some versions ask if all filesystems should be checked prior to mounting or just "dirty" ones (usually the default): ones that *fsstat* indicates were not unmounted cleanly. Here is the heart of *mountall*; it is the inner part of a loop which runs once for each filesystem on the system:

```
. . .
msg=`/etc/fsstat ${dev} 2>&1`      Check device to see if it needs fsck.
case $? in
0) # Clean
   if [ $FSCK_ALL = true ]         FSCK_ALL is set by a yes response to a prompt
   then                           earlier in the script.
      /etc/fsck -y -D ${dev}   # Fix everything; reboot if the root disk.
   fi
   /etc/mount ${dev}
   ;;
1) # Dirty
   echo "${msg}"
```

```
        echo "${dev} is being checked."
        /etc/fsck -y -D ${dev}
        /etc/mount ${dev}
        ;;
2) # Already mounted
        echo "mountall: ${dev} already mounted."
        ;;
*) # Errors
        echo "mountall: unable to fsstat ${dev}."
        ;;
esac
```

The shell variable FSCK_ALL is set by a prompt (not shown); it has the value "true" only if the administrator has explicitly requested that all filesystems be *fsck*'ed. *mountall* runs *fsstat* on the device, and then runs *fsck* on it if FSCK_ALL is true or *fsstat* returns error status 1. *fsck* runs with the options *-y -D*, which tell it to make all necessary repairs to the filesystem and to remount the root disk or reboot the system if any repairs were made there (which is done depends on the severity of the errors it found on the root disk). The remaining two *case* statement entries handle other *fsstat* error conditions. Once *fsck* completes, the filesystem is mounted.

Several of the System V initialization scripts start daemons. They are started in a manner quite similar to that used under BSD:

```
if test -x /etc/rwhod; then
    if test ! -d /usr/spool/rwho; then
        mkdir /usr/spool/rwho
    fi
        /etc/rwhod; echo " rwhod\c"
    fi
```

This example starts the *rwho* daemon, which supports the *rwho* command (a network version of *who*). It checks to make sure that *rwho*'s executable file exists and has execute access set. If so, then it creates *rwho*'s spooling directory if necessary and then starts the daemon.

These examples illustrate the way that all of the startup (and shutdown) activities get done under System V. If you need to change an initialization procedure, you'll need to modify the appropriate file(s) in */etc/init.d*. For example, to disable some network daemons your system doesn't need, comment out the appropriate lines in */etc/init.d/tcp* or */etc/init.d/nfs*. In some cases, you may decide you don't need an entire file. For example, you may not need the links to */etc/init.d/lp* if your system doesn't support local or remote printing. In such cases, remove the links from the appropriate *rcn.d* subdirectories, but *leave the master files in* */etc/init.d*, in case circumstances ever change.

If you need to add your own new scripts, put them in */etc/init.d* and create the necessary links to the appropriate *rc* subdirectories. Choose the filenames for the links carefully, so that your new files will be executed at the proper point in the sequence. If you're in doubt, put them at the end by choosing a higher number than any existing file uses.

AIX 3.1: Making System V Look Like BSD

It's possible to eliminate most of the layers of initialization scripts that are standard under System V. Consider this *inittab* file, taken from an AIX 3.1 system:

```
init:2:initdefault:
brc::sysinit:/etc/brc >/dev/console 2>&1  # Phase 2 of system boot
rc:2:wait:/etc/rc > /dev/console 2>&1  # Multi-User checks
rctcpip:2:wait:/etc/rc.tcpip > /dev/console 2>&1 # Start TCP/IP daemons
rcnfs:2:wait:/etc/rc.nfs > /dev/console 2>&1  # Start NFS Daemons
srcmstr:2:respawn:/etc/srcmstr  # System Resource Controller
cons::respawn:/etc/getty /dev/console
cron:2:respawn:/etc/cron
qdaemon:2:once:/bin/startsrc -sqdaemon
```

Other than starting a server process for the system console and executing the file */etc/brc* at boottime, nothing is defined for any run-level other than state 2 (multi-user mode). Commands for shutdown and reboot states are not needed since AIX 3.1 supports the BSD/V.4 *shutdown* command, which handles the activities performed by *rc0* and the scripts in */etc/rc0.d* internally (*shutdown* is described in the next section, "Shutting Down a UNIX System.")

When the system enters state 2, a series of initialization files are run in sequence: */etc/rc*, */etc/rc.tcpip*, */etc/rc.nfs*. Then, the AIX 3.1 system resource controller process is initiated directly from *inittab*, followed by the *cron* server and the spooler server *qdaemon* (the latter is started by the system resource controller). The */etc/rcn.d* subdirectories are not used at all. This setup is little different from that used under BSD.

One can imagine an *inittab* file that takes this approach to its logical conclusion:

```
init:2:initdefault:
cons::respawn:/etc/getty /dev/console
rc:2:wait:/etc/rc > /dev/console 2>&1
```

Such a file assumes a BSD/V.4 *shutdown* command, an *rc* script prepared to handle all startup activities (and perhaps calling *rc.local*), and no terminals other than the console (additional terminals would require at least one additional entry each—see Chapter 11, *Printers and the Spooling Subsystem*). While it's probably not worth making major modifications to existing System V systems, just make them look like BSD—*if it isn't broken*.... But if you find the System V setup unnecessarily complicated and frustrating, it might be possible to simplify it.

Shutting Down a UNIX System

From time to time, you will need to shut the system down. This will be necessary for scheduled maintenance, for running diagnostics, for hardware changes or additions, and other administrative tasks.

To shut the system down cleanly, the following actions should take place:

- Notify all users that the system will be going down, preferably with some reasonable advance warning.

- Signal all processes that they are about to be killed, allowing them time to exit gracefully (provided they've made provisions to do so).

- Place the system in single-user mode, logging all remaining users off and killing all remaining processes.

- Ensure that filesystem integrity is maintained by completing all pending disk updates.

After taking these steps, the administrator can turn the power off, execute diagnostics, or perform any other maintenance necessary.

To make sure that all of this gets done, UNIX provides the *shutdown* command. *shutdown* prints a series of timed messages to all users who are logged on, warning them that the system is going down; after sending the last of these messages, it logs all users off the system, placing the console in single-user mode.

WARNING

All UNIX systems—even 386-based microcomputers—should be shut down using the commands described in this section. This is necessary to ensure disk integrity and the "clean" termination of the various system services. *Never just turn the power off.*

The System V shutdown Command

Under System V, *shutdown* has the form:

```
# shutdown -gn -ilevel [-y]
```

where *n* is the number of seconds to wait before beginning the shutdown (the default is 60), and *level* is the run-level in which the system should be placed, usually one of the following:

0   If you intend to turn off the power.

1   Administrative state.

S   Single-user mode (the default if −i is omitted).

5   Firmware state.

6   Reboot to the *initdefault* state in */etc/inittab*.

The System V *shutdown* command will prompt for confirmation just before the system goes down; this prompt may be pre-answered *yes* by including the *-y* option on the *shutdown* command.

Many System V systems require that input to the *shutdown* command come from the system console. This is most easily accomplished by running the *shutdown* command from the console. However, *shutdown* can be executed from any terminal by redirecting standard input to the console device and including the *-y* option (so no input will actually be needed by *shutdown*). For example, the following command will reboot the system in two minutes and may be executed from any terminal:

```
# shutdown -g120 -i6 -y < /dev/console > /dev/console 2>&1
```

The command sends its output to the console terminal as well.

As we've noted, on shutdowns the *rc0* script runs the scripts contained in *rc0.d*,* in a manner similar to all the other *rc* scripts: K-files followed by S-files. In most cases, there are no S-files in *rc0.d*. Such files should only be used to perform essential cleanup activities which take very little time; otherwise, they will end up being killed as part of the shutdown process before they have a chance to finish.

---

*Some versions of *rc0* also make reference to the now obsolete directory */etc/shutdown.d*; no files should be stored there as it is maintained only for compatibility purposes.

The BSD shutdown Command

On BSD systems, the *shutdown* command has the following syntax:

```
# shutdown time message
```

where *time* can have three forms:

> +*m*
> *h*:*m*
> **now**

The first form shuts the system down in *m* minutes; the second shuts the system down at time *h* hours and *m* minutes on a 24-hour clock; and the last shuts the system down immediately. Obviously, *now* should be used with discretion on multi-user systems. *Message* is the announcement that *shutdown* sends to all users; it may be any text string. For example, the command:

```
# shutdown +60 "System going down for regular maintenance"
```

will shut the system down in one hour. It warns users by printing the message "System going down for regular maintenance" on their terminals. *Shutdown* sends the first message immediately; as the shutdown time approaches, it will repeat the warning with increasing frequency.

System V.4 provides the BSD version of *shutdown* in */usr/ucb*. AIX 3.1 supports the BSD form of the *shutdown* command, although the -*m* option must be used to specify shutting down to single-user mode.

XENIX supports a BSD-style *shutdown* command, but it requires no arguments; by default, it will prompt you for the number of minutes to wait before shutting down. Alternatively, you can specify the number of minutes to wait as its first argument. If you specify the keyword *su* as its second argument, the system will be placed in single-user mode (rather than being shut down and halted).

Some BSD-based systems support a *shutdown* configuration file */etc/rc.shutdown*, but this is not standard. If *rc.shutdown* is supported, administrators may place commands they want run at shutdown in it (for example, to cleanly terminate local programs and third party applications). If *rc.shutdown* is not supported on your system, it can be simulated by:

- Renaming the */etc/shutdown* file to something else, like */etc/shutdown.exe*.

- Creating a script named */etc/shutdown* which performs the desired actions and then calls */etc/shutdown.exe* (or whatever you've called it). The script should have the same ownership and permissions as the *shutdown* command did (although it won't need the SUID access mode *shutdown* has).

Shutdown and Automatic Reboot

Under BSD, the *-r* option to the *shutdown* command lets you shut the system down and reboot automatically as soon as the system enters single-user mode. For example, the command:

```
# shutdown -r +5 "Back up soon"
```

will shut the system down in five minutes and reboot it immediately. The AIX 3.1 *shutdown* command also supports the *-r* option.

Under System V, an automatic reboot is accomplished by specifying run-level 6 on the *shutdown* command. This form will shut down the system and take it to the system state specified in the *initdefault* entry in */etc/inittab*. For example, the following command begins the shutdown process in one minute, pre-answers yes to all prompts, and will reboot the system immediately:

```
# shutdown -y -i6 < /dev/console
```

Rebooting Immediately Under System V

Another way to quickly reboot the system under System V, when no grace period is needed, is to use the *telinit* command. *telinit* takes a run-level as its argument, and sends a signal to *init* directing it to take the system to that state. Thus, the command *telinit 6* will initiate an immediate reboot.

BSD Shutdown and Fast Reboot

Under BSD, the *-f* option to the *shutdown* command causes the system to reboot immediately after reaching single-user mode, *without* executing *fsck*. Since *fsck* is fairly time-consuming, this allows the system to reboot very quickly. It should only be used if there are no questions about the filesystem's accuracy.

The *shutdown* command specifies a fast reboot by creating the file */fastboot*. If this file exists, then the initialization scripts know to skip the *fsck* of the disks. The file is removed automatically at boottime. The *fastboot* command performs the identical function to *shutdown -f*.

Rebooting Under XENIX

On XENIX systems, there is no way to specify an automatic reboot on the *shutdown* command. However, once the shutdown process is complete, striking any key will reboot the system.

Rebooting from Single-user Mode

Under BSD, after you have shut down to single-user mode, entering CTRL-D will return the system to multi-user mode. Alternatively, the command *reboot* will halt UNIX and immediately reboot the system for normal multi-user operation. *reboot* should only be executed in single-user mode.

These two commands differ in that *reboot* halts the system before rebooting (i.e., reloads and reinitializes the kernel) while CTRL-D continues the current boot process. *reboot* will result in the disks being *fsck*ed again, while entering CTRL-D will skip this step. Thus, *reboot* should be used any time a complete boot process is needed—for example, if *fsck* had to be run manually on the root disk—while CTRL-D may be used if you know this is not needed—when the system has been taken to single-user mode for backups or some types of software upgrades. AIX 3.1 also supports the *reboot* command.

Under System V, a reboot to multi-user mode from single-user mode may be made by running the *shut down* command and specifying run-level 6 or with *tel-init 6*.

Shutdown and Halt

Under BSD, the *-h* option to the *shutdown* command lets you shut down the system to the point where power may be safely turned off. This process involves halting the CPU completely, so that UNIX is not running any more. When you do this, UNIX prints a series of messages something like the following:

```
# shutdown -h +5 "Installing a new disk."
```
...Many messages about the impending shutdown, ending with:...
```
System going down IMMEDIATELY

System shutdown time has arrived
Jul 14 14:49:21 hamlet shutdown: reboot by root:
Jul 14 14:49:25 hamlet syslogd: going down on signal 15
syncing disks... done
>
```

At this point, it is safe to remove power from the system.

Under AIX 3.1, either the *-h* or the *-v* option to *shutdown* may be used to halt the CPU.

Under System V, specifying run state 5 (firmware mode) performs a similar sort of action:

```
# shutdown -y -g0 -i5
```

The firmware state may be used to run diagnostics or to boot manually from an alternate disk.

Under V.4, the *powerdown* command may be used to shut down the system, stop all processes (including UNIX itself), and automatically remove power (assuming the hardware supports this function). It supports *shutdown*'s -y option (answer yes to all prompts) and also a -Y option, which overrides the normal 60-second pause between prompts.

On XENIX systems, use the *haltsys* command to immediately shut down the system.

Manually Halting the Processor Under BSD

If you didn't halt the CPU automatically by executing the *shutdown -h* command, you may do it manually using the *halt* command once the system has reached single-user mode:

```
# halt
```
...Messages stating that the CPU is halted...
>   *monitor prompt*

At this point, it is safe to remove power from the system. The command *fasthalt* will halt the processor and also create the */fastboot* file, which will tell *rc* to skip the *fsck* operation on the next boot.

Guaranteeing Disk Accuracy

As we've noted above, one of the important parts of the shutdown process is *syncing* the disks. The *sync* command finishes all disk transactions and writes out the up-to-date superblock, guaranteeing that the system can be turned off without corrupting the files. You can execute this command manually if necessary:

```
# sync
# sync
```

Why is *sync* executed twice (or more)? Essentially this is a bit of UNIX superstition. The *sync* command schedules, but does not necessarily immediately perform, the required disk writes, even though the UNIX prompt returns immediately. Multiple *sync* commands raise the probability that the write will take place before you enter another command (or turn off power) by taking up the time needed to complete the operation. However, the same effect can be obtained by waiting a few seconds for disk activity to cease before doing anything else. Typing "sync" several times gives you something to do while you're waiting.

There is one situation in which you do not want *sync* to be executed, either manually or automatically: when you have run *fsck* manually on the root filesystem. If you *sync* the disks at this point, you will rewrite the bad superblocks stored in the kernel buffers and undo the fixing *fsck* just did. On BSD systems, use the *-n* option to *reboot* or *shutdown* to suppress the usual automatic *sync* operation. On AIX 3.1 systems, use *shutdown -c* or *reboot -n*.

System V is smarter about this issue. The *-b* option to *fsck* automatically remounts the root filesystem or reboots the system if necessary when it has modified the root filesystem. If you run *fsck* manually on the root filesystem, be sure to include *-b* on the *fsck* command (*-b* is included on the *fsck* commands in the system initialization files). No other special actions are required to avoid *sync*ing the disks.

Disabling Logins Under BSD

On BSD systems, if the file */etc/nologin* exists, then users may not log in to the system. The file is created automatically by the *shutdown* command and removed by */etc/rc*. You can also create the file yourself if you need to. The contents of the */etc/nologin* file is used as a message when someone tries to log in. When you include a message on the *shutdown* command, it is placed in */etc/nologin* when created.

System V.4 and AIX 3.1 also use the */etc/nologin* file.

Aborting a Shutdown

The only way to abort a pending system shutdown is to kill the *shutdown* process. Determine the shutdown process' process ID by using a command like:

```
# ps -ax | grep shutdown       (BSD)
# ps -ef | grep shutdown       (System V)
```

Then use the *kill* command to terminate it:

```
# ps -ef | grep shutdown
25723 co S      0:01 /etc/shutdown -g300 -i6 -y
25800 co S      0:00 grep shutdown
# kill -9 25723
```

It's only safe to kill a *shutdown* command during its grace period; once it has actually started closing down the system, you're better off letting it finish and then rebooting.

Fake Shutdowns (BSD and AIX 3.1)

The BSD and AIX 3.1 *shutdown* commands also support a -*k* option (as does */usr/ucb/shutdown* under V.4). This option inaugurates a fake system shutdown: the shutdown messages are sent out normally, but no shutdown actually occurs. I suppose the theory is that you can scare users off the system this way, but some of them can be pretty persistent, preferring to be killed by *shutdown* rather than log out.

When the System Crashes

Even the best-maintained systems do crash from time to time. There are many causes of crashes. The most common are:

- Hardware failures: failing disk controllers, CPU boards, memory boards, power supplies, disk head crashes, and so on.

- Power failures or surges, due to internal power supply problems, external power outages, electrical storms, and other causes.

- Other environmental problems: roof leaks, air conditioning failure, etc.

- I/O problems, involving a fatal error condition rather than a device malfunction.

- Software problems, ranging from fatal kernel errors caused by operating system bugs to problems caused by user or third-party programs.

Some of these causes are easier to identify than others. Rebooting the system may seem like the most pressing concern when the system crashes, but it's just as important to gather the available information about why the system crashed, while it's still accessible.

Sometimes it's obvious why the system crashed—as when the lights go out. If the cause isn't immediately obvious, the first source of information are any messages appearing on the system console. They will still usually be visible if you check immediately, even if the system is set to reboot automatically. After they are no longer on the screen, you still may be able to find them by checking the system error log file (supported under BSD and by quite a few System V vendors as well), usually stored in */usr/adm/messages* (see the section entitled "Configuring BSD-style Error Logging," in Chapter 5, *Security*, for more details).

Beyond console messages lie crash dumps. Most systems automatically write a dump of kernel memory when the system crashes (if possible). These memory images can be examined using the *crash* command in an effort to determine what the kernel was doing when it crashed. (Obviously, these dumps will be of use only for certain types of crashes in which the system state at the time of the crash is relevant.) Using *crash* is beyond the scope of this book, but you should know where crash dumps go on your system and how to access them, if only to be able to save them for your field service engineers.

Crash dumps are usually written to the system disk swap partition. Since this area may be overwritten when the system is booted, some provisions need to be made to save its contents. BSD solves this problem via the *savecore* command, often executed automatically in *rc.local*, which usually copies the crash dump to the directory */usr/crash*, creating the files *vmcore.n* and *vmunix.n* (where *n* is an integer used to distinguish multiple memory images).

The *savecore* command is sometimes disabled in *rc.local* by default; if this is the case on your system, you should uncomment the relevant lines if you wish to save crash dumps. Once *savecore* runs, these files may examined at leisure. Over time, quite a few dump files can accumulate, so you'll need to delete unneeded ones from time to time.

If your system crashes and you are *not* collecting crash dumps by default but you want to get one, boot the system to single-user mode, and execute *savecore* by hand. Don't let the system boot to multi-user mode before saving the crash dump; once the system reaches multi-user mode, it's too late.

System V has no comparable facility. On some System V systems, the kernel information must be written to tape before rebooting the system.* You can use

---

*On a few systems, even the crash dump itself must be generated manually; on a Stardent 3000, for example, you must execute the *sysdump* command at the PROM monitor to generate a crash dump.

the *dd* command, which transfers raw data between devices, for this purpose. For example:

```
# dd if=/unix of=/dev/rmt20 bs=512
# dd if=/dev/dsk/c1d5s1 of=/dev/rmt20 bs=512 count=64
```

The first command copies the kernel image file to tape device 20 (it is needed by *crash*). The second command copies 64 512-byte data blocks from the swap partition (*/dev/dsk/c1d5s1*) to the same tape (the size of the memory system on this machine is 32 MBytes). The commands for your system may vary, but this example should give you some sense of the required procedure; check the manual pages for *dd* and *crash* for further information.

When the System Won't Boot

As with system crashes, there can be many reasons why a system won't boot. Some are hardware problems, usually identifiable via the boottime error messages. There's not a lot you can do in these cases, other than calling field service. One thing you can try is power cycling the affected device or the system. This process will clear many types of disk and disk controller problems. Once you've turned the power off, leave it off for at least ten seconds to allow the device's internal capacitors to discharge.

We've already looked at problems due to corrupted filesystems. In these cases, you'll need to run *fsck* manually (see Chapter 8, *Filesystems and Disks*).

A third major cause of boot problems is errors in initialization files. Usually, once an error is encountered, the boot will stop and leave the system in single-user mode. The incident described in Chapter 1, *Introduction to System Administration*, about the workstation that wouldn't boot ended up being a problem of this type. The user had been editing the initialization files on his workstation, and he had an error in the first line of */etc/rc* (I found out later). So only the root disk got mounted. On this system, */usr* was on a separate disk partition and the commands stored in */bin* used shared libraries stored under */usr*. So, there was no *ls*, no *cat*, not even *ed*.

As I told you before, I remembered that *echo* could list filenames using the shell's internal wildcard expansion mechanism (and it didn't need the shared library). So I typed:

```
# echo /etc/rc*
```

and found out there was an *rc.dist* file there. Although it was probably out of date, it could get things going. So I executed it manually:

```
# . /etc/rc.dist
```

The morals of this story are, of course, *test, test, test,* and that an obsessive prudence will save you every time.

4

User Accounts

Adding New Users
UNIX Groups
Standard UNIX Users and Groups

This chapter describes UNIX user accounts and related issues: how UNIX identifies users, how it associates users into groups, and so on. A large part of the chapter deals with adding new user accounts to the system, one of the first and most frequent system administrative activities. The final section of the chapter discusses the standard users and groups defined on almost every UNIX system.

From the system's point of view, a user isn't necessarily an individual person. A user is any entity that can execute programs or own files. Such users may be other computer systems; they may be particular system functions that run automatically (for example, the accounting system); or they may be groups of people with a similar function (for example, a research group). Some users only exist to own collections of public files. In most cases, however, a user means a particular individual that can log in, edit files, run programs, and otherwise make use of the system.

Each user has a *username* (occasionally called a *login name*) that identifies him. When adding a new user account to the system, the administrator assigns it a unique *user identification number* (UID). Internally, the UID is the system's way of identifying a user. The administrator also assigns each new user to one or more *groups*. A group is a collection of users who generally share a similar function.

For example, they might all work on the same project. Each group has a *group identification number* (GID) that is analogous to the UID: it is the system's internal way of identifying a group. Together, any user's UID and GID determine what kinds of access rights she has to files and other system resources. User account information is stored primarily in the *password file*, */etc/passwd*. This is an ASCII text file containing the complete list of system users, together with their user and group IDs, and a coded form of their passwords. On some older systems, this raw file is used to generate two binary, random-access database files, */etc/passwd.pag* and */etc/passwd.dir*.

The file */etc/group* lists all defined groups. This chapter describes how to add a new user or create a new group, by modifying these two files. Both */etc/passwd* and */etc/group* are public information; all users may read them, but only the superuser is allowed to modify them. A readable password file has long been considered a significant security risk; the various schemes for altering this situation are discussed in "Shadow Password Files," later in this chapter.

Adding New Users

To add a new user to the system, you must:

- Assign the user a username, a user ID number, and a primary group.

- Enter this data in */etc/passwd* and into any secondary password file in use.

- Assign a password to the new account.

- Set other user account parameters in use on your system (including password aging, account expiration date, and resource limits).

- Create a home directory for the user.

- Place initialization files in the user's directory.

- Use *chown* and/or *chgrp* to give the new user ownership of his home directory and initialization files.

- Add the user to any other facilities in use such as the quota system or the mail system.

- Define any secondary group memberships in the system group file, */etc/group*.

- Perform any other site-specific initialization tasks.

- Test the new account.

This section discusses standard UNIX account creation; alternatives supported by some implementations will be covered as appropriate.

Defining a New User Account

Normally, the file */etc/passwd* is the system's master list of information about users. To add a new user to the system, you must add a new entry to this file. This may be done by simply editing the file with any editor, or, under BSD, by using the command *vipw* to do so. The *vipw* command invokes an editor on a copy of the password file named */etc/ptmp*. This temporary password file also serves as a lock file to prevent simultaneous editing by two different users: no one else may invoke *vipw* while this file exists. The editor used is selected via the EDITOR environment variable (the default is *vi*). *vipw* creates locks to prevent simultaneous access by two different users. When you save the file and exit the editor, *vipw* performs some simple consistency checking. If this is successful, it renames */etc/ptmp* to */etc/passwd*. If necessary, *vipw* also automatically generates the password database files */etc/passwd.pag* and */etc/passwd.dir*.

If you edit the password file manually, it's a good idea to save a copy of the unedited version so you can recover from errors:

```
# cp passwd passwd.sav        Save a copy of the current file.
# vi passwd
#                             Test changed accounts.
```

Lots of people use a name like *opasswd* for the copy—"old" password—but I prefer adding a suffix so they're all together in directory listings.

If you want to be even more careful, you can copy the password file again, to something like *passwd.new* and edit that, renaming it only when you've successfully exited the editor. This will save you from having to recopy it from *passwd.sav* on those rare occasions when you totally munge the password file in the editor.

Each entry in the password file has the following form:

name:*coded-passwd*:*UID*:*GID*:*user information*:*home-directory*:*shell*

where fields are separated by colons. Blank spaces are legal only in the *user information* field. The meanings of the fields are as follows:

name   The username assigned to the user. Since usernames are the basis for communications between users, they are not private or secure information. They should be names that can be remembered easily, like the user's last name; most users will need to know the usernames of the other users on the system.

coded-passwd   The user's encrypted password.* If you are adding a user
                         who will never log in (for example, creating a user whose
                         only function is to own files), fill this field with an asterisk
                         (:*:). This prevents anyone from using this name to log in
                         (because an asterisk is not among the target characters for
                         encrypted passwords and hence can never be matched).
                         It's a good idea to initially place an asterisk in the pass-
                         word field when creating a new account. That way, if you
                         are interrupted before you've finished, system security
                         won't be compromised. A blank password field means that
                         no password will be required to log in using this account
                         (not recommended).

                         Do not attempt to place a password in this field while edit-
                         ing */etc/passwd*. After you have finished adding the user to
                         the system, assign him a password with the *passwd* com-
                         mand (see the next section).

                         Some UNIX implementations no longer keep the encrypted
                         passwords in */etc/passwd*; see "Shadow Password Files,"
                         later in this chapter.

UID   The user's identification number. Each user must have a
                         unique UID. It is a good idea to assign UIDs sequentially,
                         beginning with 100, and to keep */etc/passwd* ordered
                         according to user IDs. Conventionally, UIDs less than 100
                         are used for system accounts.

GID   Determines the user's primary group membership. This
                         number is usually the identification number assigned to a
                         group in the file */etc/group* (discussed in the section
                         entitled "UNIX Groups," later in this chapter), although
                         technically the GID need not be listed there. Under many
                         UNIX implementations, this field determines the group
                         ownership of files the user creates. In addition, it gives the
                         user access to files that are owned by the group. Conven-
                         tionally, GIDs less than 10 are used for system groups.

user-information   Usually contains the user's full name. Mail systems and
                         commands like *finger* (primarily BSD) use this

---

*Technically, the password is encoded, not encrypted. At login authentication, the entered ("clear")
and coded passwords are used to encrypt a block of zeros, and the results are compared. If they match,
then the user entered the correct password. Nevertheless, I'll follow general usage in referring to the
coded passwords stored in the password file as "encrypted."

information. This field is also called the GECOS field, after the name of the operating system whose remote login information was originally stored in the field. Sometimes GECOS is spelled GCOS.

home-directory   The user's home directory. When the user logs in, this will be the initial working directory.

shell   The program that UNIX will use as a command interpreter for this user. Whenever the user logs in, UNIX will automatically execute this program. Normally, this is usually one of */bin/sh* (Bourne shell), */bin/csh* (C shell) or */bin/ksh* (Korn shell). (Under V.4, the shells are stored in */sbin.*) *uucp* users (i.e., the *uucp* username and all usernames assigned to other systems for *uucp*) list the *uucp* command interpreter, */usr/lib/uucp/uucico*, in this field.

If this field is empty, it defaults to the */bin/sh* (or */sbin/sh* under V.4). This is conventionally the Bourne shell, although on some recent systems, including AIX 3.1, the file */bin/sh* is actually a link and thus can be used to make any shell the default shell.

Some systems allow users to change their login shell (using *chsh* or *passwd -s*). Under BSD, the legal shells are defined in the file */etc/shells*; only programs whose pathnames are listed here may be specified as password file login shells. Here is a sample */etc/shells* file:

```
/bin/sh
/bin/csh
/bin/ksh
/usr/lib/uucp/uucico
```

You may add additional entries to this file if necessary. The superuser is not held to this restriction, however, and may enter any program name into the password file shell field.

For example, a typical entry in */etc/passwd* is:

```
chavez:*:190:20:Rachel Chavez:/u/chavez:/bin/csh
```

This entry creates a user whose username is *chavez*. She hasn't been assigned a password yet; her account is currently disabled. Her UID is 190, her primary group is group 20, her full name is Rachel Chavez, her home directory is */u/chavez*, and she runs the C shell.

Newer systems with shadow password files often discourage administrators from editing the password file directly. Instead, they provide commands which act as an interface to the files. It's often a good idea to use these interface commands, especially at first. That way you'll be sure that all of the necessary files are updated when you add or modify a user account. (This is especially true under AIX 3.1, where user account information is scattered among several different files.)

Assigning User Passwords

All user accounts should have passwords.* The *passwd* command may be used to assign an initial password for a user account. When used for this purpose, it takes the relevant username as its argument. For example, the command:

```
# passwd chavez
```

will assign an initial password for the user *chavez* that we added above. You will be prompted for the password twice. The same command may also be used to change a user's password should this ever be necessary (for example, if she forgets her password). Some System V systems support a -*f* option to *passwd* which pre-expires a password, forcing the user to change it the next time he logs in.

Under AIX 3.1, whenever the superuser assigns a password to an account with *passwd* (manually or indirectly via SMIT), password will be pre-expired, and the user will be required to change it at the next login. When the superuser changes an existing user's password, AIX 3.1 prompts for the old password before asking for the new one (just as it does when changing one's own password). Either the user's old password or the root password may be entered in response to the old password prompt.

Guidelines for Choosing Passwords

Let's take a brief look at choosing passwords. The considerations discussed here apply both to choosing the root password (which the system administrator chooses) and to user passwords. In the latter case, your input usually takes the form of educating users about good and bad choices.

---

*The only possible exception I see is an isolated, non-networked system with no dialin modems at a personal residence, but even then you might need to take into account houseguests, neighborhood kids, and so on, before deciding not to use passwords. Any system in a commercial environment, even single-user systems in locked offices, should use passwords.

The purpose of passwords is to prevent unauthorized people from accessing user accounts and the system in general. What this means in practical terms is that passwords should be hard to guess, even if someone is willing to go to a fair amount of effort. The following items should be *avoided* as passwords:

- Any part of the user's name or the name of any member of the user's extended family (including significant others and pets). Your maternal grandmother's maiden name is a lot easier to find out than you think.

- Significant numbers to you or a significant person to you: social security numbers, car license, phone number, birthdates, etc.

- The name of something that is important to you, like your favorite food, recording artist, movie, TV character, place, etc. Similarly, if your thesis was on benzene, don't pick benzene as a password. The same goes for people, places, things you hate.

- Any name, numbers, people, places, or other items associated with your company or institution or its products.

- English words spelled correctly, especially if they appear in online dictionaries (assuming English is the language in use at your site). You can use the *spell* command to see if a word appears in the UNIX online dictionary:

  ```
  $ echo cerise xyzzy | spell
  xyzzy
  ```

  In this case, *spell* knows the word "cerise" (a color) but not "xyzzy" (although xyzzy is a bad password on other grounds).

  If two or more languages are in common use at your site, or in the area in which it's located, words in all of them should be avoided.

- The names of famous people, places, things, fictional characters, movies, TV shows, songs, slogans, and the like.

- Published password examples.

Avoiding passwords like the first few items in this list makes it harder for someone to figure out your password. Avoiding the later items makes it harder for someone to successfully break into an account using a brute force trial and error method, like a computer program.

Simple modifications of any of these bad passwords, created by adding a single additional character, spelling it backwards, or permuting the letters, are still bad passwords and ought to be avoided. For example, avoid not only "john" but also "nhoj" and "ohnj" and "john2." It doesn't take a password guessing program very long to try all combinations of adding one character, reversing and permuting.

Although they are risky themselves, these items can serves as the base for creating a good password. Passwords that use two or more of the following modifications to ordinary words are usually good choices:

- Embedding one or more extra characters, especially symbol and control characters.

- Misspelling it.

- Using unusual capitalization (all lowercase is not unusual).

- Concatenating two or more words or parts of words.

- Interleaving two or more words: for example, "cdaotg" interleaves "dog" and "cat." (With a little practice, some people can do this easily in their heads; others can't. If you need a one-second delay between characters as you type in such a password, don't use them.)

The table below illustrates some of these recommendations, using "StarTrek" as a base (although I'd recommend avoiding *anything* having to do with Star Trek in passwords altogether):

Bad	Good
StarTrek	StarR^TRk
sTarTrek	st^IrtRi#
trekstar	sttrAErK
StarDrek	jetr^Ekdi

(Of course, these would all be poor choices now.) Overall, the goal is that passwords should be hard to guess, for humans and programs, but be easy to remember and fast to type.

When choosing successive root passwords, try to avoid falling into a recognizable pattern. If you always, say, capitalize all the vowels, and someone knows this, you effectively lose the value of the unusual capitalization.

Some System V systems require passwords chosen by users to conform to certain rules, usually including: being at least six characters long, including at least two alphabetic characters and one numeric or special character, and having at least three characters that were not in the previous password. Others allow the superuser to set a minimum password length (see the section entitled "Setting Password Restrictions," later in this chapter). The superuser generally is not required to adhere to these rules.

Here are some general recommendations about passwords and system security:

- The root password should be changed regularly. I'm not sure it really needs to be changed religiously once a month, but it ought to be changed every time there's someone who knows it but doesn't need to. This includes not only unauthorized people learning it, but also legitimate root users who leave the system. It's also a good idea to change it once in a while when you don't think anyone who shouldn't know it does, just in case you're wrong.

- Users should be encouraged to keep their passwords secret and to choose passwords that are hard to guess (as described previously).

- There should be no unprotected accounts on the system. This includes accounts without passwords and accounts for users who have left the system, protected by their original Passwords. When a user leaves, always set her password to an asterisk (see the section entitled "Removing a User Account," later in this chapter).

- Finally, it's always a good idea to specify a minimum password length if your system lets you. I recommend setting it to 8, the maximum UNIX password length (which isn't really long enough anyway). Longer passwords can be typed in, but any extra characters are ignored.

Shadow Password Files

Some UNIX implementations support *shadow password files*: files which are protected from all access by non-root users and which store the encrypted passwords. You can tell when a shadow password file is in use if you look at the password fields in */etc/passwd*: if they are all set to "x" (or "!" under AIX 3.1), then a shadow password file is in use. Under System V, its name is */etc/shadow*; under AIX 3.1, its name is */etc/security/passwd*. The *passwd* command automatically updates the shadow password file instead of the regular password file if a shadow file exists.

System V provides the *pwconv* command to create and update a shadow password file, using the encrypted passwords and other data currently stored in */etc/passwd*. Initially, *pwconv* will create */etc/shadow* from */etc/passwd*, replacing the encrypted passwords in the latter with an "x". On an update, *pwconv* adds new users in */etc/passwd* to */etc/shadow*, removes users not in */etc/passwd* from the shadow file, and moves passwords and aging data for existing users from the password file to the shadow file, again leaving an "x" in the password field of */etc/passwd*.

Password File Permissions

The password file is usually owned by *root* and the system group (GID 0). Only the owner should have write access:

```
$ ls -l /etc/passwd
-rw-r--r-- 1 root   system   4096 Apr  1  1991 /etc/passwd
```

Shadow password files usually have the same ownership but are not accessible at all by anyone but *root*:

```
# ls -l /etc/shadow
-rw------- 1 root   system   4096 Apr  1  1991 /etc/shadow
```

The */etc/shells* file (under BSD) should have the same ownership and protections as the password file. Old and saved versions of any of these files should also be protected just like the main file; be sure to check them when you create them.

Setting Password Restrictions

Users don't like to change their passwords. System V, AIX 3.1, and XENIX provide mechanisms whereby you can force them to anyway. You can specify how long a user can keep the same password before being *forced* to change it (the *maximum password lifetime*), how long he must keep a new password before being *allowed* to change it again (the *minimum password lifetime*), the minimum password length, and sometimes some other parameters. Setting the minimum and maximum password lifetimes is referred to as specifying *password aging* information.

Before you decide to turn on password aging on your system, you should consider carefully how much "password fascism" it really needs. Forcing users to change their password when they don't want to is one of the least effective system security tactics. And preventing them from changing their new password right back to what it was before (which they liked and can remember without writing down) can also have some unexpected side effects. One potential problem with a minimum password lifetime comes at those times when a password *must be changed*—when someone who shouldn't have sees it, for example. At such times, a user might be unable to change his password even though he needs to. Of course, the superuser can always change passwords, but then the user will have to hunt down the system administrator, admit what happened, and get it changed. Or, the user may decide just to wait until the minimum lifetime expires and change it himself. You'll need to decide which is more likely on your system: users attempting to circumvent necessary password aging or users needing to be able to change their passwords at will; depending on your situation, either one could be more important for system security.

System V Password Aging

Under System V, you can use the *passwd* to specify password aging parameters as well as a password. The *-n* and *-x* options to the System V *passwd* command specify the minimum and maximum password lifetimes respectively (in days). For example, the following command sets minimum and maximum password lifetimes for user *chavez* and also sets password aging for user *chavez*:

```
# passwd -n1 -x158 chavez
```

Chavez may use the same password for 158 days, after which time she must change it. When she does change it, she must keep the new password for one day. When setting password aging, both *-x* and *-n* should be specified, even if one is set to zero.

Other useful options to *passwd* are:

-f   Force the user to change the password at the next login.

-s   List password data for the specified user.

-a   Used with *-s* to list data for all users.

-l   Lock the account so the user can't log in.

-d   Delete password for this user; no password will be required to log in to this account. This practice is not recommended.

For example, the following command displays the password information for user *chavez*:

```
# passwd -s chavez
chavez  PS  03/12/91  7  158  7
```

The first item is the username. The second item is the password status, one of: *PS* (password defined), *NP* (no password), or *LK* (account locked/disabled with a password like an asterisk; re-enable the account by assigning a new password). The third item is that date *chavez* last changed her password. The fourth and fifth columns indicate the minimum and maximum password lifetimes (in days), and the sixth column shows the number of days prior to password expiration that *chavez* will begin to receive messages to that effect. (On some systems, the user's UID, GID, home directory, and shell are also included in this display.)

When the *passwd* command is executed, password aging is enabled for that account. If -*x* and -*n* are not specified, then the values listed in the file */etc/default/passwd* are used. Here is a sample */etc/default/passwd* file:

```
MAXWEEKS=26
MINWEEKS=0
WARNWEEKS=1
PASSLENGTH=8
```

The file sets the default password aging parameters as follows: the same password may be used for at most 26 weeks (six months), users will begin to get warning messages one week before the password expires. However, they can change their new password again as soon as they want to. These settings will serve to force users to think about changing their passwords twice a year, but won't compel them to actually do so. (Note that the values here are in weeks although the *passwd* command uses days.) Finally, the minimum password length is eight characters.

To disable the password aging feature, set up a default file like the following:

```
MAXWEEKS=2000    Or some other big number.
MINWEEKS=0       Passwords can always be changed.
WARNWEEKS=0
```

You can use the -*x* option to the *passwd* command to disable password aging for a single user. Specifying a value of -1 will instantly turn off password aging for the specified user. A value of 0 will also disable password aging and will also force the user to change his password at his next login.

User-specific password aging data is stored with the encrypted password in the password file (or in the shadow password file, if one is in use). It is separated from the encrypted password by a comma. The first two characters following the comma represent the maximum and minimum password lifetime in weeks, using the following coding scheme:

.	0 weeks	A	12 weeks	a	38 weeks
/	1 week	B	13 weeks	b	39 weeks
0	2 weeks	C	14 weeks	c	40 weeks
1	3 weeks	...		...	
2	4 weeks	W	34 weeks	w	60 weeks
...		X	35 weeks	x	61 weeks
8	10 weeks	Y	36 weeks	y	62 weeks
9	11 weeks	Z	37 weeks	z	63 weeks

The remaining characters (if any) are an encoded form of the last change date. For example, the following password file entry indicates that user *martin* must change his password every 12 weeks and must keep the new one for one week (the encrypted password is fake):

```
martin:xy&%NjgMPtx*Q,A/:145:20:Gordon H. Martin:/u/martin:/bin/ksh
```

Not all System V implementations support all of these features. Older versions don't support the options to *passwd* and require the superuser to enter the password aging data into the password file by hand.

XENIX Password Aging Features

The XENIX *pwadmin* command provides the same functionality as the System V version of *passwd*, using a different set of options:

-min   Minimum password lifetime in weeks.

-max   Maximum password lifetime in weeks.

-f   Force password change at next login (as in System V).

-a   Enable password aging for the specified user, using the defaults in */etc/default/passwd*.

-n   Disable password aging for the specified user.

-d   Display password data for the specified user.

-c   Prevent the user from changing his password. For example, the following command would force user *chavez* to change her password twice a year and to keep a new password for one week. She would also have to specify a new password at her next login:

```
# pwadmin -min 1 -max 26 -f chavez
```

Setting Restrictions on Passwords Under AIX 3.1

Under AIX 3.1, several system-wide password characteristics can be specified in the *pw_restrictions* stanza of the */etc/security/login.cfg* file. Here is an example:

```
pw_restrictions:
        maxage = 26
        minage = 0
        minalpha = 0
        minother = 1
        mindiff = 4
        maxrepeats = 4
```

The *minage* and *maxage* keywords specify the minimum and maximum times between password changes in weeks. The settings above mean that a password *must* be changed at least every six months but *can* changed at any time (if *minage* were set to 1, new passwords would have to be kept for one week).

The *minalpha* keyword specifies the minimum number of letters in a valid password; the value 0 sets no minimum. The *minother* keyword specifies the minimum number of nonalphabetic characters in a valid password (these can be numbers, symbols, control characters, and so on).

The *mindiff* and *maxrepeats* keywords determine how different a new password must be from the previous password. *mindiff* says how many characters in the new password must not have been present anywhere in the old password (a fairly high value is designed to prevent users from picking a new password that is just a simple variation on the old one). The *maxrepeats* keyword specifies how many characters that were in the old password can also be in the new password.

If you don't want to put restrictions on user passwords, use the following values:

```
pw_restrictions:
        maxage = 0
        minage = 0
        minalpha = 0
        minother = 0
        mindiff = 0
        maxrepeats = 8
```

You can also disable these restrictions for an individual user by adding the flag *NOCHECK* to the user's entry in */etc/security/passwd*, the AIX 3.1 shadow password file, which also stores the encrypted passwords. The *pwdadm -q* command may be used to list a user's current status:

```
# pwdadm -q chavez
chavez:
        lastupdate = 678986374
        flags = NOCHECK
```

You can edit this file directly or use the *pwdadm* command's *-f* flag to change an entry:

```
# pwdadm -f NOCHECK martin
```

Another useful flag is *ADMCHK,* which forces the user to change his password at the next login without changing his current password. (When the superuser changes a user's password, he is also required to change it at his next login.)

Creating a Home Directory

After adding a user to the *letc/passwd* file, you must create a home directory for
the user. Use the *mkdir* command to create the directory in the appropriate location. For example:

```
# mkdir /u/chavez
```

User home directories are often located on a separate filesystem beginning at */u*
or */home* (or, on older systems, under */usr*).

Initialization Files

Next, you should give the user copies of the appropriate initialization files for the
shell the account will run. The UNIX initialization files are:

Bourne shell	*.profile*
C shell	*.login* and *.cshrc*
Korn shell	*.profile* and any file specified in the ENV environ- ment variable (if any)

These files must all be located in the user's home directory. All are shell scripts
(for their respective shell) which are executed in the standard input stream of the
login shell (i.e., as if they had been invoked with *source* (C shell) or . (Bourne or
Korn shell)). The *.profile* and *.login* initialization files are executed at login;
.cshrc is executed every time a new shell is spawned (as is the file set in ENV in
the Korn shell).

The Korn shell provides a mechanism for defining a file with a function similar to
.cshrc's. The file specified as the value of the ENV variable will be executed
each time a shell is spawned. Thus, a command like the following in the *.profile*
file will simulate *.cshrc*'s behavior:

```
export ENV=$HOME/.kshrc
```

As administrator, you should create standard initialization files for your system
and store them in a standard location. On BSD systems, this is conventionally
/usr/skel; on V.4 systems, */etc/skel* is defined for this purpose. When files are
stored in these *skeleton* directories, the filenames typically do not include the initial period. On AIX 3.1 systems, standard initialization files are stored in
/etc/security under their own names (including the period). In all cases, the standard initialization files should be writable only by *root*.

You should copy the relevant file(s) to the user's home directory after you create it. For example:

```
# cp /usr/skel/profile /u/chavez/.profile
# cp /usr/skel/login /u/chavez/.login
# cp /usr/skel/cshrc /u/chavez/.cshrc
```

There are, of course, cleverer ways to do this. I tend to copy all the standard initialization files to a new account in case the user wants to use a different shell. It is up to the user to modify these files to customize her own UNIX environment appropriately.

Depending on how you use your system, several other initialization files may be of interest. For example, many editors have configuration files, the BSD *mail* handler has an initialization file named *.mailrc*, and the C shell also supports a *.logout* file, which contains commands to be executed when the user logs out.[*]

Sample Login Initialization Files

The *.login* or *.profile* files are used to perform tasks that only need to be executed upon login, such as:

* Setting the search path.

* Setting the default file protection (with *umask*).

* Setting the terminal type and initializing the terminal.

* Setting other environment variables.

* Performing other customization functions necessary at your site.

The contents of a simple *.login* file are listed below; it will serve to illustrate some of its potential uses:

```
if (-e ~/.hushlogin) cat /etc/motd
limit coredumpsize 0k
umask 022
setenv PATH /usr/ucb:/bin:/usr/bin:/usr/local/bin:.:~/bin
setenv PRINTER ps
setenv EDITOR emacs
setenv MORE -c
setenv ARCH_DIR /u/pubg91/archdir/
mesg y
biff y
set prompt = '`hostname`-\!> '
```

---

[*]Under the Bourne shell, including a section in *.profile* headed by a *trap 0* command would perform a similar function.

```
echo -n "Enter terminal type: "; set tt=$<
if ("$tt" != "") then
  setenv TERM $tt
  tset
endif
```

This file performs the following tasks:

1. The initial command tests for the presence of a file named *.hushlogin* in the user's home directory. Such a file disables the usual display of the message of the day in */etc/motd*; this command overrides it.

2. The *limit coredumpsize 0* command sets the maximum size of a core file to zero, which has the effect of disabling their creation. Alternatively, you could set the coredumpsize limit to some reasonable value.

3. The *umask*—the default protection for new files—is set to 022 (read and execute access for group and other, all access for user owner).

4. The *setenv PATH* command sets the PATH environment variable. The remaining *setenv* commands set environment variables for this user's default text editor and printer (under System V, the latter is named LPDEST), tell the *more* command to always run with the *-c* option, and sets an environment variable used by an application on this system.

   The values of all environment variables may be displayed with the *printenv* command (C and Korn shells and newer Bourne shells) or the *env* command (Bourne shell). *printenv* can also take an argument to display the value of a selected environment variable.

5. The *mesg y* command allows messages to be sent to the user's terminal. The *biff y* command asks UNIX to notify the user whenever new mail arrives.

6. The *set prompt* command sets the prompt string to the name of the current host plus a hyphen (–) plus the current command number (as defined by the C shell's command history feature) plus a greater-than sign (>) plus a space. The prompt might look something like this on the screen:

   ```
   hamlet-10> _
   ```

   The cursor resets one space beyond the greater-than sign.

7. The final commands perform some simple terminal handling operations: prompting the user for his terminal type, setting the TERM environment variable with his (non-null) response, and executing the *tset* terminal initialization command.

We can create a very similar *.profile* file:

```
ulimit -c 0                          Available under V.4 and AIX 3.1 only.
umask 022
PATH=/usr/ucb:/bin:/usr/bin:usr/local/bin:.
LPDEST=ps
EDITOR=emacs
MORE=-c
ARCH_DIR=/u/pubg91/archdir/
mesg y
biff y
PS1="`uname -n`-\!> "
export PATH LPDEST EDITOR MORE ARCH_DIR PS1 TIMEOUT
echo "Enter terminal type: \c"; read tt
if [ "$tt" != "" ]
then
  TERM=$tt ; export TERM
  tset
fi
```

The main differences are in the *ulimit* command, the different syntax for environment variables and the required *export* commands, the substitution of *uname* for
hostname, and the different mechanism for obtaining user input (note also that the
echo command functions differently in the two shells). The prompt string,
defined via the PS1 variable, should not include the command number placeholder (!) if the file is destined for the Bourne shell.

Terminal Handling in Initialization Files

More complex terminal handling is possible than what we saw in the sample initialization files above. Here is an example from the C shell:

```
if (! $?TERM) setenv TERM unknown          If TERM is undefined, set to "unknown".
if ("$TERM" == "unknown" || "$TERM" == "network") then
    echo -n 'TERM? [vt100]: '; set tt=($<) Prompt for terminal type.
    if ("$tt" == "") set tt="vt100"        The default is vt100.
    if ("$tt" == "mac") then               If it's a Mac, set type to vt100
        set tt="vt100"; stty rows 36       and the number of rows to 36.
      endif
    setenv TERM $tt                        Set TERM environment variable.
    endif
switch ($TERM)
case "sun":                                If on a SUN and it's the
    stty crt erase ^?                      console, run suntools.
    if (`tty` == /dev/console) exec suntools
    breaksw
case "hft":                                If the type is hft and X is set
    stty erase ^H                          up, start it.
    if (-e ~/.xinitrc) open xinit
    breaksw
```

```
case "aixterm":                                   A remote session from the RS/6000,
    setenv TERM xterm; stty erase ^H              so standardize TERM's name.
    breaksw
case "iris-ansi-net":                             A remote session from an IRIS;
    setenv TERM vt100; stty crt erase ^H          pretend it's a vt100.
    breaksw
default:                                          Anything else.
  stty crt erase ^?
  tset                                            Initialize terminal.
    tset -sIQ $TERM >! ~/.ttytmp                  Set TERM and TERMCAP.
    source ~/.ttytmp; rm ~/.ttytmp
    breaksw
endsw
```

The purpose behind this approach is to allow the same *.login* file to be used on all systems where the user has an account. It takes advantage of the fact that the TERM environment variable is passed to subshells, including remote login sessions. These commands will prompt for the terminal type only if the TERM variable is undefined or is set to "unknown" or "network." Unlike the previous one, this prompt sequence sets the terminal to a default type if the user enters a carriage return.

The majority of the commands perform actions appropriate for a specific terminal type. Many of them set the appropriate erase character, via the *stty erase* command, which takes the key sequence emitted by the desired delete-character key (DELETE or BACKSPACE) as its argument.

The "default" section will be executed when the terminal type is other than the specific ones already handled by other parts of the *switch* command. It runs the *tset* command twice: once to perform standard terminal initialization and once with the *-s* option, which generates the *setenv* commands necessary to set the TERM and TERMCAP environment variables. This output is captured in a file, which is then executed using *source*. (The two *tset* commands could be combined; they are separated here for intelligibility.)

Terminal characteristics and the *stty* and *tset* commands are discussed in more detail in the section entitled "Specifying Terminal Characteristics," in Chapter 10, *Terminals and Modems*.

Shell Initialization Files

In the C shell, the *.cshrc* file performs tasks that need to be executed whenever UNIX creates a new shell: when the user executes any UNIX command except those built into the shell, runs a script or program, and so on. These tasks include setting shell variables (some of which have important functions, others of which are useful abbreviations) and defining aliases (alternate names for commands).

Unlike environment variables like TERM, shell variables and aliases are not automatically passed to new shells; therefore, they need to be established whenever UNIX starts a new shell. The contents of a simple *.cshrc* file are:

```
alias j jobs
alias h history
alias l ls -aFx
alias ll ls -aFxlg
set history = 40
set savehist = 40
set filec
```

The file initially sets up four aliases—abbreviations for commonly-used commands. Then the *set* commands set the values of some built-in C shell variables. The *history* variable turns on the C shell history mechanism and saves the last 40 commands, allowing them to be recalled, edited, and re-executed. The *savehist* variable saves the last 40 commands across login sessions in the file *.savehist* in the user's home directory. The variable *filec* enables the C shell's file completion mechanism. When it is enabled, the C shell will interactively complete filenames from their first few characters. Hitting the ESCAPE key triggers filename completion. Here is an example of it in action:

```
% ls
afilename      alongfilename      averylongfilename
% cat av<ESCAPE>                And like magic the rest of the filename appears:
               ↓
% cat averylongfilename_
```

If you type "cat av" in the directory shown and then hit the ESCAPE key, the C shell will automatically fill in the rest of the filename, leaving the cursor at the end of the line. If more than one filename matches what's been entered so far (if you'd typed only "cat a" before hitting ESCAPE in the preceding example), the C shell will beep at you (*set nobeep* disables beeping) to indicate multiple matching filenames. (Filename completion is not available in all C shell implementations.)

Under the Korn shell, a shell initialization file may be defined via the ENV environment variable (usually in *.profile*):

```
export ENV=$HOME/.kshrc
```

We can make a *.kshrc* file similar to the *.cshrc* file we looked at earlier:

```
alias j=jobs
alias h=history
alias l="ls -aFx"
alias ll="ls -aFxl"
export HISTSIZE=60           History is on by default, with size = 60.
```

The same four aliases are defined (although *ll* is defined appropriately for a System V system). The size of the history file, *.sh_history* in the user's home directory, is set to 60 commands.

System-wide Initialization Files

For Bourne and Korn shell users, the file */etc/profile* serves as a system-wide initialization file that is executed before the user's personal *.profile* file. The PATH variable is almost always defined in it; therefore it applies to users without explicit PATH variables set in their *.profile*. Sometimes a default *umask* is also specified here. Here is a sample */etc/profile* file:

```
PATH=/bin:/usr/bin:/usr/bin/X11
TZ=EST5EDT
MAIL=/usr/mail/$LOGNAME
export PATH TZ MAIL
```

This file sets the default path, timezone, and mail file location and exports these variables to the environment.

AIX 3.1 also supports an additional system-wide initialization file, */etc/environment*. This file is executed by *init*, and it affects all login shells via the environment they inherit from *init*. Under System V, additional system-wide user default characteristics are also set in the file */etc/default/login*. The keywords described in Table 4-1 are among the most important.

Table 4-1. /etc/default/login File Variables

Variable	Example	Meaning
CONSOLE	`CONSOLE=/dev/console`	Direct *root* logins are restricted to this device.
IDLEWEEKS	`IDLEWEEKS=4`	Amount of time an account can go unused before it is automatically disabled.
PASSREQ	`PASSREQ=YES`	Whether passwords are required at login.
PATH	`PATH=/bin:/usr/bin:/usr/ucb`	Default path for users.
SUPATH	`SUPATH=/etc:/bin:/usr/bin:/usr/ucb`	Default path after *su*.
TIMEOUT	`TIMEOUT=20`	Number of seconds before *login* quits.
UMASK	`UMASK=022`	Default *umask*.
ULIMIT	`ULIMIT=500000`	Default file size limit.

System-wide initialization files and the files in */etc/default* should be writable only by *root*.

Setting File Ownership

After you copy the appropriate initialization files to the user's home directory, you must make the new user their owner. To do this, execute commands like these:

```
# find /u/chavez -exec chown chavez {} \; \
    -exec chgrp chem {} \;
```

If you are working on a BSD, SunOS, AIX 3.1 system, or on a V.4 system with */usr/ucb* at the head of your search path, these commands may all be executed at once with:

```
# chown -R chavez.chem /u/chavez
```

The *-R* ("recursive") option changes the ownership on the directory and all the files it contains.

Adding the User to Other System Facilities

The user should also be added to the other UNIX facilities in use at your site. These may include the following activities:

* Assigning disk quotas (see the section entitled "Managing Disk Usage with Disk Quotas (BSD and V.4)," in Chapter 7, *Managing System Resources*).

* Defining a mail alias (see the section entitled "Sending Mail to a Group of Users," in Chapter 1, *Introduction to System Administration*).

* Setting print queue access (see the section entitled "Priorities and Permissions," in Chapter 11, *Printers and the Spooling Subsystem*).

Adding the User to Secondary Groups

Although the user's primary group is defined in the password file, he may also be designated as a member of additional groups in the group file */etc/group*. See the section entitled "UNIX Groups," later in this chapter.

Additional Tasks

Any other site-specific user account tasks, for local or third-party application, should be performed as part of the account creation process.

Testing the New Account

Minimally, you should try logging in as the new user. A successful login will confirm that the username and password are valid and that the home directory exists and is accessible. Next, verify that the initialization files have executed: for example, look at the environment variables, or try an alias that you expect to be defined. This will determine if the ownership of the initialization files is correct; they won't execute if it isn't. (You should test the initialization files separately before installing them into the skeleton directory.) Try clearing the terminal screen. This will test the terminal type setup section of the initialization file.

Using su to Recreate a User's Environment

A very useful command when debugging a user account is *su*. It can also be used for some types of testing for newly created accounts. The *su* command may also be used to recreate the environment of another user. When given a username as an argument, *su* will allow a user to temporarily become another user; *root* is simply the default username to change to if none is specified. Under this mode of operation, most of the user environment is unchanged by the *su* command: the current directory does not change, values of most environment variables don't change (including USER), and so on. However, the option "-" (a minus sign alone) may be used to simulate a full login by another user (without actually logging out yourself). This option is useful when trying to reproduce a user's problem. For example, the following command simulates a login session for user *martin*:

```
# su - martin                      No password needed when root executes su.
Erase set to Delete
Kill set to Ctrl-U
Interrupt set to Ctrl-C

Talk sense to a fool and he calls you foolish.
        -- Euripides

What next?>> _
```

In addition to new account testing, such a technique is very handy when users complain about "broken" commands and the like.

Automating the Account Creation Process

Shell scripts to automate the user account creation process are very common; there are, for example, many variations of the widely-known *adduser* script. Recent UNIX implementations attempt to incorporate some of this functionality into a standard command. The following sections describe some of the approaches in current use.

XENIX: mkuser

XENIX has long included the *mkuser* command, which is an interactive, menu-driven interface for account creation. The XENIX *mkuser* command prompts you for all needed information about the account: username, home directory location, and so forth, using information stored in */etc/default/mkuser* as defaults for the home directory location, and the protection on the home directory, profile files and mail files. Here is a sample */etc/default/mkuser* file:

```
HOME=/u
HOMEMODE=0755
PROFMODE=0755
MAILMODE=0700
```

This file sets the default location for a user's home directory to */u*/username and sets the default file modes as listed. The initialization files to be placed in the user's home directory are stored in the directories */usr/lib/mkuser/*shell where *shell* is the name of the login shell. The initialization files in these shell-specific directories do not contain the leading periods in the filenames.

System V: passmgmt

System V supports the *passmgmt* command. Its *-a* option may be used to add a user to the password files (regular and shadow). The other fields in the password file are specified using these options:

-h   Home directory.

-c   Full name field.

-u   UID (if omitted, default to the next UID).

-g   GID.

-s   Shell (defaults to */bin/sh*).

For example, the following command could be used to create user *chavez* that we created by hand previously:

```
# passmgmt -a -u 190 -g 20 -c "Rachel Chavez" -h /u/chavez \
  -s /bin/csh chavez
```

You can specify *-m* (instead of *-a*) to modify the data for an existing user.

System V.4: useradd

System V.4 adds a user creation command to the UNIX standard: *useradd*. *useradd* has two modes: defining a new user and setting system-wide defaults. Let's consider them in reverse order.

The *-D* option tells *useradd* to set system-wide default values (used when creating new users). In this mode, it has the following additional options:

-g   Set default group.

-b   Set default base directory for user home directories.

-f   Set default inactive period.

-e   Set default account expiration date.

The base directory is the directory under which users' home directories are located. For example, if user home directories have pathnames of the form */home/*username, then */home* is the base directory. The inactive period is the maximum number of days that can elapse between logins before an account is automatically disabled; the value -1 disables this feature. The expiration date option is used when setting up temporary accounts, which will automatically be disabled on the specified date. The following command illustrates the use of these options:

```
# useradd -D -g chem -b /u -f -1
```

This command sets the default group to *chem*, the base directory to */u*, and disables the inactivity feature.

When defining a new user, the *useradd* command has many options, including:

-u   UID (defaults to next highest).

-g   Primary group.

-G   List of secondary groups.

-b   Base directory for home directory.

-d   Name for home directory (defaults to the username).

-m   Create home directory in addition to defining user.

-s   Shell.

-c   Full name.

-k   Skeleton directory containing initialization files.

-e   Account expiration date.

-f   Maximum inactive period (in days).

The home directory's pathname is the concatenation of the base directory (from *-b* or *-D -b*) and the name specified to the *-d* option.

Here is the *useradd* command to create user *chavez* (given the defaults we set above):

```
# useradd -u 190 -g chem -G bio,phys -s /bin/csh \
    -c "Rachel Chavez" -m \
```

This command creates user *chavez* shown previously, creates the directory */u/chavez* if it doesn't already exist, and places *chavez* in the groups *chem, bio,* and *phys.*

A user's current attributes may be changed with the *usermod* command, which accepts these *useradd* options: *-u, -g, -G, -d, -m, -s, -c, -e,* and *-f.* In addition, it supports a *-l* option, used to change the username of an existing user. For example, the following command changes *chavez*'s username to *vasquez*:

```
# usermod -l vasquez chavez
```

V.4 also provides tools to display the attributes of user accounts. The *listusers* command without any arguments will list all defined usernames and their associated UIDs for user accounts (UID > 99). The *-g* and *-l* options may be used to limit the display to specific groups and usernames. Each takes a comma-separated list of values as its option. In all cases, the list is sorted by username, and each username will appear only once in the list (even if the user belongs to more than one listed group).

The *logins* command may be used to find potential security problems in the password file as well as to obtain more detailed information about specific users. The first sort of activity is performed by these options:

-p   List users having no password.

-d   List duplicate UIDs in the password file.

-s   List system login accounts.

-m   List users belonging to more than one group.

-x   Also display password file data: home directory, shell, password aging (if any).

-a   Also display account expiration data and maximum inactivity period (if set).

logins also supports the *-g* and *-l* options to limit the display to certain groups and usernames.

AIX 3.1: mkuser Revisited

AIX 3.1 offers another variation on these themes. Its *mkuser* command may also be used to create user accounts and update the relevant files.

Table 4-2. AIX 3.1 User Account Data Files

File	Contents
/etc/passwd	Password file: holds usual password file data.
/etc/security/passwd	Shadow password file: holds encrypted passwords, account flags, and most recent password change date.
/etc/security/user	Holds AIX-specific user account attributes.
/etc/security/limits	Holds users' system resource use limits.

mkuser has the following format:

```
# mkuser attribute=value ... username
```

where *username* is the account to be created and the *attribute-value* pairs are used to specify information about the account. The defined attributes include:

id   UID.

pgrp   Primary group.

groups   Secondary groups.

home   Home directory.

shell   Login shell.

gecos   Full name.

umask   Default umask.

expires   Account expiration date.

By default, *mkuser* also automatically creates the user's home directory and copies the *.profile* initialization file from */etc/security* to it.

For example, the following command creates user *chavez*:

```
# mkuser id=190 pgrp=chem groups=system,bio,phys \
    gecos="Rachel Chavez" home=/u/chavez shell=/bin/csh chavez
```

The *chuser* command may be used to modify the attributes of an existing user. It has the same syntax as *mkuser*.

The defaults used by *mkuser* are stored in a couple of places. The *user* stanza in */etc/security/mkuser.default* defines several attributes for ordinary users. Here is an example, customized for a specific site:

```
user:
        group = chem
        groups = science,staff
        prog = /bin/csh
        home = /u/$USER
```

The *groups* and *home* keywords are the same as those used in *mkuser* and *chuser*; here the default secondary groups set is defined as "science,staff" and the default home directory is a directory named after the username under */u*. The *prog* keyword sets the value of the *shell* attribute (here to the C shell) and the *group* keyword sets the value of the *pgrp* (primary group) attribute, in this case, to the *chem* group.

The file */etc/security/user* stores the values of user attributes other than those stored in the password file. Its *default* stanza sets the default value for most of them. Here is an example:

```
default:
        admin = false          Is this an administrative account?
        login = true           Are logins allowed?
        su = true              Can someone su to this username?
        daemon = true          Can user use cron?
        rlogin = true          Can remote logins connect via this account?
        sugroups = ALL         What groups can su to this username?
        ttys = ALL             What ttys can this user log in on?
        auth1 = SYSTEM         Method(s) used to validate user's identity.
        auth2 = NONE           SYSTEM=use normal UNIX passwords.
        umask = 022            Default file protection.
        expires = 0            Date when account expires.
```

Finally, the functioning of *mkuser* itself can be customized. *Mkuser* runs the shell script */etc/security/mkuser.sys*, which by default creates the user account (and the corresponding entries in */etc/passwd*, */etc/security/passwd*, */etc/security/user*, and */etc/security/limits*) according to the attributes listed on the command line and the defaults described above. It also creates the user's home directory and copies */etc/security/.profile* to it (reflecting AIX 3.1's default shell, */bin/ksh*). It can easily be modified to fit the requirements of your site, for example, to change the configuration files to *.login* and *.cshrc* (be sure to copy it to */etc/security/mkuser.sys.dist* first!).

Captive Accounts

Sometimes it is desirable to limit what users can do on the system. For example, when users spend all of their time running a single application program, you can make sure they stay there by making that program their login shell (as defined in the password file). Once the login process is complete, that program begins executing, and when they exit from it, they will be automatically logged out.

Not all programs can be used in this way, however. If variable input is required, for example, and there is no one way of invoking it, then simply using it as a login shell won't work. Some UNIX versions provide a *restricted shell* to address such problems.

Under System V and AIX 3.1, a modified version of the Bourne shell (most often */bin/Rsh* but sometimes stored as */lib/rsh* or */bin/rsh*), is available for creating *captive accounts*: user accounts that run only an administrator-specified set of actions and log off automatically when they are finished. For example, a captive account might be used for an operator who runs backups via a menu set up by the administrator. Or, a captive account might be used to place users directly into an application program at login. A captive account is set up by specifying the restricted shell as the user's login shell and creating a *.profile* file to perform the desired actions.

This *restricted shell* takes away some of the functionality of the shell. Specifically, users of the restricted shell may not:

- Use the *cd* command.

- Set or change the value of the PATH variable.

- Specify a command or filename containing a slash (/). In other words, only files in the current directory can be used.

- Use output redirection (> or >>).

Given these restrictions, a user running from a captive account will have to stay in whatever directory the *.profile* file places him. This directory should not be his home directory, to which he probably has write access; if he ended up there, he could replace the *.profile* file that controls his actions. The PATH variable should be set as minimally as possible.

A captive account must not be able to write to any of the directories in the defined path. Otherwise, a clever user could substitute his own version for one of the commands he is allowed to run, allowing him to break free from captivity. What this means in practice is that the user should not be placed in any directory in the path as his final destination, and that the current directory should *not* be in the search path if it is writable.

Taking this idea to its logical conclusion, some administrators set up a separate *rbin* directory—often located as a subdirectory of the captive account's home directory—containing hard links to the set of the commands the captive user is allowed to run, and then set the user's search path to point only there. If you use this approach, however, you need to be careful in choosing the set of commands you give to the user. Many UNIX commands have *shell escape* features: ways of running another UNIX command from within them. If a command supports shell escapes, the user can generally run *any* command, including a nonrestricted shell. While the path you set will still be in effect for commands run in this way, the user is not prevented from specifying a full pathname in a shell escape command. Thus, even a command as seemingly innocuous as *more* can allow a user to break free from a captive account (a shell command may be run from *more* (and *man*) by preceding it with an exclamation point(!)).

Be sure to check the manual pages carefully before deciding to include a command among the restricted set. Unfortunately, occasionally shell escapes are undocumented; this is most true in games. In many cases, shell escapes are performed via an initial exclamation point or tilde-exclamation point (~ !).

CAUTION

In general, you should be wary of commands which allow any other programs to be run within them, even if they do not include explicit shell escapes. For example, a mail program might let a user invoke an editor, and most editors allow shell escapes.

Removing a User Account

Many times, simply changing a user's encrypted password in */etc/passwd* to an asterisk is sufficient to deactivate a user's account. This method prevents file ownership problems which can crop up when a username is deleted.

When more drastic action is called for, UNIX implementations offering built-in commands for adding users also usually offer similar commands for removing them. The following commands may be used to remove the user *chavez* from the password file(s):

```
# passmgmt -d chavez      (System V)
# userdel chavez          (V.4)
# rmuser -p chavez        (AIX 3.1)
# rmuser chavez           (XENIX)
```

None of these command forms removes the user's files, however. V.4's *userdel* command supports an option to do this as well: *-r*. In the other cases, the files and home directory must be removed by hand (if desired). Indeed, the XENIX command must be executed only after the user's files and home directory are gone.

When removing a user from the system, various other actions probably also ought to be considered:

• Remove the user's mail file with a command like:

```
# rm /usr/spool/mail/username
```

• Remove the user from the mail aliases file (*/usr/lib/aliases*) or redefine the alias to send mail to someone else, for example:

```
chavez:
    \root
```

See the section entitled "Sending Mail to a Group of Users," in Chapter 1, *Introduction to System Administration*, for details on this file.

• Make sure the user hasn't left any *cron* or *at* jobs around.

• Perform any other site-specific termination activities that may be appropriate.

UNIX Groups

UNIX groups are a mechanism provided to enable arbitrary collections of users to share files and other system resources. As such, they provide one of the cornerstones of system security. We'll discuss using groups effectively as part of an overall system security plan in detail in Chapter 5, *Security*.

Groups may be defined in two ways:

- Implicitly, by GID: whenever a new GID appears in the fourth field of the password file, a new group is defined.

- Explicitly, by name and GID, via an entry in the file */etc/group*.

Although it is not required, all system groups are generally listed in the */etc/group* file.

As we've noted, the group whose GID appears in her password file entry is a user's primary group, and a user may also be a member of other secondary groups. BSD implementations don't distinguish between these two types of groups except for accounting purposes. On these systems, a user is always simultaneously a member of all of her groups for system access purposes, although her accounting records are made under the primary group.

On BSD systems, the *groups* command displays a user's group memberships:

```
% groups
chem bio phys wheel
```

The *groups* command will also take a username as an argument; in this case, it lists the groups to which user *martin* belongs:

```
$ groups martin
chem bio graphics
```

System V.4 and AIX 3.1 also provide the *groups* command.

In contrast to BSD, on many System V systems, a user may only have one active group at a time. At login, this will automatically be set to his primary group, and he must use the *newgrp* command to change it:

```
$ newgrp graphics
```

newgrp creates a new shell; all future activities will be performed with group *graphics* permissions, and accounting data will be so recorded (see the *newgrp* manual page for more details about this command).

The *id* command will display the currently active group:

```
$ id
uid=190(chavez) gid=20(chem)
```

The /etc/group File

Just as */etc/passwd* lists all the system's users, */etc/group* lists all the system's named groups. Adding a new group consists of adding a new one-line entry to this file. Each entry has the form:

group-name:*:*GID*:*additional-users*

No spaces are allowed within the line. The meanings of these fields are:

group-name	A name identifying the group. For example, a development group working on new simulation software might have the name *simulation.*
*	The second field is an artifact of earlier UNIX versions. It is unused and is usually filled with an asterisk.
GID	This is the group's identification number. By convention, standard groups like *root*, *bin*, and *sys* have consecutive group numbers, beginning with 0; by convention, groups added locally have group numbers that are multiples of 10.
additional-users	This field holds a list of users and groups that will have access to this group's files, *in addition* to those users belonging to the group by virtue of */etc/passwd* (who need not be listed). Usernames in this list must be separated by commas (but no spaces).

Here are some typical entries from an */etc/group* file:

```
chem:*:20:williams,wong,jones,root
bio:*:30:root,chavez,martin
genome:*:160:root
```

The first line defines the *chem* group. It assigns the group identification number (GID) 20 to this group. UNIX will allow all members of group 20 plus the additional users *williams*, *wong*, *jones*, and *root* to access this group's files. The *bio* and *genome* groups are also defined. User *chavez* is a member of the *bio* group, and *root* is a member of both groups. The remaining lines define the *bio* and *genome* groups.

Some UNIX implementations limit the number of groups a user can be in (often to 8 or 16).

The */etc/group* file (and any old or saved copies of it) should be owned by *root* and not writable by anyone but the owner.

System V.4 Group File Manipulation Commands

System V.4 introduces commands to manipulate the group file (rather than editing it directly). The *groupadd* command defines a new group. For example, the command:

```
# groupadd splines
```

adds a new group named *splines*. By default, it is assigned the next consecutive GID. A specific GID may be specified with the *-g* option:

```
# groupadd -g 90 splines
```

The command defines *splines* as group 90.

The *groupmod* command is used to assign a new name or group ID to an existing group. For example, the following command changes the name of the *splines* group to *graphics*:

```
# groupmod -n graphics splines
```

Similarly, the command below changes the GID of the *splines* group to 110:

```
# groupmod -g 110 splines
```

The *groupdel* command is used to delete a group definition. Its only argument is the name of the group to be removed from the */etc/group* file. Note that *groupdel* does not change any user definitions in the */etc/passwd* file that use this group. Thus, *groupdel* should only be used to remove groups with no members.

AIX 3.1 Group Sets

AIX 3.1 extends the basic UNIX groups mechanism to allow a distinction to be made between the groups a user belongs to, which are defined by the password and group files, and those that are currently active. The latter are referred to as the *concurrent group set*, or more simply as the group set. The current real group and group set are used for a variety of accounting and security functions under AIX 3.1.

As under BSD, the *groups* command lists the groups to which a user belongs. For example, when user *chavez* runs the command, the following output results:

```
$ groups
chem bio phys staff
```

The real group at login is the user's primary group, as defined in the password file. When a user logs in, the group set is set to the entire list of groups to which the user belongs. The *setgroups* command is used to change the active group set and designated real group. The command has the following options:

-a   Add the listed groups to the group set.

-d   Delete the listed groups from the group set.

-r   Specify the real group (group owner of new files and processes, etc.).

-        Reset the real group and group set to the login values.

For example, the following command adds the groups *phys* and *bio* to the user's current group set:

```
$ setgroups -a phys,bio
```

The following command adds *phys* to the current group set (if necessary) and designates it as the real group ID:

```
$ setgroups -r phys
```

Thus, *setgroups -r* is similar to System V's *newgrp* command, although it doesn't spawn a new shell.

Without any arguments, *setgroups* lists the user's defined groups and current group set:

```
$ setgroups
chavez:
     user groups = chem,bio,phys,staff
     process groups = phys,bio,chem
```

The groups labeled "user groups" are the entire set of groups to which user *chavez* belongs. The groups labeled "process groups" form the current group set. The first group listed in each group is the real group ID.

The following command deletes the *phys* group from the current group set:

```
$ setgroups -d phys
```

The *phys* group was also the current real group; when it is removed from the current group set, the next group in the list (in this case *system*) becomes the real group.

The *setgroups* command may also be used to specify the group set explicitly, by supplying the desired set of groups as its argument (without options). The first group in the list becomes the real group. For example, the command below sets the group set to *chem* and *bio*, with *chem* as the real group:

```
$ setgroups chem,bio
```

AIX 3.1 allows permissions to be set on the basis of the current group set. See the section, "Assigning User Passwords," later in this chapter for details.

Standard UNIX Users and Groups

All UNIX versions typically predefine several users. The most common are listed below. Note that the UIDs used for these standard users vary somewhat from implementation to implementation.

root   User 0, the superuser. The superuser has unrestricted access to all aspects of the system. Most administrative functions require you to log in as *root* or to use the *su* command and the superuser password to become superuser.

WARNING

The defining feature of the superuser account is UID 0, *not* the username *root*; *any* account with UID 0 is a superuser account. Multiple password file entries for UID 0 are not recommended.

daemon   UID 1, used to execute system server processes. This user only exists to own these processes (and the associated files) and guarantee that they execute with appropriate file access permissions.

bin   UID 2, owns some executables.

sys   UID 3, owns some system files.

adm   UID 4, typically owns the accounting files.

uucp   UID 5, UNIX-to-UNIX copy subsystem account. This is the user that owns the *uucp* tools and files. There may also be other *uucp*-related accounts on your system. By convention, usernames beginning with the letters "uu," "UU," and, more recently, "u" are reserved for *uucp hosts*: other computers that log in to your system to transfer mail and other files.

operator   On some BSD systems, a user with read-only access to the entire filesystem (and write access as determined for normal users). This username exists for system operators who need to do backups, initiate system shutdowns, and perform other administrative functions, but who do not need to be superuser.

nobody   Account used by the NFS product. It has the UID -2, but this sometimes appears in the password file as a very large integer (UIDs are of the unsigned data type). In the latter case, the presence of this account often breaks various user creation commands or scripts that try to automatically set the UID of the new user to the next highest available UID (since *nobody* already has a very high UID).

With the exception of *root*, these accounts are seldom used for logins. The password file as usually shipped has these accounts disabled. Be sure to check the password file on your system, however. Standard accounts without passwords can be significant security holes.

In addition to these standard UNIX accounts, individual vendors may include other usernames in the password files they ship. Some common ones are *field*, *guest*, and *demo*. These accounts will often have standard passwords (like "service" for *field*), initially set the same on all systems that vendor ships, or will not have a password at all. Be sure to change the passwords for these accounts or disable them entirely. Otherwise, they can pose a significant security risk.

Standard Groups

UNIX systems are similarly shipped with a standard */etc/group* file, holding entries for standard groups. These may include:

wheel or *system* or *root*

> GID 0. On BSD systems, members of this group are allowed to become superuser by using the *su* command, and other users may not. Under SunOS, if the wheel group has any members listed in */etc/group*, then this restriction applies; otherwise, it does not.
>
> Under SunOS, if the *wheel* group has a null user list (i.e., no additional members), then any user may *su* to root.

daemon
> This group exists to own the spooling directories (*/usr/spool/**) and programs that are responsible for transferring files. The spooling directories are temporary resting-places for files that are waiting to be printed, to be transferred by *uucp*, or to be processed by some other subsystem. Giving the group *daemon* ownership of these programs and directories provides additional security because the spooling directories and their contents are *not* public. No individual user can access them directly. Spooling programs use the SGID access mode to allow users access through the spooling programs. Consequently, users can only manipulate the files in these directories in ways allowed by these programs. They have no general ability to copy or otherwise access these files.

kmem
> GID 2 on BSD systems. This is a special group that owns some system programs needing to read kernel memory directly. These programs include *ps* and *pstat*.

sys   Under System V, the group *sys* owns various system files and the spe-
             cial files owned by group *kmem* under BSD.

tty   This group often owns all the special files connected to terminals.
             That is, it controls access to the terminals so that programs like *write*
             can let users communicate with each other through their terminals,
             but cannot write directly to other terminals.

staff   A group that may be used to own locally developed software; basi-
             cally, a group for local program development. You may wish to add
             new groups that replace the function of staff.

Usernames and group names are independent of each other and have no necessary
relationship, even when the same name is both a username and a group name.

5

Security

UNIX Lines of Defense
Preventing Security Problems
Detecting Problems

These days, the phrase "system security" is most associated with protecting against break-ins: attempts by an unauthorized person (bearing a strong resemblance to Matthew Broderick in *War Games*) to gain access to the system, whether motivated by maliciousness or mere mischievousness. In reality, however, security encompasses much more than guarding against outsiders. For example, there are often as many security issues relating to *authorized* users as to outsiders.

This chapter will discuss basic UNIX security issues and techniques. For a more detailed treatment of these topics, see the Nutshell Handbooks, *Practical UNIX Security*, by Simson Garfinkel and Gene Spafford, and *Computer Security Basics*, by Deborah Russell and G.T. Gangemi, Sr.

Security discussions often begin by considering the kinds of threats facing a system. I'd like to come at this issue from a slightly different angle by focusing on what needs to be protected. Before you can address any security-related issue on your system, you need to be able to answer the following questions:

> What are you trying to protect?
> What is of value that might be lost?

If you can answer these questions, you go a long way toward identifying and solving potential security problems. The answers to these questions might include:

- The computer itself might be stolen or damaged. What is valuable is the computer as a physical object (*loss of equipment*).

- The data on the computer might be lost, corrupted, or stolen, and that is what is most valuable (*loss of data*). If stolen, the data may be obtained by copying it electronically or by removing the medium or even the computer on which it is stored.

- The computer might be down or otherwise unusable for some period of time, and valuable time and CPU cycles would be lost (*loss of use*).

Depending on which of these concerns are relevant to you, different sorts of threats are what need to be forestalled. Physical threats include not only theft but also natural disasters (fires, pipes bursting, power failures from electrical storms, and so on). Data loss can be caused by malice or accident, ranging from deliberate theft and destruction to user errors to undebugged programs wreaking havoc. Thus, preventing data loss means taking into account not only unauthorized users getting on your system and authorized users on the system doing things they're not supposed to do, but also authorized users doing things they're allowed—but didn't mean—to do. And sometimes it means cleaning up after yourself.

Once you've identified what needs to be protected and what potential acts and/or events it needs to be protected from, you'll be in a much better position to determine what steps to take to prevent problems. For example, if theft of the computer itself is your biggest worry, then you need to think about locks more than about how often to change the root password. Conversely, if physical security is no problem but data loss is, then you need to think about ways to prevent it, from both accidental and deliberate acts, and to recover it quickly when it does occur.

The key to a well-secured system is a combination of policies that:

- Prevent every possible relevant threat, to the extent that they can be prevented—and they can't always—or the extent that you and your users are willing to accept the tradeoffs that some security measures entail. For example, isolated systems are easier to make secure than those on networks, but not everyone really wants to, say, write tapes to transfer files in the interests of enhanced security.

- Plan what to do when the worst happens anyway. For example, the best backup plans are made by imagining that tomorrow morning you will come in and all your disks will have had head crashes. It's helpful to imagine that even the impossible can happen. Thus, if it's important that certain people not have access to the *root* account, then don't leave *root* logged in on an unattended terminal, not even on the console in the locked machine room, to which they can *never* have access—never is almost always shorter than you think.

In the end, good security, like successful system administration in general, is largely a matter of planning and habit: designing responses to various scenarios in advance and faithfully, scrupulously carrying out the routine, boring, daily actions required to prevent and recover from the various disasters you've foreseen. Although it may seem at times like pounds, rather than ounces, of prevention are needed, I think you'll find that they are less burdensome than even grams of cure.

UNIX Lines of Defense

Standard UNIX offers two basic ways of preventing security problems:

* *Passwords* are designed to prevent unauthorized users from obtaining any access to the system at all.

* *File permissions* are designed to allow access to the various commands, files, programs, and system resources only to designated groups of authorized users.

In theory, passwords prevent the bad guys from getting on the system in the first place, and proper file permissions prevent normal users from doing things they aren't supposed to. On a system which is isolated both physically and electronically, theory pretty well matches reality, but the presence of networks, dialup lines, or nonsecure terminals and workstations complicates the picture enormously. For example, network access often bypasses the normal password authentication procedures; your system may be only as secure as the worst protected system on the network.

Permissions and passwords are useful only as part of an overall security strategy for your system, based upon its needs and potential threats. It may be helpful to think of them in the context of the various "lines of defense" which might be set up to protect your system from the various losses it might experience.

Physical Security

The first line of defense is the physical access to your computer. The most security-conscious installations protect their computers by eliminating all network and dialup access and strictly limiting who can get near them. At the far extreme are those systems in locked rooms (requiring a password be entered on a keypad for entrance) in restricted access areas of installations with guarded entrances (usually military or defense-related). To get onto these systems, you have to get into the site, into the right building, past another set of guards in the secure part of that building, and finally into the computer room before you even have to worry about having a valid password on the system. Such an approach effectively keeps out outsiders and unauthorized users; security threats then can come only from insiders.

Although this extreme level of physical security is not needed by most sites, all administrators will face some physical security issues. Some of the most common include:

- Preventing theft and vandalism, by locking the door or locking the equipment to a table or desk. If these are significant threats for you, you might also need to consider other aspects of the computer's physical location. For example, the best locks in the world can be basically worthless if the door has a glass window in it.

- Limiting access to the console and CPU to prevent someone from crashing the system and rebooting it to single-user mode. Even if your system allows you to disable single-user mode access without a password, there still may be issues here for you. For example, if your system is secured by a key position on its front panel, but you keep the key in the top middle drawer of your desk (right next to your file cabinet keys), or inserted in the front panel, this level of security is effectively stripped away. On V.4 systems, the same considerations apply to the firmware state's *floppy key* (a special floppy disk containing system-identification information, used if the firmware password is forgotten or unavailable) if supported.

- Controlling environmental factors, as much as is realistically possible. This concern can range from considering special power systems (backup generators, line conditioners, surge suppressors, and so on) to prevent downtime or loss of data, to fire detection and extinguishing systems to prevent equipment damage, to simple, common sense policies like not putting open cups of liquid next to your keyboard or other equipment.

- Restricting (or monitoring) access to other parts of the system, like terminals, workstations, network cables, and so on. You may want to do so not only (or even primarily) to keep unwanted users off the system but also to prevent vandalism, which occurs most frequently to these exposed parts rather than to the main system components themselves. Accessible cables are also sometimes vulnerable to tapping and eavesdropping.

- Limiting access to backup tapes. If the security of its data is important to your system, backup tapes need to be protected from theft and damage as well as the system itself. Such issues include providing safe storage areas, with at least some of them physically separated from the computer so that the backups don't, say, burn up with the machine room (this topic is discussed in detail in Chapter 9, *Backup and Restore*).

Passwords

If someone gains access to the system, or you have voluntarily given up complete physical security, passwords form the next line of defense against unauthorized users and their potential problems. As I've said before, all accounts should have passwords. There are suggestions in the section entitled "Guidelines for Choosing Passwords," in Chapter 4, *User Accounts*, designed to reduce your system's vulnerability to humans or programs successfully guessing an account's password.

The weakness with passwords is that if someone breaks into an account by finding out its password, he has all the rights and privileges granted to that account and can impersonate the legitimate user as desired. There are a variety of methods for adding additional stumbling blocks if a password is guessed, including:

- *Secondary authentication programs*, which require additional input before granting access to the system.

- *Dialup passwords*, which are essentially a second password required when logging in via a modem on the assumption that phone lines are inherently less secure than hardwired terminals or workstations.

- *Enhanced network authentication systems* like Kerberos, designed to protect networked systems and fileservers against the threats inherent in stand-alone workstations (for example, someone attempting to access information or exercise privileges gained on the workstation—usually via *su*—on a different system) and against some types of network eavesdropping.

Some of these alternatives are discussed in later sections of this chapter.

File Permissions

File permissions form the next line of defense, against both bad guys who've succeeded in breaking into an account and legitimate users trying to do something they're not supposed to. Properly set up file protection can prevent many potential problems. The most vulnerable aspects of file protection are the SUID and SGID access modes, which we'll look at in detail later in this chapter.

Some UNIX versions also provide other ways to limit non-*root* users' access to various system resources. Facilities like disk quotas, system resource limits, and printer and batch queue access restrictions protect computer subsystems from unauthorized use, including attacks by "bacteria"* designed specifically to overwhelm systems by completely consuming their resources. If someone succeeds in logging in as *root* (or breaks into another account with access to important files or other system resources), in most cases, system security is irreparably compromised. In such cases, the administrative focus must shift from prevention to detection: finding out both what has been done to the system—and repairing it—and determining how the system was compromised—and plugging that gap. Hence, the two major sections of this chapter discuss preventing and detecting security breaches in detail.

---

*It seems that no new type of security threat is uncovered without acquiring a "cute" name. *Bacteria*, also known as *rabbits*, are programs whose sole purpose is to reproduce and thereby overwhelm a system, bringing it to a standstill (from the way they consume system resources, they might equally accurately be called locusts). There are a few other creatures in the security jungle whose names you ought to be familiar with. *Viruses* are programs that insert themselves into other programs, often legitimate ones, producing noxious side-effects when their host is later executed. *Worms* are programs that move from system to system over a network, sometimes leaving behind bacteria or viruses or other nasty programs. *Trojan horses* are programs that pretend to do one thing while doing another. The most common type is a password-stealing program, which mimics a normal login sequence but actually records the password the the user types and then exits. The term is also applied to programs or commands embedded within certain types of files which get executed automatically when the file is processed (for example, *shar* archives and PostScript files are both susceptible to containing Trojan horses). *Back doors*, also called *trap doors*, are undocumented alternative entrances to otherwise legitimate programs which allow a knowledgeable user to bypass security features.

In practice, these creatures often work in concert with one another. The well-known Internet worm incident (November 1988) consisted of a worm program which moved from system to system via a back door in the *sendmail* mail handling program. It left behind other programs which, among other things, tried to discover passwords for accounts on that system. Occasionally, due to a bug, these programs behaved like bacteria, overwhelming the system by executing many simultaneous copies of themselves.

Encryption

There is one exception to the complete loss of security if the *root* account is compromised. For some types of data files, encryption can form a fourth line of defense, providing protection against *root* and other privileged accounts. Encryption is discussed further later in this chapter.

Backups

Backups provide the final line of defense against some kinds of security problems and system disasters. In these cases, a good backup scheme will almost always enable you to restore the system to something near its previous state (or to recreate it on new hardware if some part of the computer itself is damaged). However, if someone steals the data from your system but doesn't alter or destroy it, backups are irrelevant.

Backups provide protection against data loss and filesystem damage only in conjunction with frequent system monitoring, designed to detect security problems quickly. Otherwise, a problem might not be uncovered for awhile. If this occurs, then backups would simply save the corrupted system state, making it necessary to go back weeks or months to a known "clean" state when the problem finally was uncovered (and restoring by hand newer versions of files not affected by the problem).

In any case, UNIX security features are not perfect. Sites needing much more elaborate security systems should look into the many third party add-on security packages available.

Security-related Sections in Other Chapters

Security considerations permeate most system administrative activities. Security procedures work best when they are integrated with other, normal system activities. Given this reality, discussions of security issues can't really be isolated to a single chapter. Rather, they will pop up again and again throughout the book. Here is a list of other sections of this book which contain significant discussions of security and related issues.

Table 5-1. Discussions of Security Issues

Issues Discussed	Chapter Title
File ownership, file protection	Chapter 2, *The UNIX Way*.
Single-user mode.	Chapter 3, *Startup and Shutdown*.
Guidelines for choosing passwords, setting password restrictions, captive accounts, removing a user account.	Chapter 4, *User Accounts*.
Cron security.	Chapter 6, *Automating Routine Tasks*.
Monitoring system activity, process resource limits, BSD disk quotas.	Chapter 7, *Managing System Resources*.
Planning a backup schedule, storing backup media	Chapter 9, *Backup and Restore*.
BSD "secure" terminals.	Chapter 10, *Terminals and Modems*.
Priorities and permissions.	Chapter 11, *Printers and the Spooling Subsystem*.
Network security.	Chapter 12, *TCP/IP Network Management*.

Preventing Security Problems

Many security problems can be prevented by a combination of effective passwords and carefully planned filesystem protections. This section will open by discussing the security issues related to user authentication and file ownership and permissions, including the SUID and SGID access modes, which provide a way of granting intermediate privilege between that of an ordinary user and that of the superuser, but which also complicate system security enormously. The final subsections deal with some specialized security features: encryption and dialup passwords.

Password File Issues

We've already looked at the issues around password selection and aging in the section entitled "Guidelines for Choosing Passwords." It's also important to examine the password file regularly for potential account-level security problems. In particular, it should be examined for:

- Accounts without passwords.

- UIDs of 0 for accounts other than *root* (which are also superuser accounts).

- GIDs of 0 for accounts other than *root*. Generally, users don't have group 0 (named *wheel*, *system*, *sys*, *root*, or something similar) as their primary group.

- Accounts added or deleted without your knowledge.

- Its own file permissions.

Under System V and SunOS, the *pwck* command will perform some simple syntax checking on the password file and can identify some security problems with it (AIX 3.1 provides *pwdck* to check its several user account database files). *pwck* will report on invalid usernames (including null ones), UIDs, and GIDs, null or nonexistent home directories, invalid shells, and entries with the wrong number of fields (often indicating extra or missing colons and other typos). However, it won't find a lot of other, more serious security problems. You'll need to check for those periodically yourself. (The *grpck* command performs similar simple syntax checking for the */etc/group* file.)

You can find accounts without passwords with a simple *grep* command:

```
# grep '^[^:]*::' /etc/passwd
root::NqI27UZyZoq3.:0:0:SuperUser:/:/bin/csh
demo::7:17:Demo User:/u/demo:/bin/sh
::0:0:::
```

The *grep* command looks for two consecutive colons which are the first colon characters in the line. This command found three such entries. At first glance, the entry for *root* appears to have a password, but the extra colon creates a user *root* with a nonsense UID and no password; this mistake is probably a typo. The second line is the entry for a predefined account used for demonstration purposes, probably present in the password file as delivered with the system. The third line is one I've found more than once and is a significant security breach. It creates an account with a null username and no password with UID and GID 0: a superuser account. While the login prompt will not accept a null username, *su* will:

```
$ su ""        No password prompt!
#
```

The extra colon should be removed from the *root* entry, the *demo* account should be assigned a password (or disabled with an asterisk in the password field in */etc/passwd*), and the null username entry should be removed.

If your system uses a shadow password file, then that is the file you should execute the *grep* command on rather than */etc/passwd*.

Account with UID or GID 0 can also be located with *grep*:

```
# grep ':00*:' /etc/passwd
root:NqI27UZyZoq3.:0:0:SuperUser:/:/bin/csh
martin:xyNjgMPtdlx*Q:145:0:Gordon H. Martin:/u/martin:/bin/ksh
badguy:mksU/.m7hwkOa:0:203:Bad Guy:/u/bg:/bin/sh
larooti:lso9/.7sJUhhs:000:203:George Larooti:/u/martin:/bin/csh
```

The final line of output indicates why you should resist using a command like:

```
# grep ':0:' /etc/passwd | grep -v root        This won't catch everything.
```

Whoever added user *larooti* has been tricky enough to add multiple zeros as the UID and the word "root" in the GECOS field. That person has also attempted to throw suspicion on user *martin* by including his home directory in this entry. That is one of its two functions; the other is to enable the entry to pass some password file checking programs (including *pwck*). It seems unlikely, although not impossible, that user *martin* is actually responsible for the entry; *martin* could be being very devious (or monumentally stupid, which can look very similar). I wouldn't consider the home directory clear evidence either way.

You can find new accounts by scanning the password file manually, or by comparing it to a saved version you've squirreled away in an obscure location. The latter is the best way to find missing accounts, since it's easier to notice something new than that something is missing. Here is a sample command:

```
# diff /etc/passwd /usr/local/bin/old/opg
36c36,37
< chavez:9Sl.sd/i7snso:190:20:Rachel Chavez:/u/chavez:/bin/csh
---
> gull:dgJ6GLVsmOtmI:507:302:Malcolm Gull:/u/gull:/bin/csh
> chavez:9So9sd/i7snso:190:20:Rachel Chavez:/u/chavez:/bin/csh
38d38
< wang:19jsTHn7Hg./a:308:302:Rich Wang:/u/wang:/bin/sh
```

The copy of the password file is stored in the directory */usr/local/bin/old* and is named *opg*. It's a good idea to choose a relatively unconventional location and misleading names for security-related data files. For example, if you store the copy of the password file in */etc** or */usr/adm* (the standard administrative directory) and name it *passwd.copy*, it won't be hard for an enterprising user to find and alter it when changing the real file. If your copy isn't secure, then comparing against it is pointless. (The example location given above isn't an excellent

---

*There may be copies of the password file in */etc*, but these are for backup rather than security purposes.

choice either; it's merely meant to illustrate the general principle. You'll know what are good choices on your system.)

The sample output displayed previously indicates that user *wang* has been added, user *gull* has been deleted, and the entry for user *chavez* has changed since the last time the copy was updated (in this case, her password changed). This command represents the simplest way of comparing the two files. More elaborate variations are discussed in the section entitled "Example: Password File Security," in Chapter 6, *Automating Routine Tasks*.

Finally, you should regularly check the ownership and permissions of the password file (and any shadow password file in use). In most cases, it should be owned by *root* and a system administrative group, and be readable by everyone but writable only by the owner:

```
$ ls -l /etc/passwd        Use -lg on BSD systems.
-rw-r--r--   1 root     sys        1148 Jul 12 09:52 /etc/passwd
```

Secondary Login Authentication

If you feel that passwords alone are insufficient for the security needs on your system, you might want to look into a secondary authentication program. Such programs require additional information before accepting that the user is who she claims to be. For example, the program may require the user to answer several questions about their personal preferences ("Which of the following flowers do you prefer?") and then compare the responses to those given when the user was initially added to the system (the question may be multiple choice, with the four or five wrong responses chosen randomly from a much larger list). The theory behind this sort of approach is that even if someone discovers or guesses your password, they won't be able to guess your favorite flower, bird, color, and so on, and that you won't need to write them down in order to remember them either, since the questions are multiple choice. It also relies on there being enough questions and choices per question to make blind guessing extremely unlikely to succeed (accounts are automatically disabled after a small number of unsuccessful authentications).

Alternative Authentication Under AIX 3.1

Some add-on security packages for UNIX systems include secondary authentication programs or the ability to add one easily. While not providing a secondary authentication program, AIX 3.1 makes it easy to add one to the system; this facility is described in this subsection.

AIX 3.1 provides for an administrator-defined alternative login authentication method. The alternative method may be used in addition to or instead of the standard UNIX password method. An alternative authentication program must take a username as an argument and return a zero if the user passes and nonzero if the user fails the authentication process. The program must be designated an authentication program in the file */etc/security/login.cfg*. The stanza defines a name for the authentication method (uppercase by convention) and specifies the pathname of the authentication program:

```
LOCALAUTH:
     program = /etc/local_auth_prog
```

This stanza defines an authentication method LOCALAUTH using the program */etc/local_auth_prog*. The standard password authentication method is named SYSTEM.

Modifying the *auth1* user attribute is one way to define an alternative or additional authentication scheme. For example, the command below replaces the standard password authentication with the LOCALAUTH method for user *chavez*:

```
# chuser auth1=LOCALAUTH chavez
```

The command below adds LOCALAUTH as an additional authentication method, run after the standard password check for user *chavez*:

```
# chuser auth1=SYSTEM,LOCALAUTH chavez
```

local_auth_prog will be passed the argument "chavez" when user *chavez* tries to log in. Of course, it would be wise to test an additional authentication method thoroughly on a single account before installing it on the system as a whole.

Using Groups Effectively

Proper file ownerships and protections are an integral part of the total system security. The purpose of file permissions is to allow the appropriate people to use files they need and to deny access to anyone who shouldn't have access. Effective file permissions are intimately connected to the structure of your system's groups, since groups are the only method UNIX provides to refer to and operate on arbitrary sets of users at the same time.

Some sites define the groups on their systems to reflect the organizational divisions of their institution or company: one department will become one UNIX group, for example (assuming a department is a relatively small organizational unit). However, this isn't necessarily what makes the most sense in terms of system security.

Groups should be defined on the basis of the need to share files, and, correlatively, the need to protect files from unwanted access. This may involve combining several organizational units into one group or splitting a single organizational unit into several distinct groups. UNIX groups need not mirror "reality" at all if that's not what security considerations call for.

Group divisions are often structured around projects; people who need to work together, using some set of common files and programs, will become a UNIX group. Users own the files they use most exclusively (or sometimes a group administrator owns all the group's files), common files are protected to allow group access, and all of the group's files can exclude non-group member access without affecting anyone in the group. When someone works on more than one project, then he is made a member of both relevant groups.

When a new project begins, you can create a new group for it and set up some common directories to hold its shared files, protecting them to allow group access (read-execute if members won't need to add or delete files and read-write-execute if they will). Similarly, files will be given appropriate group permissions when they are created based on the access group members will need. New users added to the system for this project can have the new group as their primary group; relevant existing users can be added to it as secondary group members in the group file. Although some UNIX implementations limit the number of groups a user can belong to, the limit is usually at least eight, which is more than sufficient for most purposes. In those rare cases where a user needs to be added to more groups than the system allows, the solution is to create a second username for her, with the same home directory as the original one, and to divide the group memberships between the two usernames.

Although it is very simple, the UNIX groups mechanism works very well under most conditions, especially on BSD-based systems. Under System V, it can be inconvenient for users to have to explicitly change their active group with *newgrp* at times, but in most cases any desired file accesses can be granted—and denied—to users via the relevant groups. However, the limitations inherent in this scheme come to the surface when a user needs to access files belonging to two different groups *simultaneously*. On System V systems, where a user cannot be in more than one group at a time, merely adding the user to the second group will not help (of course, on BSD systems, where all groups are always active, this solution works fine). For System V, there are several possible approaches to this problem, all involving tradeoffs of one sort or another:

- Make the user copies of the files he needs from the second group. This approach works only if the files are relatively small (compared to the available disk space) and the user won't be making changes to the files. In the latter case, you end up with two versions that have to be merged.

- Make the user the owner of all the files he needs access to from the second group. Then, he will be able to use them even while the other group is active. The drawbacks to this approach are obvious: if the user needs only read access, for example, this is overkill. There are also many circumstances in which you wouldn't want to change its ownership just to give someone access to a file.

- Make the files world-accessible. Some systems make all files world-readable; on others, it is imprudent to do so. Again, this approach is usually overkill when all you want to do is give one additional user access.

- Write a SGID program that accesses the files. This approach will work in many cases, but it can take a while to write and debug such a program. Also, depending on the type of access needed, this may introduce new security risks. For example, if the user needs to edit these files, you could write a SGID program that starts an editor on a file, but editors typically have shell escape commands, and so the user could then perform any action as a member of the second group. Sometimes this is fine and sometimes it isn't.

Similar dilemmas are possible even on BSD systems. For example, if you want to give a user access to just one file owned by a group that she doesn't belong to, making her a member of the second group will work, but it might give her more privileges than you want to. Access control lists, a mechanism which allows file permissions to be specified on a per-user basis, are the best solution to such problems; unfortunately, no widely-adopted UNIX standard has incorporated them. The AIX 3.1 version of access control lists is described in the following section.

The SUID and SGID Access Modes

The set user ID (SUID) and set group ID (SGID) file access modes provide a way to grant users system access to which they are not otherwise entitled on a temporary, command-level basis. However, SUID access especially is a double-edged sword. Used properly, it allows users access to certain system files and resources under controlled circumstances. However, if it is misused, there can be serious negative security consequences.

SUID and SGID access are added with *chmod*'s *s* access code (and they can similarly be recognized in long directory listings):

```
# chmod u+s file(s)    (SUID access)
# chmod g+s file(s)    (SGID access)
```

When a file with SUID access is executed, the process' effective UID is changed to that of the user owner of the file, and it uses that UIDs access rights for subsequent file and resource access. In the same way, when a file with SGID access is executed, the process' effective GID is changed to the group owner of the file, acquiring that group's access rights.

The *passwd* command is a good example of SUID access. The file */bin/passwd* usually has the following permissions:

```
$ ls -lo /bin/passwd
-rwsr-xr-x  3 root      55552 Nov 29  1988 /bin/passwd
```

The file is owned by *root* and has the SUID access mode set, so when someone executes this command, his EUID is changed to *root* for that command. SUID access is necessary for *passwd* because the command must write the user's new password to the password file, and only *root* has write access to the password file (or shadow password file, if used).

The various commands to access line printer queues are also usually SUID files. On BSD, line printer commands are usually SUID to user *root* because they need to access the printer port */dev/printer* (owned by *root*). On System V systems, the printer-related commands are often SUID to the special user *lp*. In general, SUID access to a special user is preferable to SUID *root* since it grants fewer unnecessary privileges to the process.

Other common uses of the SUID access mode are the *at*, *uucp*, and mailer facilities, all of which must write to central spooling directories to which users are normally denied access.

SGID access may be illustrated by the *ps* command. The file */bin/ps* is usually SGID to the group that owns the special files used to access system memory (specifically kernel memory): group *kmem* under BSD and often group *sys* under System V (although on some older system, *ps* is installed as an SUID file to user *root*). When a user runs *ps*, the process' EGID is set to the group owner of */bin/ps*, allowing her to access the kernel memory device for that command.

Similarly, certain commands allow users (processes) to write to terminals other than their own using SGID access to the group that owns the terminal devices (*tty* under BSD or *terminal* under some System V versions). These commands include *write*, *mesg*, and, under BSD, the *dump* backup program. In the latter case, SGID access allows an unprivileged user—such as an operator—to run *dump* and get messages on any terminal where he's logged in telling him it's time to mount a new tape.

NOTE

As the examples we've considered have illustrated, SUID and SGID access for system files varies quite a bit from system to system (as does file ownership and even directory location). You should familiarize yourself with the SUID and SGID files on your system.

To be secure, an SUID or SGID command or program must not allow the user to perform any action other than what it was designed to do, including retaining the SUID or SGID status after it completes. The threat is obviously greatest with programs that are SUID to *root*. The number of SUID commands on the system should be kept to a minimum. Checking the filesystem for new ones should be part of general system security monitoring. The following command will list all files that have the SUID or SGID access mode set:

```
# find / \( -perm -2000 -o -perm -4000 \) -type f -print
```

You can compare the command's output against a saved list of SUID and SGID files, and thereby easily locate any changes to the system. You can also do a more comprehensive comparison by running *ls -l* (include *-g* on BSD systems) on each file and comparing that output to a saved list:

```
# find / -type f \( -perm -2000 -o -perm -4000 \) \
            -exec ls -l {} \; | diff - /usr/local/bin/old/fs
2d1
< -rwsr-xr-x  1 root   bin   41792 Jun 7 1988 /usr/local/bin/is
```

Any differences uncovered should be investigated right away. The file storing the expected SUID and SGID files' data can be generated initially using the same *find* command after you have checked all of the SUID and SGID files on the system and know them to be secure. The file should be hard to find or stumble onto easily. It should be located in an obscure directory under an obscure name; if you name it */usr/adm/suid.sav*, it would be pretty easy for someone trying to sneak an SUID file onto the system to find it and add their file to it. (The location in the previous example is neither a recommendation nor a particularly good choice.) The data file and any scripts which use it should be owned by *root* and be protected against all group and other access. Even with these precautions, it's important that you be familiar with the files on your system, in addition to any security monitoring you perform via scripts, rather than relying solely on data files you set up a long time ago.

Aside from commands that are part of UNIX, other SUID and SGID programs should be added to the system with care. If at all possible, get the source code for any new SUID or SGID program being considered and examine it carefully before installing the program. It's not always possible to do so for programs from third party application vendors, but such programs are usually less risky than public domain programs. Hopefully, the part requiring privileged access will be isolated to a small portion of the package (if it isn't, I'd ask a lot of questions before buying it). *Never*, ever, install public domain software that runs SUID or SGID without examining the source code. In fact, it's a bad idea to run *any* public domain program for which you don't have the source as *root*. Ways to ensure security when creating your own SUID and SGID programs are discussed in the next section.

Writing SUID/SGID Programs

Two principles should guide you in those rare instances where you need to write an SUID or SGID program:

1. *Use the minimum privilege required for the job.* Thus, whenever possible, make the program SGID instead of SUID. Ninety-nine percent of all problems can be solved by creating a special group (or using an existing one) and making the program SGID. The other one percent can be solved by creating a special user and using SUID to it. Using SUID to *root* is a bad idea because of the difficulty in foreseeing and preventing every possible complication, system call interaction, or other obscure situation which will turn your nice program into a security hole. Also, if the program doesn't need SUID or SGID access for its entire lifetime, reset its effective UID or GID back to the process' real UID or GID at the appropriate point.

2. *Avoid extra program entrances and exits.* This principle rules out many different features and programming practices. For example, the program should not support shell escapes, which allow a shell command to be executed inside of another program (for example, in *vi* you can run a shell command by preceding it with an exclamation point and entering it at the colon prompt). If an SUID program has a shell escape, then any shell command run through it will be run using the process' effective UID (in other words, as *root* if the program is SUID to *root*). To be completely secure, the program should not call any other programs because, if it does so, it inherits the security holes of the secondary program. Thus, if an SUID program lets you call an editor, and the editor has shell escapes, then it's just as if the first program has shell escapes.

This principle also means that you should avoid system calls that invoke a shell (*popen, execve, system,* and so on.) These calls are susceptible to attacks by clever users. Two well-known ones are:

- Redefining the search path: if the system call runs the shell to execute a command specified only by name (e.g., popen("ls","r")), a user could change his search path to look in the current directory before the standard system directories and create a file there named *ls*. Then, when the SUID program is run, whatever *./ls* does will be done as the privileged user.

- Redefining the internal field separator: even if the full pathname of the command is passed to the system call, in some cases the user can reset the Bourne or Korn shell's internal field separator via the IFS environment variable. The internal field separator is the character which separates arguments on the command line; usually it is set to a space. However, if a user redefined it to be the slash character, then the command */bin/ps* would be interpreted as the command *bin ps* is under normal circumstances.

Then, with a properly set search path, the user could create a file *bin* in the current directory, and the SUID program would run it (with the argument *ps*) instead of the command that was intended, again as the privileged user.

Finally, avoid writing back doors into the program.

On many systems, SUID and SGID access is ignored on shell scripts (or it causes the script to fail in the case of the C shell). However, some older systems allow SUID and SGID scripts to be used. If your system is one of them, you should still never create privileged shell scripts because it is impossible to create secure ones. You should also make sure that there are none currently existing on your system (one way to do so is to run the *file* command on all SUID and SGID files).

Search Path Issues

We touched briefly on some security issues related to the search path in the previous section. In general, it's a good idea to place the current directory and the *bin* subdirectory of the user's home directory at the end of the path list, *after* the standard locations for UNIX commands, as in the search path below:

```
$ echo $PATH
/usr/ucb:/bin:/usr/bin:/usr/bin:/usr/bin/X11:.:$HOME/bin
```

This placement closes a potential security hole associated with search paths. If, for example, the current directory is searched before the standard command locations, then it is possible for someone to sneak a file named, say, *ls* into a seemingly innocuous directory like, say, */tmp*, which performs some nefarious action instead of or in addition to giving a directory listing. Similar effects are possible with a user's *bin* subdirectory (although hopefully it would be better protected).

For similar reasons, and because of the potential for much more damage, the current directory should not even appear in *root*'s search path. Similarly, no relative pathname should appear in *root*'s search path. In addition, none of the directories in *root*'s search path should be writable by anyone but *root*; if one was, then someone could again substitute something else for a standard command, which would be unintentionally run by and as *root*.

Encryption

Encryption provides another method of protection for some types of files. Encryption involves transforming the original file (the *plain* or *clear* text), using a mathematical function or techniques. Encryption can protect the data stored in files in several circumstances, including:

- Someone breaking into the *root* account on your system and copying or tampering with them (or an authorized *root* user doing similar things).

- Someone stealing your disk or backup tapes (or floppies) or the computer itself in an effort to get the data.

- Someone acquiring the files via a network.

The common theme here is that encryption can protect the security of your data even if the files themselves somehow fall into the wrong hands. (It can't prevent all mishaps, however, like an unauthorized *root* user deleting the files, but backups will cover that scenario.)

Most encryption algorithms use some sort of a *key* as part of the transformation, and the same key is needed to decrypt the file later. The simplest kinds of encryption algorithms use external keys that function much like passwords; more sophisticated encryption methods use part of the input data as the part of the key.

UNIX provides a simple encryption program, *crypt.** *crypt* is a very poor encryption program. It uses an old encryption scheme which is very easy to break. *crypt* can be made a little more secure by running it multiple times on the same file, for example:

```
$ crypt key1 < clear-file | crypt key2 | crypt key3 > encr-file
$ rm clear-file
```

The *crypt* takes the encryption key as its argument and encrypts standard input to standard output using that key. When decrypting *encr-file*, *crypt* is again used, but the keys are specified in the reverse order. It's important to remove the original file after encryption, since having both the clear and encrypted versions makes it very easy for someone to discover the keys used to encrypt it.

Even in this mode, *crypt* is no match for anyone with any encryption-breaking skills. Nevertheless, it is still useful in some circumstances. I use *crypt* to encrypt files that I don't want anyone to see accidentally or as a result of snooping around on the system as *root*. My assumption here is that the people I'm protecting them against might try to look at protected files as *root* but won't bother trying to decrypt them. It's the same philosophy behind many simple automobile protection systems; the sticker on the window (or the device on the steering wheel) are meant to discourage prospective thieves and to encourage them to spend their energy elsewhere, but don't really place more than trivial barriers in

---

*At least in the U.S.A. Government regulations forbid the inclusion of encryption software on systems shipped to foreign sites in many circumstances.

their way. For cases like these, *crypt* is fine. If you anticipate any sort of attempt to decode the encrypted files, as would be the case if someone is bothering to break into the system in the first place, then don't use *crypt*.

Many UNIX vendors offer the Data Encryption Standard (DES) encryption system as an optional product. DES is generally regarded very secure (although no system should be considered 100 percent secure) although rumors about supposed built-in weaknesses flourish. Generally, DES encrypted files are believed to be breakable, but only at great CPU-time expense.

For all encryption schemes, the choice of a good key (or keys) is imperative. In general, the same guidelines that apply to passwords apply to encryption keys. Also, longer keys are generally better than shorter ones. Finally, don't use any of your passwords as an encryption key; that's the first thing that someone who breaks into your account will try.

It's also important to make sure that your key is not inadvertently discovered by its being displayed to other users on the system. In particular, be careful about the following:

- Clear your terminal screen as soon as possible whenever a key appears on it.

- Don't use a key as a parameter to a command, script, or program, or it may show up in *ps* displays (or in *lastcomm* output under BSD).

- Although the *crypt* command ensures that the key doesn't appear in *ps* displays, it does nothing about shell command history records. If you use *crypt* in a shell that has a command history feature, turn history off before using *crypt*, or run *crypt* via a script that prompts for it.

Dialup Passwords

Dialup passwords add another level of user authentication for systems allowing dialup access via modems. When dialup passwords are in use, users are required to provide a dialup password in addition to their username and password before being allowed access to a system over a dialup line. Dialup passwords may also be used as a way to restrict dialup access to certain users (by only telling the password to them).

Although dialup passwords are not a standard part of pre-V.4 implementations of UNIX, they are included in some implementations of both System V and BSD as an undocumented feature. To find out whether your system supports them or not, see if the string "d_passwd" appears in the *login* executable. Here are two ways of doing this:

```
% strings /bin/login | grep d_passwd          or
$ od -a /bin/login | grep 'd *_ *p *a *s'
```

The dialup password facility uses two configuration files: */etc/d_passwd*, the dialup password file (described later in this section), and */etc/dialups* (occasionally named *dial-ups*), which lists the terminal lines that are connected to dialup modems (i.e., modems that allow users to dial in to the computer system). The special file for one dialup terminal is listed on each line of the file.

For example, the */etc/dialups* file below shows that three terminal lines are connected to dialup modems:

```
/dev/tty10
/dev/tty11
/dev/tty13
```

Users who log in through one of these terminal lines must supply a dialup password (according to the */etc/d_passwd* file) in order to log in successfully. Enter all of the terminal lines connected to modems into this file.

The file */etc/d_passwd* contains a set of encrypted dialup passwords. The dialup password required depends on the user's login shell. The *d_passwd* file contains only two fields, separated by colons:

> *shell*:*encrypted-password*

where *shell* is the complete pathname of a shell that can be listed in the user's *passwd* entry. The second entry is the encrypted password. As in the */etc/passwd* file (or shadow file), this must *not* be the clear password—the password the user actually types to log in—it must be the encrypted password.

The dialup password file does not provide any support for generating the encrypted password; you must generate it yourself. First, you must choose two strings: a two-character "salt," (chosen from the letters and numbers) and an eight-character password. To encrypt the password, execute the command:

```
% echo "passwdsalt" | /usr/lib/makekey
```

(The *makekey* command may be stored in a different location on your system.) *makekey* prints the encrypted password on standard output; copy this into the *d_passwd* file. For example, if you choose 12345678 for the dialup password, and

AB for the salt, you will use the following command to generate the encrypted password:

```
% echo "12345678AB" | /usr/lib/makekey
ABk0sdfghlkdf
```

The string that *makekey* returns, represented by *ABk0sdfghlkdf*, is the *encrypted dialup password*. Copy this string into *d_passwd*.

If your system does not have the *makekey* command, encrypted dialup passwords may be generated by creating a fake user in the */etc/passwd* file, exiting and assigning it a password with the *passwd* command and then copying the string that appears in the *passwd* file into */etc/d_passwd*. **Be sure to remove the fake user afterwards.**

If passwords are stored in a shadow file, then the process in the previous paragraph will still work with the following modification. After creating the fake user and setting its password, *grep* for that user in the shadow file, for example:

```
# grep fakeguy /etc/shadow
fakeguy:4dP9/d.liOi.F:999:99::::
```

The password will be in the second field (delimited by a colon).

If you decide to use the same dialup password for all user shells (the *uucp* account's password should always be different), you should encrypt them using different salts. Their encrypted representation will look different in the file, so it will not be obvious that they are the same password. If you assign the same password to your fake user in the password file a second time, a different salt will be used by the system and a different encrypted version generated.

If you want to assign different dialup passwords to the different systems that connect to yours via *uucp*, then create hard links to */usr/lib/uucp/uucico* for each of them, assign each account a different link as its shell in the password file, and give each link a different dialup password. For example, a command like the following will create a link to *uucico*:

```
# cd /usr/lib/uucp
# ln uucico uucico1
```

After executing this command, you would edit the password file and change the shell for one of the systems' account to *usr/lib/uucp/uucico1* and include a line for */usr/lib/uucp/uucico1* in the dialup password file.

Here is a sample dialup password file:

```
/bin/sh:10gw4c39EHIAM:
/bin/csh:p9k3tJ6RzSfKQ:
/bin/ksh:9pk36RksieQd3:
/bin/Rsh:*:
```

```
/usr/lib/uucp/uucico:9919icAI1wHOgm:
/usr/lib/uucp/uucico1:s7hsieoK.jdYnP:
```

In this example, there are specific entries for the Bourne shell, Korn shell, and the C shell, as well as the uucp account. Dialup access from the restricted Bourne shell (*/bin/Rsh*) is disabled by putting an asterisk in the password field. Users who use other shells may log in from remote terminals without giving an additional dialup password. I recommend that you assign a dialup password to all shells in use at your site. If you assign a dialup password to *uucico* (or a link to it), you'll need to inform the system administrator for each *uucp* host so that he can modify the system's *uucp* dialing configuration file appropriately.

Once you have installed this file, users who log in over dialup phone lines must give the dialup password in addition to their personal password before they are allowed to log in. Dialup passwords should be changed periodically. They should also be changed whenever anyone who knows the dialup password stops using the system (as part of the general account deactivation procedure), or if there is any hint that an unauthorized user has learned it.

AIX 3.1 Access Control Lists

AIX 3.1 offers further refinements to the standard UNIX file permissions capabilities through its support for *access control lists* (ACL's), (which are also available on a few other UNIX systems). ACL's enable you to specify access for files for groups other than the file's group owner and on a user-by-user basis. ACL's effectively allow you to define sets of users which are logical combinations of the system's defined groups: users who are in both *chem* and *bio* or users in either *organic* or *analytic*.

An access control list looks like this:

attributes:		*Special modes like SUID.*
base permissions		*Normal UNIX file modes:*
owner(chavez):	rw–	*User access.*
group(chem):	rw–	*Group access.*
others:	r––	*Other access.*
extended permissions		*More specific permissions entries:*
enabled		*Whether they're used or not.*
specify r––	u:martin	*Permissions for user martin.*
deny –w–	g:organic	*Permissions for group organic.*
permit rw–	u:ng, g:bio	*Permissions for user ng when group bio is active.*

The first line specifies any special attributes on the file (or directory). The possible attribute keywords are:

SETUID   Setuid is set.

SETGID   Setgid is set.

SVTX   The sticky bit is set (for a directory).

Multiple attributes are all placed on one line, separated by commas.

The next section of the ACL lists the *base permissions* for the file or directory. These correspond exactly to the UNIX file modes. Thus, for the file we're looking at, the owner (who is *chavez*) has read and write access, members of the group *chem* (which is the group owner of the file) also have read and write access, and all others have read access.

The final section specifies *extended permissions* for the file: access information specified by user and group name. The first line in this section is either the word "enabled" or "disabled," indicating whether the extended permissions that follow are actually used to determine file access or not. In our example, extended permissions are in use.

The rest of the lines in the ACL are *access control entries* (ACE's), which have the following format:

   operation access-types user-and-group-info

where the *operation* is one of the keywords "permit," "deny," and "specify," which correspond to *chmod*'s +, −, and = operators respectively. "Permit" says to add the specified permissions to the ones the user already has, based on the base permissions; "deny" says to take away the specified access; and "specify" sets the access for the user to the listed value. The *access-types* are the same as those for normal UNIX file modes. The *user-and-group-info* consists of a user name (preceded by "u:") or one or more group names (each preceded by "g:") or both. Multiple items are separated by commas.

Some examples are probably helpful at this point. Let's look again at the ACE's in our sample ACL:

```
specify  r--     u:martin
deny     r--     g:organic
permit   rw-     u:ng, g:bio
```

The first line grants read-only access to user *martin* on this file. The second line removes read access for the *organic* group from whatever permissions a user in that group already has. The final line adds read and write access to user *ng* while in group *bio*. AIX 3.1 has extended the UNIX concept of groups to define *group sets*: the set of the groups to which the user belongs that is currently active (see the section entitled "AIX 3.1 Group Sets" in Chapter 4, *User Accounts*. By default, the current group set is all of the groups to which the user belongs.

ACL's which specify a username and group are useful mostly for accounting purposes; the previous ACL ensures that user *ng* has group *bio* active when working with this file. They are also useful if you add a user to a group on a temporary basis, ensuring that the added file access goes away if the user is later removed from the group. In the previous example, user *ng* would no longer have access to the file if she were removed from the *bio* group (unless, of course, the file's base permissions grant it to her).

If more than one item is included in the *user-and-group-info*, then all of the items must be true for the entry to be applied to a process (AND logic). Thus, in the third line, the user must be *ng*, and *ng*'s group set must include the *bio* group. Similarly, the ACE below is applied only to users that have both *bio* and *chem* in their group sets (under normal circumstances, this is equivalent to "are members of both the *chem* and *bio* groups"):

```
permit   rw-    g:chem, g:bio
```

If you wanted to grant write access to anyone who was a member of either group *chem* or group *bio*, you would specify two separate entries:

```
permit    rw-    g:chem
permit    rw-    g:bio
```

So, how is all this information processed? When a process requests access to a file with extended permissions enabled, the ACE's are read. The permitted accesses from the base permissions and *all* applicable ACE's—all ACE's which match the user and group identity of the process—are combined via a union operation. The denied accesses from the base permissions and all applicable ACE's are also combined. Then, if the requested access is permitted *and* is not denied, then it is granted. Thus, contradictions among ACE's are resolved in the most conservative way: access is denied unless it is both permitted and not denied.

For example, consider the ACL below:

```
attributes:
base permissions
    owner(chavez):   rw-
    group(chem):     r--
    others:          ---
extended permissions
    enabled
    specify      r--    u:stein
    permit       rw-    g:organic, g:bio
    deny         rwx    g:physics
```

Now suppose that the user *stein*, who is a member of both the *organic* and *bio* groups (and not a member of the *chem* group) wants write access to this file. The base permissions clearly grant *stein* no access at all to the file. The ACE's in lines one and two of the extended permissions apply to *stein*. These ACE's grant him read access (lines one and two) and write access (line two). They also deny him write and execute access (implicit in line one). Thus, *stein* will not be given write access because while the combined ACE's do grant it to him, they also deny write access, and so the request will fail.

In simple terms, in order for a certain type of access to be available to a user, the ACE's must both grant it and not deny it. Thus, line three in the ACL prevents all access by members of the group *physics* to this file, since it explicitly denies all access. This type of entry is useful because it will remain in effect regardless of the base permissions (file modes) set on the file.

WARNING

The base permissions on a file with an extended access control list may be changed with *chmod*'s symbolic mode, and any changes made in this way will be reflected in the base permissions section of the ACL. However, *chmod*'s numeric mode must not be used for files with extended permissions, since using it automatically disables them.

ACLs may also be changed with the *acledit* command. *acledit* retrieves the current ACL for the file specified as its argument and opens it for editing, using the text editor specified by the EDITOR environment variable. The use of this variable under AIX 3.1 is different than what you're used to if you're familiar with BSD systems. For one thing, there is no default (most UNIX implementations use *vi* as a default editor for commands using EDITOR if its value is unset). Secondly, AIX 3.1 requires that the full pathname to the editor be supplied, not just its name: */usr/ucb/vi*, not just *vi*.

Once in the editor, make any changes to the ACL that you wish. If you are adding extended permissions ACE's, be sure to change "disabled" to "enabled" in the first line of that section. When you are finished, exit from the editor normally. AIX 3.1 will then print the message:

```
Should the modified ACL be applied? (y)
```

If you wish to discard your changes to the ACL, enter "n"; otherwise, you should enter a carriage return. AIX 3.1 will then check the new ACL, and if it has no errors, apply it to the file. If there are errors in the ACL (misspelled keywords or usernames are the most common), you will be placed back in the editor where you can correct them and try again. AIX 3.1 will put error messages like this one at the bottom of the file, describing the errors it found:

```
* line number  9: unknown keyword: spceify
* line number 10: unknown user: chavze
```

You don't have to delete the error messages themselves from the ACL.

This is the slow way of applying an ACL. The *aclget* and *aclput* offer alternative ways to display and apply ACLs to files. *aclget* takes a filename as its argument, and displays the corresponding ACL on standard output. For example, the command below displays the access control list for the file *gold*:

```
$ aclget gold
attributes:
base permissions
     owner(chavez):  rw-
     group(chem):    r-x
     others:         r-x
extended permissions
     disabled
```

This file currently uses only the standard UNIX file modes for determining file access. The output from *aclget* may be redirected to a file for editing with the *-o* option, which takes the output filename as its argument:

```
$ aclget -o metal.acl silver = aclget silver > metal.acl
```

The *aclput* command is used to read in an ACL from a text file. By default, it takes its input from standard input, or an input file may be specified with the *-i* option. Thus, to set the ACL for the file *gold* to the one stored in the file *metal.acl*, use either of these commands:

```
$ aclput gold <metal.acl = aclput -i metal.acl gold
```

This form of *aclput* is useful if you use only a few different ACL's, which are saved as separate files to be applied in this way as needed.

To copy an ACL from one file to another, put *aclget* and *aclput* together in a pipe. For example, the command below copies the ACL from the file *silver* to the file *emerald*:

```
% aclget silver | aclput emerald
```

To copy an ACL from one file to a group of files, use one of the shell's built-in looping commands. Here are examples from the C and Korn shells:

```
% foreach f (*.dat *.old)
? aclget silver | aclput $f
? end

$ aclget -o temp.acl silver
$ ls *.dat *.old | xargs -n1 aclget -i temp.acl
```

These commands copy the ACL in *silver* to all the files ending in *.dat* and *.old*.

Detecting Problems

So far, we've looked at lots of ways to prevent security problems. The remainder of this chapter will look at ways to detect and investigate security breaches should they occur despite your best efforts to prevent them. In some cases, detecting and correcting minor security problems—like a directory that is world-writable but shouldn't be—can also prevent more serious ones which would exploit that weakness.

Monitoring the Filesystem

Setting protections properly on important files and directories is an important step in making your system secure. Making sure that the ownerships and protections remain correct over time is vital to ensuring its continuing security. This includes:

• Checking the ownership and protection of important system configuration files.

• Checking the ownership and protection on important directories.

• Verifying the integrity of important system binary files.

Possible ways to approach these tasks are discussed in the following subsections of this chapter. Each one introduces an increased level of cautiousness; you'll need to decide how much monitoring is necessary on your system.

Checking File Protection

Minimally, you should periodically check the ownership and permissions of important system files and directories. The latter are important since, if a directory is writable, a user could substitute a new version of an important file for the real one, even if the file itself is protected.

Some important system files are listed in Table 5-2 (note that filenames and locations vary somewhat). In general, these files are owned by *root* or another system user (for example, the user *uucp* owns *uucp*-related files); none of them should be world writable.

Table 5-2. Important Files for Security Monitoring

File(s)	Purpose
/.cshrc, /.login, /.logout, /.kscrc, /.profile	*root* account's initialization files.
/.forward, /.mailrc, etc	*root's* mail initialization files.
/.rhosts	**Should not exist** (see Chapter 12, *TCP/IP Network Management*).
/dev/*	Special files (the disk and memory devices are the most critical).
/etc/cron/* (V.4)	*at* and *cron* permissions files.
/etc/d_passwd	Dialup password file.
/etc/dialups	Dialup terminal line list (used for dialup passwords).
/etc/default/* (System V)	Default user and system settings.
/etc/exports	Filesystems available to other systems via NFS.
/etc/filesystems (AIX 3.1)	Filesystem configuration file.
/etc/fstab	Filesystem configuration file.
/etc/ftpusers	Users prevented from using *ftp*.
/etc/group	Group definition file.
/etc/hosts	TCP/IP network configuration file.
/etc/hosts.equiv	TCP/IP trusted hosts.
/etc/inetd.conf	Internet daemon configuration file.
/etc/init.d/* (System V)	System initialization scripts.
/etc/inittab (System V)	System configuration file.
/etc/netgroup	Netgroups definitions for NIS.
/etc/networks	TCP/IP configuration file.
/etc/passwd	Password file.
/etc/rc*	System initialization scripts.
/etc/profile	System-wide account initialization file.
/etc/protocols	TCP/IP configuration file.
/etc/remote	Modem dialer definitions (used by *tip* and *cu*).
/etc/rc?.d/* (System V)	System initialization scripts.
/etc/security/* (AIX 3.1)	User account data files.
/etc/services	TCP/IP configuration file.
/etc/shadow	Shadow password file.
/etc/shells (BSD)	List of valid shells.
/etc/swapspaces (AIX 3.1)	List of system paging areas.
/etc/syslog.conf	System logging configuration file.
/etc/ttys (BSD)	Terminal lines.

Table 5-2. Important Files for Security Monitoring (continued)

File(s)	Purpose
/etc/wtmp (System V)	Records all logins and logouts.
/etc/vfstab (V.4)	Filesystem configuration file.
/etc/utmp	Current logged in users database.
/usr/adm/*	Administrative databases and scripts.
/usr/lib/aliases	Mail aliases and groups.
/usr/lib/cron/cron.* (V.3)	*cron* permissions files.
/usr/lib/sendmail.cf	*sendmail* mailer configuration file.
/usr/lib/crontab* (BSD)	*cron* configuration file.
/usr/lib/uucp/*	*uucp* configuration files and scripts. Important configuration files include *L-devices, L.cmds, L.sys,* and *USERFILE* for *uucp* Version 2 and *Devices* and *Permissions* for the newer version of *uucp*, which System V calls the Basic Networking Utilities (BNU).
/usr/spool/cron/at.* (V.3)	*at* permissions files.
/usr/spool/cron/crontabs (System V)	*cron* configuration files.
/var/adm/* (V.4)	Administrative databases and scripts.
All SUID and SGID files	Wherever they may be.

You should be familiar with the correct ownership and protection for these files (as well as any others of importance to your system). Unfortunately, correct ownership varies from system to system. You can also facilitate the task of checking them with a script that runs a command like *ls -l* on each one, saves the output, and compares it to a stored list of the proper ownerships and permissions. Such a script can be very simple:

```
#!/bin/csh
umask 077
# Make sure output file is empty.
cp /dev/null perm.ck
alias ck "ls -lg \!:* >> perm.ck"
ck /.[a-z]*
ck /dev/{,r}disk*
. . .
ck /usr/lib/uucp/Permissions
diff /usr/local/bin/old/pm perm.ck > perm.diff
```

This script is a C shell script so that it can define an alias to do the work; you could do the same thing with a Bourne shell function. The script runs the *ls -lg* (omit the "g" under System V) command on the desired files, saving the output to the file *perm.ck*. Finally, it compares the current output against a saved data file.

If the files on your system change a lot, this script will produce a lot of false positives: files that look suspicious because their modification time changed but whose ownership and protection are correct. You can avoid this by making the *ls* command a bit more complex:*

```
ls -lg file(s) | awk '{print $1,$3,$4,$NF}' >> perm.ck
```

This command compares only the file modes, user owner, group owner, and filename fields of the *ls* command.

In addition to checking individual files, it is important to check the protection on all directories which store important files, making sure that they are owned by the proper user and are not world-writable. These directories include those containing UNIX commands (*/etc*, */bin*, */usr/bin*, */usr/ucb*, */usr/etc*, */usr/lib*, */usr/local/bin*, */sbin*, */usr/sbin*, and so on), administrative data files or scripts (*/usr/adm* or */var/adm*, */etc*'s subdirectories under System V, and so on), and the spooling directories starting at */usr/spool* or */var/spool*. Any other directory containing a SUID or SGID file should also be checked.

Computing Checksums

If someone breaks into the *root* account on your system, then she would be able to make changes to the system files we checked in the previous section without affecting the ownership or file protection. There are ways of detecting such changes, however. This section and the next one deal with methods for determining whether the contents of files have changed or not.

Checksums are one quick way to tell if a file's contents have changed. A *checksum* is a number computed from the binary bytes of the file which can be used to determine whether a file's contents are correct. Checksums are most often used to check files written to disk from tape to be sure there have been no I/O errors, but they may also be used to see if a file's contents change over time.

For example, you can generate checksums for the system commands' executable files and save this data. Then, at a later date, you can recompute the checksums for the same files and compare the results. If they are not identical for a file, then that file has changed, and someone has possibly substituted something else for the real command.

---

*The corresponding *alias* command is:

```
alias ck "ls -lg \!:* | awk '{print "'$1,$3,$4,$NF'"}' >> perm.ck"
```

The tricks with the quotes in the *awk* command are to prevent the script's arguments from being placed into the alias.

The *sum* command computes checksums; it takes one or more filenames as its arguments and displays the checksum and size in blocks for each file:

```
$ sum /bin/*
09962    4 /bin/[
05519   69 /bin/adb
. . .
```

This method is not foolproof. For example, someone could pad a smaller file with junk characters to make its checksum match the old value.

Checking Modification Dates and Inode Numbers

If you want to perform the most careful possible monitoring on the system files, then you will want to compare not only file ownership and protection (and possibly its checksum), but also its modification date, size, and inode number. To do so, use the *ls* command with the options *-lsid* (or *-lsidg* on BSD systems). These options display the file's inode number, size (in both blocks and bytes), owners, protection modes, modification date, and name. For example:

```
$ ls -lsid /etc/rc*
690  3 -rwxr-xr-x  1 root    root   1325 Mar 20 12:58 /etc/rc0
691  4 -rwxr-xr-x  1 root    root   1655 Mar 20 12:58 /etc/rc2
692  1 drwxr-xr-x  2 root    root    272 Jul 22 07:33 /etc/rc2.d
704  2 -rwxr-xr-x  1 root    root    874 Mar 20 12:58 /etc/rc3
705  1 drwxr-xr-x  2 root    root     32 Mar 13 16:14 /etc/rc3.d
```

The *-d* option allows the information on directories themselves to be displayed, rather than listing their contents.

If you check this data regularly, comparing it against a previously saved file of the expected output, you will catch any changes very quickly, and it will be very difficult for someone to modify any file without detection. However, this method inevitably requires that you update the saved data file every time you make a change yourself, or you will have to wade through lots of false positives when examining the output. As always, it is important that the data file be kept in an obscure, secure location to prevent it being modified itself.

It's possible to automate most of these activities using scripts and the *cron* facility. See the sections entitled "Example: Password File Security" and "Using cron to Automate System Administration," in Chapter 6, *Automating Routine Tasks.*

Monitoring Unsuccessful Login Attempts (AIX 3.1)

Repeated unsuccessful login attempts for any user account can indicate someone trying to break in to the system. Standard UNIX does not keep track of this statistic, but some other versions do, including AIX 3.1.

Under AIX 3.1, checking for lots of unsuccessful login attempts is relatively easy. The file */etc/security/user** includes the keyword *unsuccessful_login_count* in the stanza for each user:

```
chavez:
        admin = false
        time_last_login = 679297672
        unsuccessful_login_count = 27
        tty_last_unsuccessful_login = pts/2
        time_last_unsuccessful_login = 680904983
        host_last_unsuccessful_login = hades
```

This is clearly a lot of unsuccessful login attempts. Anything above three or so is probably worth some investigation. The following command will display the username and number of unsuccessful logins when this value is greater than 3:

```
# egrep '^[^*].*:$|gin_coun' /etc/security/user | \
  awk '{if (NF>1 && $3>3) {print s,$0}} ; {s=$0}'
chavez:    unsuccessful_login_count = 27
```

The *egrep* command prints lines in */etc/security/user* that don't begin with an asterisk and end with a colon (the username lines) and that contain the string "gin_coun" (the unsuccessful login count lines). For each line printed by *egrep*, the *awk* command checks if the value of the third field in the line is greater than three if there is more than one field in the line (the username lines have just one field). If it is, it prints the previous line (saved in the variable *s*), which contains the username, and the current line.

When the user logs in, she gets a message about the number of unsuccessful login attempts, and the field in */etc/security/user* is cleared. However, if you check this file periodically, using the *cron* facility described in the Chapter 6, you can catch most strings of unsuccessful login attempts before they are erased (see the section entitled "Automate System Administration," in Chapter 6, *Automating Routine Tasks*, for an example).

---

*The file */etc/security/failedlogin* contains a record of each unsuccessful login attempt (in *utmp* format). Another option is to write a program to examine this file to track unsuccessful login attempts; AIX 3.1 does not seem to provide any utility to summarize its contents.

Tools for Detective Work

The sections that follow discuss some of the tools UNIX provides which may be used to track down some types of security problems.

Monitoring System Activity

Regularly monitoring the processes which are running on your system is another way to minimize the likelihood of security breaches. You should do this periodically, perhaps as often as several times during the day. Very shortly, you will have a good sense of what "normal" system activity is: what programs run, how long they run for, who runs them, and so on. You'll also be in a reasonably good position to notice any unusual activity: users running different programs than they usually do, processes that remain idle for long periods of time (potential Trojan horses), and the like.

The *ps* command lists characteristics of system processes. You should be familiar with all of its options. Options which are sometimes useful for system security monitoring are listed in Table 5-3.

Table 5-3. Useful ps Options

Option	Effect
Under BSD:	
-ax	Display all system processes.
-c	Display the actual command name.
-e	Display the environment as well as the command run.
-w	Widen the output format (can be used more than once).
Under System V:	
-e	Display all system processes.
-f	Produce a "full" listing, including the process start time.

Let's look at some examples of how you might use some of these options. Under BSD, you can use -w as many times as necessary to get the entire command run by a user into the display:

```
# ps -ax | egrep 'PID|martin'
   241 co R     0:02 rm /u/martin/newest/g99/1913.exe /u/mar
# ps -axwwww | egrep 'PID|martin'
   PID TT STAT  TIME COMMAND  Output is wrapped here.
   241 co R     0:02 rm /u/martin/newest/g99/1913.exe
```

```
/u/martin/newest/g99-221.chk /u/martin/newest/g99-271.int
/u/martin/newest/g99-231.rwf /u/martin/newest/g99-291.d2e
/u/martin/newest/g99-251.scr /usr/local/src/local_g99
```

In this case, you can see all the files that were deleted by using several *w*'s.

The *-c* option will reveal the actual command executed, rather than the one typed in on the command line. This is occasionally useful for discovering programs run via symbolic links:

```
% ps aux | egrep 'PID|smith'
USER    PID %CPU %MEM   SZ  RSS TT STAT TIME COMMAND
smith 25318  6.7  1.1 1824  544 p4 S    0:00 vi
smith 23888  0.0  1.4 2080  736 p2 I    0:02 -csh (csh)
% ps -auxc | egrep 'PID|smith'
USER    PID %CPU %MEM   SZ  RSS TT STAT TIME COMMAND
smith 25318  6.7  1.1 1824  544 p4 S    0:00 backgammon
smith 23888  0.0  1.4 2080  736 p2 I    0:02 -csh (csh)
```

User *smith* evidently has a file named *vi* in his current directory which is a symbolic link to */usr/games/backgammon*.

The *-f* option under System V can help you identify processes that have been idle for a long time:

```
# ps -ef
  UID  PID PPID  C   STIME TTY    TIME COMMAND
chavez 2387 1123  0   Apr 22 ?    0:05 comp_h2o
```

This process has been around for a long time, but has accumulated very little CPU time. If today is, say, May 5th, it's time to look into this process. (Hopefully, you'd actually notice it before May 5th).

As these examples indicate, creative use of common commands is what's needed in a lot of cases. The more familiar you are with the commands' capabilities, the easier it will be to know what to use in the situations you actually face.

su Log Files

Virtually all UNIX implementations provide some mechanism for logging all attempts by users to become superuser. Such logs can be very useful when trying to track down who did something untoward as *root*. Under BSD, messages from *su* are typically written to the file */usr/adm/messages* and to the system console. Here is what they look like:

```
Mar 13 17:19:05 m10 su: BAD SU chavez on /dev/ttyp3
Mar 13 17:19:10 m10 su: chavez on /dev/ttyp3
```

The first message indicates a failed attempt by user *chavez* to enter the root password; the second indicates that she successfully became the superuser. The mechanism for sending such messages to a log file or to the system console is described in the section entitled "Logging System Messages Under BSD," later in this chapter. (SunOS and AIX 3.1 both use the BSD logging facility; it is also provided by some V.3 implementations and is a standard part of V.4.)

V.3 automatically sends messages to the file */usr/adm/sulog*, using a slightly different format:

```
SU 07/20 07:27 + ttyp0 chavez-root
SU 07/20 14:00 + ttyp0 chavez-root
SU 07/21 18:36 + ttyp1 smith-chavez
SU 07/21 18:39 + ttyp1 chavez-root
```

This display lists all uses of the *su* command, not just those used to *su* to *root*. The previous example indicates times that this can be useful: user *smith* first *su*-ed to username *chavez* and then to *root*. If you look only at *su* commands to *root*, you might mistakenly suspect *chavez* of doing something *smith* in fact did. (Under BSD, *su* log messages are always entered under the real username, ignoring any intermediate *su* commands.)

Both XENIX and V.4 use the file */etc/default/su* as the means for specifying where status messages from the *su* command will be stored. This file contains lines setting the values of various keywords. Among the available keywords are:

SULOG *path*   Pathname to the *su* logfile.

CONSOLE *device*   Device special file for the system console.

If SULOG is defined in this file, then *su* log messages will be written to the specified file; if CONSOLE is defined, then the log messages will be displayed on the system console. For example, the following */etc/default/su* file sends system messages to the file */usr/adm/sulog* and also displays them on the system console:

```
SULOG:/usr/adm/sulog
CONSOLE:/dev/console
```

The pathname */dev/console* is the usual name of the special file (device interface) for the console terminal (special files are discussed in detail in the section entitled "Devices," in Chapter 2, *The UNIX Way*).

History on the root Account

A simple way of retaining some information about what's been done as *root* is to give *root* a shell which supports a history mechanism (the C or Korn shell), and set the number of commands saved across login sessions to a large number in *root*'s initialization file. For example, the following commands will cause the last 200 commands entered by *root* to be saved:

```
set history = 200          C shell
set savehist = 200

export HISTSIZE=200        Korn shell
export HISTFILE=/var/adm/.rh
```

Under the C shell, commands are saved in the file ~/.history—/.history for *root*. Under the Korn shell, commands are written to the file named in the HISTFILE variable or to ~/.sh_history by default. Of course, a clever user can turn off the history feature, but it can also often be overlooked (especially if you don't put the command number in the prompt string).

Tracking User Activities

There are other utilities you can use to determine what users have been doing on the system, which will sometimes enable you to track down the cause of a security problem. These commands are listed in Table 5-4.

Table 5-4. Command Summary Utilities

Command	UNIX Versions	Displays Information About
last	BSD, XENIX, V.4, AIX 3.1, some V.3	User login sessions.
lastcomm	BSD, V.4, AIX 3.1	All commands executed (by user and TTY).
acctcom	System V, AIX 3.1	All commands executed (by user and TTY).
acctcms	System V, AIX 3.1	All commands executed (by time of day).

These commands draw their information from the system accounting files, the age of which determines the period of time that they cover. Note that accounting must be running on the system for any of them to be available (starting accounting is discussed in Chapter 13, *Accounting*).

The *last* command displays data for each time a user logged into the system. *last* may be optionally followed by a list of usernames and/or terminal names. If any arguments are specified, the report is limited to records pertaining to at least one of them (OR logic):

```
% last
martin    ttyp1    iago      Fri Sep 16 10:07    still logged in
ng        ttyp6              Fri Sep 16 10:00 - 10:03  (00:02)
martin    ttyp1    iago      Fri Sep 16 09:57 - 10:07  (00:09)
chavez    ttyp5              Fri Sep 16 09:29    still logged in
```

```
jackson     ttyp5                     Fri Sep 16 07:39 - 08:12  (00:32)

wtmp begins Thu Sep  1 07:15
% last chavez
chavez      ttyp5                     Fri Sep 16 09:29    still logged in
chavez      ttypc     duncan          Thu Sep 15 21:46 - 21:50  (00:04)
chavez      ttyp9                     Thu Sep 15 11:53 - 18:30  (07:23)
chavez      ttyq1                     Wed Sep 14 10:14 - 11:04  (00:45)
chavez      ttyp9                     Wed Sep 14 09:48 - 11:53 (1+02:04)
% last dalton console
dump        console                   Wed Sep 14 17:06 - 18:56  (01:49)
dalton      ttyq4     newton          Wed Sep 14 15:58 - 16:29  (00:31)
dalton      ttypc     newton          Tue Sep 13 22:50 - 00:19  (01:28)
dalton      console                   Tue Sep 13 17:30 - 17:49  (00:19)
ng          console                   Tue Sep 13 08:50 - 08:53  (00:02)

wtmp begins Thu Sep  1 07:15
```

last lists the username, ttyname, remote hostname (for remote logins), starting and ending times, and total connect time in hours for each login session. The ending time is replaced by the phrase "still logged in" for current sessions. At the end of each listing, *last* notes the date of its data file, */usr/adm/wtmp*, indicating the period covered by the report.

The username *reboot* may be used to list the times of system boots:

```
% last reboot
reboot      ~                         Fri Sep  9 17:36
reboot      ~                         Mon Sep  5 20:04

wtmp begins Thu Sep  1 07:15
```

On older System V systems, the file */usr/adm/lastlog* contains similar information to that supplied by *last* (on newer systems, however, this file may be binary or be replaced by a directory of binary files).

Under BSD, *lastcomm* displays information on previously executed commands. Its default display is the following:

```
% lastcomm
lpd       F   root      __         0.08 secs Mon Sep 19 15:06
date          martin    ttyp7      0.02 secs Mon Sep 19 15:06
sh            smith     ttyp3      0.05 secs Mon Sep 19 15:04
csh           ng        ttypf      3.45 secs Mon Sep 19 14:53
calculus  D   chavez    ttyq8      0.95 secs Mon Sep 19 15:09
more      X   ng        ttypf      0.17 secs Mon Sep 19 15:03
ruptime       martin    console    0.14 secs Mon Sep 19 15:03
mail      S   root      ttyp0      0.95 secs Fri Sep 16 10:46
```

The display lists the command name, flags associated with the process, the user-name and tty associated with it, the amount of CPU time consumed by its execution and the time the process exited. The flags may be one or more of:

S   Command was run by the superuser.

F   Command ran after a fork.

D   Command terminated with a core dump.

X   Command was terminated by a signal (often CTRL-C).

The command optionally accepts one or more image or command names, user-names, or terminal names to further limit the display. If more than one item is specified, then only lines which contain all of them will be listed (AND logic). For example, the following command lists entries for user *chavez* executing the image *calculus*:

```
% lastcomm chavez calculus
calculus      D  chavez   ttyq8     0.95 secs Mon Sep 19 15:09
calculus         chavez   ttyp3    10.33 secs Mon Sep 19 22:32
```

Under System V, the *acctcom* command produces similar information (output is shortened):

```
$ acctcom
COMMAND                        START     END       CPU
NAME       USER    TTYNAME    TIME      TIME      (SECS)
calculus   chavez  ttyq8      15:52:49  16:12:23   0.95
grep       martin  ttyq3      15:52:51  15:52:55   0.02
rm         root    tty02      15:52:55  15:55:56   0.01
```

acctcom has several useful options:

-u user   Limit the display to the specified user.

-g group   Limit the display to the specified group.

-l tty   Limit the display to /dev/*tty*.

-n pattern   Limit the display to lines containing *pattern*. The pattern can be a literal string or a regular expression. Often used to limit the display by command name.

-b   Display data in reverse chronological order.

If more than one option is specified, records must match all of them to be included (AND logic). For example, the following command displays *vi* commands run by *root*:

```
$ acctcom -a -u root -n vi /usr/adm/pacct
COMMAND                         START    END       CPU
NAME        USER    TTYNAME     TIME     TIME     (SECS)
vi          root    tty01       10:33:12 10:37:44  0.04
vi          root    ttyp2       12:34:29 13:51:47  0.11
vi          root    ttyp5       11:43:28 11:45:38  0.08
```

Unfortunately, *acctcom* doesn't display the date in each line like *lastcomm* does, but you can figure it out by knowing when its data file (*/usr/adm/pacct*) was created and watching the dates turn over in the display (records are in chronological order). If you're trying to track down a recent event, use the *-b* option.

So what can you do with these commands? Suppose you find a new UID 0 account in the password file and you know the file was all right yesterday. After checking its modification time, you can use the *su* log file to see who became *root* about that time; *last* will tell you if *root* was logged in directly at that time. Assuming *root* wasn't directly logged in, you can then use *lastcomm* or *acctcom* to find out who ran an editor at about the right time. You may not get conclusive proof as to who made the change, but it may help you to narrow the possibilities; you can then talk to those users in person. Of course, there are trickier ways of changing the password file that will evade detection by this method; there's no substitute for limiting access to the *root* account to trustworthy people. This example also illustrates the importance of detecting security problems right away (e.g., if you can't narrow down when the password file was changed very accurately, then it will be almost impossible to figure out who did it).

System V also provides the *acctcms* command (stored in */usr/lib/acct*), which lists statistics about the various commands that have been run. Its main security use is in listing commands run during offpeak hours (as defined in the file */usr/lib/acct/holidays*). If yours is a site that is pretty quiet after hours, then checking this listing periodically may turn up any suspicious activity. Here is an example of its use in this mode (output is shortened):

```
$ /usr/lib/acct/acctcms -a -o -n /usr/adm/pacct
            NON-PRIME TIME COMMAND SUMMARY
COMMAND     NUMBER      TOTAL       TOTAL
NAME        CMDS      KCOREMIN     CPU-MIN
ls          26          0.00        0.02
grep        21          0.80        0.01
more        15          0.10        0.03
. . .
sort         1          0.03        0.02
munchmunch   1          0.26        1.10
```

The *munchmunch* command might be worth looking into (for example, you could use *acctcom* to find out which user ran it).

Configuring BSD-style Error Logging

We'll close this chapter on system security by looking at a facility which lets you specify where and how some types of system messages are saved. One of the daemons started at boottime on BSD systems is *syslogd*, the system message logger. *syslogd* is also supported under V.4 and AIX 3.1, and on some V.3 systems. *syslogd* collects messages sent by various system processes and routes them to their final destination based on instructions given in its configuration file */etc/syslog.conf*. It is the way that an *su* log file is created, for example. Entries in */etc/syslog.conf* have the following format:

> *facility.level   destination*

where *facility* is the subsystem sending the message, *level* is the severity level of the message, and *destination* is the file, device, or username to send the message to. Multiple facility-level pairs may be included on one line by separating them with semicolons; multiple facilities may be specified with the same severity level by separating them with commas. An asterisk may be used as a wildcard in all three locations.

There are a multitude of defined facilities. The most important are:

kern   The kernel.

mail   The mail subsystem.

lpr   The printing subsystem.

daemon   System server processes.

auth   The login authentication system.

The severity levels are, in order of decreasing seriousness:

emerg   System panic.

alert   Serious error requiring immediate attention.

crit   Critical errors like hard device errors.

err   Errors.

warn   Warnings.

notice   Non-critical messages.

info   Informative messages.

In addition, the special levels *debug* and *none* may be used. Not all levels are used by all system facilities.

All of this will be much clearer once we look at a sample *syslog.conf* file:

```
*.err;auth.notice                    /dev/console
*.err;daemon,auth.notice;mail.crit   /usr/adm/messages
lpr.debug                            /usr/adm/lpd-errs
mail.debug                           /usr/spool/mqueue/syslog
*.alert                              root
*.emerg                              *
```

The first line prints all errors, and notices from the authentication system (indicating successful and unsuccessful *su* commands) on the console. The second line sends all errors, daemon and authentication system notices, and all critical errors from the mail system to the file */usr/adm/messages* (the conventional message file on BSD systems). The third and fourth lines send printer and mail system debug messages to their respective error files. The fifth line sends all alert messages to user *root*, and the sixth line sends all emergency messages to all users.

You may modify this file to suit the needs of your system. For example, to create a System V-style *sulog* file, add a line like the following to *syslog.conf*:

```
auth.notice                    /usr/adm/sulog
```

All messages are appended to log files; thus, you'll need to keep an eye on their size and truncate them periodically when they get too big. This topic is discussed in detail in the section entitled "Limiting the Growth of Log Files," in Chapter 8, *Filesystems and Disks*.

6

Automating Routine Tasks

Using Scripts Effectively
Periodic Program Execution: The cron
   Facility

This chapter discusses ways to automate various system management tasks. Automation offers many advantages over performing such tasks by hand, including:

* Greater reliability: tasks are performed in the same (correct) way every time. Once you have automated a task, its correct and complete performance no longer depends on your alertness or your memory.

* Guaranteed regularity: tasks can be performed according to whatever schedule seems appropriate and need not depend on your availability or even your presence.

* Enhanced system efficiency: time-consuming or resource-intensive tasks can be performed during off-hours, freeing the system for users during their normal work hours.

On UNIX systems, automation is accomplished via shell scripts and the *cron* facility, which are the subjects of the two major sections of this chapter.

In this section, we'll consider two system monitoring tasks as examples of creating and using administrative shell scripts. The discussions are meant to consider not only these tasks in themselves but also the process of and alternatives available when using scripts. All examples use the Bourne shell, but you can use any shell you choose; it's merely a UNIX prejudice that "real shell programmers use the Bourne shell," however prevalent that attitude may be.

Example: Password File Security

We discussed the various security issues surrounding the password file in Chapter 5, *Security*. The various commands used to check it and its contents could be combined easily in a shell script. Here is one version (named *ckpwd*):

```
#!/bin/sh
# ckpwd - check password file (run as root)
umask 077
cd /usr/local/bin/old    # move to dir. with stored passwd
echo ">>> Password file check for `date`"; echo ""

echo "*** Accounts without passwords:"
grep '^[^:]*::' /etc/passwd
if [ $? -eq 1 ]          # grep failed
    then
    echo "None found."
fi
echo ""

echo "*** Non-root UID=0 or GID=0 accounts:"
grep ':00*:' /etc/passwd | \
  awk -F: 'BEGIN         {n=0}
           $1!="root"    {print $0 ; n=1}
           END           {if (n==0) print "None found."}'
echo ""

sort </etc/passwd >tmp1
sort <opg >tmp2          # opg is the saved copy
echo "*** Accounts added:"
comm -23 tmp[1-2]        # lines only in /etc/passwd
echo ""
echo "*** Accounts deleted:"
comm -13 tmp[1-2]        # lines only in ./opg
echo ""
rm -f tmp[1-2]
```

```
echo "*** Password file protection:"
echo "-rw-r--r--  1 root      wheel           >>> correct values"
ls -lg /etc/passwd      # leave off "g" under System V

echo ""; echo ">>> End of report."; echo ""
```

The script surrounds each checking operation with *echo* and other commands designed to make the output more readable so that it can be scanned quickly for problems. For example, the *grep* command which searches the password file for non-root accounts with UID 0 is now preceded by an *echo* command which outputs a descriptive header, and it is piped to an *awk* command which removes the *root* entry from its output and displays the string "None found." if no other UID or GID 0 accounts are present:

```
echo "*** Non-root UID=0 or GID=0 accounts:"
grep ':00*:' /etc/passwd | \
   awk -F: 'BEGIN        {n=0}
           $1!="root"    {print $0 ; n=1}
           END           {if (n==0) print "None found."}'
echo ""
```

Instead of using *diff* to compare the current password file with the saved version, the script uses *comm* twice, to present the added and deleted lines separately (entries that have changed will appear in both lists). The script ends with a simple *ls* command; the administrator must manually compare its output to the string displayed by the preceding *echo* command. However, this comparison could be automated as well by piping *ls*'s output to *awk* and explicitly comparing the relevant fields to their correct values.

Here is some sample output from *ckpwd*:

```
>>> Password file check for Fri Jul 19 15:48:26 EDT 1991

*** Accounts without passwords:
None found.

*** Non-root UID=0 or GID=0 accounts:
badboy:lso9/.7sJUhhs:000:203:Bad Boy:/u/bb:/bin/csh

*** Accounts added:
chavez:9Sl.sd/i7snso:190:20:Rachel Chavez:/u/chavez:/bin/csh
wang:19jsTHn7Hg./a:308:302:Rick Wang:/u/wang:/bin/sh

*** Accounts deleted:
chavez:Al9ddmL.3qX9o:190:20:Rachel Chavez:/u/chavez:/bin/csh

*** Password file protection:
-rw-r--r--  1 root      wheel      >>> correct values
-rw-r--r--  1 root      wheel      1847 Jul 11 22:38 /etc/passwd

>>> End of report.
```

If you don't like all the bells and whistles, the script needn't be this fancy. For example, its two *sort*, two *comm*, and five other commands in the section comparing the current and saved password files could easily be replaced by the *diff* command we looked at in Chapter 5, *Security*, (and possibly one *echo* command to print a header). In the extreme case, the entire script could consist of just the four commands we looked at previously:

```
#!/bin/sh  # minimalist version of ckpwd
grep '^[^:]*::' /etc/passwd
grep ':00*:' /etc/passwd
diff /etc/passwd /usr/local/bin/old/opg
ls -lg /etc/passwd
```

How much complexity is used is up your to own taste and free time. More complex means it takes longer to debug.

Whatever approach you take, *ckpwd* needs to be run regularly to be effective. This can be accomplished via the *cron* facility, described later in this chapter.

Example: Monitoring Disk Usage

It seems that no matter how much disk storage a system has, the users' needs (or wants) will eventually exceed it. Keeping an eye on the situation is a very important part of system management, and this monitoring task is well-suited to automation via shell scripts. The following commands are helpful in this task:

df   Show disk use by physical device.

du   Show disk use under a directory.

These commands are discussed in detail in the section entitled "Managing Disk Space Usage," in Chapter 8, *Filesystems and Disks*. Here are some brief examples using them (from a BSD system):

```
% df                         Show how full the disks are.
Filesystem    kbytes    used    avail capacity  Mounted on
/dev/disk0a   889924  576340  224588    72%     /
/dev/disk4e   923044  806004   24732    97%     /rocks
% du /u/chavez/progs     Show space used under this directory.
43        /u/chavez/progs/new
21        /u/chavez/progs/old
123       /u/chavez/progs
% du -s ~chavez          Just give the total blocks used.
34823     /u/chavez
```

The script we'll consider in this section—*ckdsk*—is designed to compare current disk use with what it was yesterday and to save today's data for comparison tomorrow. We'll build the script up gradually, starting with this simple version:

```
#!/bin/sh
if [ ! -s du.sav ] ; then
    echo "ckdsk: can't find old data file du.sav."
    exit 1
fi
du /iago/home/martin > du.log
cat du.log | xargs -n2 cmp_size 40 100 du.sav
mv -f du.log du.sav
```

After making sure yesterday's data is available, this script checks the disk usage under the directory */iago/home/martin* using *du*, saving the output to the file *du.log*. Each line of *du.log* is fed by *xargs* to another script,[*] *cmp_size*, which does the actual comparison, passing it the arguments 40, 100, and "du.sav" as well as the line from the *du* command. Thus, the first invocation of *cmp_size* would look something like this:

```
cmp_size 40 100 du.sav 876 /iago/home/martin/bin
```
        ↑ *Output from du begins here.*

On systems without *xargs* (usually BSD systems), the following commands can substitute for the *cat* command piped to *xargs* shown previously:

```
cat du.log | \
awk "{print \"cmp_size 40 100 du.sav\", "'$1, $2}' >tmp.sh
. tmp.sh
rm tmp.sh
```

The *awk* command constructs each *cmp_size* command explicitly, placing them into *tmp.sh*, which is then executed via the shell's dot command (which reads a file's contents into the command stream, like the C shell's *source* command).

ckdsk ends by replacing the old data file with the saved output from today's *du* command, in preparation for running again tomorrow.

This simple *ckdsk* script is not very general; it works only on a single directory. After looking at *cmp_size* in detail, we'll consider ways of expanding its usefulness. Here is *cmp_size*:

```
#!/bin/sh
#   $1 (limit)=min. size for new dirs to be included in report
#   $2 (dlimit)=min. size change for old dirs to be included
#   $3 (sfile)=pathname for file with yesterday's data
#   $4 (csize)=current directory size
```

[*]On some systems, *cmp_size* could be a function defined in *ckdsk*; on others, however, *xargs* won't accept a function as the command to run.

```
#    $5 (file)=pathname of directory
#    osize=previous size (extracted from sfile)
#    diff=size difference between yesterday & today
if [ $# -lt 5 ] ; then
    echo "Usage: cmp.sh newlim oldlim data_file size dir"
    exit 1
fi
# save initial parameters
limit=$1; dlimit=$2; sfile=$3; file=$5; csize=$4
# get yesterday's data
osize=`grep "$file\$" $sfile | awk '{print \$1}'`
if [ -z "$osize" ] ; then              # it's a new dir.
    if [ $csize -ge $limit ] ; then   # report if size >= limit
        echo "new\t$csize\t$file"
    fi
    exit 0
fi
# compute the size change from yesterday
if [ $osize -eq $csize ]
then
    exit 0
elif [ $osize -gt $csize ]
then
    diff=`expr $osize - $csize`
else
    diff=`expr $csize - $osize`
fi
# check if size change is big enough to report on
if [ $diff -ge $dlimit ] ; then
    echo "$osize\t$csize\t$file"
fi
```

cmp_size first checks to see that it was passed the right number of arguments. Then it sets its arguments to shell variables for readability. The first two parameters are cutoff values for new and existing directories respectively. If the size of the directory specified as its fifth parameter has changed by an amount greater than the cutoff value, *cmp_size* will print its name and old and new sizes; otherwise, *cmp_size* will return silently. This is to allow you to tell *cmp_size* how much of a change is too small to be interesting (since you don't necessarily care about minor disk usage changes).

cmp_size finds yesterday's size by *grep*-ing for the directory name in the data file specified as its third parameter (*du.sav* is what *ckdsk* passes it). If *grep* didn't find the directory in the data file, it's a new one, and *cmp_size* then compares its size to the new directory cutoff (passed in as its first argument), displaying its name and size if it is large enough.

If *grep* returns anything, *cmp_size* then computes the size change for the directory by subtracting the smaller of the old size (from the file and stored in the variable *osize*) and the current size (passed in as the fourth parameter and stored in *csize*) from the larger. *cmp_size* then compares the size difference to the old directory cutoff (passed in as its second argument), and displays the old and new sizes if it is large enough.

This version of *cmp_size* reports on directories that either increased or decreased in size by the amount of the cutoff. If you are only interested in size increases, you could replace the *if* statement which computes the *diff* variable with a much simpler one:

```
if [ $osize -le $csize ]
then
   exit 0        # only care if it's bigger
else
   diff=`expr $osize - $csize`
fi
```

Unlike the simple version of *ckdsk*, *cmp_size* is fairly general; it could also be used, for example, to process output from the *quot* command (described in "quot: Report Usage by User (BSD, XENIX, and V.4)," in Chapter 8, *Filesystems and Disks*.

One way to make *ckdsk* more useful is to enable it to check more than one starting directory, with different cutoffs for each one. Here is a version which can do that:

```
#!/bin/sh
du_it()
{
# $1 = cutoff in blocks for new directories
# $2 = cutoff as block change for old directories
# $3 = starting directory; $4 = flags to du
du $4 $3 > du.tmp
cat du.tmp | xargs -n2 cmp_size $1 $2 du.sav
cat du.tmp >> du.log; rm du.tmp
}

umask 077
rm -f du.log du.tmp 2>&1 >/dev/null
if [ ! -s du.sav ] ; then
   echo "run_cmp: can't find old data file."
   exit 1
fi
echo "Daily disk usage report for `date`"; echo ''
df
echo ''; echo "Old\tNew"
echo "Size\tSize\tDirectory Name"
echo "------------------------------------------------------------"
du_it 40 100 /iago/home/martin
du_it 1 1 /usr/lib
du_it 1 1000 /u/\* -s
```

```
echo "----------------------------------------------------------"
echo ''
mv -f du.log du.sav
exit 0
```

This script uses a function named *du_it* to perform the *du* command and pass its output to *cmp_size* using *xargs*. The function takes four arguments: the cutoffs for old and new directories (for *cmp_size*), the starting directory for the *du* command, and any additional flags to pass to *du* (optional).

du_it saves *du*'s output into a temporary file, *du.tmp*, which it appends to the file *du.log* afterwards. *du.log* thus accumulates the data from multiple directory checks and will eventually become the new saved data file, replacing yesterday's version.

The script proper begins by removing any old temporary files from previous runs and making sure its data file (still hardwired as *du.sav*) is available. It then runs *df* and prints some header lines for the output from *cmp_size*. This version of the script then calls *du_it* three times:

```
du_it 40 100 /iago/home/martin
du_it 1 1 /usr/lib
du_it 1 1000 /u/\* -s
```

It will run *du* and compare its output to the saved data for the directories */iago/home/martin*, */usr/lib*, and all of the subdirectories of */u*, passing the *du* command the *-s* option in the latter case. In the third command, the wildcard is passed through to the actual *du* command line by quoting it to *du_it*. Different cutoffs are used for each call. When checking */usr/lib*, this version asks to be told about any change in the size of any directory (size or size change greater than or equal to one). In contrast, when checking the users' home directories under */u*, the report will include new directories of any size but only existing directories that changed size by at least 1000 blocks.

ckdsk ends by moving the accumulated output file, *du.log*, on to the saved data file, *du.sav*, saving the current data for future comparisons.

Here is some sample output from *ckdsk*:

```
Daily disk usage report for Tue Jul 30 09:52:46 EDT 1991

Filesystem        kbytes     used    avail capacity Mounted-on
/dev/dsk/c1d1s0    81952    68848    13104    84%   /
/dev/dsk/c1d1s2   373568   354632    18936    94%   /u
/dev/dsk/c1d2s8   667883   438943   228940    66%   /genome

Old    New
Size   Size    Directory Name
-----------------------------------------------------------
348    48      /iago/home/martin/g94
```

```
new       52     /iago/home/martin/test
2000     1012    /iago/home/martin
new       912    /usr/lib/acct.bio
355       356    /usr/lib/spell
34823    32797    /u/chavez
9834     3214     /u/ng
new       300     /u/park
```

The *echo* commands set off the output from *cmp_size* and make it easy to scan.

This version of *ckdsk* requires new *du* commands to be added by hand. The script could be refined further by allowing this information to be external as well. Similarly, the script currently checks all users' home directories. If only some of them need to be checked, then the final *du* command could be replaced by a loop like this one:

```
for user in chavez havel martin ng smith tedesco ; do
  du_it 1 1000 /u/$user -s
done
```

The *cron* facility is also the most sensible way to run *ckdsk*; we'll look at how it might do so in the section entitled "Execution Scheduling," later in this chapter.

Periodic Program Execution: The cron Facility

cron is a UNIX facility that allows you to schedule programs for periodic execution. For example, you can use *cron* to call a particular *uucp* site every hour, to clean up editor backup files every night, or to perform any number of other tasks. Under *cron*, administrative functions are performed silently, without any intervention by the system's users. However, *cron* is not a general facility for scheduling program execution off-hours; for the latter, use the *at* command.

For administrative purposes, *cron* is useful for running commands and scripts according to a preset schedule. *cron* can send their output to a log file or to any username via the mail system.

Execution Scheduling

The *cron* system is serviced by the *cron* daemon. What to run and when to run it are specified to *cron* by *crontab entries*, which are stored in the system's *cron* schedule. Under BSD, this consists of the files */usr/lib/crontab* and */usr/lib/crontab.local*; either file may be used to store crontab entries. Both are ASCII files and may be modified with any text editor. Since only *root* usually has access to these files, all *cron* scheduling must go through the system administrator. This can be either an advantage or a disadvantage, depending on the needs and personality of your site.

Under System V (and AIX 3.1, XENIX, and SunOS), any user may add entries to the *cron* schedule. Crontab entries are stored in separate files for each user in the directory */usr/spool/cron/crontabs* (or */var/spool/cron/crontabs* for V.4 and SunOS); users' *crontab* files are named after their username (for example, *root*'s *crontab* file is */usr/spool/cron/crontabs/root*). The *crontab* files are not edited directly by ordinary users, but are placed there with the *crontab* command (described later in this section).

crontab entries direct *cron* to run commands at regular intervals. Each one-line entry in the *crontab* file has the following format:

> *mins hrs day-of-month month weekday username cmd*   *(BSD)*
> *mins hrs day-of-month month weekday cmd*   *(System V)*

Spaces separate the fields. However, the final field, *cmd*, can contain spaces within it (i.e., the *cmd* field consists of everything after the space following *weekday*); the other fields must not contain spaces. The *username* field is used in the BSD version only and specifies the username under which to run the command. Under System V, commands are run by the user who owns the *crontab* in which they appear (and for whom it is named).

The first five fields specify the times at which *cron* should execute *cmd*. Their meanings are described in Table 6-1.

Table 6-1. Crontab Entry Time Fields

Field	Meaning	Range
mins	The minutes after the hour.	0-59
hrs	The hours of the day.	0-23 (0 = midnight)
day-of-month	The day within a month.	1-31
month	The month of the year.	1-12
weekday	The day of the week.	1-7 (1 = Monday) *BSD*
		0-6 (0=Sunday) *System V*

An entry in any of these fields can be a single number, a pair of numbers separated by a dash (indicating a range of numbers), a comma-separated list of numbers and ranges, or an asterisk (a wildcard that represents all valid values for that field).

If the first character in an entry is a number sign (#), *cron* will treat the entry as a comment and ignore it. This is an easy way to temporarily disable an entry without permanently deleting it.

Here are some example crontab entries (shown in System V format):

```
0,15,30,45 * * * *  (echo -n '    '; date; echo "") >/dev/console
0,10,20,30,40,50 7-18 * * * /usr/lib/atrun
0 0 * * *   find / -name "*.bak" -type f -atime +7 -exec rm {} \;
0 4 * * *   /bin/sh /usr/adm/ckdsk 2>&1 >/usr/adm/disk.log
0 2 * * *   /bin/sh /usr/adm/ckpwd 2>&1 | mail root
30 3 * * 1 /bin/csh /usr/lib/uucp/uu.weekly 2>&1 >/dev/null
#30 2 * * 0,6  /usr/lib/newsbin/news.weekend
```

The first entry displays the date on the console terminal every fifteen minutes (on the quarter hour); notice that multiple commands are enclosed in parentheses in order to redirect their output as a group. (Technically, this says to run the commands together in a subshell.) The second entry runs */usr/lib/atrun* every ten minutes from 7:00 a.m. to 6:00 p.m. daily. The third entry runs a *find* command to remove all *.bak* files not accessed in seven days.

The fourth and fifth lines run a shell script every day, at 4:00 a.m. and 2:00 a.m., respectively. The shell to execute the script is specified explicitly on the command line in both cases; the system default shell, usually the Bourne shell, is used if none is explicitly specified. Both lines' entries redirect standard output and standard error, sending it to a file in one case and mailing it to *root* in the other.

The sixth entry executes a C shell script named *uu.weekly*, stored in */usr/lib/uucp*, at 3:30 a.m. on Monday mornings. Notice that the command format—specifically the output redirection—is for the Bourne shell even though the script itself will be run under the C shell. The final entry would run the command */usr/lib/newsbin/news.weekend* at 2:30 a.m. on Saturday and Sunday mornings if it were not disabled.

The final three active entries illustrate three output-handling alternatives: redirecting it to a file, piping it through mail, and discarding it to */dev/null*. If no output redirection is performed, the output is sent via mail to the user who ran the command.

The *cmd* field can be any UNIX command or group of commands (properly separated with semicolons). The entire crontab entry can be arbitrarily long, but it must be a single physical line in the file.

If the command contains a percent sign (%), *cron* will use any text following this sign as standard input for *cmd*. Additional percent signs can be used to subdivide this text into lines. For example, the following crontab entry:

```
30 11 31 12 * /etc/wall%Happy New Year!%Let's make next year great!
```

runs the *wall* command at 11:30 a.m. on December 31st, using the text:

```
Happy New Year!
Let's make next year great!
```

as standard input. This entry also illustrates how *cron* makes use of the date fields under BSD. On these systems, if both the date in the month and day of the week are specified, then the crontab entry is only run when that date falls on one of the specified days of the week.

By contrast, on System V-based systems and under SunOS, the day of the week and day of the month fields are effectively OR'ed: if both are filled in, then the entry is run on that day of the month *and* on matching days of the week. Thus, the following entry would run on January first and every Monday on these systems:

```
* * 1 1 1 /usr/local/bin/test55
```

cron reads the crontab file(s) every minute to see whether or not there have been changes. Therefore, any change to its schedule will take effect within one minute.

The *cron* command starts the *cron* program. It has no options. Once started, *cron* never terminates. It is normally started automatically by one of the system initialization scripts.

Adding Crontab Entries

Under BSD, new crontab entries are created simply by editing one of the crontab files. Either crontab file may be used, although non-system-related entries may be separated out into the *crontab.local* file if desired.

Under System V, AIX 3.1, XENIX, and SunOS, the normal way to create crontab entries is with the *crontab* command, in the following manner. First, the desired crontab entries are created in a text file (usually with an editor). Then, you run the *crontab* command to install the file in the *cron* spool area. For example, if user *chavez* executes the command below, the file *mycron* will be installed as */usr/spool/cron/crontabs/chavez*:

```
$ crontab mycron
```

If *chavez* had previously installed crontab entries, they will be *replaced* by those in *mycron*; thus, any current entries that *chavez* wishes to keep must also be present in *mycron*.

The *-l* option to *crontab* lists the current crontab entries, and redirecting its output to a file will allow them to be captured and edited:

```
$ crontab -l >mycron
$ vi mycron
$ crontab mycron
```

The *-r* option will remove all current crontab entries. Under SunOS, *crontab* has an additional *-e* option which lets you directly edit your current crontab entries in a single step.

The preceding discussion describes the normal, officially recommended way of creating crontab entries, a somewhat tedious process (except under SunOS). However, the files in the *cron* spool area are just plain ASCII files. Users can't edit them directly, but you can as *root*, greatly speeding up changing them for administrative purposes.*

Under both System V and BSD, the system administrator must consider what user should execute each command run by *cron*. Under BSD, the sixth field of a crontab entry is the username under which to run the command. Under System V, crontab entries must be added to the correct *crontab* file. The following list describes common system users and the sorts of crontab entries they conventionally control:

root   General system functions and filesystem cleanup.

adm   Accounting.

uucp   *uucp* scripts.

---

*On some systems, *crontab* files are write-protected even against their owner. In this case, it may be just as fast to use the *crontab* command as to change a crontab file's protection and then edit it.

The System V cron Log File

Under System V and XENIX, cron will keep a log of its activity if the variable CRONLOG is set to YES in the file */etc/default/cron*:

    CRONLOG=YES

Logging will be sent to the file */usr/lib/cron/log* under V.3 and XENIX and to the file */usr/sbin/cron.d/log* under V.4. Under some System V versions, logging is automatic (and there is no CRONLOG variable). Under AIX 3.1, logging is automatic and goes to the file */usr/adm/cron/log*. If logging is enabled, this file should be periodically truncated, as it grows extremely quickly.

Using cron to Automate System Administration

The sample crontab entries we looked at previously provide some simple examples of using *cron* to automate various system tasks. *cron* provides the ideal way to run scripts like *ckpwd* and *ckdsk* according to a fixed schedule.

Another common way to use *cron* for regular administrative tasks is through the use of a series of scripts designed to run every night, once a week, and once a month, often named *daily*, *weekly*, and *monthly*, respectively. The commands in *daily* would need to get done every night (more specialized scripts *ckpwd* and *ckdsk* could be run from it); the other two would handle tasks to be performed less frequently.

Here are examples of what each one might do:

* *Daily*:

    — Remove junk files more than 3 days old from */tmp* and other scratch directories.

    — Run accounting summary commands.

    — Run *calendar*.

    — Rotate log files cycled daily.

    — Take snapshots of the system with *df* and *ps*.

    — Perform daily security monitoring.

* *Weekly*:

    — Remove old junk files from the system.

    — Rotate log files cycled weekly.

— Rebuild the *catman* database for use by *man -k*.

— Run *fsck -n* to list any disk problems.

• *Monthly*:

— List files not accessed that month.

— Produce monthly accounting reports.

— Rotate log files cycled monthly.

Additional or other activities might make more sense on your system. The scripts might be run late at night:

```
0 3 * * *   /bin/sh /usr/adm/daily   2>&1 | mail root
0 2 * * 1   /bin/sh /usr/adm/weekly  2>&1 | mail root
0 1 1 * *   /bin/sh /usr/adm/monthly 2>&1 | mail root
```

In this example, the *daily* script runs every night at 3:00 a.m., *weekly* runs every Monday at 2:00 a.m., and *monthly* runs on the first day of every month at 1:00 a.m.

cron need not only be used for tasks to be performed periodically forever, year after year. It can also be used to run a command repeatedly over a limited period of time, after which the crontab entry would be disabled or removed. For example, if you were trying to track certain kinds of security problems, you might want to use *cron* to run a script repeatedly to gather data. As a concrete example, consider this short script to check for large numbers of unsuccessful login attempts under AIX 3.1 (although the script applies only to AIX 3.1, the general principles are useful on all systems):

```
#!/bin/sh
date >> /usr/adm/bl
egrep '^[^*].*:$|gin_coun' /etc/security/user | \
  awk 'BEGIN {n=0}
       {if (NF>1 && $3>3) {print s,$0; n=1}}
       {s=$0}
       END {if (n==0) {print "Everything ok."}}' \
  >> /usr/adm/bl
```

This script writes the date and time to the file */usr/adm/bl* and then checks */etc/security/user* for any user with more than three unsuccessful login attempts. If you suspected someone was trying to break in to your system, you could run this script via *cron* every, ten minutes, in the hopes of isolating what accounts were being targeted:

```
0,10,20,30,40,50 * * * * /bin/sh /usr/adm/ckbdlg
```

Similarly, if you are having a performance problem, you could use *cron* to automatically run various system performance monitoring commands at regular intervals to track performance problems over time.

cron Security Issues

cron's security issues are of two main types: making sure the system crontab files are secure, and making sure unauthorized users don't run commands using it. The first problem may be addressed by setting (if necessary) and checking the ownership and protection on the crontab files appropriately. (In particular, they should not be world-writable.) Naturally, they should be included in any filesystem security monitoring that you do. Addressing the second problem is the subject of the next section.

Limiting Access to cron Under System V, XENIX, and SunOS

The files *cron.allow* and *cron.deny*,* stored in */usr/spool/cron* under V.3, */var/spool/cron* under SunOS, */usr/lib/cron* under XENIX, */usr/adm/cron* under AIX 3.1, and */etc/cron.d* under V.4, enable you to restrict access to *cron*. Both files contain lists of usernames, one per line. Access to *cron* is controlled in the following way:

- If *cron.allow* exists, then a username must be listed within it in order to access *cron*.

- If *cron.allow* does not exist and *cron.deny* exists, then any user not listed in *cron.deny* may access *cron*. *cron.deny* may be empty to allow unlimited access to *cron*.

- If neither file exists, then only root may access *cron*.

Under BSD, access to *cron* is controlled solely via the protection on the crontab files. Thus, it is imperative that they be owned by *root* and not writable by anyone other than the owner. They should be included in any filesystem security monitoring that you do.

---

*Access to the *at* command may be similarly controlled with the files *at.{allow,deny}*.

Limiting Access to cron Under AIX 3.1

AIX 3.1 handles *cron* access in a different manner. The *daemon* user account attribute determines whether users can use the *cron* and system resource controller (*src*) facilities. The value of this attribute is stored in the stanza for each user in the file */etc/security/user*; it is a binary attribute with legal values of "yes" or "no" (and their equivalents).

To prevent a user from using *cron* and *src*, you can either edit the user attributes file directly or use the *chuser* command. For example, the following command disables *cron* and *src* access for user *chavez*:

```
# chuser daemon=no chavez
```

To determine a user's current status, check */etc/security/user*:

```
chavez:
    admin = false
    unsuccessful_login_count = 0
    time_last_login = 679723651
    daemon = no
```

If a user's stanza in */etc/security/user* contains no *daemon* keyword, then it defaults to "yes."

7

Managing System Resources

Monitoring System Load
Controlling Execution Priorities
Process Resource Limits
Managing Memory
Managing Disk Usage with Disk Quotas
(BSD and V.4)

This chapter discusses the tools and facilities UNIX offers for managing the system's CPU and disk resources (including some of the limitations inherent in the UNIX approach). A large part of managing any system resource is knowing its current status and usage, and so we'll spend some time looking at ways to monitor resource and use and to track it over time. At appropriate points, we will note the effects that various conditions and options can have on system performance, but considering system performance in itself—and how to optimize it—is a vast topic beyond the scope of this book. I recommend the Nutshell Handbook *System Performance Tuning* (O'Reilly & Associates, 1990) as an excellent treatment of this subject.

Monitoring System Load

Processes are to system performance what files are to system security: the central entity over which the administrator has control. Managing CPU resources is to a great extent equivalent to managing processes. UNIX provides the ability to monitor process execution and, to a limited extent, specify their execution priorities.

By doing so, you control how CPU time is allocated. For example, you can expedite certain jobs at the expense of all others, or you can maintain interactive response times by forcing large jobs to run at lowered priority. This section discusses UNIX processes and the tools available for monitoring and controlling process execution.

The BSD command *uptime*, also available under V.4, AIX 3.1, and some V.3 implementations, will give you a rough estimate of the system load:

```
% uptime
3:24pm up 2 days, 2:41, 16 users, load average: 1.90, 1.43, 1.33
```

uptime reports the current time, the amount of time the system has been up, and three load average figures. The load average is a rough measure of CPU use. These three figures report the average number of processes active during the last minute, the last five minutes, and the last 15 minutes. High load averages usually mean that the system is being used heavily and the response time is correspondingly slow. Note that the system's load average does not take into account the priorities of the processes that are running.

What's high? As usual, that depends on your system. Ideally, you'd like a load average under, say, 3, but that's not always possible given what some systems are required to do. Ultimately, "high" means high enough so that you don't need *uptime* to tell you that the system is overloaded—you can tell from its response time.

Furthermore, different systems will behave differently under the same load average. For example, on some workstations, running a single CPU-bound background job at the same time as X windows will bring response to a crawl even though the load average remains quite "low." In the end, load averages are only significant when they differ from whatever is "normal" on your system.

The *ps* command gives a more complete picture of system activity. This utility produces a report summarizing execution statistics for current processes. From an administrative point of view, it is useful to display a lot of data about all of the processes currently running on the system; the options required to do this differ between BSD and System V. Under BSD, the command is *ps -aux*, which produces a table of all processes, arranged in order of decreasing CPU usage at the moment when the *ps* command was executed. It is often useful to pipe this output to *head*, which will display the most active processes:

```
% ps -aux | head -5
USER      PID %CPU %MEM   SZ  RSS TTY STAT  TIME COMMAND
martin  12923 74.2 22.5  223  376 p5  R     2:12 f77 -o foo foo.F
chavez  16725 10.9 50.8 1146 1826 p6  R N  56:04 g94 <Hg0.dat
ng      17026  3.5  1.2  354  240 co  I     0:19 vi benzene.txt
gull     7997  0.2  0.3  142   46 p3  S     0:04 csh
```

The meanings of the fields (as well as others displayed by the *-l* option to *ps*) in this output are given in Table 7-1.

The first line in the previous example shows that user *martin* is running a FORTRAN compilation. This process has PID 12923 and is currently running or runnable. User *chavez*'s process (PID 17026), executing the program *g94*, is also running or runnable, though at a lowered priority. From this display, it's obvious who is using most system resources at this instant: *martin* and *chavez* have about 85% of the CPU and 73% of the memory between them. However, although it does display total CPU time, *ps* does not average the %CPU or %MEM values over time in any way.

Table 7-1. ps Command Output Fields in a Nutshell

Column*	Contents
USER (BSD)	Username of process owner.
UID (System V)	Username of process owner.
PID	Process ID.
%CPU	Estimated fraction of CPU consumed (BSD).
%MEM	Estimated fraction of system memory consumed (BSD).
SZ	Virtual memory used in K (BSD) or pages (System V).
RSS	Real memory used (in same units as SZ).
TT, TTY	Terminal port associated with process.
STAT (BSD), S (System V)	Current process state; one (or more under BSD) of:
R	Running or runnable.
S	Sleeping.
I	Idle (BSD). Intermediate state (System V).
T	Stopped.
Z	Zombie process.
D (BSD)	Disk wait.
P (BSD)	Page wait.
X (System V)	Growing: waiting for memory.
K (AIX 3.1)	Available kernel process.
W (BSD)	Swapped out.
N (BSD)	Niced: execution priority lowered.
> (BSD)	Execution priority artificially raised.

Table 7-1. ps Command Output Fields in a Nutshell (continued)

Column*	Contents
TIME	Total CPU time used.
COMMAND	Command line being executed (truncated).
STIME (System V)	Time or date process started.
START (SunOS)	Time or date process started.
C (System V), CP (BSD)	Short term CPU-use factor; used by scheduler for computing execution priority (PRI below).
F	Flags associated with process (see *ps* manual page).
PPID	Parent's PID.
PRI	Actual execution priority (recomputed dynamically).
NI	Process nice number.
WCHAN	Event process is waiting for.

*Some vendors add other fields, such as the processor number for multiprocessors (e.g., the L field in *ps -l* output under Stardent UNIX) and additional or different process states (as in AIX 3.1's K code listed above). These codes contradict one another at times: for example, the 0 code under Stardent UNIX means a process that is actually running (and R means runnable) while 0 under AIX 3.1 means a nonexistent process.

A vaguely similar listing is produced by the System V *ps -ef* command:

```
$ ps -ef
   UID   PID  PPID   C    STIME    TTY   TIME CMD
   root     0     0   0 09:36:35     ?   0:00 sched
   root     1     0   0 09:36:35     ?   0:02 /etc/init
   . . .
   gull  7997     1  10 09:49:32  ttyp3   0:04 csh
 martin 12923 11324   9 10:19:49  ttyp5  56:12 f77 -o foo foo.F
 chavez 16725 16652  15 17:02:43  ttyp6  10:04 g94 <Hg0.dat >Hg0.log
     ng 17026 17012  14 17:23:12 console   0:19 vi benzene.txt
```

The columns hold the username, process ID, parent's PID (the PID of the process that created it), the current scheduler value, the time the process started, its associated terminal, its accumulated CPU time, and the command it is running. Note that the ordering is by PID, not resource usage.

AIX 3.1's version of the *ps* command supports both BSD and System V options. The BSD options are not preceded by a hyphen (which is a legal syntax variation under BSD), and the System V options are. Thus, under AIX 3.1, *ps -au* ≠ *ps au*. The command is the System V version, however, even if its output is displayed with BSD column headings. Thus, *ps aux* output is displayed in PID rather than %CPU order.

ps is also useful in pipes; a common use is:

```
% ps -aux | grep chavez
```

to see what user *chavez* has currently running.

Controlling Execution Priorities

A UNIX process has two priority numbers associated with it:

- Its *nice number*, which is its requested execution priority with respect to other processes and is settable by the process's owner and by *root*. This value appears in the NI column in *ps -l* listings.

- Its current (actual) execution priority, which is computed and dynamically updated by the operating system, taking into account the process's nice number, how much CPU time it has had recently, what other processes are runnable and their priorities, and other factors. This value appears in the PRI column in *ps -l* listings.

Under BSD, nice numbers range between -20 and 20, with -20 being the "highest" priority (the default priority is 0); under V.3, nice numbers range from 0 to 39 (the default is 20), with 0 again being the priority which will execute soonest (this changes under V.4, as we'll see). For UNIX, less is truly more. Only the superuser can specify nice numbers lower than the default. Interactive shells run at the default level.

Any user can be "nice" and decrease the priority of a processes he owns by increasing its nice number. Only the superuser can decrease the nice number of a process. This prevents users from increasing their own priorities and thereby using more than their share of the system's resources. There are several ways to specify a job's execution priority. First, there are two commands that users can use to initiate a process at lowered priority: the *nice* command built into the C shell and the general UNIX command *nice*, usually stored in */bin* (or */usr/bin*). These commands both work the same way, but have slightly different syntaxes:

```
% nice [+|-n] command
% /bin/nice -[[-]n] command
```

In the built-in C shell version of *nice*, if an explicitly signed number is given as its first argument, it specifies the amount the command's priority will differ from the default nice number; if no number is specified, the default offset is +4. With */bin/nice*, the offset from the default nice number is specified as its option and so is preceded by a hyphen; the default offset is +10, and positive numbers need not include a plus sign. Thus, the following commands are equivalent, despite looking very different:

```
% nice +6 bigjob
$ /bin/nice -6 bigjob
```

Both commands result in *bigjob* having a nice number of 6 under BSD and 26 under V.3. Similarly, the following commands both raise *bigjob*'s priority five steps above the default level (to -5 under BSD and 15 under V.3):

```
# nice -5 bigjob
# /bin/nice --5 bigjob
```

BSD and System V nice numbers always differ by 20, but identical commands have equivalent effects on the two systems.

The *-l* option to *ps* (either V.3 or BSD—the output varies only slightly) may be used to display a process' nice number and current execution priority. Here is some output from a SunOS system:

```
% ps -l
   F UID  PID  PPID CP PRI NI  SZ  RSS WCHAN        COMMAND
8201 371 8390  8219  0   1  0  24  184 socket . . . rlogin iago
8201 371 8391  8219  4   3  4  24  184 pause   . . . big_cmd
8201   0 8394     1  0  15 -5  24  184 select . . . imp_cmd
```

The column headed NI displays each process' nice number. The column to its immediate left, labeled PRI, shows the process' current actual execution priority.

Some UNIX implementations will automatically reduce the priority of processes that run for longer than 10 minutes of user CPU time. The *ps* command reports total CPU time (user time plus system time); thus, its display will usually indicate a total CPU time of more than 10 minutes when this happens.

Processes inherit the priority of their parent when they are created. However, changing the priority of the parent process does not change the priorities of its children. Therefore, increasing a process's priority number may have no effect if this process has created one or more subprocesses. If the parent process spends most of its time waiting for its children, changing the parent's priority will have little or no effect on the system's performance.

Changing a Process's Nice Number

When the system's load is high, you may wish to force CPU-intensive processes to run at a lower priority. This frees more time for interactive jobs like editing, and generally keeps users happy. Alternatively, you may wish to devote most of the system's time to a few critical processes, letting others finish when they will. The *renice* command may be used to change the priority of running processes. Introduced in BSD, *renice* is also supported under V.4. Only root may use *renice* to increase the execution priority of a process (i.e., lower its nice number). Its syntax is:

```
# renice new-nice-number pid
```

where *new-nice-number* is a valid nice number, and *pid* is a process identification number. For example, the command:

```
# renice 5 8201
```

sets the nice number of process 8201 to 5, lowering its priority by five steps.

CAUTION

Giving a process an extremely high priority may interfere with the operating system's own operation.

AIX 3.1 uses the V.3-style priority system, running from 0 (high) to 40 (low). It does support a *renice* command, however. For *renice* under AIX 3.1, the new nice number is still specified on a scale from -20 to 20; it is translated internally into the 0-40 scheme actually used. This can make for some bizarre output at times:

```
# renice 10 3769
3769: old priority 0, new priority 10
# ps -l -p 3769
       F S UID  PID PPID C PRI NI ADDR  SZ   WCHAN   TTY TIME CMD
200801 S 371 3769 8570 0 70   30 2aca  84 1d79098 pts/1 0:00 c12
```

The *renice* command reports its action in terms of BSD nice numbers, but the *ps* display shows the real nice number.

Changing Process Priorities Under V.4

V.4 by default uses time-sharing priority numbers ranging from -20 to 20, with 20 as the highest priority (the default is 0). It supports the BSD *renice* command, mapping BSD nice numbers to the corresponding time-sharing priority number, but also introduces a new command as part of its support for real-time processes, *priocntl*. The form to change the priority for a single process is:

```
# priocntl -s -p new-pri -i pid proc-id
```

where *new-pri* is the new priority for the process and *proc-id* is the process ID of the desired process. For example, the following command sets the priority level for process 8733 to -5:

```
# priocntl -s -p -5 -i pid 8733
```

The *priocntl* command has many other capabilities and uses. See the section entitled "Introducing the System V.4 Process Scheduler," later in this chapter.

Destroying Processes

Sometimes it's necessary to eliminate a process entirely; this is the purpose of the *kill* command. The syntax of the *kill* command is as follows:

```
# kill [-signal] pid
```

where *pid* is the process's identification number, and *signal* is the signal to send to the process (it is optional). The default signal is number 15, the TERM signal, which tells the process to terminate. Under System V, the signal must be specified numerically; under BSD, either the signal number or its symbolic name may be used.

Sometimes, a process may still exist after a *kill* command. If this happens, execute the *kill* command with the -9 option, which sends the process signal 9, appropriately named KILL. This almost always guarantees that the process will be destroyed. However, it does not allow the dying process to clean up, and therefore may leave the process's files in an inconsistent state.

Occasionally, processes will not die even after being sent the KILL signal. The vast majority of such processes fall into one of three categories:

- Zombies. A process in the zombie state (displayed as Z status in BSD *ps* displays and as *<defunct>* under System V). When a process is exiting, it informs its parent of its imminent death; when it receives an acknowledgment, its PID is removed from the process table. A zombie process is one in which all its resources have been freed, but the parent process's acknowledgment has not occurred. Usually, *init* will step in when the parent is gone, but very occasionally this fails to happen. Zombies are always cleared the next time the system is booted and do not adversely affect system performance.

- Processes waiting for unavailable NFS resources (for example, trying to write to a remote file on a system that has crashed) will not die if sent a KILL signal. Use the QUIT signal (3) or the INT (interrupt) signal (2) to kill such processes. See the section entitled "Mounting Remote Directories," in Chapter 12, *TCP/IP Network Management*," for full details.

- Processes waiting for a device to complete an operation before exiting. Often this means waiting for a tape to finish rewinding.

When you kill a process, you also kill all its children (i.e., unless they're catching the signal). Killing a shell therefore usually kills all the foreground and stopped background processes initiated from that shell (including other shells). Killing a user's login shell is equivalent to logging the user out. This is a useful (if somewhat painful) way to recover from certain kinds of problems. For example, if a user manages to confuse his editor by mistyping control keys and escape sequences, or enters an infinite loop that he can't terminate by normal means, killing his shell will let him regain control of the situation, possibly at the cost of some work. Use the *ps* command to determine which process is the offending user's shell. Remember that you must be superuser in order to kill someone else's process.

Introducing the System V.4 Process Scheduler

System V Release 4 introduces administrator-configurable process scheduling. One purpose of this new facility is to support *real-time processes*: processes designed to work in application areas where nearly-immediate responses to events are required (say, processing raw radar data in a vehicle in motion, controlling a manufacturing process making extensive use of robotics, or starting up the backup cooling system on a nuclear reactor). Operating systems handle such needs by defining a class of processes as real-time processes, giving them virtually complete access to all system resources when they are running. Under such instances, normal time-sharing processes will receive little or no CPU time. System V Release 4 allows a system to be configured to allow both normal time-sharing and real-time processes (although actual real-time systems using other operating systems have seldom actually done this). Alternatively, a system may be configured without real-time processes.

This section is written strictly from a theoretical point of view and is intended *only* as an introductory overview. There are as yet very few V.4 systems, and fewer still with customized schedulers. Obviously, the process scheduler facility is something to play with on an unimportant system first, not something to try on your main production system three days before an important deadline.

System V Release 4 defines three process classes: real-time, time-sharing, and system. The latter class is what is used for kernel processes (such as the paging daemon). Each process class has its own set of priority numbers. For example, real-time process priorities run from 0 to 59 (higher is better). Time-sharing processes use priority numbers from -20 to 20 by default (although the numbers used are configurable). These three class-specific priority number sets are all mapped to a single set of internal priority numbers running from 0 to 159. Figure 7-1 illustrates the default mapping.

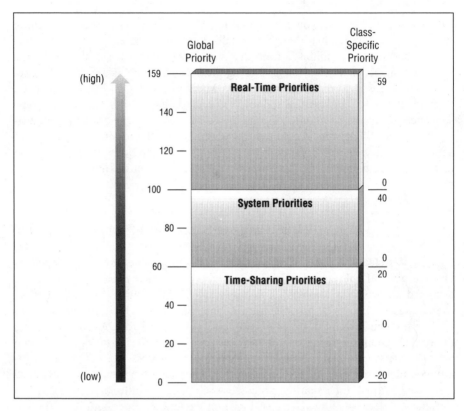

Figure 7-1. System V.4 Process Priorities (Default System Configuration)

As the diagram indicates, a real-time process will *always* run before either a system or time-sharing process since real-time global priorities—which are what is actually used by the process scheduler—are all greater than system and time-sharing global priorities. The definitions of each real-time and time-sharing global priority level are stored in the kernel and, if they have been customized, are usually loaded by one of the system initialization scripts at boottime. The current definitions may be retrieved with the *dispadmin -g* command:

```
$ dispadmin -g -c TS >/etc/new_sched.ts
# Time Sharing Dispatcher Configuration
RES=1000
```

# ts_quantum	ts_tqexp	ts_slpret	ts_maxwait	ts_lwait	PRIORITY LEVEL	
1000	0	10	5	10	#	0
1000	0	11	5	11	#	1
1000	1	12	5	12	#	2
1000	1	13	5	13	#	3
. . .						
100	47	58	5	58	#	57
100	48	59	5	59	#	58
100	49	59	5	59	#	59

Each line of the table defines the characteristics of a different priority level, numbered consecutively from 0. The *RES=* line defines the time units used in the table. It says how many parts a second is divided into; each defined fraction of a second becomes one unit. Thus, in this file, the time units are milliseconds.

The fields have the following meanings:

ts_quantum   The maximum amount of time that a process at this priority level can run without interruption.

ts_tqexp   New priority given to a process running at this priority level that gets the entire maximum run interval. In the preceding table, this has the effect of lowering its priority.

ts_slpret   New priority given to a process at this priority level when it returns from a sleep.

ts_maxwait   Maximum amount of time a process at this level can remain runnable without actually executing before having its priority changed to the value in the *ts_lwait* column. This setting affects processes that are ready to run but aren't getting any CPU time. After this interval, their priority will be increased with the preceding scheduler table.

ts_lwait   New priority given to a process that is runnable and whose maximum wait time has expired. In the preceding table, this usually increases its priority somewhat.

All text after number signs is ignored. Thus, the PRIORITY LEVEL columns are really comments designed to make the table easier to read.

From the table, it is evident how process priorities would change under various circumstances. For example, consider a level 57 process. If this process runs for its full 100 ms., then afterwards it will drop down to priority level 47, giving up the CPU to higher priority processes. If, on the other hand, it it waits for 5 ms. after being ready to run, then its priority level is raised to 58, making it more likely to be executed soon.

The *priocntl* command allows a priority level ceiling to be imposed upon a time-sharing process, which specifies the maximum priority level it can attain. This prevents a low priority process from becoming runnable and eventually marching up to the top priority level (as would happen under the preceding scheduler table) when you really want that process to run only when nothing else is around. Setting a limit can keep it below the range of normal processes. For example, the following command sets the maximum priority for process 27163 to -5:

```
# priocntl -s -m -5 27163
```

The real-time process schedule table is much simpler than the time-sharing table:

```
$ dispadmin -g -c RT
# Real Time Dispatcher Configuration
RES=1000
```

# TIME QUANTUM		PRIORITY
# (rt_quantum)		LEVEL
1000	#	0
1000	#	1
100	#	58
100	#	59

The single column in this table (the priority levels are again just comments for readability) lists the maximum uninterrupted execution interval allowed for each priority level. Processes at each level can run without interruption for the specified interval; afterwards, the scheduler will stop them and begin executing the highest priority process that is runnable (which may still be the same process). In the preceding example, higher priority levels are run for small intervals of time.

UNIX Batch Processing Facilities

Manually monitoring and altering processes' execution priorities is a crude way to handle CPU time allocation, but unfortunately it's the only way that standard UNIX offers. It is adequate for the conditions under which UNIX was developed: systems with lots of small interactive jobs. But if a system runs some large jobs as well, it quickly breaks down.

For some heavily loaded systems, after-hours execution of a few jobs may provide some relief. Standard UNIX has a limited facility for doing so via the *at* and *batch* commands. *at* allows a command to be executed at a specified time, and *batch* provides one queue from which jobs may be run sequentially in a batch-like mode. For example, if all large jobs are run via *batch*, it can ensure that only one is ever running at a time (provided users cooperate, of course). If a single, first-in, first-out queue is all that is needed, *batch* may be of some use, but if any sort of queue priority features are required, it will prove insufficient.

A true batch system supports multiple queues and allows the administrator to set in-queue priorities (for ordering jobs within a queue), queue execution priorities and resource limits (the priority and limits automatically assigned to jobs started from a queue), queue permissions (which users can submit jobs from each queue), and other parameters on a queue-by-queue basis. AIX 3.1 has adapted its print spooling subsystem to provide a very simple batch system, allowing for different job priorities within a queue and multiple batch queues, but it is still missing most important features of a modern batch system.

The Network Queueing System (NQS), available on some UNIX systems, is an excellent batch processing facility and includes full network support. Contact your vendor to see if it is available on your system.

Process Resource Limits

The 4.2 BSD version introduced a very simple level of process resource limits to UNIX. Table 7-2 lists the resources for which limits are defined and the keywords associated with each one in the C and Korn shells.

Table 7-2. Settable Resource Limits

Resource	Keyword	
	C shell	*Korn Shell*
Total accumulated CPU time (hrs:mins:secs).	*cputime*	*time*
Largest file that may be created (whether created from scratch or by extending an existing file).	*filesize*	*file*
Maximum size of the data segment of the process. On some systems this seems to imply the data+stack region (e.g., SunOS); on others just the data segment itself (e.g., AIX 3.1).	*datasize*	*data*
Maximum size of the stack segment of the process.	*stacksize*	*stack*
Maximum size of a core file (created when a program bombs).	*coredumpsize*	*coredump*
Maximum amount of memory that may be used by the process.	*memoryuse*	*memory*

Resource limits are divided into two types: soft and hard. *Soft limits* are resource use limits currently applied by default when a new process is created. A user may increase these values up to the system-wide *hard limits*, beyond which only the superuser may extend them. Hard limits are thus defined as absolute ceilings on resource use.

The C shell has two built-in commands for displaying and setting resource limits. The *limit* command displays current resource limits. The hard limits may be displayed by including the *-h* option on the *limit* command:

```
% limit                            % limit -h
cputime      1:00:00               cputime      unlimited
filesize     1048575 kbytes        filesize     unlimited
datasize     65536 kbytes          datasize     3686336 kbytes
stacksize    4096 kbytes           stacksize    262144 kbytes
coredumpsize 1024 kbytes           coredumpsize unlimited
memoryuse    32768 kbytes          memoryuse    54528 kbytes
```

The C shell *unlimit* command will raise the soft limits to the hard limits.

This mechanism is also present in V.4 and in AIX 3.1. The Korn shell equivalent command is *ulimit* (also supported in the Bourne shell under V.4). The *-a* and *-Ha* options will display the current soft and hard limits respectively; for example:

```
$ ulimit -a                        $ ulimit -Ha
time(seconds)    3600              time(seconds)    unlimited
file(blocks)     2097151           file(blocks)     2097151
data(kbytes)     65536             data(kbytes)     257532
stack(kbytes)    4096              stack(kbytes)    196092
memory(kbytes)   32768             memory(kbytes)   unlimited
coredump(blocks) 1024              coredump(blocks) unlimited
```

ulimit also changes the current value of a resource limit. Each individual limit may be increased by specifying an option letter corresponding to the first character of its name in the display. For example, the following commands increase the current CPU time limit to its maximum value and increase the memory use limit to 64 MB:

```
$ ulimit -t unlimited
$ ulimit -m 65536
```

Now for the bad news. Current UNIX resource limits are completely useless from an administrative standpoint for several reasons. First, the hard limits are often hard-wired into the kernel and cannot be changed by the system administrator. Second, users can always change their own soft limits. All an administrator can do is place the desired commands into users' *.profile* or *.cshrc* files and hope. Third, the limits are on a per-process basis. Unfortunately, many real jobs consist of many processes, not just one. There is currently no way to impose limits on a parent process and all its children. Finally, in many cases, limits are not even enforced; this is most often true of the ones you probably care about the most: CPU time and memory use. You'll need to experiment to find out which ones are in force on your system.

However, one limit which it is often worth setting in user login initialization files is the core file size limit. If the users on your system will have little use for core files, then set the limit to 0, which will prevent their creation. The commands to do this are listed below:

```
limit coredumpsize 0        ...C shell...
ulimit -c 0                 ...Korn shell...
```

AIX 3.1 includes the structure for a more elaborate version of these limits (and perhaps new ones), via the file */etc/security/limits*, which may be modified by the *chuser* command. It has stanzas of the form:

```
chavez:
       fsize = 2097151
       core = 2048
       cpu = 3600
       data = 131072
       rss = 65536          ...Memory use limit...
       stack = 8192
```

which specify the soft limits for the username which labels the stanza. To change *chavez*'s memory use limit, use a command like:

```
# chuser "rss = 102400" chavez
```

This command sets *chavez*'s default memory use limit to 100 MB, modifying or adding the *rss* line for *chavez* in */etc/security/limits*. It seems quite likely that future releases of AIX will use the */etc/security/limits* file more fully and perhaps add additional functionality.

Managing Memory

Memory resources have at least as much effect on overall system performance as the distribution of CPU time. To perform well, a system needs to have adequate memory not just for the largest jobs it will run, but also for the overall mix of jobs typical of its everyday use. For example, the amount of memory that is sufficient for the one or two big jobs that run overnight might provide only a mediocre response time under the heavy interactive use a system is expected to support in the daytime; on the other hand, an amount of memory which supports a system's normal interactive use very well might result in quite poor performance when larger jobs are run. Thus, both sets of needs should be taken into consideration when planning for and evaluating system memory requirements.

Paging and swapping are the means by which UNIX distributes available memory among current processes when their total memory needs exceed the amount of physical memory. Technically, *swapping* refers to writing an entire process to disk, thereby freeing all of its memory. A swapped-out process must then be reread into memory when execution resumes. *Paging* involves moving sections of a process' memory—in units called *pages*—to disk, in order to free up memory needed by that process or another process. A *page fault* occurs when a process needs a page of memory that is not resident and must be (re)read in from disk. On virtual memory systems, swapping occurs only rarely if at all—and usually indicates a serious memory shortage—and so the two terms are sometimes used synonymously.

In the most general sense, paging is what makes virtual memory possible, allowing a process's memory requirements to greatly exceed the actual amount of physical memory. A process's total memory requirement is generally the sum of the size of its executable image* (known as its *text segment*) and the amount of memory it uses for data. On systems without virtual memory (e.g., Crays, XENIX systems), the process must have an amount of physical memory equal to its current text and data requirements in order to run. Virtual memory systems take advantage of the fact that most of this memory isn't actually needed all the time. Information is read in from disk only as needed. The system automatically maps the *virtual addresses* (the address of a text or data location with respect to the beginning of the process' image) used internally by the program to real memory locations. When the process accesses a part of its executable image or its data not currently in memory, the kernel reads in (*pages in*) what is needed from disk, usually replacing other pages that the process no longer needs.

So, for a large program that spends most of its time in, say, two routines, only the part of its executable image containing them need be in memory while they are running, freeing up the memory the rest of the program's text segment would occupy on a non-virtual memory computer for other uses. This is true whether the two routines are close together or far apart in the executable. Similarly, if a program uses a very large data area, all of it needn't be resident in memory simultaneously if the program doesn't access it all at once.

The problem with paging comes when there is not enough memory on the system for all of the processes currently running. In this case, the kernel will apportion the total memory among them dynamically. When a process needs a new page read in and there are no free or reusable pages, then an existing page in memory is *paged out*: written out to a paging area on disk. When that page is again

---

*An exception occurs for executables which can be partially or totally shared by more than one process. In this case, only one copy of the image is in memory regardless of how many processes are executing it. The total memory used by the shared portions in these cases is divided among all processes using them in the output from commands like *ps*.

required, then it must be paged back in, probably forcing out another page. An appreciable portion of the available CPU time can be spent page faulting under such conditions, and all processes will execute much less efficiently.

Ideally, changing the execution priorities for some of the jobs would solve such a problem. Unfortunately, this isn't always the case. For example, consider two large processes on a system with only a modest amount of real memory. If the jobs have the same execution priority, they will probably cause each other to page continuously if they run at the same time. This is a case where swapping is actually preferable to paging. If one job is swapped out, then the other runs uninterrupted, and after some amount of time, the situation can be reversed; both jobs will finish much sooner this way than they will under continuous paging.

Logically, lowering the priority of one of the jobs should cause it to wait to execute until the other one pauses (e.g., for an I/O operation) or completes. On BSD systems, setting a process' nice number to 20 will produce such behavior: the process will execute only when no other process wants the CPU. On other UNIX systems, however, a minimum priority process is not handled in this way, but rather occasionally gets some execution time even when higher priority processes are runnable (reflecting a scheduling algorithm designed for lots of small interactive jobs). On such systems, running both jobs at once, regardless of their priorities, will result in some execution degradation (even for the higher priority job) due to paging. In such cases, you need to either buy more memory or not run both jobs at once.

The next subsection discusses commands you can use to monitor the memory use and paging activity on your system and get a picture of how well the system is performing. Later subsections discuss managing the system paging areas.

Monitoring Memory Use and Paging Activity

On BSD and XENIX systems, you can determine current memory use with the *vmstat* command; under System V, the command is *sar* (AIX 3.1 provides both). The most important statistics from either command are the number of running processes and the number of page-outs and swaps. You can use this information to determine if the system is paging excessively. As you gather data with these commands, you'll also need to run the *ps* command so that you know what programs are generating the memory usage you're seeing.

The following subsections discuss the memory monitoring commands and show you how to interpret their output. They provide examples of output from systems under heavy loads. It's important to keep in mind, though, that all systems from time to time have memory shortages and consequent increases in paging activity. You can expect to see similar output on your system periodically. Such activity is significant only if it is persistent. Some deviations from what is normal for your system are to be expected, but consistent and sustained paging activity does indicate a memory shortage that you'll need to deal with.

These sections provide only an introduction to serious system performance monitoring. Their goal is for you to be able to use the relevant tools and to interpret their output and isolate their important data. The next step is, obviously, to try to improve the system's performance. For information about this activity, consult the Nutshell Handbook *System Performance Tuning*, especially the chapter on memory performance.

vmstat (BSD and XENIX)

vmstat provides a number of statistics about current CPU and memory use. Its most useful mode uses this syntax:

```
% vmstat interval [count]
```

where *interval* is the number of seconds between reports, and *count* is the total number of reports to generate. If *count* is omitted, *vmstat* will run continuously until you kill it. To generate meaningful data, use an interval of at least five seconds.

Here is an example of *vmstat*'s output:

```
% vmstat 5 4
procs     memory            page                faults              cpu
r b w     avm  fre re at pi po fr de sr d0 d1 d2 d3 in sy cs us sy id
1 0 0 61312 9280  0  0 24  1  2  0  0  4  1  1 12 35 66 16 63 11 26
1 2 0 71936 3616  3  0 96  0  0  0  2 18  0  0  0 23 89 34 72 28  0
2 0 0 76320 3424  0  0  0  0  0  0  0 26  0  0  0 24 92 39 63 37  0
1 2 0 63616 3008  1  1  0  0  0  0  0 21  0  0  0 23 80 33 78 22  0
```

The first line of every *vmstat* report is an average since boottime; it should be ignored. The report is organized into sections as follows:

procs   Statistics about active processes.

memory   Memory use and availability data.

page   Paging activity.

faults   Per-device IO operations and overall system interrupt rate.

cpu   Percentage of CPU devoted to system time, user time, and left idle.

The most important columns in *vmstat*'s report are:

r   Number of runnable processes.

b   Number of "blocked" processes (waiting for I/O).

w   Number of swapped out runnable processes (should be 0).

fre   Number of memory pages on the free list.*

re   Number of page reclaims.

pi   Number of pages paged-in (includes process startup).

po   Number of pages paged-out (if >0 the system is paging).

dn   Disk operations per second on disk *n*.

us   Percentage of total CPU time spent on user processes.

sy   Percentage of total CPU time spent as system overhead.

id   Idle time percentage (percentage of CPU time not used). The first three columns tell you how many processes are currently active. The number in the *w* column should be 0, indicating no swapped-out processes; if it isn't, the system has a serious memory shortage.

The *po* column is the most important in terms of paging: it indicates the number of page-outs and should ideally be very close to zero. If it isn't, then processes are contending for the available memory and the system is paging. Paging activity is also reflected in significant decreases in the amount of free memory (*fre*), in the number of page reclaims (*re*)—memory pages which are taken away from one process because another one needs it even though the first process needs it too—and more indirectly in a high system CPU time percentage (*sy*).

High numbers in the page-ins column (*pi*) are not significant since starting up a process involves paging in its executable image and data. When a new process starts, this column will jump up, but then quickly level off again:

```
% vmstat 5
procs     memory            page                    faults
r b w    avm    fre   re at  pi  po  fr  de  sr d0 d1 d2 d3  in
. . .
0 1 0 81152 17864    0  0    0   0   0   0   0  0  0  0 10  32
1 1 0 98496 15624    0  0  192   0   0   0   0 23  0  0 65 103
2 0 0 84160 11648    0  0  320   0   0   0   0 12  0  0 66 125
2 0 0 74784  9600    0  0  320   0   0   0   0 12  0  0 42 105
2 0 0 74464  5984    0  0   64   0   0   0   0  5  0  0 23  72
```

---

*For *vmstat*, a page is always 1K, regardless of the system's actual page size.

```
2 0 0 78688  5472   0 0   0   0   0   0   0 14  0  0 44  80
1 1 0 60480 16032   0 0   0   0   0   0   0 20  0  0 48 101
^C
```

At the second data line, a compile job starts executing. There is a jump in the number of page-ins, and the available memory (*fre*) drops sharply. Once the job gets going, the page-ins drop back to zero, although the free list size stays small. When the job ends, its memory returns to the free list (final line).

Here is some output from a system under distress:

```
% vmstat 5
procs     memory            page                  faults
r b w   avm   fre  re at  pi  po  fr  de  sr d0 d1 d2 d3  in
. . .
2 1 0 43232 31296   0  0   0   0   0   0   0 23 11  2  0  39
1 2 0 46560 32512   0  0   0   0   0   0   0 27 13  1  0  40
5 0 0 82496  2848   2  0 384 608 640   0  33 19 16 15  0  56
2 3 0 81568  2304   2  0 384 448 480   0  21 24 16  7  0  62
4 1 0 72480  2144   0  0  96  96  64   0   9 13  8  1  0  28
5 1 0 72640  2112   0  0  64  32  64   0   2  8 10  1  0  32
4 1 0 73280  3328   0  0   0   0   0   0   0  3 10  0  0  41
2 1 0 54176 19552   0  0  32   0   0   0   0  4 16  1  0  44
^C
```

At the beginning of this report, this system was running well, with no paging activity at all. Then new processes start up (line 5), and both page-in and page-out activity increases (and the free list shrinks). This system doesn't have enough memory for all the jobs that want to run at this point. This is also reflected in the size of the free list. By the end of this report, however, things are beginning to calm down again as these processes finish.

vmstat's output on XENIX systems is somewhat different. Instead of page-ins and page-outs, it displays swap-ins and swap-outs (labeled *si* and *so*) since XENIX systems don't support paging. Other critical fields in its output are *swr* and *sww*, which list the swap reads and writes, respectively. Sustained non-zero values in *sww* and *so* indicate that memory is short.

sar (System V)

System V's *sar* command provides very similar data to *vmstat*. Its syntax is:

```
$ sar [options] interval [count]
```

where *interval* is the number of seconds between reports (should be at least five to produce meaningful data), and *count* is the total number of reports to produce (the default is one). *sar*'s options specify what data to include in its report; the most useful for determining memory usage are:

-p   Paging data.

-r   Free memory and swap space data.

-g   Memory performance data (V.4 only).

The reports look like this:

```
$ sar -r 5       Free memory report
hamlet hamlet 3.2 2 i386    06/24/91

08:29:49 freemem freeswp
08:29:54     184   27800
```

The first column of every *sar* report is a time stamp. This report shows the current amount of free memory available to user processes (in 512-byte blocks) and the amount of free swap space. When the amount of free memory drops significantly below its normal level, the system is short of memory.

The *-p* option shows paging data. Its output is highly implementation-specific. Here is the output from Interactive UNIX:

```
$ sar -p 5
hamlet hamlet 3.2 2 i386    06/24/91

08:31:32  vflt/s  pflt/s  pgfil/s  rclm/s
          2.59    0.60    0.00     0.00
```

Here is what it looks like on a different System V system:

```
$ sar -p 5
ilium ilium 3.3.2 12031609 IP7    06/25/91

vflt/s dfil/s cache/s pgswp/s pgfil/s pflt/s cpyw/s steal/s rclm/s
 2.59   2.40   0.20    0.00    0.00    0.60   0.00    2.99    0.00
```

(I've removed the time stamps to save space.)

Whatever its format, the most important columns in this report are *vflts/s*, the number of address translation page faults per second, and *rclm/s*, the number of page reclaims per second. *vflts/s* indicates how often processes are calling for pages not in memory which must be paged-in. Page reclaims happen when the system must free memory for one process that another process still wants. Both of them indicate processes are contending for an insufficient amount of total memory.

Both of these options can be used simultaneously; *sar* will interleave their output:

```
$ sar -pr 10 100            Output shortened.
ilium ilium 3.3.2 12031609 IP7    06/25/91

08:36:17  vflt/s  dfill/s cache/s . . . rclm/s
```

```
          freemem freeswp
          swpin/s bswin/s swpot/s bswot/s pswot/s pswch/s

08:36:20     8.96    7.96    1.00 . . .    0.00
            25290   27800
08:36:30   196.57  133.33   63.24 . . .    0.00
            23507   27800
08:36:40   193.63  147.55   46.08 . . .    0.00
            23531   27800
08:36:50   190.55  108.96   81.59 . . .    0.00
            24184   27800
08:37:00     0.50    0.50    0.00 . . .    0.00
            25378   27800
^c
```

Beginning at each time stamp, *sar* lists the output for the *-p* and *-r* options on separate lines in that order. (It looks messy, but you get used to it.) When this *sar* command was executed, the system was doing fine. At the second interval, however, the system becomes much more active as several new processes start (indicated by the number of context switches in *pswch/s* in the third line of each group). As they run, there is a lot of paging activity, but the system never has to swap out an entire job. As the processes finish, the system returns to normal.

Under V.4, *sar -g* collects together statistics related to memory usage into a single option:

```
11:23:04 pgout/s ppgout/s pgfree/s pgscan/s %s5ipf
11:23:09    0.00      0.0     0.34      1.9     0.00
```

The report shows the number of page-out operations, the number of pages paged-out, the number of reclaimed pages, the average number of pages scanned in order to find candidates to reclaim, and the percentage of inodes in System V-type filesystems removed from the free list (all per second). The most important are the page-out and page reclaim (*pgfree/s*) statistics.

Managing Paging Space

Specially designated areas of disk are used for paging. On most UNIX systems, distinct disk partitions—called *swap partitions** are used to hold pages written out from memory. In some recent UNIX implementations, paging goes to special *paging files* stored in a regular UNIX filesystem.*

On multi-user systems, if at all possible, paging should be done to multiple paging areas, spread across different physical disk drives, ideally on separate disk controllers. Performance will be improved the closer you come to this ideal.

---

*Despite their names, both swap partitions and paging files can be used for both paging and swapping.

How Much Paging Space?

There are as many answers to this question as there are people to ask. The correct answer is, of course, "It depends." What it depends on is the type of jobs your system typically executes. The canonical value of four times the amount of physical memory works only for systems with mostly small interactive processes (for example, whose typical workload is several or many people editing, and occasional compilation, and some light network activity). A single-user workstation might be able to get away with as little as two times the amount of physical memory if all it's used for is editing and small compilations. On the other hand, for real production environments running big programs, you'll see better performance with six to eight times the amount of physical memory.

Factors that will tend to increase your paging space needs include:

• Jobs requiring large amounts of memory.

• Programs that are themselves very large (i.e., have large-sized executables). This often implies the item above, but not vice-versa.

• A large number of simultaneous jobs running, even if each individual job is fairly small.

• Other demands on the system, such as moderate or heavy network traffic.

On System V systems, you can find out the locations of the paging areas and how much of it is currently in use by using the *-l* option to the *swap* command:

```
$ swap -1
path                 dev  swaplo blocks    free
/dev/dsk/c1d5s1      0,209      0 368640   91540
```

This system has about 180 MB (368640 512-byte blocks) of swap space on a single swap partition, about three quarters of which is currently in use.

Under V.4, *swap* also has a *-s* option which lists statistics about overall paging space usage. Its output looks something like this:

```
allocated  reserved     used  available
   237568     28672   266240     143360
```

Under BSD, the *pstat -s* command provides similar information:

```
% pstat -s
179232k used (20640k text), 211112k free,44832k wasted,0k missing
avail: 9*8192k 3*4096k 2*1024k 4*512k 98*128k 18*64k 828*1k
```

The first line of the output indicates that a little over half of this system's 435 MB of swap space is in use. The second line indicates the fragmentation of the available swap space, showing how many of each size of fragment there are. For example, on this system, there are nine fragments of at least 8 MB in size.

"Wasted" space refers to portions of allocated swap space that are not needed by the processes to which they are allocated—the standard BSD allocation algorithm is notoriously inefficient, as it insists on allocating swap space in segments of increasing powers of two. The first time a process requests paging space, it gets 1K; the next time it asks for some, it must take 2K, and so on, whether it wants that much or not. To see a list of swap partitions on a BSD system, look for the keyword "swap" in /etc/fstab:

```
% grep swap /etc/fstab
/dev/disk2b / swap sw 0 0
/dev/disk4b / swap sw 0 0
```

Under AIX 3.1, the command to list the paging spaces is lsps -a:

```
$ lsps -a
Page Space   Phys. Volume   Volume Group   Size    %Used   Active  Auto
hd6          hdisk0         rootvg         200MB    76      yes     yes
paging00     hdisk3         uservg         128MB    34      yes     yes
```

The output lists the paging space name, the physical disk it resides on, the volume group it is part of, its size, how much of it is currently in use, whether it is currently active and whether it is activated automatically at boottime. This system has two paging spaces totaling about 328 MB; total system swap space is currently about sixty percent full.

Activating Paging Areas

Paging areas are activated automatically at boottime. Under BSD, swap partitions are listed in the filesystem configuration file /etc/fstab (described in detail in the section entitled "The Filesystem Configuration File," in Chapter 8, *Filesystems and Disks*). Here is a sample entry:

```
/dev/disk2b / swap sw 0 0
```

This entry says that the *b* partition on disk 2 is a swap partition. This basic form is used for all swap partitions; only the name of the special file changes for swap partitions on other disks.

All swap partitions in /etc/fstab are activated automatically at boottime in /etc/rc:

```
swapon -a > /dev/console 2>&1
```

The *swapon -a* command says to activate all swap partitions. This command may also be issued manually when adding a new partition. SunOS supports paging files as well swap partitions (discussed later in this chapter), and *swapon -a* will activate them as well.

Under System V, the swap area on the root disk is activated automatically at boottime. If additional swap areas are added, then commands to activate them must be added to one of the initialization scripts. The *swap* command with its *-a* option will activate a paging area. It has the following syntax:

```
# swap -a block-special-file begin-block length
```

where *block-special-file* specifies the swap partition, *begin-block* is the offset into that area to start at (usually 0), and *length* is the length of the swap area in 512-byte blocks. For example, the following command activates a 40 MB swap partition on disk 1:

```
# swap -a /dev/dsk/c1d1s1 0 81920
```

The same command would need to be placed in a system initialization script in order for the swap partition to be activated at boottime.

Under AIX 3.1, paging areas are listed in the file */etc/swapspaces*:

```
hd6:
    dev = /dev/hd6

paging00:
    dev = /dev/paging00
```

Each stanza lists the name of the paging space and its associated special file (the stanza name and the filename in */dev* are always the same). All paging logical volumes listed in */etc/swapspaces* are activated at boottime by a *swapon -a* command in */etc/rc*. Paging logical volumes can also be activated when they are created or by manually executing the *swapon -a* command.

Creating New Paging Areas

As we've noted, paging requires dedicated disk space which is used to store paged-out data. Standard System V and BSD allow for only fixed-size dedicated disk partitions. If you need more paging space on one of these systems, you must add an additional swap partition by either buying a new disk and using some of it for swapping or by reallocating the space on one of your existing disks to add a swap partition.

Making a new swap partition on such a disk is a painful process, involving these steps:

* Performing a full backup of all filesystems currently on the device and verifying that the tapes are readable (see the section entitled "Backing Up the Filesystem," in Chapter 9, *Backup and Restore*).

- Restructuring the physical disk organization. This is only necessary on some systems, usually microcomputers (see the section entitled "Adding Disks," in Chapter 8, *Filesystems and Disks*).

- Creating new filesystems on the disk. At this point, you are treating the old disk as if it were a brand new one (see the section entitled "Remaking an Existing Filesystem," in Chapter 8.

- Informing the kernel of the new swapping areas (discussed in the previous section).

- Restoring the files to the new (smaller) filesystems (see the section entitled "Restoring Files from Backup," in Chapter 9.

Most of these steps are covered in detail in other chapters, as noted in parentheses.

Filesystem Paging

SunOS and V.4 offer a great deal more flexibility by supporting *filesystem paging*—paging to designated files within normal filesystems. Paging files can be created or deleted as needs change. Under SunOS, the *mkfile* command creates new paging files. For example, the following command will create the file */chem/page_1* as a system page file:

```
# mkfile 50m /chem/page_1
```

The *mkfile* command creates a 50 MB page file with the specified pathname. The size of the file is interpreted as bytes unless a "k" (KB) or "m" (MB) suffix is appended to it.

The new paging file must be entered into the filesystem configuration file */etc/fstab*. A paging file entry looks like this:

```
/chem/swap swap swap rw 0 0
```

The first field contains the pathname of the paging file (in place of the special file for filesystems), and the second field contains the word "swap" (instead of the mount point). The filesystem type field is also "swap", the options are set to read-write and the final two fields are 0. If you want to activate the paging file immediately, execute the command:

```
# swapon -a
```

which enables all swap areas listed in the filesystem configuration file.

Under V.4, the regular *swap* command is used to designate an existing file as a paging file by substituting its pathname for the special file name. For example, the following command adds */chem/page* as a 50 MB paging file:

```
# swap -a /chem/page 0 102400
```

If a new area is being permanently added to the paging space, then the command should be placed in one of the system initialization files (probably */sbin/rc2*).

Adding Paging Space Under AIX 3.1

Under AIX 3.1, paging is seemingly more flexible than under standard BSD and V.3. Paging space is organized as special paging logical volumes. Like normal logical volumes, paging spaces may be increased in size as desired as long as there are unallocated logical partitions in their volume group. In practice, however, most administrators allocate all available disk space to filesystems or paging spaces, and so increasing space (without adding a new disk) means following a process quite similar to the one outlined previously: backing up a filesystem (and verifying that the tapes are good) and then deleting its logical volume, recreating it at a smaller size, creating a filesystem on the new logical volume, and restoring the backed-up files. Once free space is available, you can use the *mkps* command to create a new paging space with them or use the *chps* command to enlarge an existing one. For example, the following command will create a 200 MB paging space in the volume group *myvg*:

```
# mkps -a -n -s 50 myvg
```

Once free space is available, you can use the *mkps* command to create a new paging space with them or use the *chps* command to enlarge an existing one. For example, the following command will create a 200 MB paging space in the volume group *myvg*:

```
# mkps -a -n -s 50 myvg
```

The paging space will be assigned a name like *paging*nn where *nn* is a number: *paging01*, for example. The -*a* option says to activate the paging space automatically on system bootups (its name is entered into */etc/swapspaces*). The -*n* option says to activate the paging space immediately after it is created. The -*s* option specifies the paging space's size, in logical partitions (whose default size is 4 MB). The volume group name appears as the final item on the command line.

The size of an existing paging space may be increased with the *chps* command. Here the *-s* option specifies the number of additional logical partitions to be added:

```
# chps -s 10 paging01
```

This command adds 40 MB to the size of paging space *paging01*.

Removing Paging Areas

Except for the one on the root disk, paging spaces may be removed if they are no longer needed. To remove a swap partition under BSD, remove the corresponding line from */etc/fstab*. Once the system is rebooted, the swap partition will be deactivated.

Under System V, the *-d* option to the *swap* command will deactivate a swap area. You'll also need to remove its *swap* command from the appropriate system initialization script. Here are some examples:

```
# swap -d /dev/dsk/c1d1s1 0
# swap -d /chem/page 0              ...V.4 only...
```

Once the *swap -d* command is executed, no new paging will be done to that area, and the kernel will attempt to free areas in it which are still in use as much as possible. In the case of V.4 paging files, the command marks the specified paging file for removal. It will not actually be removed until no processes are using it.

To deactivate a paging file under SunOS, remove its name from */etc/fstab* and then reboot the system (rebooting is necessary to ensure that there are no active references to the file). The file may then be removed normally with *rm*.

Under AIX 3.1, paging spaces may be removed with *rmps*. However, only inactive paging space may be removed, and there is no way to deactivate a paging space without rebooting the system. Therefore, the procedure to remove a paging space is:

```
# chps -a n paging01
# shutdown -r now               ...Or some more gentle reboot...
   ...
# rmps paging01
```

The *chps* command removes paging01 from the list to be activated at boottime (in */etc/swapspaces*). After a reboot, the *rmps* command may be used to remove the paging space.

Running Large Jobs Under XENIX

XENIX supports only swapping. To accommodate large jobs, it provides the *runbig* command to allow a process to use more memory than that usually allocated to a single-user process. The *runbig* command precedes the normal command on the command line:

```
$ runbig big_program <input.bp >big.log
```

Once the memory requirements of the command invoked with *runbig* exceed normal user process limits, the process will remain in memory until its memory requirements decrease or it completes execution. Obviously, this will have a large effect on other processes running at the time. Hence, *runbig* should be used only when interactive performance is not an issue.

Managing Disk Usage with Disk Quotas (BSD and V.4)

Disk space shortages are a perennial problem on all computers. We looked at ways to monitor disk use in Chapter 6, *Automating Routine Tasks*. For systems where direct control over how much disk space each user has is essential, disk quotas may provide a solution.

BSD supports a disk quota system, and V.4 has incorporated them into System V. The disk quota system allows an administrator to limit the amount of filesystem storage that any user can consume. If quotas are enabled, the operating system will maintain separate quotas for each user's disk space and inode consumption (equivalent to the total number of files he owns) on each filesystem.

There are two distinct kinds of quota: a *hard limit* and a *soft limit*. A user is never allowed to exceed his hard limit, under any circumstances. When a user reaches his hard limit, he'll get a message that he has exceeded his quota, and the operating system will refuse to allocate any more storage. A user may exceed the soft limit temporarily for a limited period of time; in such cases, he gets a warning message, and the operating system grants the additional storage. If his disk usage still exceeds this soft limit at the next login, the message will be repeated. He'll continue to receive warnings at each successive login until either:

- He reduces his disk usage to within the soft limit.

or:

- He's been warned a fixed number of times (or for a specified period of time, depending on the implementation); at this point, the operating system will refuse to allocate any more storage until the user deletes enough files so that his disk usage again falls below his soft limit.

The disk quota system has been designed to let users have large temporary files, provided that long-term they obey a much stricter limit. For example, consider a user with a hard limit of 15000 blocks and a soft limit of 10000 blocks. If this user's storage *ever* exceeds 15000 blocks, the operating system will refuse to allocate any more storage immediately; he will need to free some storage before he can save any more files. If this user's storage exceeds 10000 blocks, he'll get a warning but requests for more disk will still be honored. However, if this user does not reduce his storage below 10000 blocks, the operating system will eventually refuse to allocate any additional storage until it does fall below 10000 blocks.

If you decide to implement a quota system, you must determine which filesystems need quotas. In most situations, the filesystems containing user home directories are appropriate candidates for quotas. Filesystems that are reserved for public files (for example, the root filesystem) probably don't need quotas. The */tmp* filesystem doesn't usually have quotas since it's designed to provide temporary scratch space.

Preparing Filesystems for Quotas

After deciding which filesystems will have quotas, you'll need to edit their entries in the filesystem configuration file */etc/fstab* (*/etc/vfstab* under V.4). Under BSD, you need to add the keyword *quota* to the options field (the fourth field in each entry). For example, the BSD */etc/fstab* entry:

```
/dev/disk1d /chem 4.2 rw,quota 1 2
```

specifies that quotas are in effect on the */chem* filesystem, which is located on disk */dev/disk1d*. If the entry for the filesystem in question already contains the keyword *noquota*, change it to *quota*. Otherwise, add ",quota" to the end of the current list.

Under V.4, change the *rw* in the last field to *rq*; for example:

```
/dev/dsk/c1d1s2 /dev/rdsk/c1d1s2 /chem ufs 1 yes rq
```

Next, make sure that there is a file named *quotas* in the top-level directory of each filesystem for which you want to establish quotas. If the file does not exist, create it with the *touch* command:

```
# cd /chem
# touch quotas
# chmod 600 quotas
```

The file must be writable by *root* and no one else.

Setting Users' Quota Limits

Use the *edquota* command to establish filesystem quotas for individual users. This command can be invoked to edit the quotas for a single user:

```
# edquota username(s)
```

When you execute this command, *edquota* will create a temporary file containing the hard and soft limits on each filesystem for each user. After creating the file, *edquota* invokes an editor so you can modify it (by default, *vi*; you can use the environment variable EDITOR to specify your favorite editor). Each line in this file describes one filesystem:

```
fs /chem blocks (soft=20000, hard=30000) inodes (soft=0, hard=0)
```

This line specifies quotas for the */chem* filesystem; by editing it, you can add hard and soft limits for this user's total disk space and inode space (total number of files). Setting a quota to 0 disables that quota. The example specifies a soft quota of 20000 disk blocks, a hard quota of 30000 disk blocks, and no quotas on inodes. Note that the entry in the temporary file does not indicate anything about the user(s) to which these quotas apply; quotas apply to the users specified when you execute the *edquota* command.

After you save the temporary quota file and exit the editor (using whatever commands are appropriate for the editor you are using), *edquota* modifies the *quotas* files themselves. These files should never be edited directly.

The *-p* option to *edquota* lets you copy quota settings to be copied between users. For example, the command:

```
# edquota -p chavez ng martin
```

will apply *chavez*'s quota settings to users *ng* and *martin*. *edquota*'s *-t* option (present in most later versions of *edquota* although not in the original BSD implementation) is used to specify the time limits for soft quotas.

Enabling Quota Checking

The *quotaon* command is used to enable quota checking:

```
# quotaon block-special-file
# quotaon -a
```

The first command enables the quota system for the specified filesystem. The latter enables quotas on all filesystems listed with quotas in the filesystem configuration file. For example, the command:

```
# quotaon /dev/disk2e
```

enables quotas for the filesystem on disk */dev/disk2e*.

Similarly, the command *quotaoff* disables quotas. It can be used with the *-a* option to disable all quotas, or with a list of filesystem names.

The command:

```
# quotacheck block-special-file
```

checks the consistency of the *quotas* file for the specified filesystem, and checks to see that the quota files are consistent with current actual disk usage. This command should be executed after you install or modify your quota system. If used with the option *-a*, *quotacheck* will check all filesystems listed in the filesystem configuration file.

The command:

```
# repquota block-special-file
```

reports the current quotas for the specified filesystem. You may wish to report quotas on several filesystems simultaneously; to do so, you may give a list of filesystems as arguments to *repquota*.

8

Filesystems and Disks

Mounting and Dismounting Filesystems
Managing Disk Space Usage
Using fsck to Validate a Filesystem
From Disks to Filesystems
Adding Disks
Striped Disks
Floppy Disks
Disks and Filesystems Under AIX 3.1
System V.4 Additional Device
  Management Features

Managing the UNIX filesystem is one of the system administrator's most important tasks. The system administrator is responsible for ensuring that users have access to the files and data that they need and that these files and data remain uncorrupted and secure. Administering the filesystem includes tasks such as:

- Making local and remote files available to users.

- Monitoring and managing the system's (usually) finite disk resources.

- Protecting against file corruption, hardware failures, and user errors via a well-planned backup schedule.

- Ensuring data confidentiality by limiting file and system access.

- Checking for and correcting filesystem corruption.

- Connecting and configuring new storage devices when needed.

Some of these tasks—such as checking for and correcting filesystem corruption—are usually done automatically at boottime, once the initial setup is done. Others—like backups—are usually done manually on an as-needed basis. We looked at file ownership and protection in the sections " File Ownership" and "File Protection," in Chapter 2, *The UNIX Way*, and at one method of managing disk space in the section "Managing Disk Usage with Disk Quotas (BSD and V.4)," in Chapter 7, *Managing System Resources*. This chapter describes how UNIX handles disks and covers such topics as mounting and dismounting them, the filesystem configuration file, checking filesystem integrity with the *fsck* utility, and adding new disks to the system. It closes by looking at some optional disk features offered in some UNIX implementations. Backups are the subject of Chapter 9, *Backup and Restore*.

Mounting and Dismounting Filesystems

Mounting is the process which makes a disk's contents available to the system, merging it into the system directory tree. A filesystem can be mounted or dismounted: that is, it can be connected to or disconnected from the overall UNIX filesystem. The only exception is the root filesystem, which is always mounted on the root directory while the system is up and cannot be dismounted.

Thus, in contrast to some other operating systems, mounting a UNIX filesystem does more than merely make its data available. Figure 8-1 illustrates the relationship between a system's disk partitions (and their corresponding special files) and its overall filesystem. On this system, the root filesystem—the filesystem stored on the first partition of the root disk (disk 0)—contains the standard UNIX subdirectories */bin*, */etc*, and so on. It also contains the empty directories */home*, */var*, and */chem*. This filesystem is accessed via the special file */dev/dsk/c1d0s0*.*

Figure 8-1 also shows several other filesystems. One of them, accessed via the special file */dev/dsk/c1d0s8* (partition 8 of the root disk), contains the files and directories under */var*. A third filesystem—partition 9 on disk 1—is accessed via the special file */dev/dsk/c1d1s9* and contains users' home directories, located under */home*.

---

*Disk special file naming conventions are discussed in "Fixed Disk Special Files," in Chapter 2, *The UNIX Way*.

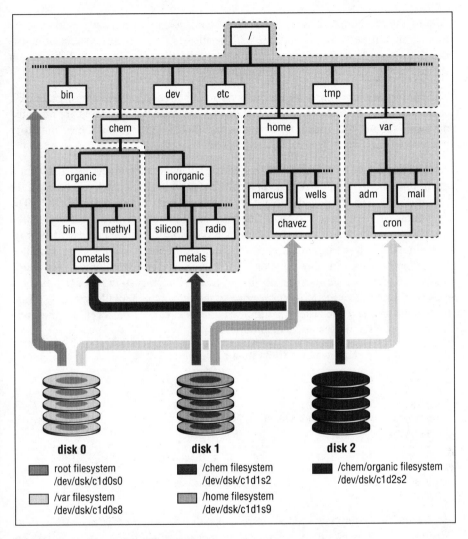

Figure 8-1. Mounting Filesystems

Another filesystem on this system is stored on partition 2 of disk 1 and is accessed via the special file */dev/dsk/c1d1s2*. Its own root directory contains the subdirectories *./organic*, and *./inorganic* and their contents. We'll call this the */chem* filesystem after its usual mounted position within the system's directory tree. When */dev/dsk/c1d1s2* is mounted, these directories will become subdirectories of */chem*.

One of the directories in the */chem* filesystem, *./organic*, is empty, and is to be used to mount yet another filesystem. The files in this fifth filesystem, on partition 2 on disk 2 and corresponding to the special file */dev/dsk/c1d2s2*, become a subtree of the *chem* filesystem when mounted.

The files in the root directory and its system subdirectories all come from disk0, as do the empty directories */chem*, */home*, and */var* before filesystems are mounted on them. Figure 8-1 illustrates the fact that the contents of the */chem* directory tree come from two different physical disks.

Note that there is no necessary connection (not even by convention) between a given filesystem and a particular disk partition (and its associated special file), for example, between the */chem* filesystem and the special file */dev/dsk/c1d1s2*. The collection of files on a disk partition can be mounted on *any* directory in the filesystem. After it is mounted, its top-level directory takes the name of the directory on which it was mounted. Effectively, the root directory of a mounted filesystem replaces the directory on which the filesystem is mounted. As a side effect, the files that were originally in the mount directory—in this example, any files that might have been in */chem* prior to mounting the new filesystem—disappear when the new filesystem is mounted and thus cannot be accessed; they will reappear once the filesystem is dismounted.

To illustrate this, let's watch a filesystem being mounted:

```
# ls -saC /chem             /chem's contents before mount.
total 20
    4 .           4 ..            12 README
# mount /dev/dsk/c1d1s2 /chem  Mount partition 2 on disk 1.
# ls -saC /chem             /chem's contents after mount.
total 48
    4 .           4 ..             4 inorganic
   32 lost+found  4 organic
# du -s /chem               /chem is much bigger.
587432    /chem
```

Before the filesystem is mounted, there is just one file in */chem* (*README*). After */dev/dsk/c1d1s2* is mounted, *README* disappears. It's still on the root disk, but can't be accessed while the */chem* filesystem is mounted. Once it is dismounted, the *README* file will reappear. After the filesystem is mounted, the subdirectories *organic* and *inorganic* appear, along with their contents (reflected in the larger amount of data under */chem*).

A filesystem can only be mounted in one place at one time; that is, a special file may only contain one directory tree. For example, the special file */dev/dsk/c1d1s2* cannot contain both the files in */chem* and the files in */tmp*. However, as we have seen previously, one filesystem can have another filesystem as a subtree within it.

The mount and umount Commands

To mount a filesystem manually, use the *mount* command as follows:

```
# mount block-special-file mount-point
```

This command mounts the filesystem located on the specified disk partition. The directory tree on this filesystem will be attached at *mount-point* within the overall UNIX filesystem. The directory *mount-point* must already exist before the *mount* command is executed. For example, the commands:

```
# mkdir /users2
# mount /dev/dsk/c1d1s8 /users2
```

mounts the filesystem located on the disk partition */dev/dsk/c1d1s8* on the directory */users2*. *mount*'s -r option may be used to mount a filesystem read-only. For example:

```
# mount -r /dev/dsk/c1d1s7 /mnt
# mount /dev/disk3b /mnt -r          XENIX and older BSD.
```

Similarly, the *umount* command may be used to dismount filesystems:

```
# umount name
```

This command dismounts the filesystem specified by *name*, where *name* is either the name of the filesystem's block special file or the name of the directory at which this filesystem is mounted.

The Filesystem Configuration File

Since mounting filesystems by hand would quickly become tedious, the required *mount* commands are executed automatically at boottime. The filesystem configuration file contains information about all of the system's filesystems, for use by *mount* and other commands. The form and name of this file varies somewhat from implementation to implementation, so we'll look at each version separately.*

---

*This section covers only local disks. "Mounting Remote Directories," in Chapter 12, *TCP/IP Network Management*, discusses mounting remote disks and their filesystem configuration file entries.

System V.3: /etc/fstab

Under V.3, */etc/fstab* has the following format:

> *block-special-file mount-loc* [*options*] [*fs-type*]

where the fields have the following meanings:

block-special-file   Special file corresponding to the desired filesystem.

mount-loc   Directory to which to attach the filesystem.

options   *-r* for mounting read-only; *-d* for a remote filesystem.

fs-type   Filesystem type string (optional).

For example, the entry (taken from a Stardent system):

```
/dev/dsk/0s1   /user3        S54K
```

indicates that the filesystem on */dev/dsk/0s1* is to be mounted on */user3*, and is of type "S54K" (System V, 4K block size). The type field is not always used, and the valid types vary from system to system.

XENIX: /etc/fstab

The */etc/fstab* file under XENIX uses a slight modification of the V.3 form. Its third field contains options to be passed on to the *fsck* and/or *mount* commands (if any), and it lacks the later fields. Here is a sample entry:

```
/dev/u /u fsckflags="-y" mountflags="-r"
```

This entry says that the disk partition accessed via the special file */dev/u* is to be mounted at */u*. The *mount* command will include the *-r* option (to mount the filesystem read-only), and when *fsck* is run on this filesystem, it will include the *-y* option (which says to repair all damage without prompting).

BSD: /etc/fstab

Under BSD, an entry in */etc/fstab* has the following form:

> *block-special-file mount-loc type opts dump-freq pass-number**

---

*Prior to NFS, colons were originally used as field separators in */etc/fstab*. On some systems, including Ultrix, colons are still used.

These fields have the following meanings:

block-special-file The name of the special file on which the filesystem resides. This must be a block device name.

mount-loc The directory at which to mount the filesystem. If the partition will be used for swapping, use / for this field.

type The kind of partition the entry refers to. The possible values are: *4.2* for normal, local partitions, *nfs* for volumes mounted remotely via NFS, *swap* for swap partitions, and *ignore*, which tells *mount* to ignore the line.

opts This field consists of one or more options, separated by commas. The *type* field, above, determines which options are allowed for any given kind of filesystem. For *ignore* type entries, this field is ignored. For *swap* entries, this field should be "sw." If the file's type is *4.2*, the options field may include the following keywords, separated by commas:

rw	Read-write filesystem.
ro	Read-only filesystem.
suid	The SUID access mode is permitted.
nosuid	The SUID access mode is not permitted.
quota	Quotas may be placed in effect.
noquota	Quotas are not in use.

Option names occasionally vary on some systems. If the filesystem type is *nfs*, many more options are supported (see the section entitled "Mounting Remote Directories," in Chapter 12, *TCP/IP Network Management*).

dump-freq A decimal number indicating the frequency with which this filesystem should be backed up. A value of 1 means backup should occur every day, 2 means every other day, and so on. This field should be 0 for swap devices.

pass-number A decimal number indicating the order in which *fsck* should check the filesystems. A *pass-number* of 1 indicates that the filesystem should be checked first, 2 indicates that the filesystem should be checked second, and so on. The root filesystem must have a *pass-number* of 1. All other filesystems should have higher pass numbers. For optimal performance, two filesystems that are on the same disk drive should have different pass numbers; however, filesystems on different drives may have the same pass number, letting *fsck* check the two filesystems in parallel. *fsck* will usually be fastest if all filesystems checked on the same pass have roughly the same size. This field should be 0 for swap devices.

Here are some typical BSD */etc/fstab* entries:

```
/dev/disk0a  /      4.2  rw          1  1
/dev/disk0b  /      swap sw          0  0
/dev/disk1e  /chem  4.2  rw          1  2
/dev/disk2e  /bio   4.2  rw,quota    1  2
```

The first entry specifies that the device */dev/disk0a* (partition *a* on disk 0) is the root filesystem. It is accessible for reading and writing, it must be backed up daily, and it is always the first filesystem to be checked by *fsck*. Partition *b* on this drive is part of the system's swap space. Therefore, it is not a filesystem, and it is not backed up. Partition *e* on drive 1 contains the */chem* filesystem. It is accessible for reading and writing, is backed up daily, and is checked for accuracy on *fsck*'s second pass. The final local entry shows partition *e* on disk drive 2, which is mounted at */bio*; it is mounted read-write and uses disk quotas. It has the same backup and *fsck* schedule as */chem*.

System V.4: /etc/vfstab

Under V.4, the filesystem configuration file changes name to */etc/vfstab*. It has the following format (very similar to the BSD version):

blk-spfile char-spfile mount-loc type fsck-pass automount? opts

The fields in a *vfstab* entry are:

blk-spfile   Block special file (to be used by *mount*).

char-spfile   Character special file (to be used by *fsck*).

mount-loc   Directory at which to mount the filesystem.

type   Filesystem type: *ufs*, *s5*, or *nfs*. V.4 filesystem types are discussed later in this chapter.

fsck-pass   A decimal number indicating the order in which *fsck* should check the filesystems. A *pass-number* of 1 means it should be checked first and is used for the root filesystem. 2 indicates that the filesystem should be checked second, and so on. For optimal performance, two filesystems that are on the same disk drive should have different pass numbers; however, filesystems on different drives may have the same pass number, letting *fsck* check the two filesystems in parallel.

automount?   The keyword *yes* or *no*, indicating whether the filesystem is to be automatically mounted by the *mountall* command.

opts   A comma-separated list of keywords.

For local filesystems, the following option keywords apply:

rw   Read-write filesystem.

ro   Read-only filesystem.

rq   Read-write filesystem with disk quotas in effect.

suid   The SUID access mode is permitted.

nosuid   The SUID access mode is not permitted.

Here is a typical */etc/vfstab* entry:

```
/dev/dsk/c1d1s2 /dev/rdsk/c1d1s2  /chem  ufs  2  yes  rw
```

This entry says that partition 2 on disk 1 is to be mounted read-write at */chem* (automatically on bootups). It is a *ufs* filesystem (BSD-style), checked during *fsck*'s second pass.

AIX 3.1: /etc/filesystems

The filesystem configuration file under AIX 3.1 is */etc/filesystems*. This file is updated automatically by various AIX 3.1 filesystem manipulation commands, including *crfs*, *chfs* and *rmfs*. */etc/filesystems* contains all of the information in */etc/fstab* and some additional data as well, arranged in a stanza-based format:

```
/:
        dev     = /dev/hd4
        vol     = "root"
        mount   = automatic
        check   = true
        free    = true
        vfs     = jfs
        log     = /dev/hd8

/u2:
        dev     = /dev/us00
        vfs     = jfs
        log     = /dev/loglv01
        mount   = true
        check   = 2
        options = rw
```

Each mount point in the overall filesystem has its own stanza, specifying which logical volume (equivalent to a disk partition for this purpose) is to be mounted there.

The most important fields are:

dev   Special file for the logical volume.

mount   Whether the filesystem is mounted automatically by a *mount all* command or not (include at boottime). *true* means that it is, *false* means that it isn't, and *automatic* is the keyword used for the root filesystem.

check   An integer indicating the order in which *fsck* should check the filesystems. A *pass-number* of 1 means it should be checked first; it should not be used for non-root filesystems. 2 indicates that the filesystem should be checked second, and so on. For optimal performance, two filesystems that are on the same disk drive should have different pass numbers; however, filesystems on different drives may have the same pass number, letting *fsck* check the two filesystems in parallel. The keyword *true* says that the filesystem should be checked but leaves it to *fsck* to decide when. The keyword *false* disables automatic checking with *fsck*; it is not recommended.

options Either *rw* (read-write) or *ro* (read-only).

vfs   Filesystem type: *vfs* for local filesystems or *nfs* for remote.

Automatic Filesystem Mounting

Regardless of its form, once the filesystem configuration file is set up, mounting may take place automatically. The commands below mount all defined filesystems:

```
# mount -a          (BSD)
# mountall          (System V)
# mount all         (AIX 3.1)
```

In addition, the *mount* and *umount* commands will now only require either the mount point or the special file name as their argument. For example, the command:

```
# mount /chem
```

looks up */chem* in the configuration file to determine what special file is used to access it and then constructs and executes the proper *mount* command.

Similarly, the command:

```
# umount /dev/disk1d
```

dismounts the filesystem on special file */dev/disk1d*. Any of the options that can be specified in the filesystem configuration file can also be included on the *mount* command. Check your system's manual page for details.

Managing Disk Space Usage

This section looks at the tools available to monitor and track system disk usage (we've already looked at them briefly in the section "Example: Monitoring Disk Usage," in Chapter 6, *Automating Routine Tasks*). It then goes on to discuss ways of approaching a perennial administrative challenge: getting users to reduce their disk use.

df: Display Filesystem Statistics

The *df* command produces a report that describes all the filesystems, their total capacities, and the amount of free space available on each one. Here is an example of its output under BSD (in this case, from a Sun):

```
Filesystem    kbytes    used    avail capacity  Mounted on
/dev/sd0a       7608    6369     478    93%     /
/dev/sd0g      49155   45224       0   102%     /corp
```

This output reports the status of two filesystems: */dev/sd0a*, the root disk, and */dev/sd0g*, the disk mounted at *corp* (containing all files and subdirectories underneath */corp*). Each line of the report shows the filesystem's name, the total number of kilobytes on the disk, the number of kilobytes in use, the number of kilobytes available, and the percentage of the filesystem's storage that is in use. It is evident that both filesystems are heavily used. In fact, the */corp* filesystem appears to be overfull. BSD UNIX holds back some amount of space in each filesystem, allocable only by the superuser (usually about 10%). A filesystem may appear to use over 100% of the available space when it has tapped into this reserve.

Under standard BSD, the *-i* option reports on inodes as well:

```
% df -i                     (Output shortened.)
Filesystem    kbytes    used    avail capacity  iused    ifree %iused
/dev/disk0a   239855  179655   36214    83%     3405   117555    3%
/dev/disk1e   635287  548513   23245    96%    35417    30119   54%
```

Under SunOS, *-i* reports only the inode data; under AIX 3.1, the *-i* option is on by default.

The System V version of *df* produces a differently formatted listing by default:

```
$ df
/           (/dev/dsk/c1d5s0 ):    11448 blocks    2520 i-nodes
/bio        (/dev/dsk/c1d5s2 ):   192984 blocks   59093 i-nodes
```

The command displays the mount point, special file, and the number of 512-byte blocks and inodes in use for each filesystem. The *-t* option may be used to display total capacity information as well. The *-v* option produces a BSD-like display.

You should run *df* frequently; administrators often put a *df* command in *root*'s initialization file (*.login* or *.profile*).

du: Report on Disk Usage

The *du* command reports the amount of disk space used by all files and subdirectories underneath one or more specified directories, listed on a per-subdirectory basis. On both System V and BSD systems, *du* reports disk usage in blocks. However, the definition of a block varies: System V uses 512-byte blocks while BSD uses 1-kilobyte blocks. A typical *du* report looks like this:

```
$ du /u/chavez
50      /u/chavez/bin
114     /u/chavez/src
. . .
34823   /u/chavez
```

This report states that in the directory */u/chavez*, the subdirectory *bin* occupies 50 blocks of disk space, and the subdirectory *src* occupies 114 blocks. Using the *du* command on users' home directories and on directories where ongoing development is taking place is one way to determine who is using the system's disk space.

The report from *du* can be inordinately long and tedious. By using the *-s* option, you eliminate most of the data; *du -s* reports the total amount of disk space that a directory and its contents occupies, but does not report the storage requirements of each subdirectory. For example:

```
$ du -s /u/chavez
34823   /u/chavez
```

reports that */u/chavez* and its contents occupy 34823 blocks, but says nothing about how storage is distributed within this directory. In many cases, this may be all the information you care about.

To generate a list of the system's directories in order of size, execute the command:

```
$ du / | sort -rn
```

This command starts at the root filesystem, lists the storage required for each directory, and pipes its output to *sort*. With the *-rn* options (reverse sort order, sort by numeric first field), *sort* orders these directories according to the amount of storage they occupy, placing the largest first.

If the directory specified as its parameter is large or has a large number of subdirectories, *du* can take quite a while to execute. It is thus prime candidate for automation via scripts and after-hours execution via *cron*.

quot: Report Usage by User (BSD, XENIX, and V.4)

One other useful command available in BSD-based versions of UNIX, under XENIX, and under V.4, is *quot*, used as follows:

```
# quot block-special-file
```

quot reports the number of kilobytes used by each user in the specified filesystem. It is run as *root* to access the disk special files. Here's a typical example:

```
# quot /dev/disk0a
/dev/disk0a:
6472    root
5234    bin
62      sys
2       adm
```

This report indicates that on the root disk 6472 kilobytes are owned by the user *root*, 5234 kilobytes are owned by user *bin*, and so on. This command can help you to spot users who are consuming excessive amounts of disk space, especially in areas other than their home directories. Like *du*, *quot* must access the entire disk and so can take an appreciable amount of time to execute.

Handling Disk Shortage Problems

The commands and scripts we've just looked at will let you know when you have a disk space shortage and where the available space has gone, but you'll still have to solve the problem and free up the needed space somehow. There is a large range of approaches to solving disk space problems, including the following:

- Buy another disk. This is always the ideal solution, but it's not always practical, unfortunately.

- Mount a remote disk that has some free space on it. This solution assumes that such a disk is available, that mounting it on your system has no security problems, and that adding additional data to it won't cause problems on its home system. (See Chapter 12, *TCP/IP Network Management*, for details on mounting remote disks.)

- Convince or cajole users into deleting unneeded files and backing up and then deleting old files they are no longer using. If you are successful, a great deal of free disk space usually results. At the same time, you should check the system for log files that can be reduced in size (discussed later in this chapter).

- When gentle pressure on users doesn't work, sometimes peer pressure will. The system administrator on one system I worked on used to mail a list of the top five "disk hogs"—essentially the output of the *quot* command—whenever disk space was short. I recommend this approach only if you have both a thick skin and a good-natured user community.

- Some sites automatically archive and then delete user files that haven't been accessed in a certain period of time (the shortest period I've ever seen used is two months). If a user wants a file back, he can send a message to the system administration staff who will read it back on. This approach is the most brutal and should only be taken when absolutely necessary. I've only ever seen it used in universities. It's also easy to circumvent by *touch*ing all your files every month.

These, then, are some of the alternatives.* In most cases, though, when you can't add any disks to the system, the most effective way to solve a disk space problem is to convince users to reduce their storage requirements by deleting old, useless, and seldom (if ever) used files (after backing them up first). Junk files abound on all systems. For example, many text editors create checkpoint and backup files as protection against a user error or a system failure. If these collect, they can consume a lot of disk space. In addition, users often keep many versions of files around (noticed most often in the case of program source files), frequently not even remembering what the differences are between them.

The system scratch directory */tmp* also needs to be cleared out periodically (as well as any other directories serving a similar function). If your system doesn't get rebooted very often, you'll need to do this by hand. You should also keep an eye on the various system spooling directories under */usr/spool* or */var/spool*, including *lp*, *mqueue*, *mail*, and *uucppublic*, as files can occasionally become stagnant there.

---

*There is another way to limit users' disk usage on some systems: disk quotas. However, quotas won't help you once the disks are already too full. Disk quotas are discussed in Chapter 7, *Managing System Resources*.

Finally, UNIX itself has a number of accounting and logging files that, if left unattended, will grow without bound. As administrator, you are responsible for extracting the relevant data from these files periodically and then truncating them. We'll look at dealing with these sources of wasted space in the following sections.

NOTE

Under some circumstances, especially on BSD systems, a filesystem's performance can begin to degrade when a filesystem is more than 90% full. Therefore, it is a good idea to take any corrective action when your filesystems reach 90% of capacity, rather than waiting until they are completely full.

Using find to Locate or Remove Wasted Space

The *find* command, previously discussed in Chapter 1, *Introduction to System Administration*, may also be used to locate potential candidates for archival and deletion (or just deletion) in the event of a disk space shortage. For example, the command:

```
$ find / -atime +60 -print
```

lists the names of all files anywhere in the system (literally, in all subdirectories under the root directory) that have not been accessed within the last 60 days. Similarly, the command:

```
$ find / -name ".BAK.*" -o -name "*~" -print
```

prints all files with names beginning with *.BAK.* or ending with a tilde, the formats for backup files from two popular text editors. As we've seen, *find* can also delete files automatically. For example, the following command deletes all editor backup files over one week old:

```
# find / /bio /corp -atime +7 \( -name ".BAK.*" \
  -o -name "*~" \) -type f -mount -exec rm -f {} \;
```

When using *find* for automatic deletion, it pays to be cautious. That is why the previous command includes the *-type* and *-mount* options (the latter would be *-xdev* under BSD) and lists each filesystem separately. With the *cron* facility, you can use *find* to produce a list of files subject to deletion nightly (or to delete them automatically).

Limiting the Growth of Log Files

If left unattended, a number of system logging files will grow without limit. The system administrator is responsible for reaping any data needed from these files and keeping them to a reasonable size. The major offenders include:

- The various system log files in */usr/adm* (or */var/logs* under V.4), which may include *sulog*, *messages*, and other files set up via keywords in files in */etc/default* (System V) or with the system log daemon in its configuration file */etc/syslog.conf* (BSD, some System V, and AIX 3.1).

- Accounting files in */usr/adm* (or */var/adm* under V.4 and SunOS), especially *wtmp* (occasionally stored in */etc*) and *acct* (BSD) or *pacct* (System V). Also, under System V, the space consumed by the cumulative summary files and ASCII reports in */usr/adm/acct/sum* and */usr/adm/acct/fiscal* are worth monitoring (under */var* in V.4). Accounting is discussed in detail in Chapter 13, *Accounting*.

- Crash dump files in */usr/crash* on BSD systems. Crash dumps should be used and then deleted or discarded.

- Subsystem log files: many UNIX facilities, such as *cron*, the mail system, and the printing system, keep their own log files. Common names and locations include:

/usr/spool/lp/log	Printing log file under BSD.
/usr/spool/lp/logs/lpsched	Changes to printer status under System V.
/usr/spool/lp/logs/requests	Individual print requests under System V.
/usr/lib/cron/log	*cron* log file.
/usr/sbin/cron.d/log	*cron* log file under V.4.
/usr/lib/spell/spellhist	*spell* history file under System V.
/usr/spool/uucp/LOGFILE	BNU *uucp* log files.
/usr/spool/uucp/SYSLOG, *usr/spool/uucp/LOG/**	Version 2 *uucp* log subdirectories (each contains multiple log files).

The various UNIX subsystems are described in later chapters of this book.

- Under AIX 3.1, the files *smit.log* and *smit.script* in users' home directories are appended to every time someone runs SMIT. They get big fast. You should watch the ones in your own and *root*'s home directories (if you *su* to *root*, the files still go in your home directory). Alternatively, you could run the *smit* command with the *-l* and *-s* options (which specify the log and script filenames respectively) and set both filenames to */dev/null*. Defining an alias is the easy way to do so:

```
alias smit="smit -l /dev/null -s /dev/null"    ...Korn shell...
alias smit "smit -l /dev/null -s /dev/null"    ...C shell...
```

There are several approaches to controlling the growth of system log files. The easiest is to truncate them by hand when they become large. This is advisable only for ASCII (text) log files. The binary accounting files need to be handled differently; they are discussed in detail in Chapter 13, *Accounting*. To reduce a file to zero length, use a command like:

```
# cp /dev/null /usr/adm/sulog
```

Copying the null device onto the file is preferable to deleting the file because in some cases the subsystem won't recreate the log file if it doesn't exist. It's also slightly preferable to *rm* followed by *touch* because the file ownerships and permissions stay the same.

To retain a small part of the current logging information, use *tail*, as in this example:

```
# cd /usr/adm
# tail -100 sulog >tmp
# mv tmp sulog
Check file ownership & protection.
```

A third approach is to keep several old versions of a log file on the system by periodically deleting the oldest one, renaming the current one, and then recreating it. Here is a script that keeps the last three versions of the *sulog* file in addition to the current one:

```
#!/bin/sh
cd /usr/adm
if [ -r sulog.1 ]; then
  mv -f  sulog.1 sulog.2
fi
if [ -r sulog.0 ]; then
  mv -f  sulog.0 sulog.1
fi
if [ -r sulog ]; then
  mv -f sulog sulog.0
fi
cp /dev/null sulog
```

There are three old *sulog* files at any given time: *sulog.0* (the previous one), *sulog.1*, and *sulog.2*, in addition to the current *sulog* file. When this script is executed, the *sulog*.n files are renamed to move them back: 1 becomes 2, 0 becomes 1, and the current *sulog* file becomes *sulog.0*. Finally, a new, empty file for current *su* messages is created. This script could be run automatically each week via *cron*, and the last month's worth of *sulog* files will always be on the system (and no more).

This approach may be modified in several ways: more than three old files can be saved, the files can be rotated daily or monthly instead of weekly, or the oldest files could be written to tape before overwritting them.

The AIX 3.1 skulker Script

AIX 3.1 provides the *skulker* script (stored in */etc*) to perform some of these filesystem cleanup operations, including the following:

- Clearing the queueing system spool areas of old, junk files.

- Clearing */tmp* and */usr/tmp* of all files over one day old.

- Deleting old news files (over 45 days old).

- Deleting a variety of editor backup files, core dump files, and random executables (named *a.out*).

The system comes set up to run *skulker* every day at 3:00 a.m. daily via *cron*, but the crontab entry is commented out. If you want to run the *skulker*, you'll need to remove the comment character from the *skulker* line in *root*'s crontab file.

Using fsck to Validate a Filesystem

A number of problems, ranging from operator errors to hardware failures, can corrupt a filesystem. The *fsck* utility ("filesystem check") checks the filesystem's consistency, reports any problems it finds, and optionally repairs them. Only under very rare circumstances will these repairs cause even minor data loss.

fsck can find the following filesystem problems:

- One block belonging to several files (inodes).

- Blocks marked as free but in use.

- Blocks marked as used but free.

- Incorrect link counts in inodes (indicating missing or excess directory entries).

- Inconsistencies between inode size values and the amount of data blocks referenced in address fields.

- Illegal blocks (e.g., system tables) within files.

- Inconsistent data in the filesystem's tables.

- Lost files (non-empty inodes not listed in any directory). *fsck* places these files in the directory named *lost+found* in the filesystem's top-level directory.

- Illegal or unallocated inode numbers in directories.

Basically, *fsck* performs a consistency check on the filesystem, comparing such items as the block free list against the disk addresses stored in the inodes (and indirect address blocks) and the inode free list against inodes in directory entries.

Under BSD, the *fsck* command is run automatically on boots and reboots. Under System V and XENIX, *fsck* is run at boottime on non-root filesystems only if they were not dismounted cleanly (e.g., if the system crashed). System administrators will need to run this utility themselves only rarely: on boots, when *fsck*'s automatic mode isn't authorized to repair all problems, after creating a new filesystem, and under a few other circumstances. Nevertheless, you need to understand how *fsck* works so that you'll be able to verify that the system boots correctly and to quickly recognize abnormal situations.

CAUTION

Except for the root filesystem, *fsck* always runs on *unmounted* filesystems. To *fsck* the root filesystem, take the system to single-user mode.

fsck has the following syntax:

```
# fsck [options] filesystem
```

where *filesystem* is the special file for the filesystem. *fsck* runs faster on a character special file. However, the block device must be used for the root filesystem. If *filesystem* is omitted—as it is at boottime—then all filesystems listed in the filesystem configuration file will be checked under BSD, all filesystems listed in */etc/checklist* will be checked if necessary under System V and XENIX, and all filesystems whose *check* keyword is not *false* will be checked under AIX 3.1.

If *fsck* finds any problems, it will ask whether or not to fix them. The example below shows an *fsck* report giving details about several filesystem errors and prompting for input as to action to take:

```
# fsck /dev/rdisk1e
/dev/rdisk1e
** Phase 1 -- Check Blocks and Sizes
POSSIBLE FILE SIZE ERROR I = 478

** Phase 2 -- Check Pathnames
```

```
** Phase 3 -- Check Connectivity
** Phase 4 -- Check Reference Counts
UNREF FILE I = 478  OWNER = 190  MODE = 140664
SIZE = 0  MTIME = Sept 18 14:27 1990
CLEAR? y       It's a socket, so it's ok to remove it.

FREE INODE COUNT WRONG IN SUPERBLOCK
FIX? y

** Phase 5 -- Check Cylinder Groups

1243 files   28347 blocks  2430 free
*** FILESYSTEM WAS MODIFIED ***
```

fsck found an unreferenced inode—an inode marked as in use but not listed in any directory. *fsck*'s output indicates its inode number, owner UID, and mode. From this information, we can figure out that the file is owned by user *chavez* and is a symbolic link. The mode is interpreted as follows:

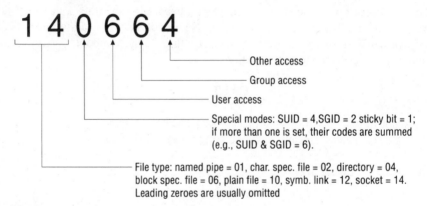

The first one or two digits of the mode indicate the file type, in this case a socket which can be safely removed.

The available options for *fsck* allow automatic correction of the filesystem to take place (or be prevented):

n   Answer no to all prompts: list but don't repair any problems found.

-y   Answer yes to all prompts; repair all damage regardless of severity. Use this option with caution.*

-p   Preen the filesystem; perform repairs that don't change any file's contents (BSD and V.4 for *ufs* filesystems).

---

*At the same time, it's not clear what alternatives you have. You can't mount a damaged filesystem, and, unless you're a real UNIX wizard, *fsck* is the only tool available for fixing the filesystem.

-b nn   Use an alternate superblock located at block *nn* (BSD and V.4 for *ufs* filesystems).

-s   Reconstruct the free list and write out to the superblock (V.3).

-q   Quiet mode: remove unreferenced named pipes and reconstruct the free list without comment.

-D   Check directories for bad blocks (V.3).

-b   Remount the root filesystem (or reboot if necessary) if it was modified (V.3).

-F type Specify filesystem type (V.4).

For BSD-type filesystems, whether on BSD or V.4 systems, *fsck* is normally run with the *-p* option. In this mode, the following problems will be silently fixed:

- Lost files will be placed in the filesystem's *lost+found* directory, named for their inode number.

- Link counts in inodes too large.

- Missing blocks in the free list.

- Blocks in the free list also in files.

- Incorrect counts in the filesystem's tables.

- Unreferenced zero-length files are deleted.

More serious errors will be handled with prompts as in the previous example.

For *ufs* filesystems under V.4, the BSD-style options are specified as arguments to the *-o* option (the type-specific options flag). For example, the following command checks the ufs filesystem on */dev/dsk/c1d0s8* and makes necessary nondestructive corrections without prompting:

```
# fsck -F ufs -o p /dev/dsk/c1d0s8
```

The *-F* qualifier is optional if it can be deduced from the filesystem's entry in the */etc/vfstab* file. Pre-V.4 versions of System V often use the following option combination in system boot scripts:

```
# fsck -y -s -D -b special-file
```

After fsck

If *fsck* modifies any filesystem, it will print a message like:

```
*** FILESYSTEM WAS MODIFIED ***
```

If the root filesystem was modified, an additional message will also appear, indicating additional action needed:

for BSD:
```
*** REBOOT UNIX ***
```

for System V:
```
***** REMOUNTING ROOT FILESYSTEM *****
```

If this occurs as part of a normal boot process, then the remount or reboot will be initiated automatically. If *fsck* has been run manually on the root filesystem on a BSD system, then the rebooting command will need to be entered by hand. Use the *reboot* command with the *-n* option:

```
# reboot -n
```

The *-n* option is very important. It prevents the *sync* command from being run, which flushes the output buffers and might very well recorrupt the filesystem. This is the only time when rebooting should occur without *sync*-ing the disks.

From Disks to Filesystems

As we've seen, the basic UNIX file storage unit is the disk partition. Filesystems are created on disk partitions, and then all of the separate filesystems are combined together into a single directory tree. This section discusses the process by which a physical disk becomes one or more filesystems on a UNIX system. It treats this topic at the conceptual level; the following section discusses the mechanics of adding a new disk to the system, including the necessary commands.

Disk Partitions

Both the System V and BSD versions of UNIX organize disks around fixed-size partitions. The locations and sizes of the partitions are determined when the disk is formatted. The UNIX operating system treats disk partitions as logically independent devices, each of which is accessed as if it were a physically separate disk. For example, one physical disk may be divided into four partitions, each of which will hold its own filesystem. Alternatively, a physical disk may be configured with only one partition (comprising its entire capacity), and several recent UNIX implementations allow several physical disks to be combined into a single logical partition, accessed as a single filesystem. AIX 3.1 carries this trend to its logical conclusion, allowing multiple physical disks to be combined into a single logical disk, which can then itself be divided into logical partitions.*

Physically, a disk consists of a stack of circular platters, forming essentially a cylinder (although there are gaps between the platters). Reading and writing is done by a series of heads which move in and out along the radius of the platters as they spin around at high speed. (The basic idea is thus not so different from an audio turntable, although both sides of the platters can be accessed at once.) Partitions consist of subcylinders of the disk: specific ranges of distance from the vertical center of the stack of platters (from, say, one inch to two inches, to make up an arbitrary example). Thus, a disk partition uses the same sized and located circular subsection on all the platters in the disk drive. Simply put, disks are divided vertically, through the platters, not horizontally.

On microcomputer systems, partitions can be defined as part of adding a new disk (see the section "Adding a Hard Disk (XENIX and Interactive UNIX)," later in this chapter). However, in most versions of System V and BSD, disk partitions are defined in advance by the operating system, and there is no easy or standardized way to change them. These predefined disk partitions comprise the only ways to use the disk drive. Some more recent implementations do provide ways of customizing these definitions; check the documentation for your system. Both System V and BSD UNIX provide a very limited amount of flexibility by defining more than one division scheme for the physical disk. Here's how this works. Each disk is divided into some number of partitions: usually eight for BSD and ten for V.4. However, the division is a logical rather than a literally physical one. Figure 8-2 depicts a common BSD-based partition scheme.

---

*AIX 3.1 uses the term "partition" in a very different way. The corresponding term for standard UNIX disk partitions under AIX 3.1 is "logical volume." See the section "Disks and Filesystems Under AIX 3.1," later in this chapter.

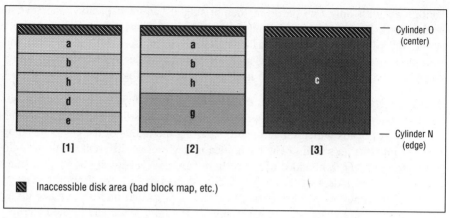

Figure 8-2. Sample BSD Disk Partitioning

Each rectangle corresponds to a different disk partition and graphically represents the partition's location within the disk. Each of the three drawings illustrates one way of dividing up the disk (imagine that the disk has been sliced along a radius and opened out). Eight different partitions are defined for the disk, named by letters from *a* to *h*.

Three drawings are needed to display all eight partitions because some of them are defined to occupy the same disk locations. The striped area at the top of each drawing indicates the part of the disk that should not be touched, containing the bad block list and other disk data. The *c* partition, as it is usually defined under BSD, comprises the entire disk, including this forbidden area; this is why the *c* partition is never used.*

There are seven other defined partitions, *a*, *b*, and *d* through *h*. However, it is not possible to use them all at one time, since some of them include the same physical areas of the disk. Partitions *d*, *e*, and *f* occupy the same space as partition *g* in the sample layout. Hence, a disk will use *either* partitions *d* through *f or* partition *g*, *but not both*. The *a*, *b*, and *h* partitions appear in both diagrams 1 and 2 because they can coexist with either scheme. (Their double appearance doesn't mean that there are two *a* partitions.)

---

*Some systems (including SunOS) have redesigned the disk drivers so that there is no forbidden area, and you can use the *c* partition to build a filesystem on the entire disk. To avoid making a BIG mistake, ALWAYS check your documentation before doing this. Assume you can't use *c* unless you're explicitly told otherwise.

This disk layout, then, offers two different ways of using the disk, divided into four or six partitions, each of which may hold a filesystem (or be used as a swap partition). Some disk partitioning schemes offer more alternative layouts of the disk. Flexibility is designed in to meet the needs of different systems.

Each of these layouts uses the disk drive as fully as possible. Furthermore, any disk drive can have any layout, and you can change a disk's layout without reformatting it (although you do need to generate new filesystems, as described later in this chapter). This flexibility has the following consequence: nothing prevents you from using a disk drive inconsistently: for example, nothing prevents you from mounting */dev/disk2d* and */dev/disk2g* from the same disk. However, this will have catastrophic consequences, since these two partitions overlap. To prevent this, you can use the *chmod* command to make the special files for partitions you do not use inaccessible. For example, the command:

```
# chmod 000 /dev/disk2g
```

makes the partition */dev/disk2g* inaccessible even to its owner, preventing you from mounting it accidentally.

Filesystems

Before any disk partition can be used, a filesystem must be built on it. Filesystems each occupy a single device, accessed with a specific special filename, however the data may actually be stored: as part or all of a single physical disk, as parts of several physical disks, as the aggregation of multiple physical disks. When a filesystem is made, certain data structures are written to disk which will be used to access and organize the physical disk space into files.

The most important of these data structures is the *superblock*. A superblock is a table that contains important information about the filesystem such as its label, size, and total number of inodes. If the superblock is damaged, the filesystem becomes unreadable. Under the System V native filesystem type, certain dynamic information about current free space is placed there too, to allow quick allocation of new files. Filesystem organization differs significantly between System V and BSD, although many V.3-based implementations have adopted the BSD form, and it is also available under V.4, so each type is described individually in the subsections that follow.

Traditional System V Filesystems

The superblock of standard System V filesystems (known as the *s5* type in V.4) also contains information about currently available free space on the disk partition. It holds the number of free inodes and data blocks, the first 50 free inode numbers, and the addresses of the first 100 free disk blocks. Following the superblock come the inodes, followed by the data blocks.

The System V filesystem was designed for storage efficiency. It tends to use a small block size of 2K bytes or less (minuscule, in fact, by modern standards). A block is the basic unit of disk storage;* all files consume space in multiples of the block size; any excess space cannot be used by other file and is therefore wasted. If a filesystem has a lot of small files, a small block size will minimize wastage and fragmentation (the extent to which files are noncontiguous). However, small block sizes are much less efficient when transferring large files.

The Berkeley Fast Filesystem

The BSD (so-called) Fast Filesystem was designed to remedy the performance limitations of the System V filesystem. It supports filesystem block sizes of up to 64KB. Since merely increasing the block size to this level would have had a horrendous effect on the amount of wasted space, the designers introduced a subunit to the block: the *fragment*. While the block remains the I/O transfer unit, the fragment becomes the disk storage unit. Each block may be divided into one, two, four, or eight fragments.

Whatever its absolute performance status, the BSD filesystem is an unequivocal improvement over System V. Hence its inclusion in V.4 as the *ufs* filesystem type. In addition to performance advantages, the BSD filesystem introduced reliability improvements as well. For example, it replicates the superblock at various points in the filesystem. If the primary superblock should be damaged, an alternate one may be used (instead of the disk becoming unreadable). The utilities that create new filesystems will report where the spare superblocks are located.

The BSD filesystem format has a more complex organizational structure as well. It is organized around *cylinder groups*: logical subcylinders of the total partition space. Each cylinder group has a copy of the superblock, a cylinder group map recording block use in its domain, and a fraction of the inodes for that filesystem (as well as data blocks). The data structures are placed at a different offset into each cylinder group to ensure that they land on different platters. Thus, in the event of limited disk damage, a copy of the superblock will still exist somewhere

---

*This "block" is not connected to the blocks used in output from commands like *df* and *du*. The latter are always 512 bytes under System V and 1K under BSD regardless of the actual filesystem block size.

on the disk, as well as a substantial portion of the inodes, enabling significant amounts of data to be potentially recoverable. In contrast, if all of the vital information is in a single location on the disk, damage there effectively destroys the entire disk.

The System V.4 bfs Filesystem

V.4 supports a third filesystem type, named *bfs*. It is used for booting only, never for user filesystems. It is a contiguous, flat filesystem (i.e., no directories), designed for quick access at boottime. The partition mounted as /*stand*, which contains the kernel image *unix* and the system configuration file *system*, is always a *bfs* filesystem.

Adding Disks

In order to make a new disk accessible to users, the following conditions must be met:

- The disk must be physically attached to the computer system. Consult the manufacturer's instructions as well as your own system's hardware documentation for the procedure.

- A suitable device driver for its disk controller must be present in the operating system. If the new disk is being added to an existing controller or you're also adding a new controller that is among those supported by the operating system, this is not a problem.

- The disk must be formatted.* Often this is done by the disk manufacturer for larger systems, although most versions of UNIX include utilities to perform this function.

- The special files required to access the disk's partitions must be created.

- A UNIX filesystem must be created on each of the disk partitions to be used.

- The new filesystems must be entered into the filesystem configuration file.

- Any site-specific activities must be performed (such as installing disk quotas).

---

*DOS uses the term "format" differently than UNIX does. Formatting a disk under DOS is equivalent to making a filesystem under UNIX (and most other operating systems). UNIX disk formatting is equivalent to what DOS call a "low level format."

The processes used to handle these activities will be discussed in the subsections that follow.

Before a new disk is added to the system, the administrator must decide how it is going to be used: which partitions will have filesystems created on them and what files (types of files) will be stored in them. The layout of your filesystems can influence your system's performance significantly. Therefore, you should take some care in planning the structure of your filesystem. For best performance, heavily used filesystems should each have their own disk drive, and they should not share a disk with a swapping partition. Preferably, heavily used filesystems should be located on drives controlled by different controllers (a disk controller acts as an interface between the raw device and the UNIX device driver; each controller can typically handle multiple disks). This setup balances the load between disk drives and disk controllers.

Adding a Hard Disk (XENIX and Interactive UNIX)

The steps required to add additional disk drive to a microcomputer system are actually more complicated that those needed for some much larger systems. Fortunately, most manufacturers provide a simple-to-use menu interface for this procedure. For example, under XENIX, the *mkdev* command may be executed from system maintenance mode (single-user mode) once the new drive has been connected to the computer. This command provides a series of menus which allow you to configure the disk and its filesystems and automatically constructs and executes the required XENIX commands. Similarly, under Interactive UNIX, you can use the *sysadm* menu interface from single-user mode to add a second hard disk: select the "diskmgmt" (choice 1) from the main menu, then "harddisk" (choice 5), and finally "addharddisk" (choice 2). The overall process is highly automated—commands are run automatically, and you are prompted for all necessary information—and proceeds as follows:

- Specify initial disk drive data. Under Interactive UNIX, you specify the controller number and drive number for the new disk. Under XENIX, you set parameters for formatting the disk if it is a non-standard model (the number of heads and cylinders, the sectors/track, and the like). If the new drive is one of the supported drives, this step may be skipped. If custom configuration is required, the *dkinit* command is executed.

- Format the disk if necessary (Interactive UNIX only). If the manufacturer of your disk states that it is pre-formatted, skip this step. Disks added to XENIX systems must be pre-formatted before invoking *mkdev*.

CAUTION

Formatting a disk destroys any data that has previously been stored on the disk. There are very few instance where it will be necessary to reformat a disk. However, if you are reformatting a disk that is already in use, and if you do not want to lose the disk's contents, *make a backup before beginning the formatting process*.

- Divide the new disk between UNIX and DOS, via the *fdisk* command. *fdisk* can divide a disk into up to four DOS partitions, not all of which need be used by UNIX (*fdisk* is modeled after the DOS utility of the same name). The UNIX partition is itself divided into partitions, which are what become separate UNIX filesystems. Microcomputer documentation thus uses the term *partition* in two distinct ways; it is the latter usage which corresponds to the standard UNIX meaning of the term.

  For a second hard disk, you should tell *fdisk* to use the entire disk for UNIX (unless you want a DOS partition for some reason).

- Scan the disk surface for defects. It is recommended that you always do the "thorough" scan.

- Divide the UNIX area of the disk into UNIX-style partitions (the command invoked by the menu system is *divvy* under XENIX and *mkpart* under Interactive UNIX). You can configure the size of these partitions and also specify how much space should be used for a swap partition (if any). XENIX also allows you to name the partitions anything you choose (answer yes to the prompt asking you if you want block control to reach the proper menu). From this menu, you should first name the partitions (the *n* option) and then create them (the *c* option). The special files corresponding to the filesystem(s) will also be created at this point, named /dev/*fsname* and /dev/r*fsname*, where *fsname* is the name you assigned.

- Create filesystems (with *mkfs*) on the partitions, check them, and create *lost+found* directories.

- Mount the new filesystems, creating the mount point directories if necessary. The filesystems are also added to the /etc/*fstab* and /etc/*checklist* as appropriate.

After the process completes, verify that the filesystems are mounted (use *df*) and have been added to */etc/fstab* and */etc/checklist*. Add any needed flags to the filesystem configuration file entries.

Adding Disks to Multi-user Systems (BSD and System V)

The discussion that follows assumes that the new disk to be added is connected to the computer and has already been formatted and is ready to accept filesystems. Many disks for popular UNIX systems arrive preformatted, so check with your disk's manufacturer. If your disk isn't preformatted, check the system documentation for the proper formatting command (often it's called *format*). Sometimes the disk formatting utility is accessible only from a menu in maintenance mode.

Once the disk is ready, creating filesystems is a relatively straightforward process. The commands used to create new filesystems are *mkfs* (System V) and *newfs* (BSD).

Making Special Files

Before filesystems can be created on a disk, the special files for the desired disk partitions must exist. Sometimes, they will already be on the system when you go to look for them. Under V.4, the autoboot process will automatically create the appropriate special files when it detects new hardware.

Otherwise, you'll have to create them yourself. Special files are created with the *mknod* command. *mknod* has the following syntax:

```
# mknod name c|b major minor
```

where the first argument is the filename, and the second argument is the letter *c* or *b*, depending on whether you're making the character or block special file. The other two arguments are the major and minor device numbers for the device. These numbers serve to identify the proper device location and device driver to the kernel. The major device number indicates the general device type (disk, serial line, etc.), and the minor device number indicates the specific member within that class.

These numbers are highly implementation-specific. To determine the numbers you need, use the *ls -l* command on some existing special files for disk partitions; the major and minor device numbers will appear in the size field. For example:

```
$ cd /dev/dsk; ls -l c1d*          ↓Major, minor device numbers.
brw-------  1 root     root     0,144 Mar 13 19:14 c1d1s0
brw-------  1 root     root     0,145 Mar 13 19:14 c1d1s1
brw-------  1 root     root     0,146 Mar 13 19:14 c1d1s2
 . . .
```

```
brw--------  1 root     root      0,150 Mar 13 19:14 c1d1s6
brw--------  1 root     root      0,151 Mar 13 19:14 c1d1s7
brw--------  1 root     root      0,160 Mar 13 19:14 c1d2s0
brw--------  1 root     root      0,161 Mar 13 19:14 c1d2s1
. . .
$ cd /dev/rdsk; ls -l c1d1*
crw--------  1 root     root      3,144 Mar 13 19:14 c1d1s0
crw--------  1 root     root      3,145 Mar 13 19:14 c1d1s1
. . .
```

The numbering pattern is pretty clear: block special files disks on controller 1 have major device number 0; the corresponding character special files have major device number 3. The minor device number of the same partition of successive disks differs by 16. So if you want to make the special files for partition 2 on disk 3, its minor device number would be 162+16 = 178, and you'd use the following *mknod* commands:

```
# mknod /dev/dsk/c1d3s2 b 0 178
# mknod /dev/rdsk/c1d3s2 c 3 178
```

Be sure to make both the block and character special files.

Under BSD, the */dev* directory includes a shell script named *MAKEDEV* which automates running *mknod*. It takes the base name of the new device as an argument and creates the character and block special files defined for it. For example, the following command creates the special files for a second SCSI disk under SunOS:

```
# MAKEDEV sd1
```

It creates the special files */dev/sd0[a-h]* and */dev/rsd0[a-h]*.

Making a New Filesystem

At the heart of this process is a program called *mkfs*, which is directly responsible for creating the new filesystem. The BSD *newfs* command is simply an easy-to-use interface to *mkfs*.

Under System V, in its simplest form, *mkfs* has the following syntax:

```
# mkfs char-spec-file size[:inodes]
```

where its required arguments are the character special file corresponding to the disk partition upon which to create the filesystem and the size of the filesystem in 512-byte blocks. The number of inodes to create may also be specified; the default is one for every 2K, under the default logical block size (I/O transfer amount) of 1024 bytes. This is almost always sufficient. Only filesystems which contain many, many tiny files will need more. A logical block size of 512 or 2048 bytes may be specified with the *-b* option (placed at the *end* of the command line).

The only unknown piece of information, then, is the size of the filesystem. There are many ways of obtaining this number. In most V.3-based implementations (including Interactive UNIX and SCO XENIX), a file named */etc/partitions* stores partition information, and you can look up the partition size there. Under V.4, the *mkfs* command has a *-m* option, which will display the command used to create an existing filesystem. You can use it to check the size of an existing filesystem on a different disk using the same partition as the one to be created.

The *newfs* command is used to create a filesystem under BSD. Its syntax is:

```
# newfs spec-file disk-name
```

where its arguments are the raw special file for the desired disk partition and the name of the disk, as defined in the file */etc/disktab*. This file defines the parameters for a number of standard disks (in a similar manner to the *termcap* and *printcap* files). Here is an example of *newfs*:

```
# newfs /dev/rdisk2g cdc-9715
```

This command builds a filesystem on the g partition of the third disk, which is a CDC 9715 model drive.

NOTE

Some operating systems, like SunOS, don't require the *disk-name* argument to *newfs* since they can figure it out from the drive itself. Now that's a utility!

The most useful options to *newfs* are:

-b size   Filesystem blocksize (default = 8192, max. = 64K).

-i bytes   Bytes-per-inode (default = 2048).

-m free   Percentage of free space reserved (default = 10).

The *-N* option to *newfs* may be used to have the command display all of the parameters it would pass to *mkfs* (which is much more elaborate under BSD) without building a filesystem.

System V Release 4 introduces a *-F* option to *mkfs*, which takes the type of filesystem to be made as its parameter: *s5* (old System V) or *ufs* (BSD fast filesystem). If the latter is specified, the *size* argument is interpreted in sectors and the number of inodes may not be specified—in other words, the command follows a BSD-like syntax. Consider the following commands:

```
# mkfs -F s5 -b 2048 /dev/rdsk/c1d1s2 409600
# mkfs -F ufs /dev/rdsk/c1d1s2 552960
```

The first command builds an *s5* filesystem on the third partition of the second disk on the second controller, using a block size of 2048 bytes. The second command builds a *ufs* filesystem on the same device, using the BSD *mkfs* syntax.

After mkfs

Once the filesystem has been created, it should be checked with *fsck* immediately, prior to initial mounting. After you have created the new filesystem and it has been checked. it should be entered into the filesystem configuration file, */etc/fstab* or */etc/vfstab*, so it will be checked and mounted automatically on future boots. It may then be mounted with the *mount* command.

Remaking an Existing Filesystem

Occasionally, it may be necessary to reconfigure a disk. For example, you might want to select a different layout, using a different set of partitions. You might want to change the value of a filesystem parameter, such as its block size. Or you might want to add an additional swap partition or get rid of an unneeded one. In order to do any of these things, you must recreate the existing filesystems.

Recreating a filesystem will destroy all the existing data in the filesystem, so it is essential to perform a full backup first (and to verify that the tapes are readable; see Chapter 9, *Backup and Restore*. For example, the following commands may be used to reconfigure a filesystem with a 16K block size under BSD:

```
# umount /chem                              Dismount filesystem.
# dump 0ds 6250 24000 /dev/disk2g           Backup.
# restore t                                 Check tape is OK!
# newfs -b 16384 /dev/rdisk2g cdc-9715      Remake filesystem.
# mount /chem                               Mount new filesystem.
# cd /chem                                  Restore files.
# restore r
```

The cautious administrator will make two copies of the backup tape. The following commands combine three filesystems on disk 1 into a single one by making a filesystem on the partition which exactly overlaps the three smaller ones:

```
# umount /dev/rdisk1d          Unmount the filesystems.
# umount /dev/rdisk1e
# umount /dev/rdisk1f          Back up all three filesystems and verify all tapes.
# newfs /dev/rdisk1g cdc-9715  Edit /etc/fstab to remove the old filesystems and
                                   add the new one.
# mount /dev/rdisk1g           Restore all files, creating any needed top-level
                                   directories first.
```

Striped Disks

Disk striping is an option that is increasingly available as an extension to UNIX, especially on high performance systems. Striping combines one or more physical disks (or disk partitions) into a single logical disk, viewed like any other filesystem device by the rest of UNIX. Disk striping is used to increase I/O performance at least as much as creating filesystems spanning more than one physical disk. Striped disks split I/O transfers across the component physical devices, performing them in parallel, and are thus able to achieve significant speedups over the performance of a single disk (although not the nearly-linear factors that are occasionally claimed). Striping is especially effective for single process transfer rates to a very large file. UNIX systems offering striped disks provide utilities for configuring physical disks into a striped device. For example, the command under Stardent UNIX looks like this:

```
# mkfarm -m 0 /c2d0s2 /c3d0s2
```

This command combines two disks into a single "disk farm" and then makes a filesystem on its associated device, */dev/rfarm/farm0*. Stardent UNIX also provides additional utilities to further configure and manage disk farms. Since there is no standard way to implement disk striping, other manufacturers who provide it will supply different—although often quite similar—commands.

The following general considerations apply to striped disk configurations:

* For maximum performance, the individual disks in the striped filesystem should be on separate disk controllers. If possible, no two disks should be on the same controller.

* The individual disks must be *identical* devices: the same size, the same layout format, and often the same brand. If the layouts are different, then the size of the smallest one is often what is used for the filesystem and any additional space on the other disks will be unusable and wasted.

- In general, disks used for file striping should not be used for any other purpose. For example, having swap partitions on disks used for disk striping will diminish their effectiveness.

- In no case should the device containing the root filesystem be used for disk striping.

NOTE

AIX 3.1 volume groups are not striped disk systems. Filesystems may span multiple physical disks, but they lack the parallel data transfer facilities and performance advantages of true disk striping.

Floppy Disks

On systems with floppy disk drives, UNIX filesystems may also be created on floppy disks. Before they can be used, floppy disks must, of course, be formatted.

The UNIX commands to do so are:

labelit   Label diskette.

format   Format diskette.

fmtflop   Format diskette (V.4).

All commands take the name of a character special file as their argument. Once a diskette is labeled and formatted, a filesystem can be built on it with *mkfs*.

For example, the following commands format and label a diskette and create a filesystem on it under Interactive UNIX:

```
# format /dev/rdsk/f05ht
# mkfs /dev/dsk/f05ht 2370:592 2 30
# labelit /dev/rdsk/f05ht extra floppy2
```

Check your operating documentation for the *mkfs* parameters recommended on your system.

Once created, floppy disk filesystems are mounted like any other filesystem. Sometimes it is useful to include *mount*'s *-r* option, which mounts a filesystem read-only.

WARNING

Like any other filesystem, floppy disk filesystems should be unmounted
(with *umount*) before removing the diskette from the drive or shutting
down the system.

Floppy Disk Special Files

Floppy disk special files often have names of the */dev/fp*n where *n* is the number
of the floppy drive. Sometimes the naming conventions are more elaborate, specifying many characteristics about the diskette, including its size and density. For
example, under Interactive UNIX floppy devices have the form:

/dev/f*nsdkh*

where the fields have the following meanings:

n   Drive number.

s   Size (*3* or *5* for 3-1/2" and 5-1/4" floppies, respectively).

d   , Density (*d, h* or *q*, for double, high, and quad, respectively).

k   Sectors/track (*8* or *9*; used only for 5-1/4", double density: *5d*).

h   How much of diskette to use (blank = all but cylinder 0, *t* = all, or *u* = all
         but cylinder 0, track 0).

For example, the special file */dev/f05d9* refers to the first floppy drive, writing
5-1/4 inch floppy disks at double density and 9 sectors/track.* The full floppy
device name is needed only for *format* operations; for all other commands, a
device name of the form */dev/rdsk/f*n (where *n* is the floppy drive number) may be
substituted.

Interactive UNIX also supports the general System V device naming conventions
for floppy disks. For example, the special file */dev/c0d0s5* refers to a floppy
diskette in drive 0. Best of all, alternate forms are also found in the directories

---

*A different naming scheme was used in earlier versions. For compatibility, the following aliases are
recognized by Interactive UNIX:

New Style	Old Style	Example
5h	q15d	f0q15dt=f05ht
5d8	d8d	f0d8dt=f05d8t
5d9	d9d	f0d9dt=f05d9t

/dev/SA and /dev/rSA, named in a more intuitive way, linked to the appropriate controller-device-section special file. For example:

```
% ls /dev/SA/disk*
disk0_1.2M    disk0_1.44M  disk0_360k   disk0_720k    disk1_1.2M
disk1_1.44M   disk1_360k   disk1_720k
```

XENIX has a substantially different floppy disk special file naming convention:

/dev/fd*ntzx*

where *n* is the drive number, *t* is the tracks per inch, *z* is either *ss* or *ds* (for single- or double-sided), and *x* is the number of tracks on the diskette. For example, the special file */dev/fd096ds9* refers to the first floppy drive, writing double-sided, 9-track diskettes at 96 tracks/inch.

Disks and Filesystems Under AIX 3.1

AIX 3.1 handles disks and filesystem management in a way completely different from standard UNIX. This section looks at the "AIX 3.1 way," especially with regard to disks.

This discussion will present the normal AIX 3.1 commands for the tasks it covers. As always, a menu-driven interface is available via SMIT. Even if you decide to use that method of executing the commands, the discussion below will aid you in navigating through its many layers of menus by providing you with a conceptual understanding of the process of filesystem creation.

In the AIX 3.1 world, you will do well to forget everything you know about disk partitions under UNIX. Not only is a completely different vocabulary employed, some UNIX terms—like partition—are used with completely different meanings. Once past the initial obstacles, the AIX 3.1 point of view is very clear and sensible. A willing suspension of disbelief will come in very handy at first, however.

Disks

To begin at the beginning, there are *disks*: real, material, solid objects that hurt your toe if they're dropped on it. There are, however, also *defined disks*, which is what a disk becomes once the operating system learns about it. Usually, AIX 3.1 will discover new devices at boottime and automatically create special files for them (like V.4). Defined disks have special filenames like */dev/hdisk1*. The *cfgmgr* command may be used to search for new devices between boots (IPL's); it has no arguments.

Before it can be used, a defined disk has to become *available*. The command below will make *hdisk1* an available disk:

```
# mkdev -l hdisk1
```

If *hdisk1* is already available, the *mkdev* command will have no effect.

Before an available disk can be used, it needs to be designated a *physical volume*. Usually, the preceding commands will take care of this. However, if you get an error message complaining that a disk isn't a physical volume, commands like the following will take care of it:

```
# chdev -l hdisk1 -a pv=clear
# chdev -l hdisk1 -a pv=yes
```

The first command resets the physical volume status, and the second makes *hdisk1* a physical volume. Some older versions of AIX 3.1 will display this symptom with the *extendvg* command (described in the next section).

Unless you're adding a third party disk yourself, you may not ever need to perform these configuration steps just described for the disks on your system; usually, they're done for you when field service installs a disk. You will probably have to create filesystems yourself, however. If you use the *df* command and don't see all the space you expect, execute the following command:

```
# lsdev -C -c disk -H
```

which says to list all the defined disks on the system. That way you will know if AIX 3.1 knows about all your disks or not.

Available physical disks are divided into *physical partitions*, whose default size is 4 MB. These are units of disk storage, but they have nothing to do with UNIX disk partitions. The *lspv* command may be used to list the characteristics and contents of physical volumes by physical partition.

Volume Groups

Physical disks must next be defined as part of a *volume group*. A volume group is a named collection of disks. Volume groups allow filesystems to span physical disks, although it is not necessary that they do so. Paradoxically, the volume group is the AIX 3.1 equivalent of the UNIX physical disk: that entity which can be split into subunits, each of which holds a single filesystem. Unlike UNIX disk partitions, volume groups are infinitely flexible in how they may be divided into filesystems.

To create a new volume group, use the *mkvg* command:

```
# mkvg -y "chemvg" hdisk1 hdisk2
```

This command creates a volume group named *chemvg* consisting of the disks *hdisk1* and *hdisk2*. The following options are useful (both take a numeric argument):

-d   Maximum number of disks in the volume group (default = 32).

-s   Physical partition size in MB: 1, 2, 4 (default), or 8.

After a volume group is created, it must be activated with the *varyonvg* command:

```
# varyonvg chemvg
```

Thereafter, the volume group will be activated automatically at each bootup. Volume groups are deactivated with *varyoffvg*; all of their filesystems must be dismounted first.

A new disk may be added to an existing volume group with the *extendvg* command. For example, the following command adds the disk *hdisk4* to the volume group named *chemvg*:

```
# extendvg chemvg hdisk4
```

The following other commands operate on volume groups:

chvg   Change volume group characteristics.

reducevg   Remove a disk from a volume group (removing all disks deletes the volume group).

lsvg   List information about volume groups.

importvg   Add an existing volume group to the system (used to move disks between systems and to activate existing volume groups after replacing the root disk).

exportvg   Remove a volume group from the system device database but don't alter it (used to move disks to another system).

Logical Volumes

Logical volumes are the entities upon which filesystems reside. They consist of some number of fixed physical partitions (disk chunks) located arbitrarily within a volume group (unless specific physical volumes are requested when the logical volume is created). Hence, logical volumes may be any size that is a multiple of the physical partition size for their volume group. They may be easily increased in size after creation while AIX 3.1 is running. There is a one-to-one correspondence between logical volumes and filesystems.

Logical volumes are divided into *logical partitions*. Many times, physical and logical partitions are identical (or at least map one-to-one). AIX 3.1 logical volumes have the capability for storing redundant copies of all data if desired; from one to three copies of each data block may be stored. If one copy is stored, then one logical partition consists of one physical partition. If two copies are stored, then one logical partition consists of two physical partitions: the two copies of the data. In other words, there is one logical partition for each discrete data block, and there is one physical partition for each copy of the data block.

The main AIX 3.1 data storage entities are illustrated in Figure 8-3. The figure shows how three physical disks are combined into a single volume group (named *my_vg*). The separate disks composing it are suggested via the dotted lines. Three user logical volumes are then defined from *my_vg* (in addition to the logging volume group required by AIX 3.1). Two of them—*lv01* and *lv02*—store a single copy of their data using physical partitions from two separate disks. The other logical volume, *lv00*, contains an equal number of physical partitions from all three disks; it stores three copies of its data (each on a separate disk), and one physical partition per disk is used in each of its logical partitions.

Logical volumes are created with the *mklv* command. A simple form of it is:

```
mklv -y "lvname" volgrp nn
```

where *lvname* is the name of the logical volume, *volgrp* is the volume group name, and *nn* is the number of logical partitions. For example, the command:

```
# mklv -y "chm00" chemvg 64
```

makes a logical volume in the *chemvg* volume group consisting of 64 logical partitions (256 MB) named *chm00*. The special files */dev/chm00* and */dev/rchm00* will automatically be created by *mklv*.

Multiple data copies may be specified with the -c option, which takes the number of copies as its argument (the default is 1). The *mklv* command has many other options, which allow the administrator as much control over how the logical volume maps to physical disks as desired, down to the specific physical partition level. However, the default settings work very well for most applications.

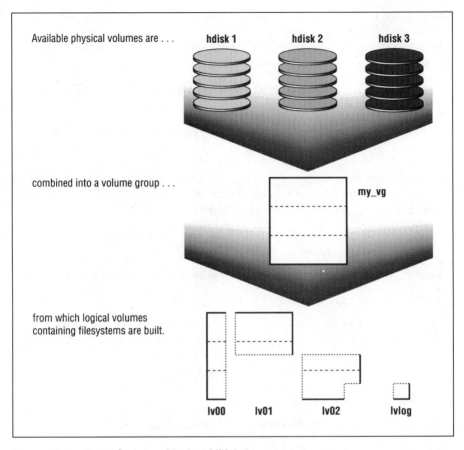

Figure 8-3. Data Storage Under AIX 3.1

The following commands operate on logical volumes:

extendlv   Increase the size of a logical volume.

chlv   Change the characteristics of a logical volume.

mklvcopy   Increase the data copies in a logical volume.

lslv   List data about logical volumes.

rmlv   Delete a logical volume.

A small logical volume in each volume group is used for logging and other disk management purposes. Such logical volumes are created automatically by AIX 3.1 and have names like *lvlog00*.

Filesystems

AIX 3.1 has a version of *mkfs*, but *crfs* is a much more useful command for creating filesystems. There are two ways to create a filesystem:

- Create a logical volume and then create a filesystem on it. The filesystem will occupy the entire logical volume.

- Create a filesystem and let AIX 3.1 create a logical volume for you automatically.

The second way is faster, but the logical volume name is nondescriptive (*lv00* for the first one so created, and so on), and the size must be specified in 512-byte blocks rather than in logical partitions (4 MB units).

The *crfs* command is used to create a filesystem. The following basic form may be used to create a filesystem:

```
crfs -v jfs -g vgname -a size=n -m mt-pt -A yesno -p prm
```

where the options have the following meanings:

-v jfs   The filesystem type is *jfs* ("journaled filesystem," using the logging logical volume in its volume group), the normal local filesystem type. The other important type is *nfs*, used for remotely mounted filesystems.

-g vgname   Volume group name.

-a size=n   Size of the filesystem, in 512-byte blocks.

-m mt-pt   Mount point for the filesystem (created if necessary).

-A yesno   Whether the filesystem is mounted by *mount all* commands.

-p prm   Access: *rw* (read-write) or *ro* (read-only).

For example, the following command will create a new filesystem in the *chemvg* volume group:

```
# crfs -v jfs -g chemvg -a size=50000 -m /organic2 -A yes -p rw
# mount /organic2
```

The new filesystem will be mounted at */organic2* (automatically at boottime) and is 25 MB in size. A new logical volume will be created automatically, and the filesystem will be entered into */etc/filesystems*. The initial mount must be done by hand.

The *-d* option is used to create a filesystem on an existing logical volume:

```
# crfs -v jfs -d chm00 -m /inorganic2 -A yes -p rw
```

This command creates a filesystem on the logical volume we created earlier. The size and volume group options are not needed in this case.

Increasing the Size of a Filesystem

A filesystem's size may be increased as long as there are free physical partitions within its volume group. There need not be any free logical partitions within its logical volume. The *chfs* command may be used to increase the size of a filesystem. For example, the following command increases the size of the */inorganic2* filesystem (and of its logical volume *chm00*) created above:

```
# chfs -a size=+50000 /inorganic
```

An absolute or relative size may be specified on the size parameter (in 512-byte blocks). The size of logical volume may be increased with the *extendlv* command, but it has no effect on filesystem size.

The following commands operate on AIX 3.1 *jfs* filesystems:

lsfs   List data about filesystems.

chfs   Change filesystem characteristics.

rmfs   Remove a filesystem, its associated logical volume and its entry in */etc/filesystems*.

Currently, there is no easy way to decrease the size of a filesystem, even if there is unused space within it. If you want to make a filesystem smaller, you need to backup up the current files (and verify that the tape is readable!), delete it and its logical volume, create a new, smaller filesystem, and then restore the files. The freed logical partitions can then be allocated as desired within their volume group; they can be added to an existing logical volume, used to make a new logical volume and filesystem, used in a new or existing paging space, or held in reserve.

Adding a Disk Under AIX 3.1

Adding a new disk under AIX 3.1 follows the same basic steps as for other UNIX systems, although the commands used to perform them are quite different. The process can be summarized as follows:

- Connect the disk drive to the computer, following the manufacturer's instructions. If you are adding a SCSI disk to the end of the chain, be sure to move the terminator to the proper location.

- If it is installed correctly, when you reboot the machine, the new drive should be detected by the operating system, and its special file will be created automatically. If the system can't find it, recheck the connections and the drive's documentation, and then run the *cfgmgr* command.

- Make the new device available with the *mkdev* command (we'll use *hdisk3* in our examples):

  ```
  # mkdev -l hdisk3
  ```

- If necessary, make the drive a physical volume; for example:

  ```
  # chdev -l hdisk3 -a pv=yes
  ```

  In a few cases, you may need to set the *pv* attribute to *clear* first.

- Add the drive to an existing volume group (or create a new volume with it). For example, the following command adds our new disk to the *chemvg* volume group:

  ```
  # extendvg chemvg hdisk5
  ```

The new disk is now ready for incorporation into the system. You can now use the logical partitions on the new disk in several ways. You can create one or more filesystems (and logical volumes), you can add them to existing filesystems, or you use them for paging by using them in an existing or new paging space.

Reorganizing the Default root Volume Group Structure

By default, the root volume group, *rootvg*, is set up with separate filesystems (and logical volumes) for the root directory, */tmp*, */usr*, and */u* (the default location for user home directories). This scheme can be wasteful since unused space in one of these filesystems is not available to the others.

Some sites choose to combine some or all of these filesystems into the root filesystem. The process for doing so is outlined below. Before beginning any of it, however, *be sure to make and verify full backups of all affected filesystems*, including the root filesystem. The methods listed below are cautious—there are other ways to achieve the same results, depending on your system configuration and degree of recklessness. All of them should be performed only when there are no users on the system.

Removing the separate */tmp* filesystem is fairly straightforward. Edit the entry for */tmp* from */etc/filesystems* so that the *mount* attribute equals *false*, and then reboot the system. Rebooting ensures that no process is using any file in */tmp*. Then execute the command:

```
# rmfs /tmp
```

This will remove the */tmp* filesystem, its entry in the filesystem configuration file, and its associated logical volume. The */tmp* in the root directory will then become the real */tmp* and not just its mount point. You can then add the space freed up to the root filesystem:

```
# chfs -a size=+80000 /
```

The value given to *size* may differ on your system.

You can consolidate the */u* filesystem into the root filesystem in a similar manner if you do so before adding any users to the system. Once */u* contains data, however, it's much more of a pain and may not be worth it. You'll need to back it up first (be sure to check that the backup tape is readable), and restore it after removing its filesystem and adding the free space to the root filesystem. Here is a snapshot of the procedure:

```
# find /u -cpio /dev/mt0 -print     Or another backup command.
# cpio -itv </dev/mt0               Verify the tape.
# unmount /u                        Unmount it.
# rmfs /u                           Remove the filesystem.
# chfs -a size+200000 /             Give its space to /.
# cpio -idv </dev/mt0               Restore the files.
```

You'll need to substitute the proper devices and sizes for your system. If you have a spare disk, you can also copy the data in */u* there instead of to tape.

Merging */usr* into the root filesystem is trickier still and to me doesn't seem worth the effort or risks involved (if you mess up, you get to restore the whole operating system from tape). The problem here is that many of the system files and shared libraries reside under */usr*. Therefore, you can only remove it from maintenance mode. Once there, the general process is the same as for */u*: back up the files (and verify the tape), remove the filesystem, add the free space to the root filesystem, and then restore the files. You'll need to do all of this from the C shell as it's the only one not dependent on anything in */usr*. To change to the C shell, use the *exec* command:

```
# exec /bin/csh
```

After you're through, reboot to multi-user mode. If you've done everything correctly, the system will come up normally, with */usr* now residing in the root filesystem.

System V.4 Additional Device Management Features

System V Release 4 introduces more advanced device management features, via device attributes and device groups. Device attributes allow device characteristics to be pre-specified to commands via a device database, and device groups allow classes of devices to be defined to enable collective management and command equivalence among them. Although we'll use disk partitions for most of the examples in this section, the features described here can apply to all device types.

Device groups are supported by some V.4 commands, such as *backup* (and support will probably increase in the future). Their advantage is that they may be specified in lieu of a particular device, and the first device within the specified group will be used. For example, if a device group is specified as the destination device to *backup*, then the first available device in the group—the first available tape drive, say—will be used for the backup operation.

The Device Database

The device database is stored in the file */etc/device.tab*. It is maintained with the *putdev* command and viewed with the *getdev* and *devattr* commands.

Devices in the device database are identified by means of *aliases*: descriptive names of the form *device-typeN* where *device-type* indicates the type of device and *N* is an integer. The following are examples of device-types:

9track   9-track tape drive.

ctape   Cartridge tape drive.

dpart   Disk partition.

disk   Physical Disk.

diskette   Diskette drive.

The *putdev* command defines or modifies a device alias in the device database. To add a device alias, the -*a* option is used, followed by the alias name, followed by zero or more attribute *keyword=value* pairs. There are a plethora of attributes. Some of the most important attributes are:

bdevice   Block special file for this device.

cdevice   Character special file for this device.

desc　　　　Brief description of the device.

type　　　　Type keyword (as described above).

capacity　　Data capacity.

dparttype　Disk partition type (for disk partitions); *fs* = filesystem.

dpartlist　　Disk partition list (for disks).

mountpt　　Mount point (for *dparttype* = *fs*).

For example, the following command defines the alias *dpart7* in the device database:

```
# putdev -a dpart7 desc="Bio filesystem" bdevice=/dev/dsk/c2d2s2 \
   cdevice=/dev/rdsk/c2d2s2 dparttype=fs type=dpart mountpt=/bio
```

The alias *dpart7* refers to partition 2 on the third disk on the third controller, mounted at */bio*.

putdev's *-m* option may be used to modify an existing device by specifying its alias and the attributes to be changed. The *-d* option may be used to remove a device database entry.

The *getdev* command may be used to list the devices in the device database. Without any arguments, it lists all defined devices:

```
# getdev
diskette1
disk1
disk2
dpart7
ctape0
 . . .
```

The *getdev* command may be used to search for devices having certain desired attributes by including a list of *attribute* = *value* pairs. The equal sign may also be replaced by "!=" to find non-matching entries. (Escape the exclamation point if you're using the C shell.) The value may be set to an asterisk to mean "that attribute is defined." The attributes are OR'ed together by default (any entry matching any one of them will be displayed). They may be AND'ed by separating them with the *-a* option.

For example, the following command lists all entries defined as disk partitions:

```
# getdev type=dpart
```

The first command below selects all devices with a nonrewinding special file specified; the second command lists all defined disk partitions that are not filesystems:

```
# getdev norewind=*
# getdev -a type=dpart 'dparttype!=fs'
```

The *devattr* command is used to display the defined attributes of a specific device. For example, the command below lists the attributes of the *dpart7* device:

```
# devattr dpart7
```

devattr can also search on attribute values in a manner identical to *getdev*.

Device Groups

V.4 also allows defined devices to be grouped together in collections known as *device groups*. Device groups are stored in the file */etc/dgroup.tab*. The *putdgrp* command is used to create a new device group. It takes the device group name and the list of devices to place in the group as its arguments. For example, the following command creates a device group named *mineallmine*:

```
# putdgrp mineallmine dpart7 dpart8 diskette9 9track4
```

If the specified groupname already exists, the listed devices are added to it. The *getdgrp* and *listdgrp* commands are used to list the names and contents of device groups respectively. They function similarly to *getdev* and *devattr*.

9

Backup and Restore

Backing Up the Filesystem
Restoring Files from Backup
Storing Backup Media
Tape Special Files

Any user of any computer system knows that files are occasionally lost. These losses have many causes: users may delete their own files accidentally, a bug can cause a program to corrupt its data file, a hardware failure may ruin an entire disk, and so on. The damage resulting from these losses can range from minor to very expensive. To ensure against them, one primary responsibility of a system administrator is planning and implementing a backup system that periodically saves all files on the system. It is also the administrator's responsibility to see that backups were performed in a timely manner and that backup tapes (and other media) are stored safely and securely.

A few years ago, 9-track tape was the only medium you'd consider using for a backup. That's no longer true; there are many different media, and selecting one can be a difficult task. Here's a quick summary of the choices you have available:

9-track tape   9-track tape is the old workhorse. Its advantage used to be that there were 9-track tape drives everywhere, so you could move tapes from one system (or site) to another without trouble. That's no longer true; 9-track tape drives are becoming rare. 9-track tape technology is very reliable and reasonably fast—in fact, extremely fast with the proper hardware (meaning: an extremely expensive tape drive, and a main-frame style I/O system). However, the tapes are bulky, the hardware is expensive, and you can't store a tremendous amount on one tape (roughly 150 MB at the highest density). In practice, this means that you can't do an unattended backup. Most modern disk drives have a capacity much greater than a single tape, so you need to mount a new reel part-way through the backup.

1/4 inch cartridge tape

1/4 inch cartridge tape is the medium of choice for most workstations. They are very reliable and the tape drives are reasonably inexpensive and standard equipment for most workstations. They are also much smaller than 9-track tapes, which is a big advantage if you have a lot of disks. The capacity of a cartridge tape is roughly the same as the capacity of a 9-track tape, so you still can't do unattended backups.

8 and 4 millimeter video tape

Lately, small video tapes have become an extremely useful medium for backup. They are very small and have an incredible capacity (2 Gigabytes or more). This makes them ideal for unattended backups: you can put a tape in at night, start a shell script that puts several filesystems on one tape, and go home. Their one disadvantage is that these tapes seem even more sensitive to heat than other types.

Floppy Disk   Floppy disk drives are everywhere; they are well-known, cheap, and reliable. However, the capacity of a floppy disk is VERY small. Unless you can isolate your backup requirements to a few files, they don't present a reasonable option. It could easily take several hundred diskettes to do a full backup of a reasonably large filesystem. If you're running UNIX on a PC, invest some money and get a cartridge tape or video tape drive.

I'll refer to "backup tapes" most of the time in this chapter. In most cases, however, what I'll be saying will apply equally well to other backup media.

Backing Up the Filesystem

The beginning and end of this section discuss general backup issues; in between, it describes the backup commands available on UNIX systems. The special filenames for typical backup devices are discussed in the section entitled "Tape

Special Files," in Chapter 9, *Backup and Restore,*" later in this chapter and in the section entitled "Floppy Disk Special Files," in Chapter 8, *Filesystems and Disks.*

Is tar Enough?

In some cases, especially single-user systems, an elaborate backup process is not needed. Rather, since the administrator and the user are one and the same person, it will be obvious which files are important, how often they change, and so on. In cases like this, the simpler tape commands, *tar* and *cpio*, may be sufficient to periodically save important files to tape (or floppy disk). For example, the following *tar* command saves all files under */u* to the default tar device (specified in the file */etc/default/tar* under System V):

```
% tar c /u
```

While the canonical model for this situation is UNIX running on a microcomputer, such a scheme may also be sufficient in many workstation environments, where each user is responsible for backing up her own files. The following commands write all files stored under */u/chavez* to tape drive 1 under AIX 3.1:

```
$ cd /u/chavez
$ tar -c -f/dev/rmt1 * .[a-z]*
```

cpio can also be used to make backups. It has several advantages:

- It can back up arbitrary sets of files; *tar* is limited to directory subtrees.

- It can back up special files and so is suitable for full system backups on small systems.

- It packs data on tape significantly more efficiently than *tar*. If fitting all your data on one tape is an issue, *cpio* may be preferable.

- On restores, it skips over bad spots on the tape while *tar* just dies.

Under its *-o* option, *cpio* copies the files whose pathnames are passed to it via standard input (often by *ls* or *find*) to standard output; you redirect standard output to use *cpio* to write to floppy disk or tape. The examples below show how *cpio* might be used for backup:

```
$ find . -print | cpio -o >/dev/rmt0
$ find . -name \*.c -print | cpio -o >/dev/rfd0
```

The first command copies all files in the current directory and its subdirectories to the tape in drive 0. The second command copies all C source files under the current directory to floppy disk. Some versions of *find* have a *-cpio* option. For those that do, the equivalent command would be:

```
$ find . -cpio /dev/rmt0
```

Check the *tar* or *cpio* manual pages for a full discussion of these commands.

Planning a Backup Schedule

It's very easy to put off doing backups, especially when you are responsible only for your own files. However, performing them regularly is essential. Basically, it's a good diea to assume that the next time you sit down at the computer, all your disks will have had head crashes, and that you will only be able to restore those files you have on backup. Keeping such a catastrophe in mind will make it obvious what needs to be backed up and how often. Backups are convenient for restoring accidentally deleted files, but they are also essential in the event of serious hardware failures or other disasters. Catastrophes *will* happen. All hardware has a finite lifetime, and eventually something will fail.

An important part of the backup process occurs before any files are copied to tape: *planning*. In planning a backup schedule, several factors need to be taken into account:

- What files are critical to users running on this system?

- Where are these files located? Are they isolated in a single filesystem, for example?

- How often do these files change?

- How quickly would they need to be restored in the event of damage or loss?

- How often are the relevant filesystems available for backup? (Ideally, backups ought not to be performed on mounted filesystems.)

For example, if your system supports a large ongoing development project, then the files on it are likely to change very frequently and will need to be backed up at least daily (probably after hours). On the other hand, if the only volatile file on your system is a large database, its filesystem might need to backed up several times every day while the other filesystems on the system could be backed up only once a week.

Basically, backups are insurance. They represent time expended in an effort to prevent future losses. The time required for any backup schedule must be weighed against the potential losses if the files are needed but are not available.

NOTE

Virtually all UNIX documentation recommends that filesystems be dismounted before a backup is performed (except for /). This recommendation is rarely followed; in practice, backups can be performed on mounted filesystems. However, users should be aware that any files they modify while a backup is in progress may not be backed up correctly.

The simplest and most thorough backup scheme is to copy all the files on the disk to tape. A *full backup* is time consuming and unwieldy; restoring a single file from a large set of tapes is inconvenient, and if the files are not changing very often, it can be a waste of time. On the other hand, if files are changing very rapidly, and 50 users will be unable to work if some of them are lost, then a full backup might be reasonable even every day. In any case, a full backup should be performed at least once each month at a typical installation; for many systems once a week is appropriate.

Incremental backups should be done more frequently. In an incremental backup, the system copies only those files which have been changed since some previous backup. We'll use the concept of a *backup level* to distinguish different backup times. Each backup type has a level number assigned to it; by definition, a full backup is level 0. Backing up the system at any level means saving all the files that have changed since the last backup at the previous level. Thus, a level 1 backup saves all the files that have changed since the last full (level 0) backup; a level 2 backup saves all the files that have been changed since the last level 1 backup, and so on. (Numeric backup levels are only supported by BSD-style backup commands, but the concept is valid for and can be implemented on any system, although you'll have to do some of the record keeping by hand.)

A typical backup strategy is to perform a full backup at the beginning of each week, and then perform a level 1 backup (all files that have changed since the full backup) each day. The following backup schedule summarizes one implementation of this plan:

Monday   Level 1 (incremental) backup.

Tuesday   Level 1 (incremental) backup.

Wednesday   Level 1 (incremental) backup.

Thursday	Level 1 (incremental) backup.
Friday	Level 0 (full) backup.

Of course, this is not the only reasonable plan. Its primary advantage is that only two sets of tapes are needed to restore the filesystem (the full backup and the incremental). Its primary disadvantage is that the daily backup tapes will gradually grow and, if the system is very active, may approach the size of the full backup tapes by the end of the week. A popular alternate plan for sites with very active systems is:

First Monday of each month	Level 0 (full).
All other Mondays	Level 1 (weekly incremental to previous Level 0).
Tuesday	Level 2 (daily incremental to previous Level 1).
Wednesday	Level 2 (daily incremental to previous Level 1).
Thursday	Level 2 (daily incremental to previous Level 1).
Friday	Level 2 (daily incremental to previous Level 1).

This plan will require three sets of tapes to do a complete restore (the most recent backup of each type).

In deciding on a backup plan, take into account how the system is used. The most heavily used portions of the filesystem (areas in which ongoing development occurs) may need to be backed up more often than the other parts (such as the root filesystem, which contains standard UNIX programs and files and which therefore rarely changes). A few parts of the system (like /tmp) need never be backed up. You may want to create some additional filesystems that will never be backed up; anyone using them would be responsible for backing up his own files.

You should also do a full backup whenever you make significant changes to the system, whether the schedule calls for one or not. This may be one of the few times that the root filesystem gets backed up, but if you ever have a problem with your system disk, you will find it well worth the effort.

Here's a trick to take care of the changes you make to configuration files between the infrequent backups of the root filesystem. Create a directory on a filesystem that is backed up regularly, and write a script to copy the important system configuration files there. It can be very simple:

```
# !/bin/sh
# cp /etc/passwd /chem/sys_config_files
# cp /etc/fstab  /chem/sys_config_files
# cp /etc/group  /chem/sys_config_files
  . . .
```

Then, create a crontab entry to run it, say, once a week, and you'll always have essentially up-to-date copies of the configuration files on tape. Then, if you ever need to retore the root filesystem, you won't need to figure out what you changed. (Creating the script is also a good way to get acquainted with all the configuration files on the system. Include anything you might ever conceivably change, and err on the side of too many rather than too few files.)

The worst part of doing backups is sitting around waiting for them to finish. Unattended backups solve this problem for some sites. If the backup will fit on a single tape, then you can leave a tape in the drive when you leave for the day, have the backup command run automatically by *cron* during the night, and pick up the tape the next morning. However, unattended backups can be a security risk; don't use them if untrusted users have physical access to the tape drive (and could steal the tape) or you can't trust users not to accidentally or deliberately write over the tape. You also won't be able to use them if the tape drive is in heavy use and can't be tied up by your tape for the entire night.

NOTE

There are a few times when simply making a backup is not enough: when making full backups for long-term storage, when remaking a filesystem, and so on. In these cases, you also need to verify that the backup tape or diskette is readable. This is done by using an appropriate restore command to list the contents of the tape or diskette. While this will not guarantee that every file is completely readable, it will raise the odds of it considerably. Backups should be verified in this way whenever you remake a filesystem, create a backup set to be stored offsite, and at any other time when the integrity of the backup is essential.

Backup Under System V.3

Backups under V.3 are performed using the *backup* command (which is really an interface to *cpio*). It can perform full or incremental backups of the filesystem, or back up a list of files or a user's home directory, to either tape or floppy disk. The *-h* option alone may be used to list the dates of the last incremental and full backup. When performing actual backups, *backup* has these options:

-c	Complete (full) backup.
-p	Partial (incremental) backup.
-f file-list	Back up the specified files (place the list in quotes).
-u user	Back up all files under *user*'s home directory.

-d *spec-file*   Specify backup target device (a character special file).

-t   The specified device is a tape device (default is floppy).

Here are some examples:

```
$ backup -c -t -d /dev/rmt/c0s0
$ backup -p
$ backup -u chavez -d /dev/rdsk/f03h
```

The first command does a full backup to the first tape drive; the second command does an incremental backup to the default floppy drive (*/dev/rdsk/f05h*); and the third command copies all files under user *chavez*'s home directory to a high density 3-1/2" floppy drive.

Backup Under BSD

The BSD *dump* utility represents the next level of sophistication for backup systems under UNIX. Although there are slight variations, the discussion here applies to UNIX implementations shown in Table 9-1.

Table 9-1. BSD-based Backup Commands

Version of UNIX	Backup Command Name
XENIX	*backup*
AIX 3.1	*backup*
V.4	*ufsbackup* (for *ufs* filesystems)
BSD	*dump*

The remainder of this discussion will use *dump* in examples, but the syntax is virtually identical for all of them.

Dump keeps track of when it last saved each filesystem, and the level at which it was saved. This information is in the file */etc/dumpdates* (*/etc/ddate* under XENIX). A typical entry in this file is:

```
/dev/disk2e    2 Sun Feb  9 13:14:56 1991
```

which indicates that the filesystem */dev/disk2e* was last backed up on Sunday, February 9th; this was a level 2 backup. If *dump* does not find a filesystem in this list, it assumes that it has not been backed up.

If */etc/dumpdates* doesn't exist, the command:

```
# touch /etc/dumpdates
```

will create it. The */etc/dumpdates* file must be owned by the user *root*.

NOTE

> If */etc/dumpdates* does not exist, *dump* will not try to create it and won't record when filesystem backups occur. Consequently, create */etc/dumpdates* before running *dump* for the first time.

The general form of a *dump* command is:

```
% dump options arguments special-file
```

where *options* is a list of options to be used for this backup, *arguments* is a list of arguments corresponding to these options, and *special-file* is the block special file corresponding to the filesystem to be backed up.*

Not all options require arguments. However, the list of arguments *must* correspond exactly, in order and in number, to the options requiring arguments. For example, consider the set of options *0sd*. The *s* and *d* options require arguments; *0* does not. Thus, a *dump* command specifying these options must have the form:

```
% dump 0sd s-argument d-argument special-file
```

Failing to observe this rule can have disastrous consequences, including destroying the filesystem (especially if run as *root*). Make sure that an argument is supplied for each option requiring one. Note too that this runs counter to the syntax of most UNIX commands, in which options and their arguments appear together. To avoid operator errors, create shell scripts that will automatically invoke *dump* with the proper options.

Take care to avoid these two potential errors in using *dump*:

1. If the tape drive specification follows the disk drive specification, the filesystem will be destroyed. In this case, *dump* tries to back up the tape drive onto the disk. The filesystem to be backed up should always be the last item on the command line.

---

*If filesystems are dismounted before backup, a character device may be used as the special file, rather than as a block device. However, since the root filesystem is always mounted, it must always be backed up as a block device.

2. If the tape drive specification is missing, the backup will be performed assuming the default 1600 BPI density value. This will mean that *dump* will run out of tape unexpectedly. On some systems, it is necessary to select the density on the tape drive's front panel in addition to specifying the correct special file.

The most important options are:

0-9   The numbers 0 through 9 indicate the *level* of the dump this command will perform. Given any level *n*, *dump* will search */etc/dumpdates* for an entry reporting the last time this filesystem was dumped at level *n-1* or lower. *Dump* then backs up all files that have been changed since this date. If *n* is zero, *dump* will back up the entire filesystem. If */etc/dumpdates* has no record of a backup for this filesystem for level *n-1* or lower, *dump* will also back up the entire filesystem. If no *level* option appears in the *dump* command, *dump* will perform a level 0 (complete) dump. This option does not require any argument.

u   If *dump* finishes successfully, this option *updates* its history file */etc/dumpdates*. It does not require an argument.

s   This option requires an argument, which specifies the *size* of the backup tape, in feet. Ballpark estimates are around 2300 for a 9-track reel-to-reel tape, 425 for a Sun cartridge tape (include the SunOS *c* option as well), and 24000 for a 8mm video tape. The value 1422 specifies a 1.44MB floppy disk (include the SunOS *D* option also). If this option is omitted, *dump* assumes a 2300-foot tape. Obviously an 8mm tape isn't 24000 feet long; that's just a number that tricks *dump* into putting the right amount of data (roughly 2 GB) on the tape. Some tape drives support a new higher-density format, so an even larger number would be appropriate.

d   This option requires an argument, which specifies the *density* of the backup tape, in bytes per inch (BPI). If this option is omitted, *dump* usually assumes 1600 BPI for tapes. This option is used by *dump* for calculation purposes.

W   This option asks *dump* to report *which* filesystems need to be backed up, without taking any action. It reads */etc/dumpdates* and */etc/fstab* to determine what filesystems need backups. If this option is present, *dump* will ignore all other options except for the dump level. It does not require an argument.

f This option states that you want to send the dump to something other than the default tape drive (i.e., to a file or to another device). If it is omitted, *dump* will send the backup to the default tape drive. If you use this option, it must have an argument, and this argument *absolutely must* be placed correctly according to the rules given above.

Typical uses of the *dump* command are:

```
% dump 1usfd 2300 /dev/rmt1 6250 /dev/disk1d
% dump 3usdf 2300 6250  /dev/rmt20 /dev/disk1d
% dump 1usDf 1422 /dev/rfd0a /dev/rsd0g
```

The first command performs a level 2 backup on the filesystem accessed via */dev/disk1d*, using a nine-track tape drive at 6250 BPI. The second command performs a level 3 backup on the same filesystem using the nine-track tape drive */dev/rmt20*, also at 6250 bpi. This corresponds to tape drive 0, without rewinding. The third command performs a level 1 backup on the */dev/rsd0g* filesystem to a floppy disk drive on a Sun system. For all three commands, *dump* will update the file */etc/dumpdates* upon completion. The command:

```
% dump 4Wd 6250 /dev/disk1d
```

does not back up any filesystems. It will print a complete list of all filesystems indicating the last time each filesystem was backed up, the level at which it was backed up, and whether or not it needs to be backed up at level 4. When the *W* option is specified, aside from the level number, all options and arguments are ignored.

Under AIX 3.1, the options are preceded by hyphens, in a more standard UNIX command syntax. For example, the following command would perform a level two backup on the indicated filesystem, sending files to tape drive 0, using a no rewind, no retension, high density access mode, and updating the */etc/dumpdates* file:

```
% backup -2 -f /dev/mt0.1 -u /dev/hd5
```

(The AIX 3.1 *backup* command also supports V.3 *backup* command options and methods. See the manual page for details.)

dump will notify the user whenever it requires some interaction. Most often, *dump* will have filled the tape currently in use and ask for another. It will also ask whether or not to take corrective actions if problems arise. In addition, *dump* prints many messages describing what it is doing, how many reels of tape it thinks it will need, and the like.

The V.4 Backup Service

System V Release 4 introduces a highly sophisticated and powerful backup facility that enables a system administrator to implement and manage an arbitrarily elaborate backup plan, spanning an entire computer network. It enables the automation of most backup tasks (except physically mounting tapes!). It may involve much more complexity than makes sense for some systems. This section will provide an overview of the backup facility under V.4, but it is not intended to be comprehensive.

The Backup Register

Backup scheduling is controlled by the configuration file */etc/bkup/bkreg.tab*. This file is accessed and modified via the *bkreg* command. The */etc/bkup/bkreg.tab* file defines each filesystem that participates in the backup system, notes how often it needs to be backed up, what special file accesses it, and other information.

The backup service is built around a notion of the *backup period*: the period of time after which the schedule repeats itself. The default period is one week, meaning that the backup schedule is the same every week. A period of four weeks would mean that the schedule might vary from week to week within a (logical) month, but would be identical from month to month. To change the backup period, the *-p* option to *bkreg* is used. For example, the following command changes the period to four weeks:

```
# bkreg -p 4
```

When used to add or modify an entry in the backup register, the *bkreg* command has a multitude of options. Some of the most useful are:

-a tag   Add an entry named *tag*.

-e tag   Edit the entry named *tag*.

-r tag   Remove the entry named *tag*.

-o oname   Originating device: filesystem to be backed up. One form for this is *mount-pt:block-special-file*.

-c when   Specifies how often the filesystem is to be backed up.

-d dg:dev   Target device, where *dg* is an optional device group name (see "Device Groups," in Chapter 8, *Filesystems and Disks*), and *dev* is the special file for a specific device. Either part may be omitted. If no device group is specified, the colon must precede the device name.

-m mkey   Backup method; two useful ones are *ffile* for a full backup and *incfile* for an incremental backup.

The *-c* option specifies how often the entry is to be backed up. Its argument has the following format:

>   *weeks:days*

where *weeks* is a comma or space-separated list of weeks (or ranges of weeks) within the backup period, and *days* is a comma or space-separated list of days or ranges of days. For example, the following string says that a backup is to be performed on Monday and Wednesday of the first and third weeks in each backup period: *1,3:mo,we*. Finally, *-c* can also take the keyword *demand* as its argument, which means that backups are performed only when requested.

Here are some example *bkreg* commands:

```
# bkreg -a chemfull -o /chem:/dev/rdsk/c1d1s2 -c 1:mo \
    -d :/dev/SA/ctape -m ffile
# bkreg -a chemincr -o /chem:/dev/rdsk/c1d1s2 -c 1-4:tu,th-fr \
    -d ctape -m incfile
# bkreg -e biofull 1:we
# bkreg -r physinc
```

The first command adds an entry named *chemfull* to the backup register, which specifies a full backup on the */chem* filesystem on the first Monday of the backup period. The second command specifies an incremental backup on Tuesdays, Thursdays, and Fridays of weeks 1 through 4 of the backup period, naming the entry *chemincr*. The *chemfull* backups go to the default cartridge tape drive, and the *chemincr* backups go to any available device in the device group *ctape*. The third command modifies an existing entry *biofull*, changing its scheduled time to the first Wednesday of the backup period, and the final command removes the entry named *physfull*.

These sample commands represent only the simplest uses of *bkreg*. For example, entries may be given priorities, and dependencies between entries may be set up. The *bkexcept* command may be used to set up exception lists for incremental backups (wildcard strings specifying files not to be backed up). Consult the relevant man pages for full details on these advanced features.

The *bkreg* command may also be used to list the contents of the backup register. The *-O* option produces a listing for each originating device (filesystem) in the backup register, and the *-R* option produces a listing by target device.

Initiating Backups

The backup service is designed assuming a distinction between the system administrator and operators. The administrator plans, sets up, and requests backup operations; the operator does the actual physical work. (In a sense, even mounting tapes is automatic under this view, from the administrator's point of view.) Backups may be initiated by the *backup* command (which bears no resemblance to its identically-named predecessor). Its simplest form is:

```
# backup
```

which reads the backup register and schedules all needed backups. Backups may be limited to a specific filesystem with the *-o* option; for example:

```
# backup -o /chem
```

Backups will be scheduled but will not actually be performed until an operator indicates all is ready by executing the *bkoper* command (no arguments are needed in its simplest form). Once he does, the backup service will inform the operator of each needed action (when and where to mount the next tape, for example), via a menu-driven interface.

The current operator is designated with the *rsnotify* command. For example, the following command designates *ng* as the operator:

```
# rsnotify -u ng
```

The backup service will send mail to the designated user whenever backups are scheduled but not started or when a backup operation requires attention.

Several other options to *backup* are of note. The *-n* option lists what operations would be performed if the *backup* command were invoked, but does not actually schedule them. The *-a* option runs *backup* in automatic mode. In this mode, *backup* will not assume that an operator is available if it needs something; the corresponding backup operation will fail instead, and *backup* will go on to the next one. The *-i* option initiates an interactive session and assumes that the person who entered the command is the operator (running *bkoper* automatically). It is useful when the administrator and operator are in fact one and the same person.

Listing Backup Status and History

The *bkstatus* command may be used to list the status of all backup operations that are in progress. Backups will be in one of the following states:

- *Active* (underway).

- *Pending* (scheduled but not started).

- *Waiting* for operator attention.

- *Suspended* (by the system administrator).

- *Failed* (or cancelled).

- *Completed*.

The *-a* option must be used for the final two categories to be included in the report (they technically aren't operations "in progress").

The *bkhistory* command is used to report on past backup operations. Its *-o* option can be used to restrict the report to a specific filesystem. For example, the following command lists completed backup operations performed on the *chem* filesystem:

```
% bkhistory -o /chem
```

This command is useful for figuring out which backup tape the file you want is on.

Other Backup Considerations

This section discusses a variety of backup issues and hints that didn't fit into the discussion of the individual commands.

When a file is accidently deleted or is otherwise lost, knowing that you have backed it up is a great relief. However, finding out which backup tape it's on may turn that relief into a headache. Once way to address this problem—and to simultaneously ensure that your backup tapes are always good—is to list their contents after they are written. If you save this information to a file, then you and your users will be able to find the files you want by *grep*ing through the most recent lists. Here is a sample script designed to back up a filesystem, verify it, and create a file listing its contents in the directory */usr/local/dump_recs*:

```
#!/bin/csh
# $1 = filesystem
# $2 = dump level (default=0)
#
if ($#argv < 1) then
    echo "do_backup: filesystem [dump-level]"
    exit 1
endif
set lev=0
if ("$2" != "") set lev=$2
set opt=$lev"ufsd"
dump $opt /dev/rmt1 24000 6250 $1
if ($status) then
  echo "do_backup: dump failed"
  exit 1
```

```
endif
restore tfv /dev/rmt1 > \
  /usr/local/dump_recs/`date | awk '{print $2 $3}'`.$lev
```

This script runs the *dump* command on the filesystem given as its first argument, using the backup level specified as its second argument (or level 0 by default). If the *dump* command exits normally, then the *restore* command is used to verify the backup and write its contents to a file whose name is the month and day and whose extension is the backup level: *Jun24.2* would be the filename for a level 2 backup done on June 24th, for example. This script is clearly geared for a BSD system, but a similar one could be created for System V.

The final stumbling block that can impede a file restoration is finding the right tape or diskette. Ideally, you should have a full set of tapes for each distinct item in your backup schedule. For example, if you do a backup every day, it's best to have five sets of tapes that you reuse each week. Labeling them clearly is a great help in finding them quickly later. Color-coded labels are favored by many sites as an effective way to distinguish the different sets of tapes.

You also need to think from time to time about the reasonable expected lifetime of your backup media. Some manufacturers recommend replacing tapes every year. This is certainly a good idea if you can afford to do so. The way that tapes and diskettes are stored also affects their lifetime: sunlight, heat, and humidity all can significantly shorten it. I always replace tapes that have failed twice, regardless of their ages; for some people and situations, a single failure is enough. I always throw away diskettes at the first hint of trouble. (Security considerations with respect to storing backup media are discussed later in this chapter.)

There are two other UNIX tape utilities you should know about, which are also of use in performing backups from time to time:

- The *dd* utility transfers raw data between devices. It is useful for converting data between systems and for reading and writing tapes from/to non-UNIX systems. It takes a number of *option* = *value* pairs as its arguments. Some of the most useful options are:

  if   Input file: source for data.

  of   Output file: destination for data.

  ibs   Input block size in multiples of 512 bytes.

  obs   Output block size in multiples of 512 bytes.

  fskip   Skip files before transferring data.

  count   The number of blocks to transfer.

conv   Keyword(s) specifying desired conversion of input data before outputting: *swap* means swap bytes, *lcase, ucase* means convert to lower/upper case, *ascii, ebcdic* means convert to ASCII/EBCDIC.

For example, the following command converts the third file on the tape in drive 0 from EBCDIC to ASCII and to lowercase, using an input block size of 1024 bytes; the command writes the converted output to the file */chem/new/data/laser*:

```
$ dd if=/dev/rmt0 of=/chem/new/data/laser \
    ibs=2 fskip=2 conv=ascii,lower
```

• The *mt* command (available under BSD, V.4, many V.3 versions, and under AIX 3.1 under the name *tctl*) is used to position tapes (to skip past backup save sets, for example), to rewind tapes, and to perform other tape manipulation. Its syntax is:

```
$ mt [-f tape-device] command
```

where *tape-device* specifies which tape drive to use, and *command* is a keyword indicating the desired action. Useful keywords include *rewind* (to rewind the tape), *status* (display device status—you can see whether it is in use, for example), *fsf n* (skip the next *n* files), and *bsf n* (skip back *n* files. For example, to rewind the tape in the second tape drive, you might use a command like:

```
$ mt -f /dev/rmt1 rewind
```

Restoring Files from Backup

All of the backup facilities described in the previous sections have corresponding file restoration facilities.

Restore Under System V.3

The V.3 *restore* command is the complement to its *backup* command. Its arguments are the list of files to be restored (wildcards are allowed in the argument list, but must be quoted to prevent expansion by the shell). It has the following options:

-c	Restore all files (a complete restore).
-i	List contents of tape/diskette (can be used to verify backups).
-o	Overwrite existing files when restoring. By default, existing files are not restored.
-d dev	Specify device to restore from.
-t	Indicates that *dev* is a tape device.

Here are some example *restore* commands:

```
# restore -c
$ restore -d /dev/rmt/c0s0 -t -o "/u/chavez/data/*.dat"
```

The first command restores all files from the diskette in the default floppy drive; existing files will not be overwritten, however. The second command restores selected files from the directory */u/chavez/data* from a tape in the first tape drive, overwriting existing files.

Restore Under BSD, AIX 3.1, XENIX, and V.4

The BSD *restore* utility retrieves files from backup tapes made with the *dump* utility. It is supported by those systems supporting a version of *dump* (although V.4 calls it *ufsrestore* and it works only for *ufs* filesystems). The command can restore single files, directories, or entire filesystems. To restore an entire filesystem, you must restore the most recent backup tapes from *each* backup level: the most recent full dump (0), the most recent level 1 dump, and so on. You must restore each level in order, beginning with level 0. If you do not, you may leave obsolete versions of some files in the system. *restore* places the files it retrieves in the current working directory. Therefore, to restore a filesystem as a whole, you may wish to create and mount a clean, empty filesystem, make the current working directory the directory where this filesystem is mounted, and then use *restore* to read the backup tapes into this directory.

If you are restoring a filesystem from a complete dump plus one or more incrementals, you will restore some files that were deleted. Incremental dumps do not keep track of deleted files; they only guarantee that you will restore the last version of any file present in a set of backup tapes. You may want to send a mail message to users asking them to re-delete any "resurrected" files.

After a full restore, you need to do a full (level 0) backup. The reason for this is that *dump* backs up files by their inode number internally, so the tape you just restored from won't match the new inodes in the filesystem (which will be assigned sequentially as files are restored).

In general, the *restore* command has the following form:

```
% restore options arguments [ files-and-dirs]
```

where *options* is a list of options, *arguments* is a list of arguments corresponding to these options, and *files-and-dirs* is a list of files and directories for *restore* to retrieve from the backup tape. If no files are listed, then the entire tape will be restored. Most options to *restore* do not have any arguments. However, as with *dump*, it is extremely important that any arguments appear in the same order as the options requiring them. And, as with *dump*, the syntax of *restore* is often non-standard.

restore places the files that it retrieves in the current working directory. When a directory is selected for restoration, *restore* will restore the directory and all the files within it, unless you have specified the *h* option (described later in this section).

I'll list *restore*'s options in a moment. Before doing so, let me note that its interactive mode—selected with the *i* option—is generally the most convenient and easy to use. The most important options are:

r   *Read* and restore the entire tape. This is a very powerful command; it should be used only to restore an entire filesystem located on one or more tapes. The filesystem into which the tape is read should be newly created and completely empty, and must not be the root filesystem.* This option can also be used to restore a complete incremental dump on top of a newly restored filesystem. That is, after using the *r* option to restore the most recent full dump, you can also use it to restore successive incremental dumps until the filesystem has been completely restored.

R   Resume a partially-completed restoration operation. With this option, *restore* requests a particular tape from a multi-volume set of dump tapes on which to restart a full restore. *Don't use this option when restoring the root filesystem.*

x   *Extract* all files and directories listed and restore them in the current directory. Each filename to be extracted must be a complete path name *relative* to the root directory of the filesystem being restored. For example, to restore the file */chem/pub/old/gold/dat* from a dump of the */chem* filesystem, you must specify the filename as *pub/old/gold.dat*. You should be in */chem* when you execute the *restore* command.

---

*See your vendor's documentation for information about restoring the root filesystem. You may have to re-install the operating system from the distribution tape, and then use *restore* to recover individual site-specific configuration files.

t   *Type* the names of the listed files and directories on the terminal if they
          appear on the backup tape. This option lets you find out whether or not a
          given file is on a particular tape more quickly than reading the entire
          tape. When used without a file list, it verifies that a *dump* tape is read-
          able. (This option is *T* under XENIX.)

f   The corresponding argument is the name of the file or device holding the
          dump. If this argument is omitted, *restore* will assume that the dump
          tape is mounted on your default tape drive. If it is present, *restore* will
          read the dump from the specified device (i.e., a special file name corre-
          sponding to a device) or the file given. Using this option improperly can
          destroy your filesystem. Be careful to have all arguments positioned
          carefully, particularly when the *f* option is in effect.

h   If a name in the list of files' *restore* is given happens to be a directory,
          restore the empty directory but do not restore the files that are within it.
          It is used to suppress restoring of entire subtrees of files. (Not supported
          in the XENIX version of *restore*.)

i   Enter interactive mode. This is described in the next subsection.

A typical usage of the *restore* command is:

```
% cd /u
% restore xf /dev/rmt16 chavez/mystuff others/myprogram
```

This restores the directory */u/chavez/mystuff* and the file */u/others/myprogram*
from a backup tape. The directories *chavez* and *others* are searched for in the current directory (and created if necessary), and then the specified subdirectory and
file are restored under them. Both of these originally resided within the */u* filesystem, from which the dump tape was made. Note, however, that the mount point
name is not used in the *restore* command. The command must be executed from
/u to restore the files to their original locations.

dump and *restore* both save files independently of where their filesystem is
mounted at the time; that is, the pathnames used by these commands are relative
to their position in their *own* filesystem, not in the overall system filesystem. This
makes sense, since the filesystem could potentially be mounted anywhere in the
overall directory tree, and files still ought to be able to be restored to their correct
location relative to the current mount point for their filesystem.

As was true for *dump*, under AIX 3.1, the *restore* command's options are preceded by hyphens, with any required arguments immediately following its option. Under AIX 3.1, the corresponding command to the previous example would be:

```
$ restore -x -f /dev/0.1 chavez/mystuff others/myprogram
```

If you need to restore some files that have been destroyed by accident, your most difficult problems will be determining which set of backup tapes contains these files and waiting for the system to read through one or more full backup tapes. If you do incremental backups, knowing when a file was last modified will help you to find the correct backup tape.

restore's Interactive Mode

Interactive mode is entered with *restore*'s *i* option (not supported by XENIX). Once there, one can scan the contents of a tape, choosing files for extraction. This mode's use is illustrated in this sample session:

```
% restore if /dev/rmt1
restore > help
Available commands are:
   ls [arg] - list directory
   cd arg - change directory
   add [arg] - add `arg' to list of files to be extracted
   delete [arg] - delete `arg' from list of files to be extracted
   extract - extract requested files
   . . .
If no `arg' is supplied, the current directory is used
restore > ls                    List current directory (on tape).
 chavez/    martin/   /ng

restore > cd chavez/vp          Change "location."

restore > ls
 v_a.c         v_a1.c        v_b3.c         v_d23.c
 v_early

restore > add v_a1.c           Select files to be restored; files are not
restore > add v_early          restored until extract is entered
restore > ls
 v_a.c         *v_a1.c        v_b3.c         v_d23.c
*v_early
restore > delete v_early       Remove a file from the extract list.
restore > extract              Selected file is extracted and written
restore > quit                 to the current directory.
```

The V.4 Restore Service

Like its counterpart for backups, V.4 restore service is designed to automate file restorations. The basic philosophy is similar to that of the backup service. There is a separation between the requesting of and the actual performance of restore operations. Unlike backup, however, anyone can request a file restoration. The restore service uses the same configuration information as the backup service, including the configuration file and the *rsnotify* command, used to designate the current operator, who will receive a mail message whenever restore operations are requested.

The following commands initiate and respond to restoration requests:

urestore   File or directory restore request command.

restore   Whole filesystem restore request command.

rsoper   Begin performing pending restore requests.

rsstatus   List all pending restore requests and their status.

ursstatus   List your own pending restore requests and their status.

Here is an example of a single file restoration command:

```
$ urestore -F /u/chavez/data/gold.data -m
```

This command requests that the most recent copy of the specified file be restored. The *-m* option tells the restore service to send mail when the request is completed if it cannot be accomplished immediately (from an online archive).

Other useful options are:

-D dir   Restore a directory and all its files.

-n   List versions of the specified item available in the backup history.

-d date   Restore the file as of the specified date (i.e., not necessarily the most recent version).

-o path   Specify alternate pathname for the restored item.

The *rsstatus* command is used to list pending restore requests. It lists the job ID (assigned when the restore request is made), file or directory to be restored, target location, the backup date, backup method (e.g., incremental or full), device type, and tape or disk labeling information for the required volume (if defined at the time of backup).

Once the "operator"—the person who will actually do the restore operation—decides to perform a restore operation, and has the required tape(s) or diskette(s), he invokes the *rsoper* command:

```
$ rsoper -d device
```

where *device* is the device where the restoration media will be read. By default, all restores pending for the volume mounted on the device will be processed (the restore service figures out which these are by reading the backup information off the volume). Restore operations may be restricted to a specific list of job IDs or usernames by using the *-j* and *-u* options to *rsoper* respectively.

Storing Backup Media

Properly storing the backup tapes or diskettes once you've made them is an important part of any backup plan. Here are some things to keep in mind when deciding where to store the ones for your system:

- *Environmental considerations*. Floppy disks and tapes like it cool, dry, and dark—the same environment used for many computer rooms. Ideally, floppy disks should be stored upright, resting on a thin edge rather than stacked on top of one another.

- *Security considerations*. Some backup media can be stored near the computer for convenience—the latest incrementals, for example. However, all of the backup tapes shouldn't be stored in the same location as the computer or a disaster there will destroy everything. At least some tapes should be some distance away (or at least in the next room). In every location where you store backup tapes, the usual physical security considerations apply: the tapes should be protected from theft, vandalism, and environmental disasters as much as is possible.

- *Offsite Backups*. Offsite backups are the last barrier between your system and total annihilation. They are full backup sets that are kept in a locked, fireproof location completely offsite. These backups should be updated on a regular basis; how often depends on how much data you can afford to lose in a truly worst-case scenario: some sites rotate off-site backups quarterly, some users and administrators take a tape offsite every week.

Tape Special Files

We'll close this look at backups and restores by discussing tape special file names. Tape special file names are among the least standardized. We'll look at several variations in this section; check your system's documentation and the contents of */dev* to see what it uses.

Special files used to access tape drives often have names of the form */dev/mt*n and */dev/rmt*n where *n* indicates the drive number and access mode. These are the files to look for first. On BSD systems, for nine-track reel-to-reel tape drives, the access mode consists of the density at which a tape is written and whether the tape is rewound after use or not. The character special files listed below all refer to tape drive 0, accessed as indicated:

/dev/rmt0	800 BPI, rewind
/dev/rmt4	800 BPI, no rewind
/dev/rmt8	1600 BPI, rewind
/dev/rmt12	1600 BPI, no rewind
/dev/rmt16	6250 BPI, rewind
/dev/rmt20	6250 BPI, no rewind

Similarly, the special files */dev/rmt1*, */dev/rmt5*, and so on refer to the second tape drive, with access method following the same sequence.

A similar format for specifying the tape access method is followed by SunOS, where tape special files can have the forms:

```
/dev/mtn
/dev/rmtn
/dev/nmtn
/dev/nrmtn
```

where *n* is the drive number and the initial "n" indicates no rewind. SunOS also supports other tape devices, named slightly differently: */dev/*st** for cartridge tape drive devices for the Sysgen SC 4000 controller (SCSI interface), */dev/*xt** for one for the Xylogics 472 controller, and similar names.

Tape device base names ("mt" above) may vary depending on the type of tape drive. For example, cartridge tape special files may have names like *ctape*n (as in V.4). System V stores tape special files in the */dev/mt* and */dev/rmt* subdirectories.

Some tape accessing schemes also include whether or not the tape should be retensioned before use. Interactive UNIX tape block special files take the following forms:

/dev/mt/c0s0	Rewind, no retension.
/dev/mt/c0s0n	No rewind, no retension.
/dev/mt/c0s0r	Rewind and retension.
/dev/mt/c0s0nr	No rewind, retension.

The corresponding */dev/rmt* are identically named. Retensioning refers to equalizing the tension on a tape. It is done by moving the tape to its beginning, then to the end of the tape, then back to the beginning; it's even slower than it sounds.

For another variation on System V, consider these tape special names taken from a Stardent UNIX system:

```
$ ls /dev/mt
0m      0mn     c0d6h   c0d6hn  c0d6l   c0d6ln  c0d6m   c0d6mn
c1d6h   c1d6hn
```

The devices beginning with "0" are for the first drive on the first controller (an initial "c0d" is omitted), the ones beginning with "c0d6" are for a second tape drive on that same controller, and the ones beginning with "c1" are for a tape drive on the second controller. The final "n"—or lack thereof—indicates whether it is a rewinding device or not, and the second-to-last letter indicates the density used: *l*ow, *m*edium, or *h*igh.

AIX 3.1 tape special file names perform perform a similar function by appending a suffix to the special file names */dev/mt*n and */dev/rmt*n (where *n* is the drive number), which also encodes a write density setting:

/dev/mt	Rewind, no retension, high density.
/dev/mt0.1	No rewind, no retension, high density.
/dev/mt0.2	Rewind, retension, high density.
/dev/mt0.3	No rewind, retension, high density.
/dev/mt0.4	Rewind, no retension, low density.
/dev/mt0.5	No rewind, no retension, low density.
/dev/mt0.6	Rewind, retension, low density.
/dev/mt0.7	No rewind, retension, low density.

10

Terminals and Modems

Terminal-Related Special Files
Specifying Terminal Characteristics
Adding a New Device
Troubleshooting Terminal Problems
Configuring a Dialin/Dialout Modem

This chapter describes how to work with terminals and modems on UNIX systems. When directly connected, both are linked to the computer over the same sort of physical medium—serial lines—and in general are accessed using the same special files. In this chapter, I'll refer to such interfaces as *terminal lines*, but be aware that what I say applies also to modems (except as noted).

The chapter opens by looking at the special files used for serial lines and other terminal sessions. It then discusses how to set the characteristics of individual terminals and generic terminal types and then goes on to consider terminal line configuration issues. The final sections describe how to add new terminals and modems and list some terminal troubleshooting hints.

Terminal-Related Special Files

The special files for serial lines vary between systems, but they often have names of the form */dev/tty*n where *n* is a one-digit (System V) or two-digit (BSD) number corresponding to the line number (beginning at 0 or 00). For example,

/dev/tty2 and */dev/tty15* correspond to the third and seventeenth serial lines on a system (it would be */dev/tty02* on a BSD system). Directly connected terminals and modems are accessed via these special files. The special file */dev/console* always refers to the system console device.

Under V.4, special files for direct terminal lines are stored in the directory */dev/term* and have names which are their line number: */dev/term/14* for example. Sometimes there are links to the older names.

The special file */dev/tty* (no suffix) serves a special purpose. It is a synonym for each process' controlling TTY. It can be used to ensure output goes to the terminal, regardless of any I/O redirection.

Systems may have other terminal special files corresponding to special devices that they support. For example, under AIX 3.1, the special file */dev/hft* is used for the "high function terminal"—the workstation console when used as an ordinary terminal (rather than as an X station). Similarly, under Stardent UNIX, special files of the form */dev/tigr*n refer to the graphics workstation shipped with most systems.

There are also other terminal devices in */dev* which are used for indirect login session via a network or windowing system; these are the *pseudo terminal* devices. Each one has two parts:

- The *master* or *control* pseudo terminal, which usually has a device name of the form */dev/pty*[p-s]n (*/dev/ptc/*n under V.4).

- The *slave* pseudo terminal (also called a *virtual terminal*), which has a device name of the form */dev/tty*[p-s]n (*/dev/pts/*n under V.4).

n is a single hexadecimal digit in both cases. The slave pseudo terminals provide a TTY-like interface to user processes not directly connected to the computer. The two parts work in pairs, having the same device number *n*, although the user only sees the virtual terminal device; this is also what appears in output from commands like *ps*.

On many workstation systems, */dev/console* is redefined depending on how the workstation is being used. When used as a regular terminal, */dev/console* refers to that terminal device. When a windowing session is running, however, */dev/console* may become one of its windows (rather than the device as a whole).

The *tty* command will display what special file is being used for any login session. For example:

```
$ hostname
hamlet
$ tty
/dev/tty12
```

```
$ rlogin duncan
Urizen Ur-UNIX* Version 9.1.3 duncan
$ tty
/dev/pts/4
```

This user is directly logged in to the thirteenth terminal line on *hamlet*. On *duncan*, his remote session is using pseudo terminal 4.

Specifying Terminal Characteristics

UNIX programs are written to be terminal independent: they don't know about or rely on the specific characteristics of any particular kind of terminal, but rather call a standard screen manipulation library which is responsible for interfacing to actual terminals. Such libraries serve to map general terminal characteristics and functions (e.g., clearing the screen) to the specific character sequences required to perform them on any specific terminal.

Terminal definitions are stored in databases on the system, and users indicate what kind of terminal they are using by setting the TERM environment variable (usually at login time—see "Terminal Handling in Initialization Files," in Chapter 4, *User Accounts*). These "databases" are handled differently under BSD and System V and are the subject of the next section.

termcap and terminfo

Programs use the name specified in the TERM environment variable as a key into the system terminal definitions database. Under BSD, terminal definitions are stored in the file */etc/termcap*; under System V, they are stored in the subdirectories of */usr/lib/terminfo*. This section provides an overview of *termcap* and *terminfo* entries. See the Nutshell Handbook *termcap & terminfo* (O'Reilly & Associates, Inc., 1991), for detailed information about the UNIX terminal definition databases and modifying or writing entries.

The BSD *termcap* database is a text file consisting of a series of entries describing the functioning of different terminals. Here is a sample entry, for a VT100 terminal:

```
d0|vt100|vt100am|dec vt100:\
     :co#80:li#24:am:\
     :ho=\E[H:\
     :ku=\EOA:kd=\EOB:
```

This sample is much shorter than an actual entry, but will serve to illustrate the features of *termcap* entries. The first line is a series of aliases for the terminal.

Any of them not containing spaces can be used as the value of the TERM environment variable. The remainder of the entry is a colon-separated series of capability codes and values. There are several kinds of capabilities. They can specify:

- Data about the terminal. In the sample entry, the *co* code tells how many columns the terminal screen has (80), the *li* code indicates how many lines it has (24), and the *am* code says that the terminal can automatically wrap long output strings onto multiple lines on the terminal screen.

- The sequence of characters to send to the terminal to get it to perform some action. In the sample entry, the *ho* code indicates what character sequence is required to move the cursor "home" (the upper left corner of the screen). In these sequences, the ESCAPE character is abbreviated \E. Thus, to get a VT100 to move the cursor to its upper left corner, you send it the sequence "ESCAPE [H."*

- The character sequence emitted when a special key is pressed. In the sample entry, the *ku* code holds the sequence for the up arrow key; on a VT100, the terminal emits "ESCAPE O A" when you press this key. Similarly, the *kd* code specifies the sequence emitted by the down arrow key.

The System V *terminfo* database is a series of binary files describing terminal capabilities. Each entry is a separate file in the subdirectory of */usr/lib/terminfo* named for the first letter of its name. For example, the *terminfo* entry for a VT100 is stored in the file */usr/lib/terminfo/v/vt100*. *terminfo* entries are compiled from source code vaguely similar to *termcap*. Here is the equivalent *terminfo* source code for the sample *termcap* entry for the VT100:

```
vt100|vt100am|dec vt100,
    am, cols#80, lines#24,
    home=\E[H,
    kcud1=\EOB, kcuu1=\EOA,
```

The following commands are available for manipulating *terminfo* entries (on System V systems):

tic   Compile *terminfo* source.

infocmp   List source for a compiled *terminfo* entry.

infocmp -C   List the equivalent *termcap* entry for a compiled *terminfo* entry (i.e., translate from *terminfo* to *termcap*).

captoinfo   Translate a *termcap* entry into *terminfo* source.

---

*This doesn't mean that if you type this sequence, the cursor will move. This discussion refers to sequences sent to the terminal *as a device*, before any interpretation.

If you need to change a *termcap* entry, you just need to edit */etc/termcap*; to change a *terminfo* entry, list its source with *infocmp*, edit it, and then recompile it with *tic*. In either case, it's wise to test the new entry by installing it under a slightly different name ("vt100t" for example) rather than merely replacing the old one. The easiest way to create a new entry is usually to find an existing one for a similar device and then rename and modify it for the new terminal type. See the Nutshell Handbook *termcap & terminfo* (O'Reilly & Associates, Inc., 1991) for details on adding new entries.

The System V commands listed previously are useful not only for modifying *terminfo* entries or creating new ones, but also whenever you need to convert an entry from one format to the other. Recently, I wanted to use an old terminal I had on an AIX 3.1 system, but the system had no *terminfo* entry for it. All I could find was a *termcap* entry for it on a BSD system, but all I had to do was extract the entry into a separate file, ship it to the AIX 3.1 system, run *captoinfo* on it, and then compile the result with *tic*.

Users can specify an alternate *termcap* or *terminfo* database with the TERMCAP and TERMINFO environment variables. If their value is a filename, that file (TERMCAP) or directory (TERMINFO) will be used instead of */etc/termcap* or */usr/lib/terminfo*. In the latter case, the named directory must contain subdirectories named for the first letter of the entries they hold, just as the standard location does. Thus, if TERMINFO is set to */u/chavez/terminfo* and TERM is set to *etchasketch*, then the file */u/chavez/terminfo/e/etchasketch* must be a compiled *terminfo* entry for that device type.

The TERMCAP environment variable can also be used to preretrieve a *termcap* entry; this feature is discussed in the next subsection.

The tset Command

Once a user has set the terminal type with the TERM environment variable, the *tset* command can be used to initialize the terminal. Without arguments, *tset* sets up the terminal, including setting the erase, kill, and interrupt characters, and sending any appropriate initialization sequences for that type. *tset* is usually included in default user initialization files (see the section entitled "Terminal Handling in Initialization Files," in Chapter 4, *User Accounts*, for examples).

Although it's most often used without options, *tset* is actually a very versatile utility. For example, it can prompt for the terminal type if desired by using its -*m* option. For example, the following command prompts the user for the terminal type, supplying *vt100* as a default, and then initializes the terminal:

```
$ tset -m ":?vt100"
TERM = (vt100)
```

If the user enters a carriage return, *tset* will use *vt100* as the terminal type; otherwise, it will use whatever type the user enters. In either case, *tset* will then initialize the terminal accordingly. Instead of *vt100*, you can use any terminal type that your system supports.

You can use *tset* to prompt for and set the TERM variable by including its hyphen option, which directs *tset* to echo the terminal type to standard output:

```
$ TERM=`tset - -Q -m ":?vt100"` ; export TERM    (System V)
% setenv TERM `tset - -Q -m ":?vt100"`            (BSD)
```

The *-Q* option suppresses the normal messages *tset* prints out.

These examples do not exhaust *tset*'s capabilities. Consult its manual page for a full description of this command.

NOTE

Default terminal types can also be specified for each serial line. We'll discuss how to do so later in this chapter. These defaults are generally propagated to the user's environment by *login* and are used by *tset* if the user doesn't specify a terminal type in any other way.

Using tset to Set the TERMCAP Environment Variable (BSD)

On BSD-based systems, *tset* can also be used to set the TERMCAP environment variable. When used this way, the entire *termcap* entry corresponding to the type named in the TERM variable becomes the value of the TERMCAP variable. Setting TERMCAP allows programs to start up more quickly since they don't need to search the *termcap* database file.

tset's *-s* option generates the shell commands necessary to set the TERM and TERMCAP environment variables (commands are generated for the shell specified in the SHELL environment variable). There are many ways of executing them; one common way is to the *eval* command:

```
$ eval `tset -sQ -m ":?vt100"`
```

(You can also include a command like this in users' initialization files.) The *tset* command in backquotes is executed first. It prompts for the terminal type, initializes the terminal, and then emits the commands necessary to set TERM and

TERMCAP, which are themselves executed by *eval*. These are the commands *tset* produces for the Bourne shell:

```
export TERMCAP TERM;
TERM=vt100;
TERMCAP='d0|vt100:co#80:li#24:am:ho=\E[H: . . .';
```

Another way to execute the emitted commands is to capture them in a file, which is then *source*d (in the C shell):

```
tset -sQ -m ":?vt100" >! ~/.tmpfile*
source ~/.tmpfile
rm ~/.tmpfile
```

These are the commands as they might appear in a user initialization file. They can also be kept in a separate file, to be *source*d whenever it is necessary to change the terminal type. The first command prompts for the terminal type and initializes the terminal. The remaining commands generate and execute *setenv* commands for TERM and TERMCAP, and then finally delete the temporary file.

What's in the temporary file? Assuming that the user selects the terminal type vt100 (i.e., assuming that she selects the default that *tset* suggests), ~/.tmpfile will look like this:

```
set noglob;
setenv TERM vt100;
setenv TERMCAP 'd0|vt100:co#80:li#24:am:ho=\E[H: ... ';
unset noglob;
```

The *set noglob* command turns off shell interpretation for the special characters (asterisks and so on), which are commonly used in *termcap* entries. Note that if something goes wrong with this sequence of commands, the *unset noglob* will never be executed, and the user will get a shell in which shell wildcards don't work. This is rare, but it's certainly confusing.

If you change your terminal type during a session, you need to reset TERMCAP or delete it before the new terminal type will take effect. This is a frequence source of confusion. Use the *unsetenv* command to remove an existing value for TERM-CAP:

```
% unsetenv TERMCAP
```

---

*If you're wondering what the exclamation point after the output redirection sign is for, it overrides the shell's *noclobber* variable, which prevents files from being accidentally overwritten. With the exclamation point, any existing file will be overwritten anyway.

The stty Command

While *tset* performs type-specific terminal initialization, the *stty* command can be used to specify generic terminal and terminal line characteristics (such as parity). Its general syntax is:

```
$ stty option [value] . . .
```

Not all options require values. *stty*'s options are not preceded by hyphens, although some options have a hyphen as the first character of their name; options often come in pairs—like *echo* and *-echo*—where the second form means the negative of the first (in this case "no echo").

stty has a large number of options (whose names vary somewhat between BSD and System V); the most useful are listed in Table 10-1.

Table 10-1. Commonly Needed stty Options

Option*	Meaning	Example
n	Baud rate.	9600
rows *n*†	Lines on the screen.	rows 36
columns *n*†	Columns on the screen.	columns 80
erase *c*	Set the delete previous character to *c*.	erase ^h
kill *c*	Set the erase command character to *c*.	kill ^u
intr *c*	Set the interrupt character to *c*.	intr ^c
eof *c*	Set the end-of-file character to *c*.	eof ^d
susp *c*†	Set the suspend job character to *c*.	susp ^z
lnext *c*†	Set the literal next character to *c*.	lnext ^v
werase *c*†	Set the word erase character to *c*.	werase ^w
reprint *c*‡	Set the reprint line character to *c*.	reprint ^r
oddp‡	Enable odd parity.	oddp
evenp‡	Enable even parity	evenp
-parity	No parity is generated or detected.	-parity
markp**	Enable mark parity.	markp
cstopb	Use two stop bits.	cstopb
-cstopb	Use one stop bit.	-cstopb
sane	Reset many options to reasonable settings.	sane

*SunOS uses the System V option forms except, oddly, for *rprnt*.
†BSD, SunOS, and V.4 only.
‡Under BSD, these options are *rprnt*, *odd*, and *even*.
**V.4 only.

For example, the *werase* option tells *stty* which character, when typed, should erase the previous word. By default, it's CTRL-W. Try it; many UNIX users aren't even aware that this feature exists. Likewise, the *reprint* option tells *stty* which character, when typed, will make the system reprint the line you're currently typing. The *sane* option just might help you to get your house in order if you accidentally do something that confuses your terminal.

Among the most useful *stty* options is *erase*, which defines the control sequence that erases the previous character (performed by the Delete or Backspace key). If the key is not currently working properly on your terminal—if the key is echoed as ^H or ^? instead of removing the previous character:

```
$ grpe^H^H^U
```

a command like the following will fix it:

```
$ stty erase ^h
```

This command sets the erase character to CTRL-H, the sequence emitted by the backspace key. You can type the desired keystroke in as *erase*'s argument or use the symbolic form: the caret character followed by the appropriate letter for that control sequence. Case does not matter, and this symbolic form may be used for any *stty* option requiring a character as its value. The code for the backspace key is "^?".

The *stty* command may also be used to display the current terminal settings. On a BSD system, the command is:

```
% stty everything
new tty, speed 19200 baud, 48 rows, 80 columns
even odd -raw -nl echo -lcase -tandem tabs -cbreak
crt: (crtbs crterase crtkill ctlecho) -tostop
-tilde -flusho -mdmbuf -litout -pass8 -nohang
-pendin -decctlq -noflsh
erase  kill   werase rprnt  flush  lnext      Output wrapped.
^?     ^U     ^W     ^R     ^O     ^V
susp   intr   quit   stop   eof
^Z/^Y  ^C     ^\     ^^/^]  ^D
```

Under System V, the command is *stty -a*, and the output is in a somewhat different order.

Note the difference between the information that *termcap* and *terminfo* provide and the information that *stty* provides. *termcap* and *terminfo* provide generic information about all terminals of a given type. *stty* provides information about the current setting of options that are, for the most part, supported by many terminals. For example, the *vt100* entries provide fairly complete information about the features specific to VT100 terminals. However, by themselves, *termcap* and *terminfo* and *tset* do not support users who like or require particular terminal options—for example, users who like "#" as an erase character (a feature of old UNIX systems), or whose terminal only runs at 2400 baud. *stty* allows a user to specify options like these. It is particularly useful when a user logs in to another system remotely; in this situation, the properties of the remote connection often don't correspond exactly to the default settings and must be explicitly changed.

stty Under AIX 3.1

AIX 3.1 supports both the BSD and System V forms of *stty*, depending on the line discipline of the terminal line; the System V form is the default. To switch between the two modes, use the *disp* option to *stty*. *disp* specified the line disciplines and accepts the keyword *bsd* or *posix* (essentially equivalent to V.4 here) as its argument. For example, the following command switches to the BSD line discipline:

```
$ stty disp bsd
```

Adding a New Device

To add a new serial line device to the system, you must:

- Physically connect the terminal or modem to the computer.

- Determine the special file in */dev* that communicates with the terminal.

- In the case of terminals, make sure a *termcap* or *terminfo* entry exists for the kind of terminal you are adding. If one doesn't, you will have to create one.

- Add or modify an entry in the relevant configuration files.

- Force *init* to reread the terminal configuration information.

Each of these steps will be considered in turn.

Making the Physical Connection

This section discusses issues related to making the physical connection between a terminal or modem and the computer.[*] The serial cables used to connect computers or terminals to modems are commonly called RS-232 cables; technically, the conform to the Electronic Industries Association (EIA) RS-232C standard. By extension (really by bending, if not breaking, the standard), RS-232 cables have

---

[*]This section on cables is reprinted from the Nutshell Handbook *Managing uucp and Usenet* (O'Reilly & Associates, Inc., 1990).

come to be used to connect computers to all kinds of serial devices—terminals, printers, and ports on other computers, as well as just modems.

RS-232 cables consist of up to 25 wires, each with a specific function and each intended to carry a different signal. Only two of the wires are commonly used for data transmission; the rest are used for various kinds of control signals.

A piece of equipment (a computer or a modem) sends a signal across the cable by applying a small positive or negative voltage to a specific pin in the cable's end connector. The signal is carried across the wires in the cable to the corresponding pin at the other end, where it is detected by another piece of equipment. The voltage either may be held high (positive) as a go-ahead signal or may pulse quickly to convey data, with the sequence of negative and positive voltages being interpreted as binary codes.

Unfortunately, as it has now come to be applied, the RS-232 standard is rather broad and leaves a lot up to the equipment manufacturer. All that is "standard" is the function of each of the 25 pins found in the connectors on each end of a serial cable. All 25 pins are rarely used. Instead, different pieces of equipment require different signals to operate. To make things even more complicated, connectors with only 9 pins are becoming increasingly common. Fortunately DB25-to-9 pin adapters are readily available.

If you buy all of your equipment—computer, terminals, modems, printers, etc.—from a single manufacturer, you can probably also buy the exact cables needed to connect the various pieces. If, like most UNIX establishments, you mix and match hardware, you will probably end up building your own cables (or having them built for you).

We cannot describe here the mechanics of actually building a cable; what follows is a brief introduction to RS-232. You should be warned that RS-232 is a complex subject and seems to arouse near-religious opinions in some readers. We have tried to negotiate this subject with care. However, we are aware that some readers may find fault with our treatment, which reflects RS-232 as it is commonly practiced, rather than as it "should be" in an ideal world. Our objective is simply that, after reading this section, you should be able to figure out what kind of cable you need to connect either to a modem or directly to another system. You may then be able to buy the cable from an electronics supply store or, if you are handy with tools, build it yourself.[*]

---

[*]Works providing more detailed and extended treatments of RS-232 and serial communications in general are listed in the Bibliography.

Many of the signals defined by the RS-232 standard are rarely used. Table 10-1 lists the signals that are important for our present purposes.

Table 10-2. RS-232 Signals and Their Functions

Pin Number	Function	Direction DTE DCE
1	Frame Ground.	↔
2	Transmit Data (TxD).	→
3	Receive Data (RxD).	←
4	Request to Send (RTS).	→
5	Clear to Send (CTS).	←
6	Data Set Ready (DSR).	←
7	Signal Ground (GND).	↔
8	Data Carrier Detect (DCD).	←
20	Data Terminal Ready (DTR).	→
22	Ring Indicator (RI).	←

Only two of the 25 pins are used for data transmission:[*]

    2   Transmit Data
    3   Receive Data

These two lines are used differently by computers and modems. The RS-232 standard defines two types of equipment: Data Terminal Equipment (DTE) and Data Communications Equipment (DCE). Most (but not all) computers are DTE; modems are always DCE.

DTE uses pin 2 to transmit data and pin 3 to receive it, and DCE does the reverse.

To connect a terminal or computer to a modem or printer (DTE↔DCE), you want to make the connection *straight through*:

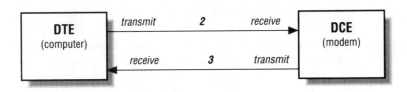

---

[*]The standard also calls for secondary transmit and receive lines, but they are rarely implemented.

To make a connection between two computers (DTE←→DTE), or a between terminal and a computer, you need a cable with lines 2 and 3 *crossed*:

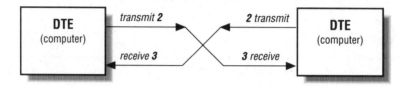

This is often called a *null-modem* or *modem-eliminator* cable.

If you do not know whether a device is DTE or DCE, you can always tell by measuring the voltage on pins 2 and 3. The transmitter should always have a negative voltage, even when idle. If pin 2 is negative, the device is DTE. If pin 3 is negative, the device is DCE.

Hardware Handshaking

Pin 7 is the signal ground. It provides the reference voltage against which other signals are measured. It should be connected straight through. A pin is said to be "asserted" when a voltage greater than ± 3 volts (relative to signal ground) is present on the pin. On the data lines, a voltage more negative than -3 volts is considered a binary 1, and a voltage more positive than +3 volts is considered a binary 0. (Serial drivers usually assert voltages of ± 12 volts to allow a noise margin.)

On the control lines, a positive voltage is considered the "on" state and a negative voltage is considered "off." This is the direct opposite of the case for the data lines.

Other than the data transmission lines (pins 2 and 3) and the signal and frame ground lines (pins 1 and 7), the remainder of the RS-232 lines shown in Table 10-1 are control lines. Most types of equipment (including modems) are not happy just to receive a stream of data. They need to feel more in control through a process called *handshaking*. In handshaking, some preliminary communication between the two pieces of equipment must take place before data can be sent.

Let's consider what type of handshaking might be necessary between a computer and a modem in order to dial up another computer system.

First of all, on an outgoing call, the computer needs to know that the modem is available to make the call. Then the modem needs to tell the computer that it has made a connection.

A computer (DTE) asserts pin 20 (Data Terminal Ready) to show that it is ready. A modem (DCE) asserts pin 6 (Data Set Ready). When the modem makes a connection with another modem on the other end, it asserts pin 8 (Data Carrier Detect) to let the computer know that a connection has actually been established. Most UNIX systems in the U.S.A. ignore DSR and simply rely on DCD alone for this type of handshaking (although European systems often use DSR) DTR is asserted when a program such as *getty* or *uucico* opens the device with an *open* system call. The *open* sleeps on the line until DCD is asserted by the modem or terminal on the other end of the line. These voltages usually remain high during the entire transmission:

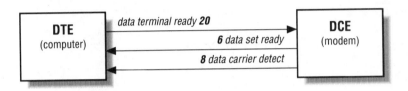

If the voltage on pin 20 drops, it tells the modem that the computer is unable to continue transmission, perhaps because it is down. The modem will hang up the phone if a call is in progress. If the voltage on pin 8 drops, it tells the computer that the modem no longer has a connection. In both cases, these pins give a simple "Yes/No" report on the state of the transmission. This form of handshaking is sometimes referred to as *modem control.*

There is a further level of handshaking that is used to control the rate of data transmission. Particularly when transmitting large amounts of data at high speed, it is possible that one end of a link may try to send data faster than the other can receive it. To keep this from happening, there is a "flow-control handshake" that allows either end to prevent the other from sending any more data until it gets the go-ahead.

In the RS-232 standard, flow control is defined only for half-duplex connections—that is, for connections in which data can be transmitted only in one direction at a time. However, the standard has been adapted, *de facto*, for full-duplex communications as well.

In the half-duplex standard, the DTE asserts RTS when it wants to send data. The DCE replies with CTS when it is ready, and the DTE begins sending data. Unless RTS and CTS are both asserted, only the DCE can send data.

However, in the full-duplex variations, RTS/CTS is used as a kind of "throttle." The signals have the opposite meaning than they do for half-duplex communications.

Whenever a DTE device is able to *accept* data, it asserts pin 4, Request to Send. If the DCE is ready to *accept* data, it asserts pin 5, Clear to Send. If the voltage on RTS or CTS drops at any time, this tells the sending system that the receiver is not ready for more data: "Whoa! Hold on till I get my buffers cleared." Since this flow control handshake is implemented in the serial port hardware, it is considerably more efficient and reliable than the CTRL-S/CTRL-Q (XON/XOFF) handshake that can be performed in software.

If both types of handshaking are used, the entire conversation between computer and modem might go something like this (a plus sign signifies raising the voltage on the line, and a minus sign signifies dropping the voltage):

Table 10-3. Computer-modem Communications

Device	Signal	Meaning
Computer	DTR +	I want to call another system. Are you ready?
Modem	DSR +	I'm turned on. Go ahead and dial.
Modem	DCD +	I've got your party, sir.
Computer	RTS +	Can I send data now?
Modem	CTS +	Sure. Go ahead.
Computer	TxD ...	Data sent out.
Modem	... RxD	Data received.
Modem	CTS -	Hold on for a moment!
Modem	CTS +	I'm OK again. Shoot!
	...	Previous four steps may be repeated, with either device in the sending role, and either device using flow control.
Computer	DTR -	I'm done. Please hang up.
Modem	DCD -	Whatever you say.

Pulling the Wool Over Their Eyes

All of the above sounds good in theory, but in practice, it will not always work. Connecting a computer to a modem is generally easy, since a DTE to DCE connection is what RS-232 was made for. A straight-through cable connecting pins 1 through 8 and 20 (or all 25 pins) will usually do the trick. You should be able to get suitable cables at most computer or electronics stores.

Things can get quite a bit more complicated for a direct connection between two computers or between a terminal and a computer.

Just as the function of pins 2 and 3 is asymmetrical between DTE and DCE devices, so too is the function of pins 6, 8, and 20. A DTE device (a computer or terminal) asserts DTR (pin 20) and expects to receive DSR (pin 6) and DCD (Data Carrier Detect). A DCE device (a modem) asserts DSR and DCD and expects to receive DTR. If you connect two DTE devices with a straight-through cable, no handshaking can occur.

On many UNIX systems, there is a clear symptom of this problem. The system asserts pin 20 when it wants to open a serial port. The success of the *open* call is dependent on getting back a response on DCD (or possibly DSR). The remote computer, not being designed as DCE, will never respond, and whatever process tried to read or write from the port will hang.

To get around the handshaking problem, a null-modem cable can cross some of the control lines as well as the data lines:

This allows DTR (pin 20) on each DTE interface to drive both DSR (pin 6) and pin 8 (DCD) on the other. That is, whenever either side asserts DTR, the other side thinks it is getting DSR and DCD.

Some publications suggest that you can fake out pins 4 and 5 by tying them together at each end of the cable. As a result, whenever the computer looks for a go-ahead signal, it gets it—from itself. This is really a poor practice. It will generally work if you are simply connecting terminals, since people cannot type fast enough to ever require the computer to cry uncle. (Even with terminals, there can be problems. For instance, a function key programmed to send a long string of characters—or a PC trying to upload a file—can send too fast for a loaded system to capture them all. Dropped characters can result, unless the system can rely on the flow-control handshake.)

For direct connections between two computers, you should always connect pins 4 and 5, crossed so that the two DTE interfaces will converse correctly (unless, of course, one of the two computers has a DCE interface, in which case the cable should be straight through).

Here is the pinning for a full null-modem cable:[*]

```
         DTE                    DTE
          1 ──────────────────── 1
          2 ──────╲    ╱──────── 2
          3 ──────╱  ╲────────── 3
          4 ──────╲    ╱──────── 4
          5 ──────╱  ╲────────── 5
       ┌  6                  6  ┐
       │  7 ──────────────────── 7  │
       └  8 ──────╲    ╱──────── 8  ┘
         20 ──────╱  ╲────────── 20
```

You should only do this for a null-modem cable, since a modem really does require the DTR/DCD handshaking signals. If you use a cable like this with a modem, it will not know to hang up when the computer closes the port and drops (deasserts) DTR. This can result in very large telephone bills!

A tip: if you are stringing cables through walls or ceilings, you should use straight-through cables with all necessary lines, then use secondary cables to do any null-modem tricks. This will give you more flexibility in the long run.

Note also that though the official distance limit for RS-232 cables is 50 feet, in practice, they can be used over much larger distances.

Like all generalities, the advice given above may be insufficient. Finding the right cable can be simple and straightforward. Or it can be a seemingly hopeless task for which no one has the right advice. You should be sure to read the documentation for the devices you are trying to connect. It may be difficult to

---

[*]Pin 1 is a safety ground and should be connected at one end (the host end of a computer-modem connection or either end of a direct link between two computers) and left unconnected at the opposite end of the cable. In a proper RS-232 implementation, pin 1 of the port is connected internally to the ground of the system. RS-232C actually says to connect at both ends, with the break done inside the modem. The proposed RS-232D standard says to connect only at the DTE end, as we have described here. But many manufacturers erroneously attach signal ground and frame ground inside the modem.

We have had a lot of controversy from our readers and reviewers over the proper use of pin 1. As noted in the latest BSD 4.3 UUCP documentation: "Proper earth grounding can make RS-232C connections virtually immune to electrical noise and lightning; improper grounding can make the system much more vulnerable. Whether or not pin 1 should be used is a tricky problem in electrical engineering, and sites that are very concerned about noise and lighting protection should have their entire communications network analyzed by a professional. At the very least, Frame Ground must not be confused with or connected to the Signal Ground, pin 7."

translate the raw description given for each device into the information necessary to connect them to one another, but you will succeed if you persevere.

The use of a device called a breakout box can be invaluable if you are trying to build your own cable. (You can usually pick one up at any electronics supply store. A good breakout box is expensive ($200-$300) but worth the investment if you plan to build cables.) The breakout box allows you to easily rearrange the wires in a cable for testing purposes and includes LEDs that display which signals are actually active at any point.

A final word of caution: many devices (such as terminals or modems) allow you to configure the serial connection by setting internal DIP switches. For instance, on a Hayes modem, if switch 1 is down, the modem will force its own DTR high, so that it can answer the telephone even if the computer itself is not asking for a connection. Don't do this! Check your modem to make sure someone else has not done it either, since it can complicate the search for the correct cable. Be sure to read the manufacturer's documentation for details like this that may affect the operation of the RS-232 link.

Gather the Necessary Data

Once you've physically connected the device to the computer, you need to assemble the information you'll need to configure the line:

- The appropriate special file: each possible terminal line connector on a computer corresponds to a particular special file in the directory */dev*. These special files usually have filenames of the form *tty*n, where n is a one or two-digit decimal number and corresponds to each successive serial port. Thus, the first serial port is */dev/tty0* (or 00), the second is */dev/tty1* (or 01), and so on. There are often labels near the RS-232 connectors on the system. If so,, the port number is usually encoded within it somehow (e.g., its last two digits). Consult the documentation to find out how to determine port numbers on your system.

- If the device is a terminal, the name of the corresponding *termcap* or *terminfo* entry.

- Other line and device characteristics needed by the various configuration files. The most crucial of these is the line speed (or maximum device speed, which ever is determinant).

Once you have this information, you are ready to modify the appropriate configurations files, which are described in the next section.

Terminal Line Configuration Files

The configuration files relevant to terminal lines are very different between BSD and System V. The two versions are treated separately.

BSD Configuration Files

Under 4.3 BSD, the following configuration files are used for terminal lines:

/etc/ttys Terminal line configuration file.

/etc/gettydefs Generic line definitions.

/etc/termcap Terminal type definitions database.

/etc/ttytab SunOS terminal line configuration file.

The file */etc/ttys* lists all available terminals on a 4.3 BSD system. It must have an entry for every terminal port in use; it may also have entries for ports that are unused, or turned off. When you add a new device or change the one connected to any port, you must modify */etc/ttys* so that it describes the correct device for that line.

Each entry in this file has four fields:

> *terminal-port command terminal-type status*

Fields are separated by one or more spaces or tab characters. Comments begin with a number sign and may be placed at the end of an entry or as separate lines. The fields have the following meanings:

terminal-port The name of the special file in */dev* that communicates with the line. All serial RS-232 peripherals (e.g., terminals, serial printers, and modems) have port names of the form *tty*nn, where *nn* is a two-digit hexadecimal number. Virtual terminal devices are also listed in */etc/ttys*.

command The command that *init* should execute to monitor this terminal line. For terminals and modems, the program used is *getty*. If *init* must *not* create a process to monitor this line, this field should contain the keyword *none*. This is the case for all terminals where no one will log in: printers, terminals used purely as displays, and the like. Alternatively, the field may contain a special-purpose command for special kinds of terminal initialization (e.g., window systems). If the command is longer than a single word (it typically will be), the entry must be enclosed within quotation marks. Use a full pathname for all commands.

terminal-type   Usually, the name of a terminal type described in */etc/termcap*. If a terminal type is included, the TERM variable will be set to this value at login. Alternatively, the field's contents need not be a type of terminal at all. In this case, the field's value functions as a keyword, which can be used by user initialization files or the *tset* command.[*] Commonly used keywords are:

> *network*   Used for virtual terminal devices.
>
> *unknown*   Used for lines without a specific attached terminal (including modem lines).
>
> *dialup*   Another type sometimes used for modem lines.

status   Zero or more keywords, separated by spaces. The following keywords are supported:

> *on*   Line is enabled, and *command* will be run by *init*.
>
> *off*   Line is disabled, and the entry is ignored.
>
> *secure*   Allow *root* logins.
>
> *window=cmd*   *init* should run *cmd* before the one in field 2.

Off status is used for lines that are down, not in use, or for which no command should be run (e.g., a line connected to a dialout modem). Multiple keywords should not be enclosed in quotation marks, even though they are separated by spaces. For virtual terminals, the status field should be blank (not *on*).

BSD Secure Terminals

If you wish to allow people to log in as *root* on a specific terminal, place the keyword *secure* in the status field for its terminal line. Conversely, you can prevent users from logging in as *root* by omitting or deleting the keyword *secure* from this field. For security reasons, do not give secure status to any modem or PBX-switched circuit. Network terminals also should not be given secure status; denying it means that anyone wanting to become *root* via a network session will need to know both a user account password and the *root* password.

---

[*]What I'm calling "keywords" have *termcap* entries like the following:

```
sa|network:\
    :tc=unknown:
```

This entry defines a "terminal type" *network* whose only characteristic equivalences it to the *unknown* terminal type.

The BSD getty Program and /etc/gettytab

The command field usually contains a *getty* command, which has the following syntax:

```
"getty gettytab-entry"
```

where *gettytab-entry* identifies a particular entry in the file */etc/gettytab*, specifying the characteristics of this terminal line. This file is similar in form to */etc/termcap*. The first line of each entry identifies two or more synonymous names that identify the entry; any name not containing spaces can be used as a valid argument to *getty*. Subsequent lines describe various line characteristics. Here are some sample lines:

```
default:\
    :ap:fd#1000:sp#1200:
    :im=\r\n\r\nUrizen Ur-UNIX* (%h) (%t)\r\n\r\n:
2|std.9600|9600-baud:\
    :sp#9600:
g|std.19200|19200-baud:\
    :sp#19200:
d1200|Dial-1200:\
    :nx=d2400:fd#1:sp#1200:
d2400|Dial-2400:\
    :nx=d1200:fd#1:sp#2400:
```

The names *std.n* are traditionally used for standard terminal lines, running at *n* baud. Thus, *std.9600* in the previous example refers to terminal lines at 9600 baud. Autobaud modems are set to the type corresponding to their maximum speed. These entries frequently set only the *sp* (line speed) characteristic.

The entries whose names begin with "d" are an older style of dialup line. The *nx* characteristic indicates the "next label": the entry that should be used next if a break is received on the line; it is designed to enable cycling through various baud rates. The sample entries oscillate between 1200 and 2400 baud, but actual *gettytab* files usually have a ring of four or more entries.

The *default* entry sets defaults for all entries; characteristics sets in individual entries inherit—and can override—the settings here. It is also where the system pre-login greeting message is set, via the *im* capability. The entry in the previous example will display a message like the following:

```
Urizen Ur-UNIX* (hamlet) (tty01)
```

("%h" inserts the hostname, "%t" inserts the TTY name, and "\r" and "\n" insert returns and newlines, respectively.)

Sample Entries from /etc/ttys

Now that we've looked at all the pieces, here are several typical entries from an *letc/ttys* file:

```
# name    getty                    type        status
console  "/etc/getty std.9600"    vt100       on secure
tty00    "/etc/getty std.19200"   aaa         on
tty01    "/etc/getty std.4800"    dialup      on    # 555-1111
tty02    none                     unknown     off # dialout line
tty03    "/etc/getty std.19200"   vt100       off
ttyp0    none                     network
ttyp1    none                     network
```

The first entry describes a VT100 terminal, used as the system console through the special file */etc/console*. It is enabled and secure (i.e., users may log in on it as *root*), and it runs at 9600 baud. Generally, it's a bad idea to change the console definition that comes with your system.

The second entry describes the terminal on the first terminal line(*/dev/tty00*). This terminal has type *aaa*, corresponding to an Ann Arbor Ambassador terminal. Whenever the terminal line is idle (i.e., whenever a user logs out or when the system enters multi-user mode), *init* runs the command */etc/getty std.19200* on this line. This uses the *std.19200* entry in */etc/gettytab* to provide information about the terminal line. This terminal is enabled, but it is not secure, meaning that users may not use it to log in as *root*.

The third entry (for */dev/tty01*) describes a dialup modem running at 1200 baud. The third serial line (*/dev/tty02*) is used for a dialout modem; no command is run for this line, and it is disabled by the status *off*, ensuring that it will be available for dialout. The fourth terminal line (*/dev/tty03*) is configured for a VT100 terminal, but it is currently disabled.

The final two lines are for virtual terminal devices for network use. The command field for all virtual terminals should contain the keyword *none*.

NOTE

Lines used for serial printers, dialout modems, and other terminal-like output devices should also appear in */etc/ttys*. The command field of these entries should be *none*, and their status field should contain the *off* keyword.

If you were to add a device to serial line 7 on this system, you would need to add an entry to *etc/ttys* for */dev/tty06*:

```
tty06    "/etc/getty std.19200"    unknown    on
```

This entry will cause a *getty* process to be spawned for this line whenever it is idle. The line is enabled, but does not specify a default terminal type.

Pre-4.3 Versions of /etc/ttys (4.2 BSD and XENIX)

Some older Version 7-based operating systems, such as 4.2 BSD and XENIX, use a different format for the */etc/ttys* file. A sample entry might be:

```
17tty04
```

This entry has three fields: two one-character fields, followed by a TTY name. The first field is 0 or 1, depending on whether the terminal line is enabled (1) or not (0). The second field is the label in the first field of the */etc/gettytab* file (the one-character version of the entry label). Like the longer version in the 4.3 BSD version of */etc/ttys*, this label serves as an index into that file and tells the *getty* program about the characteristics of that terminal line. (*getty* is the only terminal line server that can be run.) Thus, the previous entry describes the fifth serial line (*/dev/tty04*), which is enabled and uses the entry labeled *7* in */etc/gettytab*, the 4800 baud line type.

The default terminal type for each terminal line may be specified in the */etc/ttytype* file. It has entries of the form:

terminal-type line-name

where *terminal-type* is the name of a *termcap* entry, and *line-name* is the name part of the special filename (i.e., without "/dev/"). For example, the following entry sets the default terminal type to *vt220* for the second terminal line:

```
vt220 tty01
```

Under XENIX, a terminal line must also be explicitly enabled with the *enable* command, for example:

```
# enable tty04
```

The *disable* command is similarly used to disable a terminal line.

SunOS Terminal Configuration Files

SunOS uses the file */etc/ttytab*, having a form identical to the 4.3 XENIX */etc/ttys*. At boottime, *init* uses it to automatically generate a 4.2 BSD-style */etc/ttys* file. A typical entry in */etc/ttytab* is:

```
ttya "/usr/etc/getty std.9600" xterm on
```

getty's argument—*std.9600* in this case—is an index into the */etc/gettytab* as under BSD.

System V Configuration Files

System V also uses the *getty* program to handle terminal lines, but it is started in a different way. The System V terminal configuration files are:

/etc/inittab	System initialization configuration file.
/etc/gettydefs	Terminal line definition file.[*]
/usr/lib/terminfo/?/*	Terminal type configuration database.

The lines in */etc/inittab* to start *getty*s look like this:

```
co:234:respawn:/etc/getty console 9600
t0:234:respawn:/etc/getty tty0 9600
t1:234:respawn:/etc/getty tty1 9600
t2:234:respawn:/etc/getty tty2 m9600
t3:234:off:/etc/getty tty3 m2400
```

Starting at the left, the fields are the *inittab* identifier (some implementations allow names up to 14 characters long), the run levels to which the entry applies, the action to take, and the process to initiate: */etc/getty* (described in the next section). The action field for terminal line entries holds either *off* (for lines not in use) or *respawn*, which says to start another *getty* as soon as one exits.

The first three lines from the example *inittab* file start the system console and the first two terminal lines, passing *getty* the line name and a second argument which in this case corresponds to the baud rate. The third terminal line on this system is a 9600 baud modem. The fourth terminal line is configured for a 2400 baud modem but is currently disabled.

---

[*]Some System V implementations use a BSD-style *gettytab* file instead of *gettydefs*.

The System V getty Program and /etc/gettydefs

The System V *getty* command is slightly different than under BSD. Under System V, *getty* takes two arguments: the TTY name, corresponding to the name part of the special filename (i.e., without "/dev/"), and a label to look up in the /etc/gettydefs file, which holds generic line definitions. The label is often the same as the line speed. Here are some sample entries (the blank lines which must separate entries in the *gettydefs* file are removed):

```
$ cat /etc/gettydefs | grep -v '^$' | head -6
9600#B9600 CLOCAL#B9600 SANE TAB3 CLOCAL#login: #4800
9600#B9600 CLOCAL#B9600 SANE TAB3 CLOCAL#login: #9600
19200#B19200 CLOCAL#B19200 SANE TAB3 CLOCAL#login: #19200
m9600#B9600#B9600 SANE TAB3 HUPCL#login: #m4800
m4800#B4800#B4800 SANE TAB3 HUPCL#login: #m2400
m2400#B2400#B2400 SANE TAB3 HUPCL#login: #m9600
```

Each line in /etc/gettydefs describes one operating mode. The fields are:

label#initial flags#final flags#login prompt#next label

The *label* is used to refer to the entry on the *getty* command. The initial and final flags are set on the device during the periods before and after *login* is executed, respectively. Commonly used flags are:

B*n*   Baud rate of *n* baud.

CLOCAL   Local directly connected line.

HUPCL   Hangup on close (useful for modems).

TAB3   Tabs are sent to the terminal as spaces.

SANE   Set various parameters to "reasonable" values (as in *stty*).

The fourth field in the *gettydefs* file holds the login prompt used on that line. The *next label* field indicates which label should be used next if a break is received on the line. It is designed to enable cycling through various baud rates on dialup lines. If the *next label* is the same as the *label*, no such cycling will occur; this is how hard-wired lines are set up.

When adding a new device, you'll need to add a new line to /etc/inittab (or modify an existing one). For example, to add a 19.2 Kbaud terminal to the fifth direct terminal line, you would add a line like the following to /etc/inittab:

```
t4:234:respawn:/etc/getty tty4 19200
```

This terminal line is given the label *t4*. It is accessed through /dev/tty4, and its line is described by the *19200* entry in /etc/gettydefs. A *getty* will be started for the line each time it becomes idle when the system is at run level 2, 3, or 4.

Setting Default Terminal Types Under System V

The default terminal type for each terminal line may be specified in the */etc/ttytype* file. It has entries of the form:

> *terminal-type line-name*

where *terminal-type* is the name of a *terminfo* entry, and *line-name* is the name part of the special filename (i.e., without "/dev/"). For example, the following entry sets the default terminal type to *adm3a* for the fourth terminal line:

```
adm3a tty3
```

Changes to Terminal Handling Under V.4

With V.4, terminal lines are handled in a somewhat different manner. Instead of an individual *getty* process for each line, the *ttymon* port monitor oversees all the terminal lines and performs all the *getty* functions. The *ttymon* process is a server that runs continuously while the system is up; it is started automatically when the system is booted to multi-user mode.

The configuration file used by *ttymon* is */etc/ttydefs*. It is viewed and maintained by the *sttydefs* command. Currently, *ttydefs* holds essentially the same data as *gettydefs*, but the standard AT&T documentation states that its format will probably change in the future; the *sttydefs* interface is an attempt to provide continuity across such potential changes.

The *sttydefs* command has three main options, *-a*, *-l*, and *-r*, which add, list, and remove entries from the */etc/ttydefs* file, respectively. When adding an entry, the following additional options are available:

-n   Next label.

-i   Initial flags.

-f   Final flags.

-b   Set autobaud on terminal line.

The next label, initial flags, and final flags have the same meanings as they do in the */etc/ttydefs* file, but their use has been greatly expanded. Any flags accepted by the *stty* command are accepted in this field, separated by spaces. The *-a* and *-r* options require and the *-l* option accepts a label for the */etc/ttytab* entry.

For example, the commands below add a new entry named *hft* and delete an entry named *vt52* from the */etc/ttydefs* file:

```
# sttydefs -a hft -n hft -i "9600 erase ^h" \
    -f "9600 sane crt erase ^?"
# sttydefs -r vt52
```

Terminal lines are put under the control of *ttymon* with the *pmadm* command. The following form may be used to determine which lines are currently managed by *ttymon*:

```
# pmadm -l -p ttymon
```

The *-l* option says to list information about the port monitor named in the *-p* option.

The command form for adding a new port to *ttymon*'s set is quite complex and is best illustrated with a canonical example:

```
# pmadm -a -p ttymon -s 21 -i root -f u -v `ttyadm -V` \
    -m "`ttyadm -d /dev/term/21 -l 9600 -s /usr/bin/login \
    -m ldterm -p \" login: \"`"
```

Since *pmadm* is a complicated and completely general port monitor administration utility, V.4 provides some auxiliary commands to help generate its required input. The auxiliary command for terminal lines is *ttyadm*.

Let's take the preceding command apart:

pmadm -a	*Add a port to ttymon's control.*
-p ttymon	*Controlling port monitor's name.*
-s 21	*Database label (usually the line number).*
-i root	*Run service (specified below) as root.*
-f u	*Create a wtmp entry for the port.*
-v `ttyadm -V`	*Version # of the port monitor admin. file.*
-m "`ttyadm ...`"	*Monitor-specific data (see below).*
ttyadm -d /dev/term/21	*Special file for port.*
-l 9600	*Line type (label in /etc/ttydefs).*
-s /usr/bin/login	*Service program.*
-m ldterm	*Additional modules.*
-p \" login: \"	*Prompt to use.*

This command adds (*-a*) the port controlled by the special file */dev/term/21* (*-d* to *ttyadm*) to the port monitor *ttymon*'s control (*-p*). The *pmadm* command uses the *ttyadm* command twice to format its input correctly: the output of *ttyadm* is placed into the *pmadm* command via backquotes. The second *ttyadm* command does most of the work. It specifies that the */usr/bin/login* service will execute at that port when connection is requested (*ttyadm -s*); the login prompt will be:

```
login:
```

The terminal line's configuration corresponds to the entry labeled "9600" in the */etc/ttydefs* file (*ttyadm -l*).

Obviously, the new V.4 port monitor facility is quite complex. Consult the system documentation and the manual pages for *pmadm, ttyadm,* and *ttymon* for more details.

Configuring Terminal Lines Under AIX 3.1

AIX 3.1 uses *inittab* but not *gettydefs*. The *getty* command requires only one argument, the name of the port to watch, for example:

```
/etc/getty tty0
```

Terminal line characteristics are stored in the Configuration Database and may be set or changed with the *chdev* command. For example, the following command enables logins on */dev/tty0*, setting the line speed to 19200 baud, setting the *stty* modes before a login to *hupcl, cread,* and *tab3*, and the *stty* modes after *login* is executed to *cread, echoe,* and *cs8*:

```
$ chdev -l tty0 -a login=enable -a speed=19200 \
  -a term=vt100 -a runmodes='hupcl,cread,tab3' \
  -a logmodes='cread,echoe,cs8'
```

As under V.4, any *stty* options may be used for the initial and final flags set with the *runmodes* and *logmodes* attributes.

Starting the Terminal Line

The final step in installing a new serial device is (re)starting its line. To start up a terminal line, you must force the program *init* to reread the terminal line initialization information. When it does, *init* becomes aware that the device has been added and takes the appropriate action (usually starting a *getty* process for it).

Under BSD, the command:

```
# kill -HUP 1
```

sends a hangup (HUP) signal (signal number 1) to *init*. *init* catches this signal and interprets it as a command to reread initialization information *without* interrupting the system's activity; *kill* is being used in its generic, signal-sending capacity rather than to terminate a process. Therefore, by modifying the configuration files and executing the command *kill -HUP 1*, you add a new terminal without rebooting the system or otherwise interrupting the system's normal operation.

On System V systems, the *-q* option to *init* performs the same function:

`# init -q` *(minus sign before option incorrect for V.3)*

After you execute this command, check the new terminal. It should have a login prompt and allow you to login normally. If it does not, try checking the items in the next section.

Troubleshooting Terminal Problems

Messed-up terminals are an occasional problem that system administrators have to deal with. When a terminal is hung (when it won't respond to any input) or seems to have gone crazy, here are some things to try that address the most common things that might be wrong:

- If the user knows what she did last, try to undo it. For example, if she was experimenting with *stty* options, try a *stty sane* command.

- If the terminal doesn't respond at all, the user might have accidentally hit CTRL-S, the pause key, the hold screen key, or something else that will temporarily stop output. Try entering CTRL-Q and then these other keys to see if things get going again.

- Check the terminal settings via its setup menu. In particular, is its baud rate set correctly?

- Try entering the *reset* command. If it doesn't work, try preceding and following it with a line feed (CTRL-J if the terminal has no line feed key): ^J*reset*^J.

- If the user has turned the power off and back on, check other settings like the emulation mode that might have been reset to a wrong value. If the user hasn't cycled power, try this yourself; there are some conditions that only cycling the power will clear. Leave the terminal off for about 10 seconds to allow the internal capacitors to discharge completely.

- Next, go to another terminal and try to kill the program that was running. It may be that the program—and not the terminal—is hung. Use the *ps* command with its *-t* option to limit the display to the desired terminal. *-t* takes the device name as its argument, in the same form in which it appears in the TTY column of *ps*'s output. For example, the following command displays the processes for */dev/tty15*:

```
$ ps -t15
```

- If nothing else works, trying killing the user's login shell. If the terminal doesn't come back after a few seconds, try cycling the power again.

- If cycling the power and killing everything in sight doesn't bring the terminal back, check the connections. Has the RS-232 line fallen off the back, for example? (In some cases, you'll want to check this first.) If a cable is loose, it will eventually fall due to gravity alone, even if the terminal hasn't moved an inch in months.

For a new terminal, try checking these items:

- Is the terminal plugged into the correct RS-232 connector on the back of the system? It is easy to lose track of a cable between the terminal and the computer. Good record keeping and labeling will help eliminate this problem.

- Is the terminal port enabled and does it specify an appropriate way to call *getty*?

- Is the *getty* process running? Use *ps* piped to *grep* to count the number of *getty* processes and verify that the right number are present.

- Are you using the right kind of cable? If not, a command like the following will hang:

```
# cat file > /dev/ttyn
```

Don't forget to kill the process once you've verified that it is hung.

Configuring a Dialin/Dialout Modem

A longstanding deficiency of many UNIX implementations is the inability for the same modem to be used to dialin and dialout (not simultaneously, of course). System V and SunOS each provide different solutions for this problem. SunOS fixes this problem by allowing the administrator to create two different special files for the terminal line to which the modem is attached. The dialin device is usually named */dev/ttyd*n, where *n* is a number indicating which modem line it is (the lines are conventionally numbered sequentially, beginning with 0, regardless of which terminal line they correspond to), and the corresponding dialout device for the same line has a name of the form */dev/cua*n. This is the special file that would be used for outgoing *uucp* sessions and with *tip* and other programs that can place outgoing calls. The dialin device, */dev/ttyd*n, would be entered into */etc/ttytab*.

The two special files differ only in their *minor device number* (their subtype within their device class), which are offset by 128. You can use the *ls -l* command to find the major and minor device numbers for a special file; they appear in the size field.

You would use the *mknod* command if you need to create one or both of these special files. For example, the following commands may be used to create the special files for a dialin-dialout modem (the first one on the system) on the second terminal line (which is usually named */dev/ttyb*):

```
# mknod /dev/ttyd0 c 12 1
# mknod /dev/cua0 c 12 129
```

These commands both create character special files (the *c* code letter) for device class 12 (terminal lines). Once you've done this, create a normal dialin entry in */etc/ttytab* for */etc/ttyd0*, and create a normal dialout entry for */etc/cua0*. For example:

```
# The following entries represent the same physical modem
ttyd0  "/usr/etc/getty d2400" unknown on   # dialin entry  (line enabled)
cua0   none                   unknown off  # dialout entry (dialin disabled)
```

Once you've done this, use */dev/ttyd0* whenever you need to refer to the dialin modem, and */dev/cua0* when you need to dial out. See the SunOS *zs* manual page for full details on SunOS dialin/dialout lines and the section "Making Special Files," in Chapter 8, *Filesystems and Disks* for more on creating special files with *mknod*.

Under System V, the *uugetty* command is used in place of *getty* as the terminal line server process for a dialin/dialout modem. Here is a sample *inittab* entry:

```
m0:234:respawn:/usr/lib/uucp/uugetty -r -t 60 tty00 9600
```

The *-r* option tells *uugetty* to wait to read a character before issuing the login message (users will need to hit a carriage return to get the login prompt when dialing into this line). A line linked by two modems must use *uugetty -r* at each end. The *-t* option specifies the timeout period (in seconds) for the login prompt. The final two arguments are the same as for *getty*: the terminal line and the *gettydefs* entry label (usually specifying the line speed).

On more recent System V implementations, *uugetty* is no longer necessary. Instead the devices *ttyd*n and *acu*n are used for dialin and dialout access on the same line (respectively), in a similar scheme to SunOS. The */dev/ttyd*n device would be the one listed in */etc/inittab*.

11

Printers and the Spooling Subsystem

The BSD Spooling System
System V Printing
The AIX 3.1 Queueing System
Troubleshooting Printers

This chapter discusses the printing subsystems of the various UNIX versions we are considering. Nowhere is there more variation among the different versions than in how printing devices and spooling to them is handled. The BSD, System V, and AIX 3.1 spooling subsystems are discussed individually in this chapter.

In this chapter, I'll talk almost exclusively about "print" jobs, but the discussion applies equally well to other hard copy devices (such as plotters).

Any spooling system includes the following parts:

- User commands to initiate printing. The user specifies the file to print, which device to print it on if there is more than one possibility, and any other necessary instructions. BSD calls them print *jobs* while System V and AIX 3.1 refer to them as print *requests*.

- Queues to store and sequentially process print jobs. In its simplest form, a queue is basically a line waiting to use a specific device.

- Spooling directories to hold pending jobs. Under BSD, the entire file to be printed is copied to a spooling directory. Under AIX 3.1 and System V, by default only a small request file is generated, and the file is accessed in its original location at the proper time.

- Server processes to transfer jobs from the spooling directory to the device.

- Administrative commands to start and stop the subsystem or specific printers and to manage queues and individual print jobs.

The BSD Spooling System

The BSD operating system includes a standard line-printer spooling system. The subsystem can maintain multiple printers, printers at local and remote sites, and multiple print queues. This system can be adapted to support laser printers, raster printers, and other types of devices. As shipped, the spooling system supports a standard line printer.

The spooling system is a collection of five programs and several files. The key pieces to this system are:

lpr   Adds a job to a print queue by copying the file into its spooling directory. Strictly speaking, it queues the job rather than printing it; the *lpd* daemon handles the actual sending of files to printer devices. When a job is submitted, it is assigned a job ID number, which is used to refer to it in subsequent commands.

lpq   Lists jobs that are currently in the print queues.

lprm   Removes jobs from the printing queues. This program will only allow users to remove their own jobs; no user other than *root* can delete someone else's job from a print queue.

lpd   The printer daemon, responsible for sending data from the spooling directory to a printer.

lpc   The administrative interface to the printing subsystem.

/etc/printcap Printer configuration file, containing entries describing each printer on the system.

The printcap File

The file */etc/printcap* lists all devices serviced by the spooling system. BSD systems are usually shipped with a standard version of */etc/printcap* that describes many common printers, all commented out. Therefore, you can usually configure */etc/printcap* by activating the proper entry for your printer and making some minor modifications to customize that entry for your site. This section discusses how to make these modifications.

NOTE

The *printcap* file is not merely a printer characteristics database, but a required configuration file. Although the *printcap* file resembles the *termcap* file in many ways, there is a significant difference between them. The active entries in the *printcap* file (i.e., not commented out) define actual printers on the system.

Here are some sample *printcap* entries for a standard lineprinter and a laser printer:

```
# line printer -- system default printer
lp|line printer:\
    :sd=/usr/spool/lp:if=/usr/lib/lpf:lf=/usr/adm/lpd-errs:\
    :lo=lp0LOCK:lp=/dev/lp:pl=66:pw=132:af=/usr/adm/lpacct
# laser printer
ps|3rd Floor Laser Printer:\
    :sd=/usr/spool/ps:br#9600:\
    :rw:sh:lo=lock:mx#10000:\
    :af=/usr/adm/ps_acct/lp3:\
    :lf=/usr/spool/ps/log:\
    :lp=/dev/null:\
    :cf=/usr/lib/pscif:df=/usr/lib/psdvi:\
    :gf=/usr/lib/psgraph:if=/usr/lib/pspf:\
    :nf=/usr/lib/ips:rf=/usr/lib/psfort:\
    :tf=/usr/lib/pscat:vf=/usr/lib/ps:
```

The lines beginning with a number sign are comments. Individual items in a *printcap* entry are separated by colons. The first line in each holds the names of the printer: *lp* and *ps* in our example. The remaining fields describe the printer's characteristics and use. The most important ones in the example have the following meanings:

af   Accounting file pathname.

br   Baud rate.

lf   Error log file pathname.

lo   Lock filename.

lp   Device special file.

mx   Maximum file size (0=no limit).

pl   Page length in lines.

pw   Page width in characters.

sd   Spooling directory.

sh   Suppress burst (header) page.

Thus, the first entry describes a line printer accessed via */dev/lp*. Its pages are 132 characters wide and 66 lines long. It uses the spooling directory */usr/spool/lp*. Its error messages are written to the file */usr/adm/lpd-errs*, and its accounting data goes to the file */usr/adm/lpacct*. The second entry describes a laser printer accessed via */dev/ps* at 9600 baud. On this printer, the maximum file size is 10000 blocks, and burst pages are suppressed. It uses the spooling directory */usr/spool/ps*, the accounting file */usr/adm/ps_acct*, and the error log file */usr/spool/ps/log*. The final four lines of the entry specify programs used as inter-faces to this printer for different circumstances and file types. See the *printcap* manual page for full details on *printcap* entry fields.

Setting the System Default Printer

The system default printer is defined as the entry named *lp* in the */etc/printcap*. This is usually the one accessed via the special file */dev/lp*, but it needn't be; you can assign the alias *lp* to any printer that you desire.

Users can specify their own default printer via the PRINTER environment vari-able. On user printer-related commands, the *-P* option may also be used to spec-ify a specific printer. For example, the following command sends a file to the printer *ps*:

```
% lpr -Pps listing.ps
```

Spooling Directories

A spooling directory holds files destined for a particular printer until the the dae-mon, *lpd*, can print them. Spooling directories are conventionally located in */usr/spool*. Each printer must have its own spooling directory.

All spooling directories must be owned by the special user *daemon* and belong to the group *daemon* and have access mode 755 (read and execute access for every-one, read, execute, and write access for user). This protection scheme gives the spooling system sole write access to files that have been spooled, forcing users to use the spooling system and preventing anyone deleting someone else's pending files or otherwise misbehaving.

To create a new spooling directory called */usr/spool/newps*, execute the following commands:

```
# cd /usr/spool
# mkdir newps
# chown daemon.daemon newps
# chmod 755 newps
# ls -ld
drwxr-xr-x  2 daemon   daemon       2048 Apr  8 09:44 newps
```

You will have to create new spooling directories when you add additional printers.

The Spooling Daemon

The BSD spooling daemon is */usr/lib/lpd*. It is started by */etc/rc* at boottime:

```
if [ -f /usr/lib/lpd ]; then
    rm -f /dev/printer /usr/spool/lpd.lock
    /usr/lib/lpd; echo -n ' printer' >/dev/console
fi
```

If the server program is readable, then *rc* removes the old lock file and socket and then starts the daemon (it will create its own lock file and communications interface).

As */etc/rc* is delivered, the commands for *lpd* may be commented out and will need to be activated when you install the first printer.

Occasionally, the spooling daemon gets hung. The main symptom of this is a queue with jobs in it but nothing printing. In this case, you should kill the old daemon and start a new one:

```
# ps aux | grep lpd
root      5990 2.2  0.8 1408  352 p0 S      0:00 grep lpd
root       208 0.0  0.2 1536   32 ?  I      0:00 (lpd)
# kill -9 208
# /usr/lib/lpd
```

Managing Queues

The program *lpc* is used to perform most administrative tasks connected with the spooling system under BSD, including shutting down a printer for maintenance, displaying a printer's status, and manipulating jobs in print queues. The command to invoke the line printer control utility is simply *lpc*:

```
# lpc
lpc>
```

lpc is now running, and issues its own prompt. *lpc* has a number of internal commands:

status *printer*
Display status of the line printer daemon and queue for the specified printer.

abort *printer*
Terminates any printing in progress immediately and disables all printing on *printer*. It does not remove any jobs from the queue; any jobs currently in the queue will be printed when the printer is restarted. To restart the printer, use the *start* command. *abort* is useful when the spooling system reports that a daemon is present but nothing appears to be happening. *abort* is an immediate version of *stop*.

stop *printer*
Stops all printing on *printer* after the current job has finished. Users can still use *lpr* to add new jobs to the queue, but they won't be printed until the printer is started again. This command lets you stop the printer in a clean way, and is usually used when you need to add supplies or perform routine maintenance.

start *printer*
Restarts printing on *printer* after an *abort* or *stop* command.

disable *printer*
Prevents users from putting new jobs into the queue for *printer*. The superuser can still add jobs to the queue, and printing will continue. Disabling its queue, waiting for all pending jobs to finish, and then stopping the printer is the most graceful way to turn off a printer.

enable *printer*
Allows users to spool jobs to the queue again. *enable* restores normal operation after the *disable* command.

down *printer*
Stops printing and disables the queue for *printer*. *down* is equivalent to *disable* plus *stop*.

up *printer*
Enables the queue and starts printing on *printer*. *up* is equivalent to *enable* plus *start*.

For all of the *lpc* commands, the keyword *all* can be substituted for the printer name to act on every printer on the system.

Here are some examples of *lpc*'s commands:

```
# lpc                          Invoke lpc.
lpc> status ps                 What's going on on printer ps.
ps:
     queuing is enabled
     printing enabled
        5 entries in spool area
     daemon started
lpc> disable ps                Block new jobs on ps.
ps:
     queuing disabled
lpc> stop ps                   Stop printing on ps.
ps:
     printing disabled
lpc> quit                      Exit lpc.
#
```

Single *lpc* internal commands can also be executed from the UNIX command line by including it as *lpc*'s arguments:

```
# lpc up ps
#
```

Manipulating Individual Print Jobs

The *lpc* commands we've considered so far manipulate devices and their queues. In this subsection, we'll look at ways to manage individual print jobs.

Use the BSD *lpq* command to list the contents of a queue. For example, the following command lists the jobs in the queue for printer *ps*:

```
% lpq -P ps
Rank   Owner      Job  Files       Total Size
1st    chavez     15   11726.f     74578 bytes
2nd    martin     16   fpppp.F     12394 bytes
. . .
```

lprm can be used to remove individual print jobs. Its syntax is:

```
#  lprm -P printer jobs-to-remove
```

The jobs to be removed may be specified in various ways: as a list of job IDs and/or usernames (in the latter case, all jobs belonging to the specified users will be removed), or with a single hyphen, in which case all jobs will be removed when the command is run by *root*. So, to remove job 15 from the queue *ps*, use the command:

```
# lprm -P ps 15
```

To move a job within its print queue, use *lpc*'s *topq* command:

```
lpc> topq printer jobs-to-move
```

The *jobs-to-move* may be specified as a list of job IDs and/or usernames (to select all jobs belonging to those users). *topq* will move the specified jobs to the top of the queue for *printer*. If more than one job is specified, then the jobs take on the order they are listed in on the command line. At the end, the leftmost job will be at the top of the queue.

Adding a New Printer

In order to add a new printer to a BSD system, you must:

- Physically connect the printer to the computer. If you are using a serial line, a modem cable is usually the correct choice.

- For serial line printers, create or modify an entry in the terminal line configuration file */etc/ttys* (*/etc/ttytab* under SunOS). The entry should have status *off*, type *unknown*, and the keyword *none* in the command field (see the section "BSD Configuration Files," in Chapter 10, *Terminals and Modems*).

- If this is the first printer on the system, verify that the lines in */etc/rc* to start the *lpd* server are active.

- Add an entry for the printer to */etc/printcap*. If you are adding a new printer of the same type as an existing one, copy its entry, changing the name, special file, spool directory, accounting file, error log file, and any other relevant characteristics to the values for the new printer. If the new printer is the first of its type, then uncomment out the lines for its type in */etc/printcap*, and then edit these same fields. Printer manufacturers also often can provide *printcap* entries for their printers.

- Create a spooling directory for the printer (as discussed previously).

- Create the printer's accounting file (defined in the *af* field of their *printcap* entry) with the *touch* command; for example:

```
# touch /usr/adm/lp_acct/ps3
# chown daemon /usr/adm/lp_acct/ps3
# chmod 755 /usr/adm/lp_acct/ps3
```

As in this example, printer accounting files are usually stored in the home directory of user *adm*—*/usr/adm* on BSD systems and */var/adm* on SunOS system—or a subdirectory under it, and must be owned and writable by user *daemon*.

- Start the printer and its queue:

  ```
  # lpc up ps3
  ```

- Test the new printer by spooling a small file. Troubleshooting hints are discussed in the final section of this chapter.

Remote Printing

The BSD spooling system can also send files to printers on remote hosts (i.e., to systems other than your own, generally a printer on the same network). This requires a slightly different *printcap* entry. Here is a typical description for a remote printer:

```
# Remote line printer entry
remlp|print on hamlet's letter quality printer:\
    :lp=:rm=hamlet:rp=lp2:sd=/usr/spool/remlp
```

This entry specifies the properties of a printer named *remlp*. The empty *lp* field shows that this entry describes a remote printer, and the *rm* field indicates the destination system for remote printing (in this case, the host *hamlet*). The *rp* field holds the name of the target printer on the destination host. Thus, in this example, send a file to the printer *remlp* will result in its being printed by printer *lp2* on system *hamlet*. Note that this entry does not contain any specific details about the remote printer other than its name. The local host does not know, or care, what kind of printer is connected to the remote system. That is defined in the remote system's own *printcap* file.

To allow a remote system to print on the local system, its hostname must be listed in the file */etc/hosts.lpd* or */etc/hosts.equiv*. If the first file exists, the hostname must appear in it or remote printing requests will be refused. If its *printcap* entry contains the *rs* characteristic, then only remote users with accounts on the local system will be allowed to use the printer. If */etc/hosts.lpd* does not exist, the */etc/hosts.equiv* file is checked (see the section entitled "Host Level Equivalence," in Chapter 12, *TCP/IP Network Management*, for more on */etc/hosts.equiv*).

System V Printing

The System V printing system is used on a wide range of systems, from micro-computers with a single printer to high-end mainframes with many printers. This section will describe the standard System V printing subsystem, as implemented through V.3; its final subsection will discuss enhancements to the basic system introduced in some V.3 versions and standard in V.4.

The System V spooling subsystem has the following major components:

- User commands: *lp* (to initiate print requests), *cancel* (to cancel a pending request), and *lpstat* (to list queue contents). When a user submits a print job, it is assigned a unique *request ID* which is used to identify it thereafter. Under System V, request IDs usually consist of the printer name and a number: PS-1023 for example.

- The spooling daemon *lpsched*, responsible for carrying out print requests by sending data to the appropriate printer.

- Administrative commands, including *accept, reject, enable, disable, lpadmin, lpmove,* and *lpusers* (all described in this section). These commands are stored in */usr/lib*, which may need to be added to *root*'s search path.

- Spooling directories under */usr/spool/lp/request* named for each printer. These hold print request information, but by default the actual file to print is not copied. Thus, changing or deleting a file before it is printed affects the final output. The -c option to *lp* can be used to copy the file to the spool area when it is submitted for printing.

Device Classes

Print requests are sent to the queue for a *destination*. Destinations may be either a specific printer (or other device) or a *device class*, which provides a mechanism to group similar devices and declare them to be equivalent to and substitutable for one another. For example, all of the laser printers can be grouped into a class *laser*; users may then spool a print request to destination *laser*, and it will be printed on the first available device in the class. All of the devices within a device class share a single queue.

What the *lp* command actually does is to place a print request into a queue, either for a specific device or a class containing several devices; sometime later, the print service daemon, *lpsched*, actually sends the job to the printing device. We'll discuss how to place specific printers into device classes later in this section.

Setting the System Default Destination

The system default destination is set by the system administrator with the *-d* option to the *lpadmin* command. For example, the following comand sets the default destination to the device *PS2*:

```
# lpadmin -dPS2
```

The command *lpstat -d* will list the current system default destination:

```
$ lpstat -d
system default destination: PS
```

Users may set an alternate default destination for themselves with the LPDEST environment variable. For example, the following commands set this user's default destination to the device class *laser*:

```
$ LPDEST=laser; export LPDEST
```

Obtaining Destination Status Information

The *lpstat* command can provide status information about current printing queues and devices. *lpstat*'s most useful options for this purpose are:

-alist   Indicate whether the queues for the printers in *list* are accepting jobs or not.

-clist   Display the members of the listed classes.

-olist   List print requests. In this case, *list* may include request IDs, printer names, and class names. In the latter case, all requests for these printers and classes will be displayed.

-plist   Display the current status of the specified printers.

-ulist   Display the status of all jobs belonging to the specified users.

-vlist   Display the special file used by the specified printers.

-s   Summary: list all classes and their members and all printers and their associated devices.

-t   Display all status information.

All lists are comma separated; enclose them in quotes if they contain special characters that have meaning to the shell. If the list is omitted, then all entities of the specified type are assumed. For example, *lpstat -uchavez, jones* lists all jobs belonging to users *chavez* and *jones*, and *lpstat -u* lists all jobs belonging to all users. Similarly, *lpstat -c* may be used to list the members of all defined classes. Without any options, *lpstat* displays all requests that were submitted by the user executing the *lpstat* command (*lpstat* alone is thus equivalent to *lpstat -u$USER*).

For example, the following command lists all jobs in the queue for printer *PS*:*

```
$ lpstat -oPS
PS-1139    chavez     89427   May 25 07:19 on PS
PS-1140    martin    302052   May 25 07:21
PS-1141    ng         58357   May 25 07:26
PS-1142    ng          9846   May 25 07:26
```

The following command displays the current status of destinations *PS* and *PS2*:

```
$ lpstat -pPS,LP2
printer PS now printing PS-1139.  enabled since May 13 22:12
printer LP2 is idle.  enabled since May 13 22:12
```

The following command indicates whether the queue for device class *laser* is accepting new jobs or not:

```
$ lpstat -alaser
laser accepting requests since Jan 23 17:52
```

The following command displays the special file used as an interface for *PS*:

```
$ lpstat -vPS
device for PS: /dev/tty0
```

Manipulating Individual Print Requests

Under System V, the system administrator may cancel any pending job using the *cancel* command, which takes the request IDs of the jobs to be cancelled or a destination as its argument. In the first case, the specified requests are cancelled, even if they are currently printing; in the second case, whatever request is currently printing on that printer will be terminated.

---

*As illustrated in this example, the arguments to options for commands in the System V spooling system are not preceded by a space under V.3. The System V.4 syntax is more flexible.

Pending print jobs may also be moved between print queues with the *lpmove* command, which has the following syntax:

```
# lpmove request-id(s) newprinter      Move some requests.
# lpmove oldprinter newprinter         Move all requests.
```

The first form moves the specified jobs to the new printer designated as the command's final argument; the second form moves all jobs currently queued for *oldprinter* to *newprinter* (useful when a printer has gone down and an alternate is available). Note that if *oldprinter* and *newprinter* are in the same class, then an *lpmove* is not necessary: since the same queue feeds both devices, jobs will automatically be routed to the second printer if the first one goes down. *lpmove* can only be used when the printing service is shut down (see the section entitled "Starting and Stopping the Print Service," later in this chapter).

Controlling Print Queues

The *accept* and *reject* commands may be used to permit and inhibit spooling to a print queue; both take a list of destinations as their argument. With its *-r* option, *reject* may also specify a reason for denying requests, which will be displayed to users attempting to send jobs to that queue. For example, the following commands close and then reopen the queue associated with the printer PS:

```
# reject PS
# accept PS
```

The following command closes the queue for the destination class *laser*:

```
# reject -r"There is no paper in the entire building..." laser
```

accept and *reject* don't affect whether pending jobs continue to print or not. The *enable* and *disable* commands are used to control the status of a particular printing device. They both take a list of printers as their arguments; in this case, since actual devices are being controlled, destination classes are not valid arguments. *disable* also has a *-r* option to allow an administrator to specify a reason that a printer is going down. It also has a *-c* option, which automatically cancels any jobs that are currently printing on the specified device(s). By default, jobs printing when the *disable* command is executed will be reprinted on another printer in the same class (if any) or when the device comes back up. For example, the following commands disable and then re-enable the device PS:

```
# disable -r"Changing toner cartridge; back by 11" PS
# lpstat -pPS
Printer PS disabled since May 24 10:53 -
    Changing toner cartridge; back by 11
# enable PS
```

Starting and Stopping the Print Service

Print requests are actually handled by the *lpsched* daemon, which is started automatically at system boottime, usually by a file like */etc/rc2.d/S85lp*. The commands look something like these:

```
if test -x /usr/lib/lpshut -a -x /usr/lib/lpsched; then
    /usr/lib/lpshut > /dev/null 2>&1
    rm -f /usr/spool/lp/SCHEDLOCK /usr/spool/lp/FIFO
    /usr/lib/lpsched
fi
```

These commands first check to make sure the server startup and shutdown programs are available. Then, the print service is shut down (if it is running), *lpsched*'s lock file and named pipe are deleted, and then the new server is started (it will create its own lock file and named pipe).

The *-r* option to *lpstat* may be used to determine if the printing scheduling daemon is running or not:

```
$ lpstat -r
scheduler is running
```

The printing service may be shut down with the *lpshut* command. This command disables all devices but does not prevent requests from being added to queues. The print service may be restarted with the command *lpsched*. Neither command requires any arguments.

Managing Printers and Destination Classes

The *lpadmin* command is used to define and modify the characteristics of printer devices and classes. It should only be used for such purposes when *lpsched* has been stopped with *lpshut*.

The *-p* option is used to specify the printer to be affected by the *lpadmin* command. *-p* many be used on every *lpadmin* command. It also has many other options to perform various administrative functions within the spooling system.

To add a new printer to the system, the following command format is used:

```
lpadmin -pprinter -vspecial-file interface-option
```

where *printer* is the name to be given to the printer and *special-file* is the pathname to the special file through which the system communicates with the printer.

The interface option has one of the following forms:

-e printer   Copy an existing printer's interface.

-m model   Specify printer by model type (give its filename in */usr/spool/lp/model*).

-i interface-path   Specify a printer interface program (full pathname).

The purpose of these options is to specify which printer interface program is to be used with the new printer. A printer interface is a shell script which performs the various tasks necessary to prepare the printer for printing (such as setting line options with the *stty* command and downloading special control codes) and spools the desired files to the device.

The easiest option to use is *-e*, which says to use the same interface as an existing printer. For example, the following command defines a new printer *PS4*, attached via */dev/tty02*; it is the same model as the existing printer *PS3*:

```
$ lpadmin -pPS4 -ePS3 -v/dev/tty02
```

For a new printer type, you may find an appropriate interface program already on the system. Interface programs for many printer types are stored in the directory */usr/spool/lp/model*; when a printer is defined using one of them, it is copied to the directory */usr/spool/lp/interface*. Most UNIX systems come with many interface programs for many printer models. Interface programs are often available from the manufacturer of the printer and with typesetting packages like *troff*. The *-m* option specifies the filename of an interface program in */usr/spool/lp/model*. For example, the following command defines a new printer *tek1* using the interface program */usr/spool/lp/model/tek4693* and attached via */dev/tty05*:

```
$ lpadmin -ptek1 -v/dev/tty05 -mtek4693
```

The *-i* option is used to specify a custom interface program. An interface program may range from very simple to quite complex. By convention, it takes the following arguments:

$1   Job ID.

$2   Username.

$3   Job title.

$4   Number of copies.

$5   Printer-specific options.

$6 . . .   Files to be printed.

Here is an extremely simple interface program:*

```
#!/bin/sh
job=$1; user=$2; title=$3; copies=$4; printer=`basename $0`
star="*****************************************************"
# Do banner page
echo "\014c"
echo "\n\n\n$star"
banner $title
echo "\n\n\nUser: $user"
echo "Job: $job"
echo "Printer: $printer"
echo "Date: `date`"
echo "\014c"
# Print files
shift;shift;shift;shift;shift # throw away non-file arguments
files="$*"
while [ $copies -gt 0 ]
do
    for file in $files
    do
        cat "$file" 2>&1
        echo "\014c"
    done
    copies=`expr $copies - 1`
done
```

When it is invoked, standard output from the script will go to the printer. This script first prints a banner page, using the user's title and including other data like his username, the printer name, and the date. It then sends the appropriate number of copies of each file to the printer, placing a formfeed after each file and copy.

If there is no existing interface program for your printer, you can try writing one yourself. The simplest way to do so is to use one of the existing programs as a starting point.

lpadmin can also change the characteristics of an existing printer. If the printer defined with the *-p* option already exists, then any *lpadmin* command will change its characteristics.

The *-x* option removes the definition of a printer from the system. With *-r* or *-x*, if the specified printer is the only member of its class, then that class is removed as a side effect of removing the printer from the class or the system.

---

*Actually, the simplest possible interface program is probably:

```
#!/bin/sh
cat $6 2>$1
```

It ignores all five initial arguments and can print only one file at a time.

The *-c* option is used to place a printer into a class. For example, the command:

```
# lpadmin -pPS2 -claser
```

will add the printer *PS2* to the class *laser*, creating the class if it does not already exist. The *-r* option may be used to remove a printer from a class. For example, the following command removes the printer *PS1* from the class *laser*:

```
# lpadmin -pPS1 -rlaser
```

You can also place the printer into a destination class as you create it:

```
# lpadmin -pPS5 -v/dev/tty2 -mps -claser
```

This command creates a printer *PS5*, a PostScript printer accessed via */dev/tty2*, and adds it to the class *laser*.

Adding a New Printer

Now that we've looked at all of the pieces, we're ready to add a new printer to the system. In order to add a new printer to a System V system, you must:

- Physically connect the printer to the computer. If you are using a serial line, a modem cable is usually the correct choice.

- For serial line printers, set run level field for the port's entry in */etc/inittab* to *off*.

- If this is the first printer on the system, make sure that there is a link from */etc/init.d/lp* to an "S" and "K" file in the boot subdirectories (*/etc/rc0.d* and usually */etc/rc2.d*). If there aren't, you'll need to create them; for example:

```
# ln /etc/init.d/lp /etc/rc0.d/K25lp
# ln /etc/init.d/lp /etc/rc2.d/K85lp
# ln /etc/init.d/lp /etc/rc2.d/S85lp
```

  The numbering scheme and filenames used vary from system to system.

- Shut down the printing service with *lpshut*. Then add the new printer to the system with *lpadmin*. If this is the first printer on the system, log in as the user *lp* before executing *lpadmin*; this will ensure that the permissions of the printing services data files and spooling directories are set correctly.

- Start the printer and its queue; for example:

```
# accept PS3
printer "PS3" now accepting requests
# enable PS3
printer "PS3" now enabled
```

- Test the new printer by spooling a small file. Troubleshooting hints are discussed in the final section of this chapter.

Enhancements to the System V Printing System

Some versions of V.3—such as Interactive UNIX—significantly expand the functionality of the basic print service described so far, while retaining its basic structure. Enhancements to V.3 (which become standard with V.4) include the following:

- Support for *forms* on individual printer devices. Forms are output variations within a device (often different types of paper).

- Support for multiple character sets on individual printer devices.

- Automatic alerts when forms or print wheels need changing or when a printer needs attention.

- Optional banner pages on printouts.

- Ability to limit access to printers by username.

- Job priorities within print queues.

- Specification of more printer attributes via *lpadmin*.

- Printer type definitions, defined via the *terminfo* database.

- Support for remote printing.

- Built-in features for PostScript printing.

Some of the most interesting features are introduced in the sections that follow. For a full description of the V.4 print service, as implemented on your system, consult your system documentation.

Additional Options to lpadmin

The following options are among the many options added to *lpadmin* in some V.3 versions which are standard under V.4:

-*f*   Specify allowed forms for a printer or class.

-*U*   Specify dialing information for printing via modem.

-*T*   Specify a printer type (definitions are in the *terminfo* database).

-*o*   Specify additional printer characteristics.

-*S*   Define names for the character sets available on the destination.

-*I*   Define the types of jobs the printer can handle.

-*D*   Create a description of the printer for use in status displays.

This group of options describes the variations that are possible within a single printer (or destination class). The -*f* option is used to specify forms allowed (or not allowed) on a destination device. Forms are alternate print media supported by the same device, for example, different sizes of paper or literally differently printed forms (such as invoices or checks). Forms are defined via the *lpforms* command and are then applied to the different devices and classes. Similarly, the -*S* option may be used to define the available character sets on a device.

The -*I* option is used to define the types of files that can be printed at the destination. -*I* is designed to enable fully automated printing. Ideally, once all destinations are configured with -*I*, the print service will have the ability to figure out where to print a request based upon the file's characteristics—known as its *content type*—without the user having to specify a destination at all (the user can specify the file's *content type* with the -*T* option to *lp.*) The content types are defined by the system administrator. UNIX implementations including this feature also provide *filters* to convert content types to one another; the *lpfilter* command installs and manages these filter programs. See the *lp, lpfiler,* and *lpadmin* manual pages and your system documentation for details on content types in the spooling system.

The -*T* option allows printers to be defined based upon type definitions in the *terminfo* database. It can replace the model or interface information required by earlier versions. The -*o* option allows additional characteristics of the device to be specified as part of its definition.

Here is an example, illustrating some of these options:

```
# lpadmin -p xx2 -v /dev/term/13 -T "whiz1,wow5" \
   -I "simple,fortran,postscript" -S "cs0=usa,cs1=kanji" \
   -f "allow:invoice,plain,secret" -o width=14i \
   -D "WhizBang Model 2883/XX2 Printer" -c xxptr
```

This command defines a truly remarkable printer, attached via */dev/term/13,* named *xx2,* and described as a "WhizBang Model 2883/XX2 Printer." The printer supports two different printer types (perhaps in two modes): *whiz1* and *wow5.* It can handle plain ASCII files, text files with FORTRAN carriage control information, and PostScript output. It has two built-in character sets: the default one is given the synonym *usa* and the alternate one given the name *kanji.* The allowed forms on this device are *invoice, plain,* and *secret.* The printer has a width of 14 inches (which overrides the default definitions in the *terminfo* definitions for *whiz1* and *wow5*). The destination *xx2* also becomes part of the class *xxprt*.

Priorities and Permissions

The *-u* option to *lpadmin* allows access to destinations to be restricted to (or denied to) specific users. By default, all users are allowed to use any destination. With the *-u* option, the system administrator can set up an allow list and a deny list, on a destination-by-destination basis.

For any destination, if the allow list exists, then the only users whose usernames appear in it will be allowed access to it. If there is no allow list, then those users appearing in the deny list will be denied access to the printer. If both lists exist, the deny list is ignored. Allow and deny lists do not affect *root* or the special user *lp*.

Usernames are specified in the following form:

```
host!username
```

where *host* is a hostname and *username* indicates the user on that host. Either part is optional. Either part may also be replaced by the keyword *all*, which acts as a wildcard for that component. A missing *host* corresponds to the local system. Here are some examples (assume the local system is *portia*):

!chavez	User *chavez* on *portia*.
hamlet!chavez	User *chavez* on *hamlet*.
chavez	User *chavez* on any system (=all!chavez).
hamlet!all	All users from *hamlet*.
!all	All local users.

For example, the following command allows only users on *hamlet* and *duncan* to user destination *PS1*:

```
# lpadmin -p PS1 -u 'allow:duncan!all,hamlet!all'
```

The following command prevents user *martin* on the local system and user *wang* on any system from using destination *laser*:

```
# lpadmin -p laser -u 'deny:!martin,wang'
```

Requests in destination queues are assigned priority numbers in some implementations. These priorities determine the order in which requests get printed (the default is their order of submission). Priorities range from 0 to 39, with lower numbers meaning higher priorities (meaning printed sooner).

The *lpusers* command allows the system-wide printing priority level and priority limit to be specified on a user-by-user basis. The -*d* option is used to set the system default priority: the priority level a request will be assigned when no explicit priority is set on the *lp* command. For example, the command below sets the system default priority to 15:

```
# lpusers -d 15
```

The priority of an individual print request may be specified with the -*q* option to *lp*:

```
$ lp -d laser -q 25 long_file
```

This user has lowered the priority of this print request by setting the priority level to 25. Similarly, the following command queues a print request at higher than normal priority (by specifying a lower priority level):

```
$ lp -d laser -q 10 imp_file
```

The system administrator can set limits on how much a user can lower the priority level for his requests. These limits, in combination with the system default printing priority, can effectively set different printing priorities for different classes of users.

The -*q* option to the *lpusers* command specifies priority level limits. The -*u* option specifies one or more users to whom the specified limit applies. If no users are specified, then -*q* sets the default priority limit; this limit is used for users who do not have a specific value assigned. If -*u* is used without -*q* (i.e., no priority is specified), then the limits for the specified users are reset to the system default priority limit. Here are some examples:

```
# lpusers -d 15                        System default priority level.
# lpusers -q 10                        System default priority limit.
# lpusers -q 5 -u chavez,wang,gull     These users' limit is 5.
# lpusers -q 0 -u martin               martin's limit is 0.
# lpusers -u ng                        ng's limit is 10.
```

First, the system default priority level and limit are set to 15 and 10, respectively. Thus, for this system, nonprioritized jobs are given a priority level of 15, and in general users may increase their priority by specifying a priority level as low as 10. However, the users *chavez, wang*, and *gull* may specify a level as low as 5 and user *martin* may specify one as low as 0, effectively granting him almost immediate access to a printer if desired. Finally, the priority limit for user *ng* is reset to 10.

The system administrator may change the priority of a pending print request using *lp -q* in conjunction with the *-i* option, which specifies a request-ID. For example, the command below lowers the priority setting to 2 for print job PS-313:

```
# lp -i PS-313 -q 2
```

This option may be used to rearrange jobs within a print queue.

The *-H* option to *lp* allows a fast method to move a job to the head of a queue. By specifying the *immediate* keyword as its argument, the specified job advances at once to the top of the queue:

```
# lp -i PS-314 -H immediate
```

Two successive jobs sent to the top of the queue in this manner will print in reverse chronological order: the job sent most recently will print first.

If you want a job to immediately start printing without even waiting for the current job to finish, the current job may be suspended with the *hold* keyword. For example, the following commands start up request PS-314 as soon as possible:

```
# lp -i PS-314 -H immediate
# lp -i PS-209 -H hold
```

How this will affect a PostScript printer, which can sometimes retain a printing state across jobs, is uncertain. It's usually better to let the printing job finish.

If you do suspend a printing job, you can restart it later by specifying the *resume* keyword to *lp -H*:

```
# lp -i PS-209 -H resume
```

Remote Printing

The new *lpsystem* command, along with the *-S* option to *lpadmin*, is used to set up remote printing under the V.4 print service. Setting up a queue to print on a remote system is easy:

- Register the remote system name using *lpsystem*.

- Set up a queue using *lpadmin*.

The *lpsystem* command simply makes the print service aware of the existence of remote systems to which printing may be directed:

```
# lpsystem hamlet
# lpsystem -p bsd duncan
```

The first command designates *hamlet* as a remote printing host; the second command designates a BSD system named *duncan* as a remote printing host.

Setting up a queue is equally straightforward:

```
# lpadmin -p xxl -s hamlet
# lpadmin -p todun -s 'duncan!laser'
```

The first command sets up a queue which will send print jobs to destination *xxl* on *hamlet*. The second command defines a destination *todun* which will route jobs to the destination *laser* on *duncan*. The second form is required if there is already a local queue with the same name as the one on the remote host.

To enable remote users to print to a queue on the local system, the remote system must be registered with the *lpsystem* command described above. Then, the local port monitor must be configured to notify the print service of incoming print requests. For example, to configure remote printing over TCP/IP from another System V system, use a command like:

```
# pmadm -a -p tcp -s lp -i root -V `nlsadmin -V` \
     -m "`nlsadmin -o /var/spool/lp/fifos/listenS5`"
```

As we saw before with the terminal port monitor, *pmadm* again relies on an accessory utility to generate and retrieve its arguments, in this case *nlsadmin*. This command adds a service named *lp* to the port monitor *tcp*'s control.

To allow access from a BSD system, you need to know its TCP/IP address. After the system is registered using *lpsystem*, that command's -A option will list systems and their addresses. Note the address of the system in question, and then execute the following command:

```
# pmadmin -a -p tcp -s lp -i root -V `nlsadmin -V` \
     -m "`nlsadmin -o /var/spool/lp/fifos/listenBSD \
     -A'\xaddress'`"
```

In this command, *address* is the remote BSD system's TCP/IP address as displayed by *lpsystem -A*.

Support for PostScript Devices

The V.4 print service contains many enhancements to support printing to Post-Script devices. These include:

- The ability for the *lp* command to specify page ranges, portrait or landscape mode, image magnification and multiple spreads per physical page via the *lp* command when the request is made (-P specifies page ranges, and -y requests special printing modes).

- Automatic downloading of fonts.

- Filters to convert other file types to PostScript.

PostScript fonts are stored in directories under */usr/share/lib/hostfontdir*, named for the typeface family (e.g., *helvetica*); subdirectories hold the versions of the family (e.g., *bold, italic,* and so on).

The file */usr/share/lib/hostfontdir/map* is an ASCII configuration file that shows the mapping between the *hostfontdir* directory tree and the PostScript font names. It contains entries of the form:

```
Helvetica-Bold /usr/share/lib/hostfontdir/helvetica/bold
```

When a font is added to the system, the system administrator must update the map configuration file to make the new font available to users.

Each PostScript destination device also has a configuration file listing the fonts it stores internally (i.e., that don't need to be downloaded). These files are kept in */etc/lp/printers/*printer_name*/residentfonts*. Fonts listed in this file will not be downloaded to local printers or transmitted to remote printers across the network.

The AIX 3.1 Queueing System

AIX 3.1 offers a third approach to printing. It is based upon AIX 3.1's general queueing system, which may be used for any queue-related purpose; printing is but one predefined way to use it. The queueing system's general operation is illustrated in Figure 11-1. Jobs are submitted to a queue by users using the *enq* command (or another user command that calls *enq*). Files spooled with *enq* are linked to the spooling area by default, so if it changes or is deleted before the job actually prints, the output will be affected. *enq*'s *-c* option may be used to copy the file to the spooling area. Print requests are stored in */usr/lpd*; spooled files are stored in */usr/spool/qdaemon*.

NOTE

AIX 3.1 also supports the BSD and System V user print commands: *lp, cancel, lpstat, lpr, lpq,* and *lprm*.

The queues are monitored by the *qdaemon* server, which schedules and initiates jobs. When it is time for a job to execute, the *qdaemon* sends its file to the queue's *backend* program for processing. In the case of printing on the local system, the program is */usr/lpd/piobe*, but in theory any program may be used as a backend (see "Using the Queueing System as a Batch Service," in Chapter 11, *Printers and the Spooling Subsystem* later in this section). The output of the backend program is then sent to a specified physical device in the case of local printing. It may also be directed to a file.

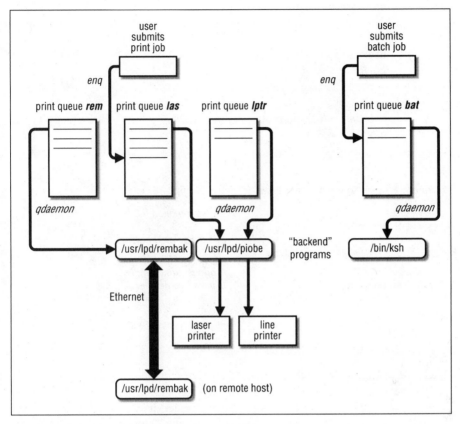

Figure 11-1. The AIX 3.1 Queueing System

The /etc/qconfig File

Queues are defined in the */etc/qconfig* file. Each queue has one or more associated *queue devices*, which are the entities which map one-to-one with physical printers.

In general, a print queue definition has the following form:

```
queue-name:
   device = qdev1 [,qdev2 ... ]
   attribute = value
   . . .
qdev1:
   backend = /usr/lpd/piobe
   attribute = value
   . . .
[qdev2:
   backend = /usr/lpd/piobe
   attribute = value
   . . .
...]
```

Here are two sample print queues from */etc/qconfig*:

```
lp0:                              A queue named lp0.
    device = dlp0
dlp0:                             lp's associated device.
    backend = /usr/lpd/piobe

laser:                            A queue named laser.
    device = dlas1,dlas2          laser's two devices.
    acctfile = /usr/adm/qacct
dlas1:
    backend = /usr/lpd/piobe
dlas2:
    backend = /usr/lpd/piobe
```

Each full definition has several parts. First comes the queue definition, beginning with a header line consisting of the queue name followed by a colon. In the example, *lp0* and *laser* are the two queue header lines. Next, indented with respect to the header, are queue attribute definitions. The queue *lp0* has only one attributer defined: its device, *dlp0*. *laser*'s stanza specifies two devices, *dlas1* and *dlas2*, and a file in which to place accounting data defined.

The definitions for a queue's devices must immediately follow the queue definition. Hence, *dlp0* is defined after *lp0*, and *dlas1* and *dlas2* are defined after *laser*. In all three cases, only one queue device attribute is specified: the backend program, which is set to the standard local printing backend */usr/lpd/piobe*.

When a queue has multiple associated queue devices, then it is used to feed jobs to all of the devices, which are assumed to be equivalent. When it is time for a job to be spooled, *qdaemon* will send it to the first available device for its queue.

Queue and Device Attributes

In addition to *device*, the available attributes for queues include:

acctfile   Accounting file pathname (default = no accounting file).

discipline   Job selection algorithm: *fcfs* = first come, first served or *sjn* = shortest job next (default=*fcfs*).

up   Set to *TRUE* or *FALSE*, depending on whether the queue is enabled or disabled.

In addition to *backend*, the available attributes for queue devices include:

align   Whether to send a form feed before starting job (default = *TRUE*).

header   When should a header page be placed before a job? Possible keywords are: *never* (default), *always*, and *group* (print header only once for multi-file print jobs).

trailer   When a trailer page should be sent (same keywords as *header*).

file   Whether or not to copy the file to the spool area by default. *TRUE* means files should be copied, and *FALSE* (the default) means they are only linked.

Two points need to be kept in mind concerning defining or modifying queue definitions. First, queue attributes should not be changed while that queue is up; rather, the queue should be stopped with the *enq -D* command (described in the section entitled "Managing Queues and Devices," later in this chapter).* You may have to wait for current jobs to complete.

Second, although the */etc/qconfig* file is currently editable with a text editor, AIX 3.1 documentation discourages this practice. The alternate method for modifying its contents is to use the *{mk,ch,rm}que* and *{mk,ch,rm}quedev* families of commands. Here are some examples of their use:

```
# mkque -q hp
# mkquedev -q hp -d hpdev -a "backend = /usr/lpd/piobe"
# chque -q laser -a "discipline = sjn"
# chquedev -q laser -d dlasl -a "header = never"
# rmquedev -q tek -d dtek
# rmque -q tek
```

---

*Current documentation says to stop the entire queueing system with *enq -G* before changing queue attributes. However, *enq -G* merely stops and then immediately restarts the *qdaemon* rather than shutting down the queueing system as the documentation implies.

The first command creates a queue named *hp*; the second command creates its queue device. (The spaces around the equal sign are required.) The third command changes the *discipline* attribute for queue *laser* to *sjn* (shortest job next). The fourth command changes the *header* attribute for the *laser* queue's device *dlas1* to the value *never*. The final two commands remove the queue device for the queue *tek* and then the queue itself (queues can be deleted with *rmque* only after all their devices are gone).

As is true of all currently-editable AIX 3.1 configuration files, using the interface commands may be required in the future, especially if the file format changes or information from it is merged into the device configuration database (which would not get updated by simply editing the file). Check the *README* files for future operating system releases carefully.

Having said this, I must confess to editing the */etc/qconfig* file by hand except when enabling or disabling queue (via the *up* attribute), when I use *chque*.

Controlling Queues and Print Jobs

This section will discuss the commands to manage queue and device status and to alter the priorities of pending jobs.

The *enq* command is the main interface to the printing system. It can be used by users to initiate print requests and by the system administrator to alter the status of print jobs and queues. On all *enq* commands, the *-P* option is used to specify the desired queue; if it is omitted, then the system default queue—the first one listed in */etc/qconfig* will be Used.* *enq*'s most important administrative options are described individually in this section.

Listing Queue Status and Contents

The *-q* option to *eng* may be used to display the status of a queue. For example, the following command lists the status of the queue *laser3*:

```
$ enq -q -P laser3
Queue   Dev    Status     Job Files  User       PP  %  Blks Cp Rnk
------- -----  ---------  --- ------  --------   --- -- ----- -- ---
laser3  dlas3  RUNNING    30  1213.f  chavez     10  43   324  1   1
               QUEUED     31  hpppp   martin              41  1   2
               QUEUED     32  fpppp   martin              83  1   3
               QUEUED     33  x27j.c  gull               239  1   4
```

---

*Users can set their own default printer via the PRINTER environment variable.

When a queue is down, the first line of the display will look like this:

```
laser3  dlas3  DOWN
```

Other options which list queue contents are:

-A   List all queues.

-L   Long listing format.

-u users Limit display to the specified users' jobs.

Deleting Print Jobs

To delete a job in a print queue, use the form:

```
# enq -x job-number
```

where *job-number* is the job number of the job to be removed; since job numbers are unique across the entire queueing system, the queue name isn't needed. All jobs in a queue may be deleted with the form:

```
# enq -P queue -X
```

where *queue* is the queue name. If the specified queue is used for remote printing (described later in this chapter), the command will only affect jobs that haven't yet been transferred to the remote system.

Here are some examples:

```
# enq -x 12
# enq -X -P laser
```

The first command deletes print job 12; the second command removes all jobs from the queue *laser*.

NOTE

Without a queue name, the *-X* option currently (as of version 3005) deletes all jobs in all queues. This is in direct contradiction to the current documentation, which emphatically states that there is no way to do this very thing.

Print Job Priorities

Jobs are assigned priorities within the queue. Together with the queue discipline, these priorities determine the order of printing (the queue discipline applies to all jobs with the same priority). Priorities range from 0 to 20 for ordinary users; users in the group *system* may use priorities up to 30. Any user may alter the values for her own jobs; the system level (21-30) are the only way for an administrator to guarantee that a job he moves up will stay above the others. Higher-numbered jobs print sooner.

Users can assign a priority to a job when they submit it with *enq*'s *-R* option. To change the priority of a pending job, use the *-a* option to *enq*:

```
# enq -# job-number -a prio
```

where *job-number* is the job number of the job to be altered, and *prio* is the new priority level. For example, the following command changes the priority of job number 45 to 22:

```
# enq -# 45 -a 22
```

Managing Queues and Devices

The following options control individual device status:

-D Designate a device as down; no more jobs will be sent to it, but current jobs will finish.

-U Bring a device back up.

-K Same as *-D*, but current jobs are killed.

All of these options require that a queue be specified using the *-P* option. If a queue has only one device, then the queue name alone will suffice to designate the device. If more than one device is controlled by the queue, you must specify which one you want by appending its name to the queue name, using a colon as separator. For example, the following command brings the *dlas1* device of the queue *laser* down:

```
# enq -P laser:dlas1 -D
```

Jobs can still be sent to the queue even when its device(s) are down. An entire queue may be disabled by changing its *up* attribute in */etc/qconfig* to *FALSE*. For example, the following command disables the queue *laser*:

```
# chque -q laser -a "up = FALSE"
```

The spaces around the equal sign, the quotation marks, and the uppercase letters on the keyword are all required.

When a queue has been disabled, its devices are automatically taken down; they will need to be brought back up (with *enq -U*) when the queue is re-enabled.

Adding a New Printer

To add a printer to the queueing system, these steps must be taken:

- Physically connect the device to the system.

- Make a device and special file for that printer. I find it's easiest to use SMIT for this step. Enter the command *smit pdp*, and then select "Add a Printer/Plotter" from the menu. Choose the correct printer type from the list; then specify the controller and line to which the printer is attached.

- Configure a queue device for the printer, either by adding one to an existing printer or creating a new queue and associated device.

- Create a virtual printer for the device, specifying its characteristics and associating it with the queue and/or queue device you created. Creating a virtual printer is done using the *mkvirprt* command. This command is menu-driven, and will prompt for the name of the printer device (special filename), the queue and queue device, and the printer type (use the same type as when you made the printer device). To obtain a list of the predefined supported printers, use the command:

  ```
  # lsdev -P -c printer | more
  ```

  There's a lot of output; hence the pipe to *more*.

Configuring Remote Printing

The following queue form in */etc/qconfig* is used to send print jobs to a print queue on another host:

```
rem0:
      host = laertes
      s_statfilter = /usr/lpd/aixshort
      l_statfilter = /usr/lpd/aixlong
      rq = laser
      device = drem1
drem1:
      backend = /usr/lpd/rembak
```

The *rem0* queue will send remote print jobs to the queue *laser* on the system *laertes*. The backend program for remote printing is */usr/lpd/rembak*. If the remove system is a BSD system, then the filters */usr/lpd/bsdshort* and

/usr/lpd/bsdlong should be substituted for the AIX 3.1 filters in the queue definition. There is no provision for submitting jobs to a System V-type remote print
service. It is possible that one could send remote jobs to a V.4 system by using its
BSD incoming print request configuration command with the AIX 3.1 system's
TCP/IP address; I have not tried this, however.

AIX 3.1 runs the BSD *lpd* daemon and uses the */etc/hosts.lpd* (or */etc/hosts.equiv*)
file to allow remote BSD systems to send print jobs to its queues, as described
previously in the BSD section of this chapter.

Using the Queueing System as a Batch Service

The printing system represents but one use of the AIX 3.1 queueing system.
Since potentially any program may be used as a queue backend program, many
other uses are possible. One such use is as a simple batch system. Here is a
sample configuration:

```
batch:
    device = batdev
    discipline = fcfs
batdev:
    backend = /bin/csh
```

By specifying a shell as the backend program, users may submit shell scripts to
the queue. The *qdaemon* will manage this queue, sending one script at a time to
be processed by the shell. Shell scripts could be used to run any desired program.
For example, the following script could be used to run a program *bigmodel*:

```
#!/bin/csh
ln -s ~chavez/output/bm.scr fort.8
ln -s ~chavez/output/bm.out fort.6
bigmodel <<END >& ~chavez/output/bm.log
140000
C6H6N6
Na
Hg
END
```

This file illustrates several important features about running programs from shell
scripts (in this case, a FORTRAN program):

- The symbolic links set up at the beginning of the file are used to associate
  FORTRAN unit number and files. By default, I/O to unit *n* uses a file named
  fort.n. Symbolic links allow a user to specify any desired paths.

- The form "<<END" is used to place standard input for a command or program
  within the shell script. All lines up until the string following the two less-than
  signs are interpreted as input to the command or program.

- The queueing system has no provision for saving job output, so the script must handle this itself.

Once set up, the *enq* command may be used as an interface to such a batch queue, allowing users to submit jobs to the queue and the administrator to delete them, alter their priority, and manage the status of the batch queue in the same manner as for print queues.

Troubleshooting Printers

This section contains strategies and suggestions for approaching various printing problems. If you've installed a printer but nothing prints on it, check the following items:

- Make sure you're using the right kind of cable. Check the printer's documentation for the manufacturer's recommendations.

- Make sure the connections are good and that you've specified the right port in the configuration file or commands. If you're using a serial line, make sure the line has been deactivated in */etc/ttys* or */etc/inittab*. Kill the *getty* process watching that line if you haven't rebooted the system.

- Verify that its queue is set up correctly. Send a file to it and then make sure something appears in the spool directory (use the *-c* option on the printing command under System V and AIX 3.1). If it doesn't, the protection on the spooling directories or files may be wrong. In particular, *root* may own something it shouldn't.

  On System V systems, the spool directories under */usr/spool/lp/request* are usually owned by the user *lp* and are protected 755 (write access only for the owner). In addition, the files in */usr/spool/lp* should also be owned by user *lp*. Under BSD, the spool directories are owned by user *daemon* and also protected 755. Under AIX 3.1, pending requests are stored in */usr/lpd/qdir*, owned by user *root* and group *printq* and protected 775, and spooled files are stored in */usr/spool/qdaemon*, owned by user *bin* and group *printq* and protected 775.

- Removing and reading the queue will sometimes fix things. This works when the queue configuration looks okay, but is actually messed up by an invisible junk character somewhere. It also works when you remember something you forgot the first time when you recreate the queue.

If a printer suddenly stops working, try the following:

- Is the daemon still running? If not, restart it. If it is, it may still be worth stopping and restarting it if no other jobs are printing:

```
# kill -9 pid-of-lpd-process        (BSD)
# /usr/lib/lpd
# lpshut; lpsched                   (System V)
# enq -G                            (AIX 3.1)
```

- Aborting the current job may clear up the problem if it was having some problem (the technical term is "wedged").

- Power cycling the device will clear most device hangups, although you will almost always lose the job that was printing at the time.

12

TCP/IP Network Management

About TCP/IP Networking
Monitoring the Network
Adding a New Host
Network Security
NFS and NIS
TCP/IP Networking and AIX 3.1

These days, few computers exist in isolation. Networking is a way of life. This chapter provides an overview of TCP/IP networking under UNIX. Its goal is to enable you to perform everyday network management tasks, including monitoring network traffic, adding new hosts to the network, and mounting remote disks and exporting local disks with the Network File System (NFS). For a more detailed discussion of TCP/IP and NFS, including their initial configuration, refer to the Nutshell Handbook *Managing NFS and NIS* (O'Reilly & Associates, 1991).

About TCP/IP Networking

UNIX networking is typically conducted via Ethernet, a high speed local area network that allows a large number of systems to communicate through a single cable. Basic networking terminology is explained below, illustrated by Figure 12-1.

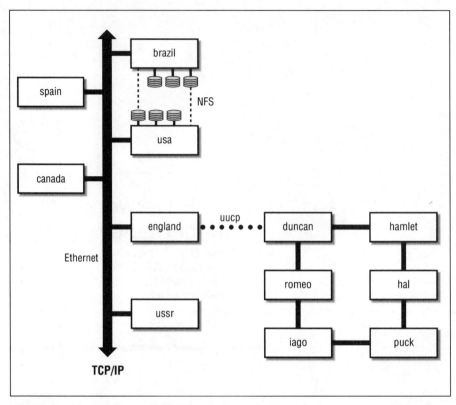

Figure 12-1. A Typical Network

Figure 12-1 depicts several kinds of network connections. Each computer system is known as a *host* (also known as *nodes* in other networking lexicons). The systems named for countries are all connected in a *local area network*, as are those with men's names. The country hosts are connected via an Ethernet; the other hosts are connected in some other way. The advantage of Ethernet is illustrated in the diagram. All hosts on an Ethernet are logically connected to every other host: to communicate with any other host, a system sends a message out on the Ethernet, where it arrives at the target host in one step (one *hop*). By contrast, for the other network, messages between *duncan* and *puck* must be handled by two other hosts first, taking three hops.

If I am logged in to, say, *spain* (either by direct terminal connection or via a modem), then *spain* is said to be the *local* system, and *brazil* is a *remote* system with respect to processes running on *spain*. A system that performs a task for a remote host is called a server; the host for whom the system is performed is called the client. Thus, if I request a file from *brazil*, that system is a server for the client *spain* (for that transaction).

england and *duncan* are *gateway hosts* because they connect two discrete networks, connected via *uucp* over a telephone line.

The Network File System (NFS) facility allows TCP/IP hosts to share disks, with remote filesystems being merged into the local directory tree. *brazil* and *usa* each effectively have access to four disk drives, even though they both only have three disks physically connected to them.

TCP/IP provides a number of user commands to access remote systems. The most important of these commands are:

- *rcp* lets users copy files between UNIX hosts.

- *rlogin* lets users log in to remote UNIX systems from their local terminal session.

- *rsh* lets users execute a single command on a remote UNIX host.

- *ftp* allows users to copy files between the local system and any reachable system. It is thus a generic version of *rcp*.

- *telnet* allows a user to log in to any reachable remote system on which she has an account, both Ux and non-UNIX, although it's mainly used for the latter. It is thus a generic version of *rlogin*.

Hostnames

Every system on a network has a *hostname*. This name is unique within the network. Hostnames let users refer to any computer on the network by using a short, easily remembered name rather than the host's network address (described in the next subsection). Hostnames should be easily remembered, relatively easy to spell, and may have at most 14 characters.

Network Addresses

Each system on a TCP/IP network has a *network address* that is unique for all hosts on the network. If the system is connected to the Department of Defense Internet, its host address is assigned by the Network Information Center. Networks that are not connected to the Internet still generally use network addresses that obey the Internet numbering conventions. An Internet network address is a sequence of four bytes. Network addresses are written in several forms, but the most important is:

a.b.c.d

where *a*, *b*, *c*, and *d* are all integers. The address is split into two parts: the first part identifies the network, the second identifies the host within the network. The size of these parts vary. The first byte of the address (*a*) determines the address type (called its *class*), and hence the number of bytes allocated to each part. Table 12-1 shows how this works.

Table 12-1. Internet Address Types

Range of a	Address Class	Network portion	Host portion
1-126	Class A	*a*	*b.c.d*
128-191	Class B	*a.b*	*c.d*
192-224	Class C	*a.b.c*	*d*

A Class "A" address is good for a network with many, many number of hosts (like the Internet); a Class "C" network address is good for a network with relatively few hosts. There are very few Class A networks; these network numbers are typically reserved for major national networks.

Most sites that are not on Internet use 192 or 193 for *a*. They then use *b* and *c* to identify particular subnetworks within a larger network; and they use *d* to identify any individual host on any subnetwork. If your site already is part of some networking scheme, you *must* be consistent with whatever usage is already established.

When you add a new host to an existing network, the unique network address you assign it must fit in with whatever system is already in use at your site. The network portion of the address is assigned by Internet's Network Information Center for sites on the Internet; sites not on the Internet often select 192 or 193 for *a*; they then set *b* and *c* to 1, and use *d* to identify individual hosts. This means that the network number is 193.1.1, and that you can have up to 254 hosts on the network (you shouldn't use 0 or 255 for address components).

For more than 255 hosts, just grab more network numbers: 193.1.2, 193.1.3, and so on.* *Gateways* are used to connect the networks to each other. Gateways are

---

*Using *b* and *c* to split a large network into smaller networks is sometimes called *subnetting*. This really isn't correct usage, but it's descriptive. However, you should know that subnetting really means borrowing additional network bits from the host portion of the address.

nothing more than computers that are connected to two networks, and can there-fore move data between the two networks. There are special-purpose computers that are designed to be gateways and nothing else, but most sites only add an additional Ethernet interface to a less-used workstation.

By convention, the network address 127.1 is used as a *loopback address*: data sent to it is transmitted back to the same host. The loopback address is used for testing. This address is usually given the hostname *localhost* in the */etc/hosts* file (described later in this chapter).

The Host Table /etc/hosts

The file */etc/hosts* is your computer's list of the hosts in the local network (includ-ing itself). You must edit */etc/hosts* whenever you add a new system to the local network. When you add a new system to an existing network, you will have to edit the */etc/hosts* file on every system on the UNIX local network and take what-ever action is equivalent for hosts running other operating systems.

Here is a sample */etc/hosts* file showing a small local network:

```
# Loopback address for localhost
#
127.1           localhost
# Our hostname and address
193.0.0.1       spain
# Other hosts
193.0.0.2       brazil
193.0.0.3       india.galxu.edu india
193.0.0.4       france gaul
193.0.0.5       greece olympus achaia
```

Lines beginning with # are comments and are ignored. Aside from the comments, each line has three fields: the *network address* of a host in the network, the host's *hostname*, and any *aliases* (or synonyms) for the host. Every */etc/hosts* file must contain at least two entries: a loopback address for debugging purposes (by con-vention, 127.1), and the address by which the local system is known to the rest of the network. The other lines describe the other hosts in your local network. This file may also include entries for hosts that are not on your immediate local net-work.

After the lines for the loopback address and the local system, the example */etc/hosts* file continues by listing the network addresses for all other systems in the local network. The example file shows four hosts on the network in addition to the local host (*spain*), for a total of five hosts. The other hosts are *brazil, india, france*, and *greece*. The last two hosts have several aliases, or synonymous host-names: *gaul* is a synonym for *france*, and *olympus* and *achaia* are synonymous names for the host *greece*. A hostname may have as many aliases as desired; each alias is separated from the previous name by one or more spaces.

Here is a somewhat more complex */etc/hosts* file:

```
# loopback address
127.1           loopback
# calexico network
193.0.9.1       joyce
193.0.9.2       proust
193.0.9.251     mann        # gateway to LAN 10
193.0.9.252     dalton-gw
# mexicali network
193.0.10.1      priestley
193.0.10.2      lavoisier
193.0.10.3      berthollet
193.0.10.26     dalton      # gateway to LAN 9
193.0.10.38     mann-gw
```

193.0.9 is one local network, and 193.0.10 is another, distinct one. The hosts *mann* and *dalton* serve to bridge the two networks; they are both connected to their own local network (on its Ethernet, for example) and to each other (by, say, a T1 line). They are both listed as members of both networks in the */etc/hosts* file. On their non-local network, however, the characters "-gw" are appended to their names to form unique hostnames for every distinct network address.

Network Daemons

The UNIX TCP/IP network services are supported by a number of *daemons*. These are programs that run in the background and either provide services directly or maintain tables that are used by other network programs. A full discussion of TCP/IP daemons is beyond the scope of this chapter, but you do need to be aware of the general functioning of the most important of them.

inetd   The Internet services daemon is the main TCP/IP server. It is responsible for overseeing virtually all network operations. It performs its job by overseeing a host of other daemons, each specialized for one specific task. The servers managed by *inetd* are listed in the */etc/inetd.conf* file.

rwhod   The remote *who* daemon is a program that periodically broadcasts information to every other host on the network. The information it sends tells who is logged in at this host, how long they have been logged in, how long the host has been up, and some other status data. Users can then find out the status of the system with the *rwho* and *ruptime* commands.

routed   The *route* daemon maintains dynamic information about the networks with which your system communicates, used in determining the routes by which to transfer data. It is designed to replace a static routing table built by a number of *route* commands during the boot process.

named   Previously, the */etc/hosts* file had to list all the hosts your host communicated with via TCP/IP. This function is now superseded by the *named* daemon. If *named* is running, */etc/hosts* need only contain information about the hosts on your local network or hosts that you access frequently; when your host needs the address of a system that is not listed in */etc/hosts*, it will refer to *named* for the address.

timed   The *time* daemon makes sure the system clocks are synchronized on all systems in the network. It has two modes. It can run as a master and be assumed to have the correct time. Other systems will synchronize their clocks with it. Or it can run as a slave and be told the correct time by a master system. Obviously, there has to be at least one *timed* process on the system that is capable of running as a master. If more than one is, only one of them is the master at any given time; when the master system goes down, then one of the slaves capable of being a master becomes the new master.

Disabling Unnecessary Daemons

You can decide to disable the remote who, name, route, or time daemons in the interests of system performance. Each places a small but measurable load on the system. If you disable *rwhod*, then the *rwho* and *ruptime* commands won't work. If you disable *named*, the */etc/hosts* must list all the hosts on the network with which your system communicates via TCP/IP. If you disable *timed*, you will have to synchronize the various system clocks by hand with the *date* command.

Things are a little more complex in the case of *routed*. If you disable *routed*, the system's boot scripts must set up all necessary network routes for the gateways on your network. You can live without the *routed* daemon if:

- Your network has no gateways; in this case, you won't have any *route* commands in your boot scripts at all.

- Your network has a single gateway; in this case, a command like the following is executed by one of your boot scripts:

```
route add default gateway 1
```

where *gateway* is the name of the gateway host to your other networks.

If your network has two or more gateways, we highly recommend that you use the *routed* daemon.

To disable a daemon, comment out the lines which enable it in your system initialization files. For example, the following lines are typical of those used to start *rwhod*:

```
if [ -f /etc/rwhod ]; then
    /etc/rwhod; echo -n ' rwhod' >/dev/console
fi
```

To disable this daemon, add comment marks (#) to the beginning of these three lines.

Monitoring the Network

The *netstat* command is used to monitor a system's TCP/IP network activity. It can provide some basic data about how much and what kinds of network activity is going on. *netstat* is provided by BSD, AIX 3.1, V.4, and some V.3 implementations.

Without arguments, *netstat* lists all active network connections with the local host. In this output, it is useful to filter out lines containing "localhost" to limit the display to interesting data:

```
# netstat | grep -v localhost
Active Internet connections
Proto Recv-Q Send-Q  Local Address   Foreign Address  (state)
tcp        0    737  hamlet.1018     duncan.shell     ESTABLISHED
tcp        0      0  hamlet.1019     portia.shell     ESTABLISHED
tcp      348      0  hamlet.1020     portia.login     ESTABLISHED
tcp      120      0  hamlet.1021     laertes.login    ESTABLISHED
tcp      484      0  hamlet.1022     lear.login       ESTABLISHED
```

```
tcp      1018      0  hamlet.1023    duncan.login    ESTABLISHED
tcp         0      0  hamlet.login   lear.1023       ESTABLISHED
```

On this host—*hamlet*—there are currently two connections each to *portia*, *lear*, and *duncan*, and one connection to *laertes*. All but one of the connections to *lear* are outgoing: the address form of a hostname with a number appended indicates the originating system for the connection. The *.login* suffix indicates a connection made with *rlogin* or with *rsh* without arguments; the *.shell* appendix indicates a connection servicing a single command.

The "Recv-Q" and "Send-Q" columns indicate how much data is currently being transferred between the two systems via each connection. These numbers indicate current, pending data (in bytes), not the total amount transferred since the connection began.

Another useful mode is to provide an time interval as *netstat*'s argument (in seconds—make it at least 5). This produces an entirely different display:

```
# netstat 5 | awk 'NR!=3 {print $0}'
      input    (en0)     output              input  (Total)    output
  packets errs  packets errs colls packets errs packets errs colls
  47      0     66       0    0    47      0    66       0    0
  114     0     180      0    0    114     0    180      0    0
  146     0     227      0    0    146     0    227      0    0
  28      0     52       0    0    28      0    52       0    0
  ^c
```

This command will display network statistics every five seconds. The *awk* command throws away the first line after the headers, which displays cumulative totals since the last reboot. This output is in two parts: it includes two sets of "input" and "output" statistics. The left half of the table (the first five columns) shows the data for the primary network interface; the second half shows total values for all network interfaces on the system. On this system, like many others, there is only one interface, and so the two sides of the table are identical.

The "input" columns show data for incoming network traffic, and the "output" columns show data for outgoing traffic. The "errs" columns show the number of errors that occurred while transferring the indicated number of network packets (a *packet* is the unit of network data transfer). These numbers should be low: less than one percent of the number of packets. Larger values indicate serious network problems.

The "colls" column lists the number of collisions. A *collision* occurs when two hosts on the network try to send a packet at exactly the same time. When this happens, each host will wait a random amount of time before retrying the transmission; this method virtually eliminates repeated collisions by the same hosts with the same packets. The number of collisions is a measure of how much network traffic there is on the system since the likelihood of a collision happening is directly proportional to the amount of network activity. Collisions are only recorded by transmitting hosts; systems which only receive network data won't count any collisions whatever the network traffic.

On some systems, collision data isn't tracked separately, but rather is merged in with the output errors figure.

Adding a New Host

To add a new system to the network, you must:

- Physically connect the system to the network.

- Perform any other network configuration required by its UNIX implementation (e.g., AIX 3.1 requires some additional steps; see the section entitled "TCP/IP Networking and AIX 3.1," at the end of this chapter).

- Assign a hostname and network address to the system (or find out what has been assigned by the network administrator).

- Add a line for this host to the */etc/hosts* file on every system. Create an */etc/hosts* file on that system (this is most easily accomplished by copying one on another system once the network is minimally set up).

- Make sure the network daemons are started at boottime on the local system. Under BSD, make sure the relevant lines are not commented out in */etc/rc* and */etc/rc.local*. Under System V, make sure there are links to */etc/init.d/tcp* (sometimes called *network*) in */etc/rc0.d* and */etc/rc2.d* or */etc/rc3.d*.

Once everything is ready and the daemons are running on the new system, test the network setup and connection with the *ping* command. *ping* is a simple utility that will tell you whether the connection is working and the basic setup is correct or not. It takes a remote hostname as its argument:

```
$ ping hamlet
PING hamlet: 56 data bytes
64 bytes from 193.0.9.3: icmp_seq=0. time=0. ms
64 bytes from 193.0.9.3: icmp_seq=1. time=0. ms
64 bytes from 193.0.9.3: icmp_seq=4. time=0. ms
^c
----hamlet PING Statistics----
5 packets transmitted, 5 packets received, 0% packet loss
round-trip (ms)  min/avg/max = 0/0/0
```

From this output you can tell that *hamlet* is receiving the data sent by the local system, and the local system is receiving the data *hamlet* sends. On some systems, *ping*'s output is much simpler, but still answers the same central question: "Is the network working or not?" Here is *ping's* output:

```
$ ping duncan
duncan is alive
```

On such systems, try the *-s* option if you want more detailed output.

Network Security

Unless special steps are taken, users must enter a password each time they want access to the other hosts on the network. While this might be tolerable when you log in remotely with *rlogin*, it is inconvenient if you only want to run a single command on the remote machine using the *rsh* command. Most importantly, you can't use the remote copy command *rcp* at all, because *rcp* does not know how to ask for passwords.

To allow remote access without passwords, there is a two-level equivalence system for UNIX hosts connected with TCP/IP. The system determines permission by looking in two files on the remote host: */etc/hosts.equiv* and *.rhosts* in the user's remote home directory. As the system administrator, you must construct and maintain these files to allow remote access as conveniently as possible, given the level of security you need.

Host Level Equivalence

The first level of equivalence is the host level. Each host has an */etc/hosts.equiv* file. This file is simply a list of hostnames, each on a separate line. For example, the file for the system *france* might read:

```
spain
italy
france
```

None, any, or all of the hosts in the system may be put in an */etc/hosts.equiv* file. It is convenient to include the host's own name in */etc/hosts.equiv*, thus declaring a host equivalent to itself. When a user from a remote host attempts an access (with *rlogin*, *rsh*, or *rcp*), the host checks the file */etc/hosts.equiv*. If the host requesting access is *not* listed in */etc/hosts.equiv*, a password will be required. If the host requesting access (that is, the host on which the user executes the command) is in the */etc/hosts.equiv* of the target machine. The target machine then checks its own */etc/passwd* file to see if it contains an account with the same username as the user on the remote system. If it does, then the remote access is permitted without requiring the user to enter that account's password. Only the */etc/hosts.equiv* file of the target machine matters; the contents of */etc/hosts.equiv* on the user's own host are irrelevant.

If the user is trying to log in under a different username (by using the *-l* option to *rsh* or *rlogin*), the */etc/hosts.equiv* file is not used. The */etc/hosts.equiv* file is also not enough to allow a superuser on one host to log in remotely as root on another host. This is helpful when systems on the network have different system administrators and root passwords.

As system administrator, then, you do two things to allow a user password-free access. First, give the user an account of the same name on each host. Each of their accounts must have the same username. Then edit */etc/hosts.equiv* on each of these remote hosts by adding the hostname of the user's local (home) host on a separate line.

When you make hosts equivalent with the */etc/hosts.equiv* file, you make any account name that is on both systems equivalent (with the exception of *root*). If these accounts belong to different users, they probably should not be equivalent. If you are the system administrator for both hosts, you can avoid this problem by making sure that identical account names always refer to the same user. If this is awkward or if you are not the account administrator for both hosts, the account level equivalence described in the next section must be used.

For networked workstations, it's generally not a good idea to put the workstations' hostnames in the *hosts.equiv* file on the file server system. The server should always be protected by passwords due to the inherent vulnerability of workstations.

Account Equivalence

There are various reasons for using account level instead of host level equivalence for password-free operation of the network:

- Users have different account names on the different hosts.

- A user may want to allow a different user on another machine with a different account name equivalent access to his account, if, for example, both users are working on the same project.

- Host-level equivalence is simply too broad for your security needs.

Account equivalence uses a file called *.rhosts* in the home directory of the target account. Each line of *.rhosts* consists of a *hostname* and, optionally, a list of *usernames*:

```
hostname    [username . . .]
```

Each line means that *username* is allowed to log in to this account from *hostname*. If *username* is not present, then only the same username as the owner of the *.rhosts* file resides can log in from *hostname*.

For example, consider the following *.rhosts* file in the home directory of a user named *wang*:

```
england    guy donald
russia     felix
usa        felix
england    kim
prc
```

The *.rhosts* allows the user *felix* to log in from the host *russia* or *usa*, users named *guy, donald,* or *kim* to log in from the host *england*, and a user named *wang* to log in from the host *prc*.

If a remote access is attempted and the access does not pass the host level equivalence test, the remote host then checks the *.rhosts* file in the home directory of the target account. If it finds the hostname and username of the person making the attempted access, the remote host allows the access to take place without requiring the user to enter a password.

WARNING

Account level equivalence should never be used for the superuser. Passwords should always be required to gain access to *root* accounts. There should be no *.rhosts* file in the root directory.

NFS and NIS

Remote logins and file copy commands represent only the most basic potential of networking. Ideally, networking ought to provide a way for computing resources to be fully shared among all component systems, in as user-transparent a manner as possible. Sun's Network File System (NFS) and Network Information Services (NIS) facilities are a step along this road, and they have been implemented by virtually every UNIX vendor at this point.

NFS enables filesystems physically residing on one computer system to be used by other computers in the network, appearing to users on the remote host as just another local disk. NIS, formerly known as the Yellow Pages (the *yp* prefix is still used in many command names), provides network-based system configuration administration, enabling a variety of system configuration tasks (including managing user accounts) to be centralized for an entire network. NFS and NIS both run on top of TCP/IP, using its protocols and capabilities and by some non-UNIX operating systems as well.

A full discussion of NFS and NIS is beyond the scope of this book. See the Nutshell Handbook *Managing NFS and NIS* (O'Reilly & Associates, 1991) for further information. The sections that follow provide a brief introduction to some of their main functioning and features.

About NFS

Several methods for sharing disks over a network have been developed. Sun's Network File System has emerged as the clear standard for sharing disks among UNIX systems and, with increasing frequency, between UNIX and non-UNIX systems.*

The following configuration files are used by NFS:

/etc/fstab Remote filesystems are entered into the filesystem configuration file, using only a slightly varied form from regular entries. (Note that under V.4, this file is */etc/vfstab*.)

/etc/exports This file controls which filesystems on the local system are available to the various remote hosts.

The following discussion is only an overview of NFS. Many implementations have much more functionality. Check your vendor's documentation to determine your system's capabilities.

NFS Daemons

NFS uses a number of daemons to handle its services. These services are started at boottime in the */etc/rc.local* file under BSD. The commands to start NFS daemons are stored in the */etc/init.d/nfs* under System V, which is linked to

---

*The other major file sharing systems are RFS, available for XENIX and System V systems, and AFS, which is just emerging from the research community, and doesn't yet belong to any standard x versions.

the */etc/rc0.d* and */etc/rc.2* directories when NFS is installed. The most important daemons are:

nfsd   Handles filesystem exporting.

rcp.mountd   Handles mount requests.

portmap   Facilitates initial connection between local and remote servers.

Mounting Remote Directories

Once NFS is running, remote filesystems may be entered into the filesystem configuration file in order to allow them to be automatically mounted at boottime. The format for an NFS */etc/fstab* entry is:

```
remote-host:remote-pathname local-mount-loc nfs options 0 0
```

where the first field is a concatenation of the remote hostname and the pathname to the mount point of the desired filesystem on the remote host, joined with a colon. For example, to designate the filesystem mounted at */organic* on host *duncan*, use the form:

```
duncan:/organic
```

mount-loc is the location on the local host where the remote filesystem is to be mounted. The type field should be set to *nfs*, and the dump frequency and *fsck* pass fields should hold zeros.

In addition to those for local filesystems, there are many additional options available for remote filesystems, including the following (the V.4 defaults are shown):

ro, rw   Designate readonly and read-write filesystems (default = *rw*).

suid, nosuid SUID modes on the remote filesystem are/are not respected (*suid*). If *nosuid* is used, SUID files on the remote filesystem will not run as *root* locally.

bg   If the NFS mount of this filesystem fails on the first try, continue retrying in the background. This is useful to speed up booting when remote filesystems are unavailable.

retry=n   Number of mount retries before giving up (100000).

timeo=n   Set the timeout—the length of time to wait for the first try of each individual NFS request before giving up—to the specified number of tenths of seconds. Each subsequent retry doubles the previous timeout value.

retrans=n   Retransmit a request *n* times before giving up (3).

soft, hard   Quit/continue trying to connect even after the *retrans* value is met.

intr   Allow an interrupt to kill a hung process.

rsize=n   The size of the read buffer in bytes.

wsize=n   The size of the write buffer in bytes.

The *soft* and *hard* options are worth special mention. They define the action taken when a remote filesystem becomes unavailable (perhaps because the remote system went down). If a remote filesystem is mounted as *hard,* then NFS will try to complete any pending I/O request forever, even after the maximum number of retransmissions is reached; if it is mounted *soft,* then an error will occur and NFS will cancel the request.

If a remote filesystem is mounted *hard* and *intr* is not specified, then the process will be hung (until the remote filesystem reappears). For a terminal process especially, this can be quite annoying. If *intr* is specified, then sending an interrupt signal to the process will kill it. For a terminal, this can be done by typing CTRL-C (although it won't die instantly; you'll still have to wait for the timeout period). For a background process, sending a INT (2), or QUIT (3) signal will usually work (again not necessarily instantaneously):

```
# kill -QUIT 3421
```

NOTE

Sending a KILL signal (-9) will not kill a hung NFS process.

It would seem that mounting filesystems *soft* would get around the process hanging problem. This is fine for filesystems mounted readonly. However, for a read-write filesystem, a pending request could be a write request, and so simply giving up could result in corrupted files on the remote filesystem. Therefore, read-write remote filesystems should always be mounted *hard,* and the *intr* option should be specified to allow users to make their own decisions about hung processes.

Here are some example */etc/fstab* entries for remote filesystems:

```
duncan:/benzene /rings nfs rw,hard,bg,intr,retrans=5 0 0
portia:/propel /peptides nfs ro,soft,bg,nosuid 0 0
```

The first command mounts the filesystem mounted at */benzene* on the host *duncan* under */rings* on the local system. It is mounted read-write, hard, with interrupts enabled. The second command mounts the */propel* filesystem on the host *portia* under */peptides*; this filesystem is mounted readonly, and the SUID status of any of its files is ignored on the local host.

Under V.4, a hyphen is placed in the fsck-device and fsck-pass fields of */etc/vfstab* for remote filesystems:

```
/dev/dsk/c1d1s2  /dev/rdsk/c1d1s2  /chem   ufs  1  yes  rw,nosuid
duncan:/benzene  -                 /rings  nfs  -  yes  rw,hard,bg,intr
```

Under AIX 3.1, remote filesystems have stanzas in */etc/filesystems* like local ones, with some additional keywords:

```
/rings:
    dev       = /benzene
    vfs       = nfs
    nodename  = duncan
    mount     = true
    options   = bg,hard,intr
```

The *nodename* attribute holds the remote hostname, the *dev* attribute holds the pathname of the filesystem on the remote system, the *options* attribute now holds NFS-related options, and the filesystem type in the *vfs* field is *nfs*.

Once defined in the filesystem configuration file, the short form of the *mount* command may be used to mount the filesystem. For example, the following command mounts the proper remote filesystem at */rings*:

```
# mount /rings
```

The *mount* command may also be used to mount remote filesystems on an ad-hoc basis, for example:

```
# mount -t nfs -o rw,hard,bg,intr duncan:/ether /mnt
```

This command mounts the */ether* filesystem from duncan under /mnt on the local system. The V.4 command is slightly different, using *-F* instead of *-t* to specify the filesystem type. The filesystem type is often superfluous.

Exporting Local Filesystems

The */etc/exports* file controls the accessibility of local filesystems to network access. Its traditional form consists of a series of lines containing a filesystem mount point and followed by one or more hostnames:

```
/organic    spain canada
/inorganic
```

This export configuration file allows the hosts *spain* and *canada* to remotely mount the */organic* filesystem and any remote host to remotely mount the */inorganic* filesystem.

More recent NFS implementations, such as SunOS, have extended its syntax and functionality. Any filesystem, directory, or file can be exported, not just the entire filesystem. And there is greater control over the type of access allowed. In its simplest form, this new version of /etc/exports consists of lines of the form:

```
pathname options
```

where *pathname* is the name of the file or directory to which network access is to be allowed; if *pathname* is a directory, then all of the files and directories below it within the same filesystem are also exported, but not any filesystems mounted within it. *Options* specifies the type of access to be given and to whom. Here is a very simple example of /etc/exports:

```
/organic    -rw=spain, -ro=brazil:canada, -anon=-1
/inorganic
```

This file allows the host *spain* to mount /organic for reading and writing, the hosts *brazil* and *canada* to mount it readonly, and maps *anonymous* users—usernames from other hosts that do not exist on the local system and the *root* user from any remote system—to the UID -1. This is a code to NFS not to allow such a user access to anything. The UID -2 may be used to allow anonymous users access only to world-readable files. If you modify /etc/exports, then the *exportfs* command must be run to put the new access restrictions into effect. The following command will put all of the access information in /etc/exports into effect:

```
# exportfs -a
```

The *showmount* command may be used to list exported filesystems (using its -e option) or other hosts that have remotely mounted local filesystems (-a). For example, the following command shows that the hosts *spain* and *brazil* have mounted the /organic filesystem:

```
brazil:/organic
spain:/organic
```

This data is stored in the file /etc/rmtab. This file is saved across boot, so the information in it can get quite old. You may want to reset it from time to time by copying /dev/null onto it.

Exporting Filesystems Under V.4

Under V.4, filesystem exporting is done via the /etc/dfs/dfstab configuration file, which stores the *share* commands needed to export filesystems. The following *dfstab* file is equivalent to the *exports* file we looked at previously:

```
share -F nfs -o rw=spain,ro=brazil:canada,anon=-1 /organic
share -F nfs /inorganic
```

For example, the first line exports the */organic* filesystem: it allows *spain* to mount it for reading and writing and *brazil* and *canada* to mount it readonly. Requests from usernames without accounts on the local system are denied.

These same commands need to be executed to immediately put these access restrictions into effect between boots.

NIS

The Network Information Service is a distributed database service that allows a single set of system configuration files to be maintained for an entire local network of computers. For example, with NIS, a single password file can be maintained for an entire network of computers almost automatically (you do still have to add or modify entries on one copy by hand). This section will provide a brief description of NIS. Consult your system documentation for details. The following command may be used to locate the relevant manual pages:

```
# man -k NIS
```

or, on older systems:

```
# man -k yellow
```

NIS defines three classes of systems within a network (illustrated in Figure 12-2).

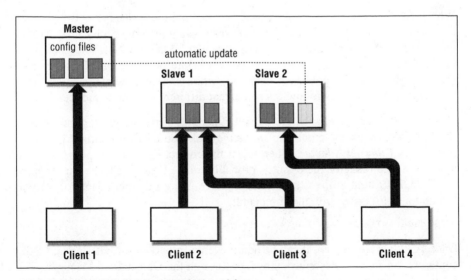

Figure 12-2. NIS System Relationships

There is one computer designated as the *master* host: the host where the permanent copies of the system files are stored and where they must be updated. The master automatically propagates copies of and changes to configuration files to the group of computers designated as *slaves*. Slaves have exact copies of all configuration files from the master. They exist to facilitate requests for data from *clients*: systems that do not contain copies of the configuration data.

The figure shows four clients, each requesting data. Three of them request it from slave systems and one from the master system, which acts as a *server* for data requests just as slaves do. The requests for data from clients 1 through 3 will be honored. However, the request to slave 2 from client 4 come while an automatic update is in progress; it will not be honored until slave 2's data is completely updated by the master.

TCP/IP Networking and AIX 3.1

The AIX 3.1 operating system on RS/6000 series workstations implements standard TCP/IP networking. This section discusses AIX 3.1 eccentricities in these matters and offers some advice about what choices to make in light of them. My first piece of advice: it's best to configure both TCP/IP and NFS via SMIT; AIX 3.1 has made the process much messier than under BSD or V.4, and SMIT makes it a bit easier.

When initially configuring TCP/IP, usually you should use the *en0* network interface (labeled "Standard Ethernet"). Best results in a heterogeneous UNIX TCP/IP network seem to come from using this "Standard Ethernet Network Interface," rather than the "IEEE 802.3 Ethernet Network Interface" (*ie3*). The latter correctly implements the published standard, while similarly labeled implementations from other vendors follow the somewhat different common practices.

You also may need to change the default Ethernet adapter connector from *bnc* to *dix*. To do so, enter the command *smit eadap*, choose *Change / Show Characteristics of an Ethernet Adapter*. Then select the correct Ethernet adapter if there is more than one (usually there isn't), probably *ent0*. Finally, change the *Adapter CONNECTOR* field to *dix*. If you know you're using Ethernet adapter *ent0*, you can do this a lot faster with the command:

```
# chdev -l ent0 -a 'bnc_select=dix'
```

Once TCP/IP is configured, it can be administered in two ways: via standard BSD configuration files, as described above, or through the Object Data Manager. The latter is the default. If you wish to administer networking via the standard configuration files, then you must do the following:

- Edit the file */etc/rc.net* and comment out all of the lines prior to the header line:

      # Part II - Traditional Configuration.

- Uncomment out the *hostname* command line and the *ifconfig* command lines for the loopback and for your network type.

  Add any additional arguments to the *ifconfig* commands that your site uses (check your other systems and the *ifconfig* manual page). You may also want to add a broadcast *ifconfig* command. The completed lines might look something like this:

      /bin/hostname portia   >>$LOGFILE 2>&1
      /etc/ifconfig lo0 loopback up >>$LOGFILE 2>&1
      /etc/ifconfig en0 `hostname` -trailers up >>$LOGFILE 2>&1
      /etc/ifconfig en0 broadcast brcast >>$LOGFILE 2>&1

- Uncomment and modify the *route* commands if appropriate.

By default, TCP/IP daemons are administered by the System Resource Controller, an AIX 3.1 facility to automate the starting, stopping, and monitoring of server processes. The daemons may be started in the traditional manner by moving the *rctcpip* entry in */etc/inittab* before the *srcmstr* entry:

    rctcpip:2:wait:/etc/rc.tcpip >/dev/console 2>&1 # TCP/IP daemons
    srcmstr:2:respawn:/etc/srcmstr   # System Resource Controller

The *rc.tcpip* file is set up so that SRC manages the TCP/IP daemons if it is running when *rc.tcpip* is invoked, but the daemons are started as independent servers if SRC is not running.

The *rc.nfs* initialization file, however, is not set up in this way, and assumes that SRC is running, using it to start all of its daemons. Rewriting *rc.nfs* along the lines of *rc.tcpip* may lead to unpredictable results—I've not felt brave enough to try it. Thus, if you use NFS or NIS, it is probably best to leave the TCP/IP daemons under SRC control as well and learn to use the ODM to reconfigure the network, using SMIT or *chssys* and related commands directly.

13

Accounting

Standard Accounting Files
BSD Accounting
System V Accounting

This chapter describes the UNIX accounting system. In general, UNIX provides user-based process accounting. That is, the operating system tracks system usage by recoding statistics about each process that is run, including its UID. In addition, records are kept of the image that was run by the process and the system resources (such as memory, CPU time, and I/O operations) that it used.

The accounting system is designed for tracking system resource usage, primarily so that users can be charged money for them. The data collected by the accounting system can also be used for some types of system performance monitoring. See the Nutshell Handbook *System Performance Tuning* (O'Reilly & Associates, 1990) for a detailed treatment of this topic.

The accounting systems under BSD and System V are quite different, but they are both based upon very similar raw data. Hence, the sort of information that may be gleaned from them is essentially identical, although output methods and formats are very different. And they suffer from the same limitations. For example, neither system provides for any project-based accounting.

As with all accounting systems, the UNIX accounting software places a small but detectable load upon the system. Under BSD, accounting is usually enabled in new systems, but may be disabled if desired; the process for doing so is described later in this chapter. Under System V, accounting is initially disabled and must be set up by the system administrator.

Standard Accounting Files

When accounting is enabled, the UNIX kernel writes a record to a binary data file as each process terminates. These records (which vary slightly between the two versions) are stored in the home directory of the standard user *adm* (conventionally UID 4), located and named as follows:

BSD-style accounting:

BSD	*/usr/adm/acct*
SunOS	*/var/adm/acct*

System V-style accounting:

V.3	*/usr/adm/pacct*
V.4	*/var/adm/pacct*
AIX 3.1	*/usr/adm/pacct**
XENIX	*/usr/adm/pacct* (only a very simple subset)

NOTE

In the rest of this chapter, for convenience I'll use the form ˜*adm* to refer to the home directory of the *adm* user in accounting file pathnames. Be aware, though, that the Bourne shell doesn't support tilde expansion.

Records written by the accounting system to the raw accounting file contain the following data about the process:

- Image name.

- CPU time used (separated into user and system time).

---

*AIX 3.1 also supports the BSD accounting commands.

- Elapsed time taken.

- Time the process began.

- Associated user and group IDs.

- Memory usage (BSD: average; System V: raw accesses).

- Number of characters read and written.

- Number of disk I/O blocks read and written.

- Initiating TTY.

- Various flags associated with the process, including its exit status.

- Other accounting data is stored in these files:

/etc/utmp   A binary log file containing data about each currently logged-in user. *login* enters a record for each successful login, which is then cleared by *init* at logout.

˜adm/wtmp   A binary log file that records each login and logout (stored in */etc* under V.3).

˜adm/lastlog   A database containing the date and time of the last login for each user.

▒ BSD Accounting ▒

BSD accounting uses the following additional accounting summary files:

˜adm/savacct   The standard summary file. Accounting records are merged into this file by the *sa* utility.

˜adm/usracct   The user-based summary file. This file is maintained and accessed by the *-m* option of the *sa* utility.

These files store processed, summarized versions of the raw accounting data collected in the *˜adm/acct* accounting file. They are maintained by the *sa* command and are useful in keeping the size of the accounting file to a manageable level.

Enabling and Disabling Accounting

By default, accounting is enabled. Specifically, this means that both of the following conditions are fulfilled:

- The *accton* command has been executed since the system was last booted.

- The accounting file specified by the *accton* command exists.

An *accton* command is usually included in the distributed version of the initialization file */etc/rc*. It specifies the file ~*adm/acct* as the accounting file, and a zero-length version of this file is often distributed with the BSD operating system. The relevant lines from */etc/rc* are:

```
if [ -f /usr/adm/acct ]; then
        accton /usr/adm/acct; echo -n ' accounting' >/dev/console
```

The *accton* command enables accounting when an accounting file is specified as its argument. (Without an argument, the command disables accounting—discussed in the section, "Administrative Accounting Options.") Once the command is executed, accounting records will be written automatically to the accounting file.

Merging Accounting Records into the Summary Files

The accounting file will grow without bounds if allowed to do so. Its contents may be processed and merged into the accumulated accounting summary files with the *sa* command. When invoked with its *-s* option, the *sa* command processes raw accounting records and places condensed summary information into the summary files. Here is an example of its use:

# accton	*Briefly disable accounting.*
# cd /usr/adm	*Move to accounting directory.*
# mv acct acct.sav	*Rename accounting file.*
# touch acct	*Recreate accounting file.*
# accton acct	*Restart accounting.*
# sa -s acct.sav >/dev/null	*Merge into standard summary file.*
# rm -f acct.sav	*Delete saved accounting records.*

The accounting file is renamed prior to invoking *sa* so that processes that terminate during processing are recorded. The output from *sa* is piped to */dev/null* to discard the report it generates. Alternatively, it could be sent to a file.

A script could be created which runs these commands, so that they could be executed as needed by the system administrator or automatically via the *cron* facility.

Administrative Accounting Options

Given the default accounting setup, administrators have a number of options, which are detailed in the following list:

- *Leave things as they are.* Many sites will find this default setup fits their needs perfectly. Accounting will be started and maintained automatically without administrator intervention, but processing the file and controlling its size will be the administrator's responsibility.

- *Disable accounting.* To do so, execute the *accton* command without an argument:

  ```
  # accton
  ```

  Accounting will now cease, and no further records will be written to the accounting file until it is re-enabled. In addition, you'll need to comment out the *accton* command in */etc/rc.*

  If desired, the accounting file may be deleted after accounting is disabled. However, two points must be noted in this event. First, The *accton* command without an argument is the only way to disable accounting. *Deleting the accounting file will not diminish accounting overhead* since the kernel will still attempt to keep and write records but have no place to put them.

  Second, when accounting is subsequently re-enabled, the accounting file will need to be recreated by hand; the accounting software will not automatically create the file if it does not already exist. Use the *touch* command to create a zero-length file before restarting accounting:

  ```
  # touch /usr/adm/acct
  # accton /usr/adm/acct
  ```

- *Change the accounting file.* This may be done by disabling accounting and then re-enabling it with a different file; for example:

  ```
  # accton
  # touch /sysadmin/accounts
  # accton /sysadmin/accounts
  ```

  The commands in the previous example replace the default accounting file with a file of the administrator's choosing. Records in the original and new accounting files may be merged into the same summary file if desired (discussed later).

- *Place all or part of the accounting system on a manual basis.* The system administrator may decide to handle some or all accounting functions manually. If this option is chosen, then the relevant lines in */etc/rc* should be commented out, and the system administrator will be responsible for starting accounting when desired.

- *Automate accounting completely.* Simple scripts can be written to process raw accounting records into the summary files and even to produce desired accounting reports. They can be run on a periodic basis via *cron*.

After a Crash

The accounting system is designed to handle system shutdowns and bootups automatically. However, special steps must be taken in the event of a system crash. In order for the accounting system to accurately record data for processes that were running when a system crash occurred, the administrator must manually close out outstanding accounting records. These records need to be saved or processed *before* accounting is started. If accounting is started automatically in the */etc/rc* file (as is the default), this process needs to occur before */etc/rc* is executed. The easy way to accomplish this is to boot to single-user mode after the crash.

The accounting file may be saved by renaming it using a *mv* command such as the following:

```
# mv /usr/adm/acct /usr/adm/acct.sav
# touch /usr/adm/acct
```

The second command recreates the accounting file, readying it for new records when accounting is started in */etc/rc*.

At this point, the system may be booted multi-user. Once booting is complete, the following commands will close out the accounting records that were pending at the time of the crash:

```
# sa -s /usr/adm/acct.sav >/dev/null
# rm -f /usr/adm/acct.sav
```

These commands update the summary files and then delete the saved accounting file. These commands may be stored in a file as a shell script for ease of execution.

Image-Based Resource Use Reporting: sa

The *sa* utility produces system usage reports based upon the image (command) that was executed. That is, in most cases its statistics are organized and presented by image name, rather than by user or project. *sa* reads the raw accounting file and its summary file */usr/adm/savacct* to accumulate its data. Without any options, *sa* produces a report like the following (output has been shortened):

```
# sa
   11238  412355.91re    5017.62cp      14avio  148k   login
    4299    1782.32re    1000.28cp     122avio   73k   ld
   12648    1335.62re     639.28cp      12avio   26k   as
    6489    1121.66re     541.82cp      50avio   10k   makemake.c
       4     627.93re     258.43cp       3avio    0k   splice
     225    6623.90re     248.56cp    2545avio    8k   find
```

In this default output, the image name appears in the final (rightmost) column. The numerical fields in *sa*'s output are identified by their suffixes, which have the following meanings:

Table 13-1. sa Output Suffixes

Suffix	Data
none	Number of times called.
cp, cpu	CPU time (system + user) in minutes.
re	Elapsed time in minutes.
avio	Average number of I/O operations per execution.
k	Average (over CPU time) memory used during execution in kilobytes.
k*sec	Cpu storage integral in kilo-core seconds.
tio	Total I/O operations for all executions.
s	System CPU time in minutes.
u	User CPU time in minutes.

Not all data appear in every report. The first five items appear in the default output. The other items appear in reports generated by the various options.

sa's output may be sorted in a number of different ways by selecting an appropriate option, as shown in Table 13-2.

Table 13-2. sa Options

Option	Sorting Item
-b	Average total CPU time per execution.
-d	Average number of disk I/O operations.
-D	Total number of disk I/O operations.
-k	CPU time-averaged memory usage.
-K	CPU-storage integral.
-n	Number of calls.

The *-D* option produces a report containing the total I/O use by the command; lines are sorted according to this total:

```
# sa -D
  225    6623.90re    248.56cp    572608tio    8k   find
 4299    1782.32re   1000.28cp    522580tio   73k   ld
 9205   58785.98re    188.08cp    497421tio    9k   makenv
   56    9610.25re     80.79cp    495507tio   18k   buildsystem
   20      50.27re     14.79cp    369163tio   11k   ncheck
```

Here is the output from the *-b* option, which sorts by average CPU time:

```
# sa -b
    4     627.93re    258.43cp      3avio    0k   splice
    4    6680.53re    162.02cp     26avio   20k   timed*
   11     294.67re     50.19cp   5961avio   14k   fsck
    2       8.75re      7.39cp   1055avio    2k   code
    3    3843.47re      7.91cp  47323avio    1k   update*
```

In addition, the *-r* option may be used to reverse the order of the sort (low to high instead of high to low). The *-m* option produces a listing of the total number of processes and CPU time for each user:

```
# sa -m
root     247648   19318.90cpu   7698005tio   3793802k*sec
chavez        2       3.67cpu         0tio   1013391k*sec
martin        4       7.33cpu         0tio   2024939k*sec
daemon     7799    2742.86cpu   1616886tio    488234k*sec
wang          6    2956.44cpu   1067648tio    406004k*sec
```

The *-l* option may be used to separate user and system time in *sa*'s output:

```
# sa -l
11238   412355.91re   4691.13u   326.49s    14avio   148k   ccom7
 4299     1782.32re    861.52u   138.76s   122avio    73k   ld
12648     1335.62re    567.13u    72.15s    12avio    26k   as
    4      627.93re    252.13u     6.30s     3avio     0k   splice
```

Alternate summary files may be specified with the *-S* and *-U* options; both should be followed by a pathname. *-S* indicates an alternative to */usr/adm/savacct*, and *-U* specifies an alternative to the per-user summary file */usr/adm/usracct*. Processing may be limited to the raw accounting file with the *-i* option.

As we've seen, the *-s* option updates the summary file and truncates the raw accounting file.

Connect Time Reporting: ac

The *ac* utility reports on user connect time. It gets its data from the */usr/adm/wtmp* file, containing records on user logins and logouts. Without any options, *ac* displays the total connect time (in hours) for all users for the lifetime of the *wtmp* file:

```
# ac
        total  5501.06
```

The command may also be followed by one or more usernames, in which case the total for those users is displayed:

```
# ac chavez wang fine
        total  1588.65
```

The *-p* option breaks down connect time by user:

```
# ac -p
        ng          30.61
        chavez     685.25
        martin       0.04
        wang       170.77
        sysadmin    44.84
        fine       732.78
```

Usernames may be specified with *-p* to limit *ac*'s scope:

```
# ac -p chavez wang fine
        chavez  685.25
        wang    170.77
        fine    732.78
        total  1588.79
```

The *-d* option breaks down the display by date:

```
# ac -d
Sep  1  total    77.32
Sep  2  total   228.78
Sep  3  total   260.82
Sep  4  total   120.30
# ac -d chavez wang fine
Sep  1  total    11.83           The total for these users is displayed.
```

```
Sep  2  total   20.36
Sep  3  total   41.00
Sep  4  total    7.14
```

Using *-d* and *-p* together produces a summary of login activity broken down by user and by date:

```
# ac -d -p chavez wang
        chavez   16.07
        wang      4.55
Sep  1  total    20.62
        chavez   15.87
        wang     20.15
Sep  2  total    36.01
        chavez   22.82
        wang     17.68
Sep  3  total    40.50
        chavez   24.36
        wang     12.17
Sep  4  total    36.53
```

The form *ac -d -p* would produce a similar listing including all users.

Connect times for an individual user might exceed 24 hours in a single day; this is easily accounted for by the fact that users may log in at more than one terminal or have more than one session on a single terminal at the same time.

System V Accounting

System V accounting is much more elaborate than under BSD. It is a complex system of commands, and shell scripts and C programs, called by one another in long sequences, all purported to be totally automated and requiring little or no intervention. In reality, it's a design only a fervent partisan could love. Standard documentation alternates between assuring the reader that the system is robust, reliable, and trouble-free and describing complicated procedures for patching corrupted accounting data files. *Caveat emptor.*

The *adm* user's home directory contains an *acct* subdirectory under System V, which itself contains three subdirectories:

~adm/acct/fiscal   Reports by fiscal period (usually month), and old binary fiscal period summary files.

~adm/acct/nite   Daily binary summary file, daily processed accounting record, raw disk accounting records, and status, error log, and lock files.

~*adm/acct/sum*   Binary daily and current fiscal period cumulative summary files and daily reports.

In addition to the *wtmp* and *pacct* files discussed above, there are several other raw data files generated by the accounting system under System V:

~*adm/acct/nite/diskacct* Raw disk usage data.

~*adm/fee*   Administrator-entered additional charge records, using the *chargefee* command. *chargefee* allows an administrator to record charges for special services not covered by the accounting system; these charges will automatically be incorporated into the accounting system. It takes two arguments: a username and the number of units to be charged to that user. For example, the following command charges user *chavez* 10 units:

```
# chargefee chavez 10
```

Figure 13-1 illustrates the general flow of data in the System V accounting system, beginning with the raw data files discussed previously. Commands and the operating system enter data into the raw data files, which are processed by a series of utilities, producing several intermediate binary summary files and finally culminating in ASCII reports suitable for use by the system administrator. All of this processing can be handled automatically by *cron* once accounting is set up.

The accounting utilities are stored in the directory */usr/lib/acct*.

Setting Up Accounting

While accounting is not enabled by default under System V, it is to a large extent pre-set up. The following steps are necessary to enable accounting:

*   Create an accounting starting entry in the */etc/rc2.d* directory by linking the file */etc/init.d/acct* to */etc/rc2.d/S22acct*. On moving to multi-user mode, the file executes the command:

    ```
    /bin/su - adm -c /usr/lib/acct/startup
    ```

    The *startup* script calls the *accton* command to initiate accounting.

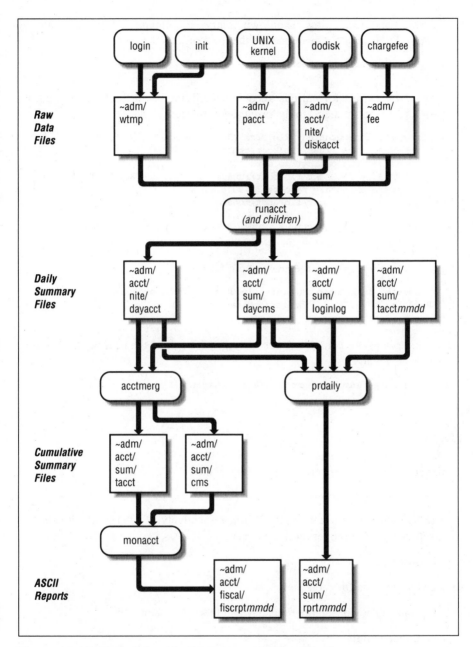

Figure 13-1. Accounting Under System V (Simplified)

- Create an accounting shutdown entry by linking the same file to
  /etc/rc0.d/K22acct. On shutdown, the file executes the command:

  ```
  /usr/lib/acct/shutacct
  ```

- Add *cron* entries for various accounting utilities. Add the following entries
  (or a variation on them) to the *crontab* file for user *adm*:

  ```
  # control accounting file size (3:30 a.m. daily)
  0  *  *  *  *  /usr/lib/acct/ckpacct
  # process accounting raw data (4:30 a.m. daily)
  30 4  *  *  *  /usr/lib/acct/runacct 2> /usr/adm/acct/nite/fd2log
  # generate monthly reports (5:30 a.m. on the first)
  30 5 1  *  *  /usr/lib/acct/monacct
  ```

Under V.4, the second entry should pipe standard error to
/var/adm/acct/nite/fd2log .

Add the following entry to the *crontab* file for *root*:

```
# generate disk usage raw data (10:30 p.m. on Saturdays)
30 22  *  *  7  /usr/lib/acct/dodisk
```

Once these steps are completed, accounting will begin at the next boot. Or it may
be started manually:

```
# /bin/su - adm -c /usr/lib/acct/startup
```

Accounting Reports

Daily accounting reports are stored in files named:

```
~adm/acct/sum/rprtmmdd
```

where *mm* and *dd* are the month and day, respectively. Each report file contains
five separate reports, covering these areas:

- Per-user usage.

- Last login time for each user.

- Command use, for the previous day and the previous month.

- Terminal activity.

Here is a sample of the daily per-user usage report, the most useful section of the daily report file from an accounting perspective:

```
March  7 10:43 1991   DAILY USAGE REPORT FOR hamlet                    Page 1
```

UID	LOGIN NAME	CPU PRIME	(MINS) NPRIME	KCORE–MINS PRIME	NPRIME	CONNECT PRIME	(MINS) NPRIME	DISK BLOCKS	# OF PROCS	# OF SESS	# DISK SAMPLES	FEE
0	TOTAL	40	101	9	34	393	124	0	1186	19	0	0
0	root	5	10	2	11	102	12	0	1129	10	0	0
473	wang	35	91	7	23	291	112	0	57	9	0	0

The times of day corresponding to prime and non-prime usage is defined in the file */etc/acct/holidays*, which the administrator must configure. The resources used during prime and non-prime hours are totaled separately by the accounting system (to allow for different charge rates).

The first line of the report is a total line, giving total system usage. After that, there is one line per UID. The fields have the following meanings:

UID	UID.
LOGIN NAME	Username.
CPU	Total CPU time for all of the user's processes in minutes.
KCORE-MINS	Total memory used by running processes, in kilobyte-minutes. Basically, this field is a function of the product of the memory used times the length of use, summed over all of the user's processes. It is an indication of how much memory the user's processes consumed, but is not an accurate measure of actual memory use.
CONNECT	Total connect time (how long the user was logged in).
DISK BLOCKS	Average total amount of disk space used by the user.
# PROCS	Total number of processes belonging to this user.
# SESS	Number of distinct login sessions.
# DISK SAMPLES	Number of times *dodisk* was run during the accounting period, giving a measure of how many values the DISK BLOCKS field is averaged over. If *dodisk* has not run, this field and the DISK BLOCKS field will contain a 0.
FEE	Total fees entered with *chargefee*.

The daily and monthly command use reports in the same file show system resource usage by command name, including the number of times each command was run and the total CPU time, memory use, and I/O transactions it consumed. The terminal activity report shows the percentage of time each terminal line was in use over the accounting period, the total connect time accumulated on it, and the number of distinct login sessions. The last login report displays the date of the last login for each UID defined in the */etc/passwd* file.

The monthly accounting reports are stored in files named:

```
~adm/acct/fiscal/fiscrptnn
```

where *nn* is the month. They are very similar to the daily reports just described.

Accounting Under XENIX

XENIX uses the System V accounting file */usr/adm/pacct*, but does not include the elaborate structure available in System V. It provides the utility *acctcom* (also available in System V) to display the data collected in the accounting data file. The *acctcom* command displays one line for each record in the data file, each of which corresponds to one process. *acctcom*'s options allow you to specify a subset of the total records in the data file for display. The most useful options are:

-b	Display records in reverse-chronological order (backwards).
-t	Display separate system and user CPU times.
-u user	Limit to *user*'s processes.
-s time	Limit to processes started after *time*.
-e time	Limit to processes in existence before *time*.
-n regexp	Limit to commands matching the regular expression.
-C value	Limit to processes using more than *value* CPU time.
-I n	Limit to processes transferring > *n* characters.

If more than one display limiting option is specified, only processes satisfying all of the criteria are displayed.

Accounting Under AIX 3.1

The AIX 3.1 accounting system implements System V accounting. However, the BSD accounting commands are also supported. Administrators may choose either set to administer accounting.

AIX 3.1 extends standard System V accounting into another area: printer-usage. The data file */usr/adm/qacct* is conventionally used to store printer usage data which can be merged into the general accounting system. Printing accounting is enabled by adding an *acctfile* keyword to the queue definition in */etc/qconfig*:

```
laser:
    device = dlas1,dlas2
    acctfile = /usr/adm/qacct
dlas1:
    backend = /usr/lpd/piobe
dlas2:
    backend = /usr/lpd/piobe
```

This line may be added with an text editor, by using the *chque* command, or by using SMIT, but in any case, the queue should be stopped first (with *enq -D*) and then restarted after reconfiguration. See the section entitled "The AIX 3.1 Queueing System," in Chapter 11, *Printers and the Spooling Subsystem*, for details.

Boottime accounting initiation is set up slightly differently under AIX 3.1, since it uses BSD-style boot scripts. The following line needs to be added to the */etc/rc* file by the administrator to turn on accounting at boottime:

```
/bin/su - adm -c /usr/lib/acct/startup
```

There are already commands in */etc/shutdown* to turn off accounting:

```
if [ -x /usr/lib/acct/shutacct ]
then
    /usr/lib/acct/shutacct
fi
```

The following additional setup steps are required under AIX 3.1:

- The subdirectories under */usr/adm/acct* will have to be created by hand:

```
# cd /usr/adm/acct
# mkdir fiscal nite sum
# chown adm.adm fiscal nite sum
# chmod 775 fiscal nite sum
```

- Add an *acctfile* line to the appropriate stanza(s) in the */etc/qconfig* file to enable printer usage accounting.

- Add an *account* line to the */etc/filesystems* stanza for each filesystem for which you want to collect disk accounting data:

```
/chem:
        dev= /dev/us00
        vfs= jfs
        log= /dev/logus00
        mount= true
        check= true
        options= rw
        account= true
```

Bourne Shell Programming Appendix

Basic Syntax
The if Statement
Other Control Structures
Getting Input: The read Command
Other Useful Commands
Functions

The purpose of this appendix is to review major Bourne shell programming features. It is not intended as a comprehensive treatment of Bourne shell programming. Rather, it is designed less to make you able to write Bourne shell scripts that to be able to understand and modify the system administration scripts on your system. (At this point, virtually all system scripts are Bourne shell scripts, although this will undoubtedly change as the Korn shell becomes more widely available.) As much as possible, the examples come from actual system scripts.

Basic Syntax

This section reviews some basic syntactic features of the Bourne shell, in a somewhat random order.

Lines in shell scripts beginning with number signs are comments:

```
# Start or stop the lp scheduler
```

The first line of a shell script usually looks like this:

```
#!/bin/sh
```

This identifies the shell the script is designed for, in this case, the Bourne shell.

The Bourne shell offers some syntactic flexibility over other shells. For example, quotes stay in effect across physical lines, as in this example we looked at in Chapter 6, *Automating Routine Tasks*:

```
echo "*** Non-root UID=0 or GID=0 accounts:"
grep ':00*:' /etc/passwd | \
   awk -F: 'BEGIN      {n=0}
           $1!="root"  {print $0 ; n=1}
           END         {if (n==0) print "None found."}'
```

Note that the arguments to the *awk* command extend across three lines, a construct much more readable than forcing them onto one line.

Another construct you'll see quite often is this redirection of standard output to a file and standard error onto to standard output (and thus to the same file):

```
/usr/lib/lpshut > /dev/null 2>&1
```

In this case the file is */dev/null*, but the concept applies whether output goes to a file, to */dev/console*, or gets thrown out.

The dot Command

The so-called "dot" command—a period followed by a filename—is used to run commands from a file in the same shell as the command itself. (The second file thus functions like an include file.) For example, the following command executes the contents of */etc/rc.newfeatures* as if they were part of the same script:

```
. /etc/rc.newfeatures
```

Placing some commands in a separate file is a way of isolating their function.

Return Codes and the exit Command

On UNIX systems, commands return a zero when they terminate normally and a nonzero value when they don't. The *exit* command may be used in scripts to return an explicit value; it takes the return value as its argument. Here is a typical use of *exit*:

```
echo "configure network FAILED"
exit 1
```

This command, from a TCP/IP startup file, terminates the script and returns a non-zero value (indicating an error).

The pipe forms "&&" and "||" are conditional pipe joins. When the shell encounters them, it checks the exit value of the previous element in the pipe before deciding whether to execute the next segment. For &&, the next segment is executed only if the previous one completed successfully; for ||, the next segment executes when the previous one fails. Here is an example with &&:

```
grep chavez /etc/passwd && grep chavez /etc/group
```

If "chavez" is found in the password file, the same string is searched for in the group file; if it isn't, the second command doesn't execute. Both constructs can be used together:

```
/usr/local/cksecret && echo "Everything ok." || mail root < slog
```

If the script *cksecret* returns a 0, then a message will be sent to standard output; otherwise, the contents of the *slog* file are mailed to *root*. (The && has to come before the || for this to work right.)

Argument Symbols and Other $ Abbreviations

Bourne shell scripts can be passed arguments like any command. The first nine arguments can be referred to by the abbreviations $1 through $9. The *shift* command is one way to access later arguments. Here is an example of how it works:

```
$ cat show_shift
#!/bin/sh
echo $1 $2 $3
shift
echo $1 $2 $3
$ show_shift a1 a2 a3 a4
a1 a2 a3
a2 a3 a4
```

After the *shift* command, all parameters are shifted one slot to the left, or down, depending on how you want to look at it. In any event, their parameter numbers are reduced by one.

The form $# is a shorthand for the number of arguments passed to the script. Thus, for the *show_shift* command in the previous example, $# would have been 4 (before the *shift* command was executed).

There are two shorthand forms for all the arguments passed to a script: $@ and $*. The two forms are usually equivalent. One case when they are not is when they are enclosed in quotation marks, where:

```
"$*" = "$1 $2 $3 $4 ... $n"
"$@" = "$1" "$2" "$3" "$4" ... "$n"
```

You'll usually see the $@ form in system scripts.

There are a couple of other dollar sign abbreviations which appear from time to time. Although they're not related to script arguments, I'll list them here:

$?   Exit status of previous command.

$$ PID of this shell's process.

$!   PID of the most recently started background job.

We'll see examples of them in this appendix.

Parameter Substitution

Shell scripts can also define variables, using the same syntax as environment variables:

```
name=value
```

Variables are dereferenced by putting a dollar sign in front of their name: $*name*. The variable name may be surrounded with braces to protect it from surrounding text. For example:

```
$ cat braces
#!/bin/sh
item=aaaa
item1=bbbb
echo ${item}1 $item1
$ braces
aaaa1 bbbb
```

The first command displays the value of the variable *item* followed by a 1; the second command displays the value of the variable *item1*.

There are more complex ways of conditionally substituting variable values. They are summarized in the following table.

Table 1. Conditional Variable Substitution

Form	Value Used (or Action Taken)	
	If *var* is set	If *var* is unset
${*var-string*}	$*var*	*string*
${*var+string*}	*string*	null
${*var=string*}	$*var*	*string* (and run *var=string*)
${*var?string*}	$*var*	(echo *string* and then exit)

Here are some examples:

```
$ name=rachel                    Set name.
$ echo ${name-tatiana}           name is set so use it.
rachel
$ echo ${name2-tatiana}          name2 is unset so use "tatiana."
tatiana
$ echo ${name=tatiana}           name is set so use it.
rachel
$ echo ${name2=tatiana}; echo $name2
tatiana                          name2 is unset so use "tatiana,"
tatiana                          and give name2 that value too.
$ echo ${name+tatiana}           name is set so use "tatiana."
tatiana
$ echo ${name3+tatiana}          name3 is unset return nothing.

$ name4=${name3?"no name given"}; echo $name4
name3: no name given             name3 is unset, so echo "name3:", then the
                                 string, and then exit (name4 is not set).
$ dir=${name-`pwd`}; echo $dir
rachel                           name is set, so use it (pwd isn't run).
$ dir=${name3-`pwd`}; echo $dir
/u/chavez
```

As the final two examples indicate, commands can be included in the *string*, and they will only be executed if that portion of the structure is used.

The if Statement

With this section, we begin looking at Bourne shell control structures: programming features seldom used on the command line. The first construct we will consider is *if*, used for conditional command execution. Here is the basic syntax of an *if* statement and a simple *if* example:

```
if condition
then
    commands
fi

if [ -f /usr/lib/lpd ]; then
    /usr/lib/lpd; echo -n ' printer' >/dev/console
fi
```

The *if* command runs the commands in *condition*. If it (or they) return a true value (zero exit status), the *commands* are executed; if it returns a false, nonzero status, then the script jumps to the command after *fi*.

The example checks for the file */usr/lib/lpd* and starts the daemon if it's there. We'll look at the condition more closely a little later. Notice the placement of the *then* command. *then* must appear to the shell as a separate command, or you'll get an error. So it either must be on a new line after the *if* command, or be separated from the *if* command by a semicolon. The same rules hold true for the *fi* command that ends the *if* construct.

There are more complex forms of *if*:

```
strings /vmunix | grep UNIX > /tmp/motd
head -1 /etc/motd | grep UNIX >/tmp/th
if [ -z /tmp/th ]                  Was there any output from grep?
then
    cat /etc/motd >>/tmp/motd
else
    tail +2 /etc/motd >>/tmp/motd
fi
mv /tmp/motd /etc/motd
```

This example illustrates the if-then-else construct. It updates the UNIX version string in the message-of-the-day file. First, it gets the current UNIX version string out of the kernel file */vmunix* and puts it in the file */tmp/motd* (this is a BSD system). Then, it checks whether the string "UNIX" appears in the first line of */etc/motd*. The condition in the *if* command checks whether the output from *grep* is zero lines long (meaning no line matched). If it is, then the entire contents of */etc/motd* are appended to */tmp/motd* by the *tail* command. Otherwise—when "UNIX" does appear in the first line of */etc/motd*—then its entire contents are appended to */tmp/motd*. Finally, the new message file replaces the current one.

Here is an example of the most complex form of *if*:

```
set `who -r`                  Determine previous run level (9th field)
if [ $9 = "S" ]               Previous level was single-user mode.
then
    echo "The system is coming up. Be patient."
elif [ $7 = "2" ]             Current run level is level 2.
    echo "Changing to state 2."
```

```
else
    echo "Changing to state 3."
fi
```

The *elif* command allows *if* statements to be chained together. It functions as an *else* for the current *if* and as the beginning of a new one. The final *else* covers the case of all false conditions and ends the entire chain.

The test Command, aka [

The most common way to construct a condition command for an *if* command is with the *test* command. It has two forms:

```
test condition
[ condition ]
```

test evaluates *condition* and returns either a 0 or 1, depending on whether it is true (0) or false (1). (This polarity matches up with *if*'s sense of true and false.)

The open bracket ([) command is a link to *test* and works exactly the same. It makes for more readable scripts, so you'll seldom see *test*. If the [form is used, a final closed bracket (]) is included to keep *test* from complaining. Note that there must be spaces after [and before].

The following options are used to construct conditions with *test* and [:

For testing file characteristics:

-s *file*   *file* > 0 length.

-r *file*   *file* is readable.

-w *file*   *file* is writable.

-x *file*   *file* is executable.

-f *file*   *file* exists and is a regular file.

-d *file*   *file* is a directory.

-c *file*   *file* is a character special file.

-b *file*   *file* is a block special file.

-p *file*   *file* is a named pipe.

-u *file*   *file* has SUID set.

-g *file*   *file* has SGID set.

-k *file*   *file* has sticky bit set.

For testing and comparing strings:

-z *string*	*string*'s length is 0.
-n *string*	*string*'s length is greater than 0.
string1 = *string2*	The two strings are identical.
string1! = *string2*	The two strings are different.
string	*string* is not null.

For testing and comparing integers:

i1 -eq *i2*	*i1* is equal to *i2*.
i1 -ne *i2*	*i1* is not equal to *i2*.
i1 -gt *i2*	*i1* is greater than *i2*.
i1 -ge *i2*	*i1* is greater than or equal to *i2*.
i1 -lt *i2*	*i1* is less than *i2*.
i1 -le *i2*	*i1* is less than or equal to *i2*.

Logical operators:

! *condition*	NOT operator: negates *condition*.
cond1 -a *cond2*	AND operator: returns true only if both conditions are true.
cond1 -o *cond2*	OR operator: returns true if either condition is true.
\(\)	Used for grouping conditions.

Here are some simple examples:

```
if [ $9 = "S" ]              If the 9th argument is S.
if [ -s /etc/ptmp ]          If /etc/ptmp is not empty.
if [ $# -lt 4 ]              If the number of arguments is < 4.
if [ ! -f /etc/.fsckask ]    If the plain file /etc/.fsckask does not exist.
if [ $? -eq 0 ]               If the last command succeeded.
if [ $? -ne 0 ]              If the last command failed.
```

Here are some examples placed in context:

```
# get pid of lpsched
pid=`/bin/ps -e | grep ' lpsched$' | sed -e 's/^ *//' -e 's/ .*//'`
if [ "${pid}" != "" ]   # if we found an lpsched process ...
then
    /bin/kill ${pid}    # kill it
fi
```

```
if [ -r /fastboot ]          If there is a readable file /fastboot
     skip the fsck
elif [ $1x = autobootx ]     otherwise if argument 1 was "autoboot"
     do the fsck
fi


if [ -d /etc/rc0.d ]         If there is a directory named /etc/rc0.d
then
     run the K files
fi


if [ -x /etc/inetd ]         If the file /etc/inetd is executable,
then
   /etc/inetd                then start the daemon.
   echo "inetd"
fi


if [ "${BOOT}" = "yes" -a -d /etc/rc0.d ]
then                         If this is a boot and there is an rc0.d directory
                             run the files in /etc/rc0.d
fi
```

Other Control Structures

The while and until Commands

The *while* statement is one way to create a loop. Its syntax is:

```
while condition    --or--    until condition
do                           do
   commands                     commands
done                         done
```

In the *while* form, the *commands* are executed until the *condition* becomes false. In the *until* form, they are executed until the *condition* becomes true. Here is an example of *while*:

```
cat /etc/fstab |
while read DEVICE MOUNT_DIR READONLY FS DUMMY1 DUMMY2
do
     fsck (if required) and mount the device
done
```

This loop takes each line of */etc/fstab* in turn (sent to it via *cat*) and performs an appropriate action for the corresponding device. The *while* loop will end when *read* (described later) returns a nonzero status, indicating an end-of-file.

The case Command

The *case* command is a way to perform a branching operation. Here is its syntax:

```
case str in
  pat1)
    commands
    ;;
  pat2)
    commands
    ;;
    . . .
  patN)
    commands
    ;;
  *)
    commands
    ;;
  esac
```

The value in *str* is compared against each of the values in *pat1* through *patN*. When a match is found, the corresponding commands are executed. The double semicolons end each section. Wildcards are allowed in the patterns, and the pattern consisting of a single asterisk serves as a default (if no other pattern is matched) when placed at the end of the *case* command.

Here is an example we looked at in some detail in Chapter 3, *Startup and Shutdown*:

```
etc/fsck -p >/dev/console
case $? in                    Check return value and do the appropriate thing.
  0)
    date >/dev/console
    ;;
  2)
    exit 1
    ;;
  4)
    /etc/reboot -n
    ;;
  *)
    echo "Unknown error in reboot" > /dev/console
    exit 1
    ;;
  esac
```

In this example, different commands are run depending on the return value from *fsck*.

Another typical example comes in the files in */etc/init.d* on System V systems. Here is an abbreviated example:

```
#! /bin/sh
# Start or stop the lp scheduler

case "$1" in
  'start')
      /usr/lib/lpsched and other commands
      ;;

  'stop')
      /usr/lib/lpshut > /dev/null 2>&1
      ;;

  *)
      echo "usage: $0 {start|stop}"
      ;;
esac
```

This script takes different actions depending on whether it is passed *start* or *stop* as its argument. Which argument it gets depends on whether it is invoked as an S-file or a K-file, as we noted in Chapter 3, *Startup and Shutdown*.

The for Command

The *for* command is another way to create loops. Here is its syntax:

```
for var [in list]
do
    commands
done
```

If a *list* is included, the variable *var* is set to each value in turn, and the loop is then run using that value. If no list of values is specified, then $@ (all script arguments) is used.

Here is an example:

```
for d in /tmp /usr/tmp /chem/tmp ; do
    find $d ! -name tmp -type d -exec rmdir {} \;
done
```

This loop removes empty subdirectories from under */tmp*, */usr/tmp*, and */chem/tmp* in turn, while not removing those directories themselves (via *! -name tmp*—of course, it won't remove */tmp/tmp* either).

The Null Command

Occasionally, you'll run across a command consisting of just a colon:

```
:
```

It's used when all the work is done in the control statement and the body of the loop is empty.

Sometimes this command is used as a comment character (since its arguments will be ignored):

```
: attempt to ship remaining files
uucico -r
```

This practice is not recommended, since a line like the following:

```
: Hourly cleanup script @(#)cleanup.hourly 2/4/90
```

(part of which was produced by a source control system) will produce an error:

```
./cleanup.hourly: syntax error at line 2: `(' unexpected
```

The syntax still has to work for the arguments even on a null command.

Getting Input: The read Command

The *read* command reads one line from standard input and assigns the next word in the line to each successive variable specified as its arguments; extra words are assigned to its final argument. For example:

```
$ cat file.dat | while read x y z
> do echo $x $y $z; done
a b c
d e f
...
```

read can be used either for reading sequentially through a file (as in the earlier example with *while*) or for getting runtime input from the user. Here is an example using *read* for command input:

```
echo "fsck all disks? [y] \c" (read ans; echo $ans; exit) < /dev/console &
proc=$!; sleep 10
kill -9 $proc > /dev/null 2>&1 &
```

These commands print a message on the screen asking whether to run *fsck* on every disk, and then use *read* to get the user's answer. If the user doesn't answer within 10 seconds, then the background process running *read* is killed. Recall that "$!" refers to the PID of the most recent background process. If the user has answered, the process will no longer exist.

Other Useful Commands

This section briefly describes other commands that you may encounter in system scripts.

set

The *set* command sets the values of $1 through $n to the words given as its arguments. It is often used with a backquoted command to assign the argument identifiers to the command's output. Here is an example of its use:

```
$ who -r
     .      run-level 2  Aug 21 16:58    2     0     s
$ set `who -r`
$ echo $6
16:58
```

expr

The *expr* command is used to evaluate various expressions. It has a lot of uses, but one common one in shell scripts is integer arithmetic. Here is a very simple example of its use in this mode:

```
$ cat count_to_5
#!/bin/sh
i=1
while [ $i -le 5 ] ; do
  echo $i
  i=`expr $i + 1`      # add one to i
done
$ count_to_5
1
2
3
4
5
```

See the manual page for full details on *expr*. Integer arithmetic is included within the Korn shell, so you can expect constructions like the previous to gradually die away.

eval

The *eval* command executes its argument as a shell command. It is used to execute commands generated by multiple levels of indirection. Here is a silly example:

```
$ a=c; b=m; c=d; cmd=date
$ eval $`echo $a$b$c`
$cmd
Tue Mar 12 15:45:42 EDT 1991
```

Here is a real example that we looked at in Chapter 10, *Terminals and Modems*:

```
eval `tset -sQ -m ":?vt100"`
```

This command runs the commands to set the TERM and TERMCAP environment variables generated by *tset -s*.

Functions

Bourne shell scripts can define functions within them.* Functions have all the same syntactic features as the scripts themselves, including their own arguments. Within a function, the argument and other shorthand forms refer to its own arguments.

The basic function syntax is:

```
fname ()
{
  commands
}
```

Here is a sample function, followed by an example of its use:

```
sserv()
{
# sserv: function to start a server
# args: $1=daemon pathname; $2!="" means use startsrc
#
if [ $# = 0 ] ; then
```

---
*Many Bourne shell implementations do not support functions.

```
    echo "sserv: srver name required."; return 1
fi
if [ ! -x $1 ] ; then return 1 ; fi
if [ -n "$2" ] ; then
   startsrc -s `basename $1`
else
   $1
fi
}
sserv /etc/syslogd $USE_SRC
```

The *sserv* function starts a server process on an AIX 3.1 system, either in the conventional way from the command line or via the *startsrc* command (which uses the system resource controller subsystem, a general server management facility). The pathname of the server to start is specified as *sserv*'s first argument, and whether to use *startsrc* or not is specified by the second argument (any non-null value uses it).

The function begins by making sure it was passed one argument; it exits if it wasn't. Note that *return* is used instead of *exit* in functions. Then it makes sure the pathname it was passed is executable, and then finally it starts the daemon.

The example invocation of *sserv* uses an environment variable USR_SRC as its second argument. If is defined, then *startsrc* will be used; otherwise, only one argument will be passed to *sserv*.

Bibliography

This bibliography lists specialized works on various system administrative and related topics. It is organized by subject.

Shell Programming and UNIX Internals

Brian Kernighan and Rob Pike, *The UNIX Programming Environment* (Prentice Hall, 1984).
> The standard work on Bourne shell programming.

Maurice J. Bach, *The Design of the UNIX Operating System* (Prentice Hall, 1986).
> This classic work covers the System V version, but much of what it says applies to all UNIX versions.

Security

Simson Garfinkel and Gene Spafford, *Practical UNIX Security* (O'Reilly & Associates, 1991).
> An excellent treatment of the theory and practice of securing a UNIX system.

Cliff Stoll, *The Cuckoo's Egg* (Doubleday, 1989).
> A very entertaining and educational account of a widely-publicized security incident involving computers, break-ins, and espionage.

Networking

John Quarterman, *The Matrix: Computer Networks and Conferencing Systems Worldwide* (Digital Press, 1990).
> A good overall introduction to networking and the plethora of protocols, implementations, and options.

Hal Stern, *Managing NFS and NIS* (O'Reilly & Associates, 1991).
> This book focuses on NFS and NIS, but it also includes a fair amount of general TCP/IP information as well.

Grace Todino and Tim O'Reilly, *Using uucp and Usenet* (O'Reilly & Associates, 1989).

Tim O'Reilly and Grace Todino, *Managing uucp and Usenet* (O'Reilly & Associates, 1989).
> These two books are indispensable if your site uses uucp. You'll find plenty of material relevant to administering uucp in *Using* as well as *Managing*.

System Tuning

Mike Loukides, *System Performance Tuning* (O'Reilly & Associates, 1990).
> A careful, thorough look at optimizing performance on a UNIX system.

Terminal Lines and Data Communications

> John McNamara, *Technical Aspects of Data Communications* (Digital Press, 1982).

Joe Campbell, *C Programmer's Guide to Data Communications* (Sams, 1987).
> Two good treatments of serial communications and the RS-232 standards.

John Strang, Tim O'Reilly and Linda Mui, *Termcap and Terminfo* (O'Reilly & Associates, 1989).
> A guide to modifying and writing termcap and terminfo entries. It also includes full descriptions of all terminal capabilities specifiable in the two databases.

Index

About the Author

Æleen Frisch has been a system administrator for about ten years. Her first major job was managing several VMS VAXen each running 16 CAD/CAM workstations. (Thus, UNIX is a second language for her, but few people notice her accent.) Currently, Æleen spends some of her time looking after a small but very heterogeneous network of UNIX-based workstations and the rest doing freelance technical and marketing writing.

Æleen is a third generation native Californian, currently living in exile in Connecticut. She has a B.S. in Literature from Caltech (with a minor in CS if they had minors), and has just finished a Ph.D. in English/Cultural Studies from Pitt. (Her thesis used literary techniques to study late eighteenth-century political and scientific texts and practice and twentieth-century feminist discourse.) In the time freed by finally finishing her degree, Æleen plans to get back to painting, writing poetry and fiction, and lounging (not necessarily in that order).

Colophon

Our look is the result of reader comments, our own experimentation, and distribution channels.

Distinctive covers complement our distinctive approach to technical topics, breathing personality and life into potentially dry subjects. UNIX and its attendant programs can be unruly beasts. Nutshell Handbooks help you tame them.

The animal featured on the cover of *Essential System Administration* is an armadillo. This insect-eating mammal is native to South America and has spread through the southern United States. Unlike most insectivores, the armadillo has teeth—simple rootless pegs set far back in its mouth. These teeth allow it to supplement its diet of termites, scorpions and other insects with snakes, poultry, fruit, and eggs.

The armadillo's name, "little armored thing," was given to it by the Spanish when they invaded the New World. This "armor" is an outer layer consisting of numerous bony plates with a horny covering. This shell is hinged at the middle of the back, allowing the front and hind sections freedom of movement. In some species, this covering extends over the face and tail as well as the torso and limbs.

Armadillos range in size from the great armadillo, at 5 feet in length, to the fairy armadillo at 5 inches. The most common of the armadillos, the 9-banded armadillo, is about the size of a house cat.

Edie Freedman designed this cover and the entire UNIX bestiary that appears on other Nutshell Handbooks. The beasts themselves are adapted from 19th-century engravings from the Dover Pictorial Archive.

The text of this book is set in Times Roman; headings are Helvetica; examples are Courier. Text was prepared using SortQuad's sqtroff text formatter. Figures are produced with a Macintosh. Printing is done on a Tegra Varityper 5000.

SYSTEM
ADMINISTRATION

Books from O'Reilly & Associates, Inc.

Fall/Winter 1994-95

"Good reference books make a system administrator's job much easier. However, finding useful books about system administration is a challenge, and I'm constantly on the lookout. In general, I have found that almost anything published by O'Reilly & Associates is worth having if you are interested in the topic."
— *Dinah McNutt*, UNIX Review

TCP/IP Network Administration

By Craig Hunt
1st Edition August 1992
502 pages, ISBN 0-937175-82-X

A complete guide to setting up and running a TCP/IP network for administrators of networks of systems or lone home systems that access the Internet. It starts with the fundamentals: what the protocols do and how they work, how to request a network address and a name (the forms needed are included in an appendix), and how to set up your network. Beyond basic setup, the book discusses how to configure important network applications, including sendmail, the r* commands, and some simple setups for NIS and NFS. There are also chapters on troubleshooting and security. In addition, this book covers several important packages that are available from the Net (such as *gated*). Covers BSD and System V TCP/IP implementations.

"Whether you're putting a network together, trying to figure out why an existing one doesn't work, or wanting to understand the one you've got a little better, *TCP/IP Network Administration* is the definitive volume on the subject."
—Tom Yager, *Byte*

Managing Internet Information Services

By Cricket Liu, Jerry Peek, Russ Jones,
Bryan Buus & Adrian Nye
1st Edition Fall 1994 (est.)
400 pages (est.), ISBN 1-56592-062-7

This comprehensive guide describes how to set up information services to make them available over the Internet. It discusses why a company would want to offer Internet services, provides complete coverage of all popular services, and tells how to select which ones to provide. Most of the book describes how to set up email services and FTP, Gopher, and World Wide Web servers.

"*Managing Internet Information Services* has long been needed in the Internet community, as well as in many organizations with IP-based networks. Although many on the Internet are quite savvy when it comes to administering these types of tools, MIIS will allow a much larger community to join in and perhaps provide more diverse information. This book will be a welcome addition to my Internet shelf."
—Robert H'obbes' Zakon, MITRE Corporation

Linux Network Administrator's Guide

By Olaf Kirch
1st Edition Fall 1994 (est.)
400 pages (est.), ISBN 1-56592-087-2

A UNIX-compatible operating system that runs on personal computers, Linux is a pinnacle within the free software movement. It is based on a kernel developed by Finnish student Linus Torvalds and is distributed on the Net or on low-cost disks, along with a complete set of UNIX libraries, popular free software utilities, and traditional layered products like NFS and the X Window System.

Networking is a fundamental part of Linux. Whether you want a simple UUCP connection or a full LAN with NFS and NIS, you are going to have to build a network.

Linux Network Administration Guide by Olaf Kirch is one of the most successful books to come from the Linux Documentation Project. It touches on all the essential networking software included with Linux, plus some hardware considerations. Topics include serial connections, UUCP, routing and DNS, mail and News, SLIP and PPP, NFS, and NIS.

DNS and BIND

By Paul Albitz & Cricket Liu
1st Edition October 1992
418 pages, ISBN 1-56592-010-4

DNS and BIND contains all you need to know about the Internet's Domain Name System (DNS) and the Berkeley Internet Name Domain (BIND), its UNIX implementation. The Domain Name System is the Internet's "phone book"; it's a database that tracks important information (in particular, names and addresses) for every computer on the Internet. If you're a system administrator, this book will show you how to set up and maintain the DNS software on your network.

"*DNS and BIND* contains a lot of useful information that you'll never find written down anywhere else. And since it's written in a crisp style, you can pretty much use the book as your primary BIND reference."
—Marshall Rose, *ConneXions*

sendmail

By Bryan Costales, with Eric Allman & Neil Rickert
1st Edition November 1993
830 pages, ISBN 1-56592-056-2

This Nutshell Handbook® is far and away the most comprehensive book ever written on sendmail, the program that acts like a traffic cop in routing and delivering mail on UNIX-based networks. Although sendmail is used on almost every UNIX system, it's one of the last great uncharted territories—and most difficult utilities to learn—in UNIX system administration. This book provides a complete sendmail tutorial, plus extensive reference material on every aspect of the program. It covers IDA sendmail, the latest version (V8) from Berkeley, and the standard versions available on most systems.

"The program and its rule description file, sendmail.cf, have long been regarded as the pit of coals that separated the mild Unix system administrators from the real fire walkers. Now, sendmail syntax, testing, hidden rules, and other mysteries are revealed. Costales, Allman, and Rickert are the indisputable authorities to do the text."
—Ben Smith, *Byte*

Essential System Administration

By Æleen Frisch
1st Edition October 1991
466 pages, ISBN 0-937175-80-3

Like any other multi-user system, UNIX requires some care and feeding. *Essential System Administration* tells you how. This book strips away the myth and confusion surrounding this important topic and provides a compact, manageable introduction to the tasks faced by anyone responsible for a UNIX system.

If you use a stand-alone UNIX system, whether it's a PC or a workstation, you know how much you need this book: on these systems the fine line between a user and an administrator has vanished. Either you're both or you're in trouble. If you routinely provide administrative support for a larger shared system or a network of workstations, you will find this book indispensable. Even if you aren't directly responsible for system administration, you will find that understanding basic administrative functions greatly increases your ability to use UNIX effectively.

Computer Security Basics

By Deborah Russell & G.T. Gangemi Sr.
1st Edition July 1991
464 pages, ISBN 0-937175-71-4

There's a lot more consciousness of security today, but not a lot of understanding of what it means and how far it should go. This handbook describes complicated concepts, such as trusted systems, encryption, and mandatory access control, in simple terms. For example, most U.S. government equipment acquisitions now require Orange Book (Trusted Computer System Evaluation Criteria) certification. A lot of people have a vague feeling that they ought to know about the Orange Book, but few make the effort to track it down and read it. *Computer Security Basics* contains a more readable introduction to the Orange Book—why it exists, what it contains, and what the different security levels are all about—than any other book or government publication.

"A very well-rounded book, filled with concise, authoritative information…written with the user in mind, but still at a level to be an excellent professional reference."
—Mitch Wright, System Administrator, I-NET, Inc.

Practical UNIX Security

By Simson Garfinkel & Gene Spafford
1st Edition June 1991
512 pages, ISBN 0-937175-72-2

Tells system administrators how to make their UNIX system— either System V or BSD— as secure as it possibly can be without going to trusted system technology. The book describes UNIX concepts and how they enforce security, tells how to defend against and handle security breaches, and explains network security (including UUCP, NFS, Kerberos, and firewall machines) in detail. If you are a UNIX system administrator or user who deals with security, you need this book.

"The book could easily become a standard desktop reference for anyone involved in system administration. In general, its comprehensive treatment of UNIX security issues will enlighten anyone with an interest in the topic."
—Paul Clark, Trusted Information Systems

PGP: Pretty Good Privacy

By Simson Garfinkel
1st Edition Winter 1994-95 (est.)
250 pages (est.), ISBN 1-56592-098-8

PGP, which stands for Pretty Good Privacy, is a free and widely available program that lets you protect files and electronic mail. Written by Phil Zimmermann and released in 1991, PGP works on virtually every platform and has become very popular both in the U.S. and abroad. Because it uses state-of-the-art public key cryptography, PGP can be used to authenticate messages, as well as keep them secret. With PGP, you can digitally "sign" a message when you send it. By checking the digital signature at the other end, the recipient can be sure that the message was not changed during transmission and that the message actually came from you. The ability to protect the secrecy and authenticity of messages in this way is a vital part of being able to conduct business on the Internet.

PGP: Pretty Good Privacy is both a readable technical users guide and a fascinating behind-the-scenes look at cryptography and privacy. Part I of the book describes how to use PGP: protecting files and email, creating and using keys, signing messages, certifying and distributing keys, and using key servers. Part II provides background on cryptography, battles against public key patents and U.S. government export restrictions, and other aspects of the ongoing public debates about privacy and free speech.

System Performance Tuning

By Mike Loukides
1st Edition November 1990
336 pages, ISBN 0-937175-60-9

System Performance Tuning answers the fundamental question: How can I get my computer to do more work without buying more hardware? Some performance problems do require you to buy a bigger or faster computer, but many can be solved simply by making better use of the resources you already have.

"This book is a 'must' for anyone who has an interest in making their UNIX system run faster and more efficiently. It deals effectively with a complex subject that could require a multi-volume series."
—Stephan M. Chan, *ComUNIXation*

Managing UUCP and Usenet

By Grace Todino & Tim O'Reilly
10th Edition January 1992
368 pages, ISBN 0-937175-93-5

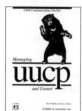

For all its widespread use, UUCP is one of the most difficult UNIX utilities to master. This book is for system administrators who want to install and manage UUCP and Usenet software.

"Don't even TRY to install UUCP without it!"—Usenet message 456@nitrex.UUCP

"If you are contemplating or struggling with connecting your system to the Internet via UUCP or planning even a passing contact with Usenet News Groups, this book should be on your shelf. Our highest recommendation." —*Boardwatch Magazine*

Managing NFS and NIS

By Hal Stern
1st Edition June 1991
436 pages, ISBN 0-937175-75-7

Managing NFS and NIS is for system administrators who need to set up or manage a network filesystem installation. NFS (Network Filesystem) is probably running at any site that has two or more UNIX systems. NIS (Network Information System) is a distributed database used to manage a network of computers. The only practical book devoted entirely to these subjects, this guide is a "must-have" for anyone interested in UNIX networking.

termcap & terminfo

By John Strang, Linda Mui & Tim O'Reilly
3rd Edition April 1988
270 pages, ISBN 0-937175-22-6

For UNIX system administrators and programmers. This handbook provides information on writing and debugging terminal descriptions, as well as terminal initialization, for the two UNIX terminal databases.

"I've been working with both termcap and terminfo for years now, and I was confident that I had a handle on them, but reading this remarkable little book gave me some valuable new insights into terminal setting in UNIX." —*Root Journal*

X Window System Administrator's Guide: Volume 8

By Linda Mui & Eric Pearce
1st Edition October 1992
372, pages, ISBN 0-937175-83-8

As X moves out of the hacker's domain and into the real world, users can't be expected to master all the ins and outs of setting up and administering their own X software. That will increasingly become the domain of system administrators. Even for experienced system administrators X raises many issues, both because of subtle changes in the standard UNIX way of doing things and because X blurs the boundaries between different platforms. Under X, users can run applications across the network on systems with different resources (including fonts, colors, and screen size). Many of these issues are poorly understood, and the technology for dealing with them is in rapid flux.

This book is the first and only book devoted to the issues of system administration for X and X-based networks, written not just for UNIX system administrators, but for anyone faced with the job of administering X (including those running X on stand-alone workstations).

Note: The CD that used to be offered with this book is now sold separately, allowing system administrators to purchase the book and the CD-ROM in quantities they choose. *The X Companion CD for R6*, estimated release November 1994.

The X Companion CD for R6

By O'Reilly & Associates
1st Edition Fall 1994 (est.)
(Includes CD-ROM plus 80-page guide)
ISBN 1-56592-084-8

The X CD-ROM contains precompiled binaries for X11, Release 6 (X11R6) for Sun4, Solaris, HP-UX on the HP700, DEC Alpha, IBM RS6000, and other industry-standard platforms. It includes X11R6 source code from the "core" and "contrib"directories and X11R5 source code from the "core"and "contrib" directories. The CD also provides examples from the O'Reilly *X Window System* series and *The X Resource* journal.

The package includes an 80-page booklet describing the contents of the CD-ROM, how to install the R6 binaries, and how to build X11 for other platforms. O'Reilly and Associates used to offer this CD-ROM with Volume 8, *X Window System Administator's Guide* of the *X Window System* series. Offering it separately allows system administrators to purchase the book and the CD-ROM in any quantities they choose.

AUDIOTAPES

O'Reilly now offers audiotapes based on interviews with people who are making a profound impact in the world of the Internet. Here we give you a quick overview of what's available. For details on our audiotape collection, send email to **audio@ora.com**.

"Ever listen to one of those five-minute-long news pieces being broadcast on National Public Radio's 'All Things Considered' and wish they were doing an in-depth story on new technology? Well, your wishes are answered."

—Byte

Global Network Operations

Carl Malamud interviews Brian Carpenter,
Bernhard Stockman, Mike O'Dell & Geoff Huston
Released Spring 1994
Duration: 2 hours, ISBN 1-56592-993-4

What does it take to actually run a network? In these four interviews, Carl Malamud explores some of the technical and operational issues faced by Internet service providers around the world.

Brian Carpenter is the director for networking at CERN, the high-energy physics laboratory in Geneva, Switzerland. Physicists are some of the world's most active Internet users, and its global user base makes CERN one of the world's most network-intensive sites. Carpenter discusses how he deals with issues such as the OSI and DECnet Phase V protocols and his views on the future of the Internet.

Bernhard Stockman is one of the founders and the technical manager of the European Backbone (EBONE). EBONE has proven to be the first effective transit backbone for Europe and has been a leader in the deployment of CIDR, BGP-4, and other key technologies.

Mike O'Dell is vice president of research at UUNET Technologies. O'Dell has a long record of involvement in data communications, ranging from his service as a telco lab employee, an engineer on several key projects, and a member of the USENIX board to now helping define new services for one of the largest commercial IP service providers.

Geoff Huston is the director of the Australian Academic Research Network (AARNET). AARNET is known as one of the most progressive regional networks, rapidly adopting new services for its users. Huston talks about how networking in Australia has flourished despite astronomically high rates for long-distance lines.

The Future of the Internet Protocol

Carl Malamud interviews Steve Deering, Bob Braden,
Christian Huitema, Bob Hinden, Peter Ford, Steve Casner,
Bernhard Stockman & Noel Chiappa
Released Spring 1994
Duration: 4 hours, ISBN 1-56592-996-9

The explosion of interest in the Internet is stressing what was originally designed as a research and education network. The sheer number of users is requiring new strategies for Internet address allocation; multimedia applications are requiring greater bandwidth and strategies such as "resource reservation" to provide synchronous end-to-end service.

In this series of eight interviews, Carl Malamud talks to some of the researchers who are working to define how the underlying technology of the Internet will need to evolve in order to meet the demands of the next five to ten years.

Give these tapes a try if you're intrigued by such topics as Internet "multicasting" of audio and video, or think your job might one day depend on understanding some of the following buzzwords:

- IPNG (Internet Protocol Next Generation)
- SIP (Simple Internet Protocol)
- TUBA (TCP and UDP with Big Addresses)
- CLNP (Connectionless Network Protocol)
- CIDR (Classless Inter-Domain Routing)

or if you are just interested in getting to know more about the people who are shaping the future.

Mobile IP Networking

Carl Malamud interviews Phil Karn & Jun Murai
Released Spring 1994
Duration: 1 hour, ISBN 1-56592-994-2

Phil Karn is the father of the KA9Q publicly available implementation of TCP/IP for DOS (which has also been used as the basis for the software in many commercial Internet routers). KA9Q was originally developed to allow "packet radio," that is, TCP/IP over ham radio bands. Phil's current research focus is on commercial applications of wireless data communications.

Jun Murai is one of the most distinguished researchers in the Internet community. Murai is a professor at Keio University and the founder of the Japanese WIDE Internet. Murai talks about his research projects, which range from satellite-based IP multicasting to a massive testbed for mobile computing at the Fujisawa campus of Keio University.

Networked Information and Online Libraries

Carl Malamud interviews Peter Deutsch & Cliff Lynch
Released September 1993
Duration: 1 hour, ISBN 1-56592-998-5

Peter Deutsch, president of Bunyip Information Services, was one of the co-developers of Archie. In this interview Peter talks about his philosophy for services and compares Archie to X.500. He also talks about what kind of standards we need for networked information retrieval.

Cliff Lynch is currently the director of library automation for the University of California. He discusses issues behind online publishing, such as SGML and the democratization of publishing on the Internet.

European Networking

Carl Malamud interviews Glenn Kowack and Rob Blokzijl
Released September 1993
Duration: 1 hour, ISBN 1-56592-999-3

Glenn Kowack is chief executive of EUnet, the network that's bringing the Internet to the people of Europe. Glenn talks about EUnet's populist business model and the politics of European networking.

Rob Blokzijl is the network manager for NIKHEF, the Dutch Insitute of High Energy Physics. Rob talks about RIPE, the IP user's group for Europe, and the nuts and bolts of European network coordination.

Security and Networks

Carl Malamud interviews Jeff Schiller & John Romkey
Released September 1993
Duration: 1 hour, ISBN 1-56592-997-7

Jeff Schiller is the manager of MIT's campus network and is one of the Internet's leading security experts. Here, he talks about Privacy Enhanced Mail (PEM), the difficulty of policing the Internet, and whether horses or computers are more useful to criminals.

John Romkey has been a long-time TCP/IP developer and was recently named to the Internet Architecture Board. In this wide-ranging interview, John talks about the famous "ToasterNet" demo at InterOp, what kind of Internet security he'd like to see put in place, and what Internet applications of the future might look like.

John Perry Barlow
Notable Speeches of the Information Age

USENIX Conference Keynote Address
San Francisco, CA; January 17, 1994
Duration: 1.5 hours, ISBN 1-56592-992-6

John Perry Barlow—retired Wyoming cattle rancher, a lyricist for the Grateful Dead since 1971—holds a degree in comparative religion from Wesleyan University. He also happens to be a recognized authority on computer security, virtual reality, digitized intellectual property, and the social and legal conditions arising in the global network of computers.

In 1990 Barlow co-founded the Electronic Frontier Foundation with Mitch Kapor and currently serves as chair of its executive committee. He writes and lectures on subjects relating to digital technology and society and is a contributing editor to *Communications of the ACM, NeXTWorld, Microtimes, Mondo 2000, Wired*, and other publications.

In his keynote address to the Winter 1994 USENIX Conference, Barlow talks of recent developments in the national information infrastructure, telecommunications regulation, cryptography, globalization of the Internet, intellectual property, and the settlement of Cyberspace. The talk explores the premise that "architecture is politics": that the technology adopted for the coming "information superhighway" will help to determine what is carried on it, and that if the electronic frontier of the Internet is not to be replaced by electronic strip malls, we need to make sure that our technology choices favor bi-directional communication and open platforms.

Side A contains the keynote;
Side B contains a question and answer period.

O'Reilly & Associates—
GLOBAL NETWORK NAVIGATOR

The Global Network Navigator (GNN)™ is a unique kind of information service that makes the Internet easy and enjoyable to use. We organize access to the vast information resources of the Internet so that you can find what you want. We also help you understand the Internet and the many ways you can explore it.

In GNN you'll find:

Navigating the Net with GNN

 The *Whole Internet Catalog* contains a descriptive listing of the most useful Net resources and services with live links to those resources.

 The *GNN Business Pages* are where you'll learn about companies who have established a presence on the Internet and use its worldwide reach to help educate consumers.

 The *Internet Help Desk* helps folks who are new to the Net orient themselves and gets them started on the road to Internet exploration.

News

NetNews is a weekly publication that reports on the news of the Internet, with weekly feature articles that focus on Internet trends and special events. The Sports, Weather, and Comix Pages round out the news.

Special Interest Publications

Whether you're planning a trip or are just interested in reading about the journeys of others, you'll find that the *Travelers' Center* contains a rich collection of feature articles and ongoing columns about travel. In the *Travelers' Center*, you can link to many helpful and informative travel-related Internet resources.

The *Personal Finance Center* is the place to go for information about money management and investment on the Internet. Whether you're an old pro at playing the market or are thinking about investing for the first time, you'll read articles and discover Internet resources that will help you to think of the Internet as a personal finance information tool.

All in all, GNN helps you get more value for the time you spend on the Internet.

 The Best of the Web

GNN received "Honorable Mention" for **"Best Overall Site," "Best Entertainment Service,"** and **"Most Important Service Concept."**

The *GNN NetNews* received "Honorable Mention" for **"Best Document Design."**

Subscribe Today

GNN is available over the Internet as a subscription service. To get complete information about subscribing to GNN, send email to **info@gnn.com**. If you have access to a World Wide Web browser such as Mosaic or Lynx, you can use the following URL to register online: http://gnn.com/

If you use a browser that does not support online forms, you can retrieve an email version of the registration form automatically by sending email to **form@gnn.com**. Fill this form out and send it back to us by email, and we will confirm your registration.

O'Reilly on the Net—
ONLINE PROGRAM GUIDE

O'Reilly & Associates offers extensive information through our online resources. If you've got Internet access, we invite you to come and explore our little neck-of-the-woods.

Online Resouce Center

Most comprehensive among our online offerings is the O'Reilly Resource Center. Here, you'll find detailed information and descriptions on all O'Reilly products: titles, prices, tables of contents, indexes, author bios, CD-ROM directory listings, reviews...you can even view images of the products themselves. We also supply helpful ordering information: how to contact us, how to order online, distributors and bookstores around the world, discounts, upgrades, etc. In addition, we provide informative literature in the field, featuring articles, interviews, bibliogrphies, and columns that help you stay informed and abreast.

 The Best of the Web

The *O'Reilly Resource Center* was voted "**Best Commercial Site**" by users participating in "Best of the Web '94."

To access ORA's Online Resource Center:

Point your Web browser (e.g., **mosaic** or **lynx**) to:
http://gnn.com/ora/

For the plaintext version, **telnet** or **gopher** to:
gopher.ora.com
(telnetters login: **gopher**)

FTP

The example files and programs in many of our books are available electronically via FTP.

To obtain example files and programs from O'Reilly texts:

ftp to:
ftp.uu.net
cd published/oreilly
or
ftp.ora.com

Ora-news

An easy way to stay informed of the latest projects and products from O'Reilly & Associates is to subscribe to "ora-news," our electronic news service. Subscribers receive email as soon as the information breaks.

To subscribe to "ora-news":

Send email to:
listproc@online.ora.com

and put the following information on the first line of your message (not in "Subject"):
subscribe ora-news "your name" **of** "your company"

For example:
subscribe ora-news Jim Dandy of Mighty Fine Enterprises

Email

Many other helpful customer services are provided via email. Here's a few of the most popular and useful.

Useful email addresses

nuts@ora.com
　For general questions and information.

bookquestions@ora.com
　For technical questions, or corrections,
　concerning book contents.

order@ora.com
　To order books online and for ordering questions.

catalog@ora.com
　To receive a free copy of our magazine/catalog,
　"ora.com" (please include a snailmail address).

Snailmail and phones

O'Reilly & Associates, Inc.
103A Morris Street, Sebastopol, CA 95472
Inquiries: **707-829-0515, 800-998-9938**
Credit card orders: **800-889-8969**
FAX: **707-829-0104**

O'Reilly & Associates—
LISTING OF TITLES

INTERNET

!%@:: A Directory of Electronic Mail
    Addressing & Networks
Connecting to the Internet:
    An O'Reilly Buyer's Guide
Internet In A Box
MH & xmh: E-mail for Users & Programmers
The Mosaic Handbook for Microsoft Windows
The Mosaic Handbook for the Macintosh
The Mosaic Handbook for the
    X Window System
Smileys
The Whole Internet User's Guide & Catalog

SYSTEM ADMINISTRATION

Computer Security Basics
DNS and BIND
Essential System Administration
Linux Network Administrator's Guide
    (Fall 94 est)
Managing Internet Information Services
    (Fall 94 est.)
Managing NFS and NIS
Managing UUCP and Usenet
sendmail
Practical UNIX Security
PGP: Pretty Good Privacy (Winter 94/95 est.)
System Performance Tuning
TCP/IP Network Administration
termcap & terminfo
X Window System Administrator's Guide:
    Volume 8
X Window System, R6, Companion CD
    (Fall 94 est.)

USING UNIX AND X

BASICS

Learning GNU Emacs
Learning the Korn Shell
Learning the UNIX Operating System
Learning the vi Editor
SCO UNIX in a Nutshell
The USENET Handbook (Winter 94/95 est.)
Using UUCP and Usenet
UNIX in a Nutshell: System V Edition
The X Window System in a Nutshell
X Window System User's Guide: Volume 3
X Window System User's Guide, Motif Ed.:
    Volume 3M
X User Tools (10/94 est.)

ADVANCED

Exploring Expect (Winter 94/95 est.)
The Frame Handbook (10/94 est.)
Making TeX Work
Learning Perl
Programming perl
sed & awk
UNIX Power Tools (with CD-ROM)

PROGRAMMING UNIX, C, AND MULTI-PLATFORM

FORTRAN/SCIENTIFIC COMPUTING

High Performance Computing
Migrating to Fortran 90
UNIX for FORTRAN Programmers

C PROGRAMMING LIBRARIES

Practical C Programming
POSIX Programmer's Guide
POSIX.4: Programming for the Real World
    (Fall 94 est)
Programming with curses
Understanding and Using COFF
Using C on the UNIX System

C PROGRAMMING TOOLS

Checking C Programs with lint
lex & yacc
Managing Projects with make
Power Programming with RPC
Software Portability with imake

MULTI-PLATFORM PROGRAMMING

Encyclopedia of Graphics File Formats
Distributing Applications Across DCE and
    Windows NT
Guide to Writing DCE Applications
Multi-Platform Code Management
Understanding DCE
Understanding Japanese Information
    Processing
ORACLE Performance Tuning

BERKELEY 4.4 SOFTWARE DISTRIBUTION

4.4BSD System Manager's Manual
4.4BSD User's Reference Manual
4.4BSD User's Supplementary Documents
4.4BSD Programmer's Reference Manual
4.4BSD Programmer's Supplementary
    Documents
4.4BSD-Lite CD Companion
4.4BSD-Lite CD Companion:
    International Version

X PROGRAMMING

Motif Programming Manual: Volume 6A
Motif Reference Manual: Volume 6B
Motif Tools
PEXlib Programming Manual
PEXlib Reference Manual
PHIGS Programming Manual
    (soft or hard cover)
PHIGS Reference Manual
Programmer's Supplement for R6
    (Winter 94/95 est.)
Xlib Programming Manual: Volume 1
Xlib Reference Manual: Volume 2
X Protocol Reference Manual, R5: Vol. 0
X Protocol Reference Manual, R6: Vol. 0
    (11/94 est.)
X Toolkit Intrinsics Programming Manual:
    Volume 4
X Toolkit Intrinsics Programming Manual,
    Motif Edition: Volume 4M
X Toolkit Intrinsics Reference Manual: Vol.5
XView Programming Manual: Volume 7A
XView Reference Manual: Volume 7B

THE X RESOURCE

A QUARTERLY WORKING JOURNAL FOR X PROGRAMMERS

The X Resource: Issues 0 through 12
    (Issue 12 available 10/94)

BUSINESS/CAREER

Building a Successful Software Business
Love Your Job!

TRAVEL

Travelers' Tales Thailand
Travelers' Tales Mexico
Travelers' Tales India (Winter 94/95 est.)

AUDIOTAPES

INTERNET TALK RADIO'S "GEEK OF THE WEEK" INTERVIEWS

The Future of the Internet Protocol, 4 hrs.
Global Network Operations, 2 hours
Mobile IP Networking, 1 hour
Networked Information and
    Online Libraries, 1 hour
Security and Networks, 1 hour
European Networking, 1 hour

NOTABLE SPEECHES OF THE INFORMATION AGE

John Perry Barlow, 1.5 hours

O'Reilly & Associates—
INTERNATIONAL DISTRIBUTORS

Customers outside North America can now order O'Reilly & Associates books through the following distributors. They offer our international customers faster order processing, more bookstores, increased representation at tradeshows worldwide, and the high quality, responsive service our customers have come to expect.

EUROPE, MIDDLE EAST, AND AFRICA
(except Germany, Switzerland, and Austria)

INQUIRIES
International Thomson Publishing Europe
Berkshire House
168-173 High Holborn
London WC1V 7AA
United Kingdom
Telephone: 44-71-497-1422
Fax: 44-71-497-1426
Email: ora.orders@itpuk.co.uk

ORDERS
International Thomson Publishing Services, Ltd.
Cheriton House, North Way
Andover, Hampshire SP10 5BE
United Kingdom
Telephone: 44-264-342-832 (UK orders)
Telephone: 44-264-342-806 (outside UK)
Fax: 44-264-364418 (UK orders)
Fax: 44-264-342761 (outside UK)

GERMANY, SWITZERLAND, AND AUSTRIA
International Thomson Publishing GmbH
O'Reilly-International Thomson Verlag
Attn: Mr. G. Miske
Königswinterer Strasse 418
53227 Bonn
Germany
Telephone: 49-228-970240
Fax: 49-228-441342
Email: gerd@orade.ora.com

ASIA
(except Japan)

INQUIRIES
International Thomson Publishing Asia
221 Henderson Road
#05 10 Henderson Building
Singapore 0315
Telephone: 65-272-6496
Fax: 65-272-6498

ORDERS
Telephone: 65-268-7867
Fax: 65-268-6727

AUSTRALIA
WoodsLane Pty. Ltd.
Unit 8, 101 Darley Street (P.O. Box 935)
Mona Vale NSW 2103
Australia
Telephone: 61-2-979-5944
Fax: 61-2-997-3348
Email: woods@tmx.mhs.oz.au

NEW ZEALAND
WoodsLane New Zealand Ltd.
21 Cooks Street (P.O. Box 575)
Wanganui, New Zealand
Telephone: 64-6-347-6543
Fax: 64-6-345-4840
Email: woods@tmx.mhs.oz.au

THE AMERICAS, JAPAN, AND OCEANIA
O'Reilly & Associates, Inc.
103A Morris Street
Sebastopol, CA 95472 U.S.A.
Telephone: 707-829-0515
Telephone: 800-998-9938 (U.S. & Canada)
Fax: 707-829-0104
Email: order@ora.com

TO ORDER: **800-889-8969** (CREDIT CARD ORDERS ONLY); **ORDER@ORA.COM**

Here's a page we encourage readers to tear out...

O'REILLY WOULD LIKE TO HEAR FROM YOU

Please send me the following:

❏ **ora.com**

O'Reilly's magazine/catalog, containing behind-the-scenes articles and interviews on the technology we write about, and a complete listing of O'Reilly books and products.

❏ *Global Network Navigator*™

Information and subscription.

Please print legibly

Which book did this card come from?

_____

Where did you buy this book?
  ❏ Bookstore ❏ Direct from O'Reilly
  ❏ Bundled with hardware/software ❏ Class/seminar

Your job description: ❏ SysAdmin ❏ Programmer
  ❏ Other _____

What computer system do you use? ❏ UNIX
  ❏ MAC ❏ DOS(PC) ❏ Other _____

Name	Company/Organization Name

Address	

City	State	Zip/Postal Code	Country

Telephone	Internet or other email address (specify network)

Nineteenth century wood engraving
of the horned owl from the O'Reilly
& Associates Nutshell Handbook®
Learning the UNIX Operating System

O'Reilly & Associates, Inc., 103A Morris Street, Sebastopol, CA 95472-9902

PLACE
STAMP
HERE

NO POSTAGE
NECESSARY IF
MAILED IN THE
UNITED STATES

BUSINESS REPLY MAIL
FIRST CLASS MAIL   PERMIT NO. 80   SEBASTOPOL, CA

Postage will be paid by addressee

O'Reilly & Associates, Inc.
103A Morris Street
Sebastopol, CA 95472-9902